LLEWELLYN'S

COMPLETE BOOK OF

MINDFUL LIVING

LLEWELLYN'S

COMPLETE BOOK OF

MINDFUL LIVING

AWARENESS AND MEDITATION PRACTICES FOR LIVING IN THE PRESENT MOMENT

Robert Butera, PhD, and Erin Byron, MA

LLEWELLYN PUBLICATIONS
Woodbury, Minnesota

FIRST EDITION
First Printing, 2016

Book design by Rebecca Zins

Cover design by Kevin R. Brown

Cover images: iStockphoto.com/5312674/©PixelEmbargo, iStockphoto.com/6269367/
©Dee-Jay, iStockphoto.com/18277883/©vectorbomb, iStockphoto.com/58268338/©sumkinn,
Shutterstock.com/191037557/©Roberto Castillo, Shutterstock.com/258023690/©Titova E

Forgive and Be Free: A Step-by-Step Guide to Release, Healing & Higher Consciousness
by Ana Holub © 2014 Llewellyn Worldwide, Ltd., 2143 Wooddale Drive,
Woodbury, MN 55125. All rights reserved; used by permission.

*Taming the Drunken Monkey: The Path to Mindfulness, Meditation, and Increased
Concentration* by William L. Mikulas © 2014 Llewellyn Worldwide, Ltd., 2143 Wooddale
Drive, Woodbury, MN 55125. All rights reserved; used by permission.

Meditation for Your Life: Creating a Plan That Suits Your Style by Robert Butera © 2012 Llewellyn Worldwide,
Ltd., 2143 Wooddale Drive, Woodbury, MN 55125. All rights reserved; used by permission.

Llewellyn is a registered trademark of Llewellyn Worldwide Ltd.

Library of Congress Cataloging-in-Publication Data
Names: Butera, Robert, 1964– writer of introduction. | Byron, Erin, 1973–
    writer of introduction.
Title: Llewellyn's complete book of mindful living : awareness and meditation
    practices for living in the present moment / Robert Butera, PhD and Erin
    Byron, MA.
Description: First edition. | Woodbury : Llewellyn Worldwide, Ltd, 2016. |
    Series: Llewellyn's complete book series ; # 9
Identifiers: LCCN 2015046695 (print) | LCCN 2016000914 (ebook) | ISBN
    9780738746777 | ISBN 9780738750835 ( )
Subjects: LCSH: Meditation. | Mindfulness (Psychology)
Classification: LCC BL627 .L59 2016 (print) | LCC BL627 (ebook) | DDC
    158.1/2—dc23
LC record available at http://lccn.loc.gov/2015046695

Llewellyn Publications
A Division of Llewellyn Worldwide Ltd.
2143 Wooddale Drive
Woodbury, MN 55125-2989
www.llewellyn.com
Printed in the United States of America

Contents

Contents

• • • • • • •

||||||||||||||||||||||||||||||||||||||||||||||||||||||||||

For the Love of Your Body • 201

||||||||||||||||||||||||||||||||||||||||||||||||||||||||||

For Reaching Potential • 235

• • • • • • •

Contents

• • • • • • •

INTRODUCTION

Mindfulness practice has become increasingly popular in the last twenty years. From counseling offices to research papers, management strategies to mealtimes, it seems like mindful living approaches are being investigated and applied all over the place. The path of mindful living can be likened to walking a labyrinth. Labyrinth walking is a meditative practice that, like most mindfulness practices, is a tool for physical, mental, and spiritual healing and awakening. Labyrinths exist in addiction treatment centers, church courtyards, trauma clinics, hospices, and chronic pain centers. From above, a labyrinth looks like a brain, with its folds leading as a single path to the core. When inside the labyrinth the middle point is always visible to the walker, just as the truth of the present moment is visible to us when we become mindful. A labyrinth walk begins at the outside; people carry their intentions to the center and back again. Similarly, meditation carries us to the core of ourselves, where insight lives. Often, a personal transformation occurs as a result of mindfulness practice, be it labyrinth walking, conscious eating, grounding, or simply focusing on the breath.

Whether you are a longtime mindfulness practitioner or are brand new to the idea of a mindful lifestyle, this book offers you the chance to explore many facets of mindfulness. You don't even have to be experienced in mindfulness or meditation—you can access it from a range of interests, experiences, and intentions about mindful living. Enjoy learning about a variety of discussion topics and mindfulness practices, as well as some research, philosophy, and practical

· · · · · · · ·

exercises. You will be inspired to take control of your well-being, overcome negative thoughts and emotions, and achieve calmness, focus, better health, and happiness!

How You Can Benefit

If you are interested in greater insight and awareness, you can use this book. From executives seeking to build a stronger company to homemakers wanting greater happiness to people struggling with chronic illness or spiritualists on the path of enlightenment, the tools and techniques offered here can assist you in attaining your personal goals.

Many areas of your life can be transformed! If you are a beginner, the chapters within this book will give you fundamental skills to build a mindfulness practice using simple, accessible techniques. Some proven benefits mindfulness and meditation can bring you include (but are not limited to) stress reduction; improved sleep; optimal weight; pain reduction; increased energy; regulated blood pressure, hormone levels, and nervous system activity; improved immune function; decreased anxiety and depression; increased productivity; improved concentration and other cognitive faculties; improved relationships (including the relationship with yourself); greater sense of compassion for yourself and others; clearer decision-making abilities; greater adaptability to change...and the list goes on and on.

There are many approaches to mindfulness and many styles of meditation. By applying what you learn here, you will be able to choose the approaches that work best for you and relate to the areas of life you are working on. This book demonstrates, in a systematic and customizable way, how to apply mindfulness practices to improve your health in many areas of life.

What Mindfulness Is

Mindfulness techniques have been around for millennia, performed by Buddhists as a means of "insight meditation," or awareness practice. At its simplest, mindfulness is the act of bringing full consciousness to the present moment, observing what is being taken in by the senses and occurring around us, as well as noticing the inner flow of emotion and thought. Mindfulness brings nonjudgmental attention to your present experiences; in other words, you do not filter your thoughts, feelings, and experiences as "good" or "bad"; just let them be. When you are freed from judgment it is easier to take in a complete experience rather than avoiding what you think might be bad. As you cultivate the objective witness within, you gain a better understanding of your mental and emotional habits, as well as chronic habits. This is not only relaxing and empowering but also helps lend courage to changing your ineffective thought, emotional, or behavioral patterns in a nonthreatening, objective way.

In the late 1970s Jon Kabat-Zinn founded mindfulness-based stress reduction (MBSR). Originally these practices were for the chronically ill; however, it wasn't long before the techniques

• • • • • • • •

were being applied to the field of mental health. Currently these techniques are used in hospitals, schools, businesses, addiction clinics, prisons, and many other institutions as a means of facilitating personal responsibility and a greater sense of well-being.

Mindfulness practices can be used anytime, anywhere, by anyone. Formal training and a formal setting are not necessary, which are two of the reasons mindfulness is so popular. Mindfulness techniques bring you a clear picture of inner and outer reality, and from this objective, nonjudgmental awareness you are empowered to consciously create a life of alignment with what you really want and who you want to be.

There are a variety of mindfulness techniques beyond the simple one described above, of bringing full consciousness to what is happening in the now. Mindfulness of the breath, classical yoga, conscious walking, body scan relaxation, and many other techniques bring attention and insight to the present moment, focusing on various areas of awareness.

Meditation is often a way to access mindful consciousness. Both meditation and mindfulness train your mind to be more objective, focused, and calm. Both require practice and are skills that are strengthened over time. Although mindfulness is the main focus of this book, meditation is mentioned in a number of chapters because it helps steady your mind and improve focus; these are important skills in a mindfulness practice. Mindfulness is a type of meditation based on cultivating awareness and relating to ongoing movement in the internal and external world. Other forms of meditation such as visualization or contemplation are concentration styles that typically involve sitting in silence. Mindfulness, however, can be performed during any activity, even doing the dishes or having a conversation.

How to Use This Book

This book is divided into five parts. The first part, For Basic Understanding and Practice, gives you a foundation of mindfulness practices as well as explains the mindfulness and meditation process in more detail. It is an excellent lead-in for the novice and can help elaborate and affirm the understanding of more experienced practitioners. You begin with practices you might typically think of when you hear "mindfulness" and "meditation" and from there progress into more unexpected and beneficial topics of health, love of your body, reaching your potential, and subtle energy/spirit.

Following the first part you will dive into mindfulness for all levels of health. Aspects of your physical, mental, and spiritual well-being are included in part two and offer you a great deal of insight into common issues such as sleep, grief, mindful eating, chronic health conditions, and connection to your pets and the earth. The third part, For the Love of Your Body, addresses how to mindfully live through enjoyment within your body and touches on body image, movement practice, and sex.

· · · · · · · ·

You will find further inspiration in the fourth section, For Reaching Potential, which includes a variety of topics for manifesting and creating prosperity and healing in many realms, including your relationships, your emotional world, and the world at large. Part five, For Subtle Energy and Spirit, shares exposition and practices with you for greater spiritual connection through your inner and energetic awareness.

Each part of the book includes a range of ideas, practices, and inspiration for you to bring specific benefits of mindfulness into everyday life. You receive a base understanding of each topic through exposition as well as the all-important opportunity for personal application. Chapters include a combination of background discussion, example stories, and something for you to engage with through your own experience via practices and exercises. As you continue to foster mindfulness with this book, write down what arises within you. You may get a special journal to hold your feelings and insights. There are also suggestions for journaling included in many of these chapters.

Every chapter is written to bring you insight and upliftedness, and can be read as a stand-alone topic. You can read through the book in whatever order you choose, selecting chapters that pique your curiosity and focusing your attention there without needing to peruse all the material that comes before. Enjoy going through the book in your own way, guided by your areas of interest and individual needs as you delve into the variety of topics.

A Variety of Contributors

This book is a team effort. A variety of leaders in the field of meditation and mindfulness came together to contribute chapters on their specific areas of expertise. Each author has a strong personal and professional background in the topic they offer. At the end of each chapter there is a full biography for each contributor so that you can learn more about them and seek out their greater bodies of work to enhance your practice.

Michael Bernard Beckwith, William L. Mikulas, Amy B. Scher, and Keith Park give you foundational ideas on mindful practice and stress reduction. Danielle MacKinnon, Angela Wix, Rachel Avalon, Melissa Grabau, Sarah Bowen, Jeanne Van Bronkhorst, and Servet Hasan share facets of health-related mindfulness practices. Inspiring love for your body, Rolf Gates, Melanie Klein, and Mark A. Michaels and Patricia Johnson offer wisdom and guidance. Ana Holub, Guy Finley, Jack Canfield, Deborah Sandella, Tess Whitehurst, Alexandra Chauran, and Shakta Khalsa inspire you to reach a higher potential through your mindful endeavors. Thomas Moore, Cyndi Dale, and Sherrie Dillard offer perspectives on the more subtle spiritual aspects of mindfulness practice. Each of these unique voices rings with truth and enthusiasm so that you, the reader, have access to a complete guide for mindful living.

The voices of the book's introduction, as well the introductions to each section, are offered by Robert Butera and Erin Byron, who also contribute chapters. Robert and Erin have a combined fifty-year practice in meditation and mindful living. Robert is the author of *Meditation for Your Life* and creator of the Meditation for Your Type Teacher Training. Erin also trains meditation and yoga teachers and is co-author of *Yoga Therapy for Stress and Anxiety* with Robert Butera. Robert and Erin created Comprehensive Yoga Therapist Training, one of the first programs accredited by the International Association of Yoga Therapists. This background in meditation and yoga therapy has given Robert and Erin great insight into the power of mindfulness and meditation. When we witness our inner experiences objectively, there is great potential for improvement in our lives.

This book was written with you, the reader, in mind. Knowing that mindfulness is a deeply personal path, this book is designed so that you can begin at the place that is most relevant for you, immediately applying the information and practices therein. You do not need to read from cover to cover. Trust yourself, and let your curiosity and natural attention set your focus. We wish you the best on this path of mindful living.

For Basic Understanding and Practice

In this beginning section you have the opportunity to explore various meditation and mindfulness practices. The diverse authors provide perspectives on and approaches to mindful living in order to give you a foundation of practice. Through this section you will learn about the connection between mindfulness and meditation, common approaches to both, how to avoid obstacles that may arise, and strategies to cope when they do. Setting an intention for your journey is one of the best ways to cultivate a strong mindfulness custom, helping you be clear on why you are doing this and staying motivated through the process. Important points throughout this section include a range of suggestions on how to establish a mindfulness routine, options of what to do within that routine (including concentration, breathing, and relaxation techniques), and mental techniques to enhance your focus and well-being.

Erin Byron and Michael Bernard Beckwith, in their respective chapters, share knowledge on embarking upon and staying motivated with a mindfulness practice. William L. Mikulas and Robert Butera elaborate on your options for connecting focus and relaxation through the breath. Amy B. Scher's chapter gives you direct tools to overcome negativity, Keith Park elaborates this with mindful problem-solving skills, and Robert Butera's chapter supports your awareness of how to transform unwitting stressful habits into a mindful lifestyle. Whether you are a novice or an experienced practitioner, you will gain a clear understanding of mindfulness basics from this section.

The Mind in Mindfulness Meditation

ERIN BYRON, MA

Mindfulness is the practice of turning on awareness. In mindfulness practice we learn to observe the breath, physical sensations, emotions, and mental processes. We expand our awareness of the interconnectivity between our thoughts, feelings, breath, body, behavior, and life choices. Through mindfulness we can even change the shape and function of our brains. As mindfulness practice develops, we realize more clearly that everything is changing. Reality is impermanent: our thoughts and feelings pass, our relationships shift, our careers alter, our interests evolve, and so on. The purpose of mindfulness meditation is to attend fully to the present moment without our habitual filters of judgments, expectations, or preconceived ideas and programming that ultimately sabotage our efforts. We witness our passing perceptions without needing to create a story around them, which brings clarity. Although it takes time and effort to establish a meditation practice, there are ways to ensure that you stay on the path and keep your practice vital. We will discuss all of these things in this chapter.

Mindfulness in Breath, Body, and Emotion

One of the simplest ways to cultivate focus is by bringing the awareness to the breath. Breath is such an important part of mindfulness and meditation that it bears repeating. Robert Butera's chapter on deep breathing focuses on the role of breath and gives you many ideas of how to use it to quiet your mind. Since you are always breathing, the breath can be a constant reminder of the present and an anchor to ongoing awareness. Additionally, bringing attention to the breath often deepens its rhythm and steadies its quality, which in turn has a calming, centering effect on the mind. It is relevant to acknowledge what you see, hear, smell, taste, and feel. Notice any judgments, wishes, and habitual thoughts, as well as become aware of how you carry your body. Give mindful attention to your posture and breath while sitting or standing; notice and release hunched shoulders, tensions in the forehead, rapid breathing, or a clenched jaw. This relaxation can extend from the breath and body into the mind by bringing greater awareness to feelings and emotions.

EXERCISE: **Mindful Breathing**

The following practice is a basic mindful breathing exercise. This is something you can practice in a dedicated way, in sacred space, or as a regular meditation. You may also perform this exercise during everyday life: while at work, in line at the store, speaking with friends, doing everyday chores, or falling asleep.

1: Be in a comfortable position with the spine erect so that the area where the breath flows is open.

2: Notice the depth and pace of your breath. Where does the air flow into your body? What parts of your torso remain still or closed? What is the length of each inhale, exhale, and the pauses between the breaths?

3: Allow your abdominal diaphragm to move the breath, if it isn't already. With each inhale the diaphragm curves into the belly as the lower lobes of the lungs inflate, thereby expanding the abdominal area. You may notice your lower ribs flaring front, sides, and back. The upper rib cage, in a full breath, also moves to the sides and back so that the rib cage is opening in a tubular fashion, not lifting up. There is a slight lift in the upper chest toward the collarbones as the lungs inflate fully. On an exhale allow the lungs to release in all directions. Be patient with yourself, as many of us have have locked up parts of the nose, sinuses, trachea / windpipe, lungs, diaphragm, and other associated musculature after many years of stress. The main point is to unite the mind with the breath.

By witnessing the movement of the breath, you calm your nervous system, balance the mind, and relax the body. These internal conditions set the stage for a greater power of focus in your mindfulness practice. Furthermore, attention to the breath gives you an ongoing focus for your mindfulness practice. The continual movement of the breath reminds us that the mind will also continue to move, as will emotions and life circumstances. Remain mindful of your breathing and stay connected to each moment of your life.

· · · · · · · ·

Mindfulness easily translates from a physical awareness of breath to other bodily sensations. By attuning to ongoing physical feedback, we have more awareness of our everyday experiences. For people who have suffered in their bodies through chronic illness, pain, or abuse, the ability to be present in the body offers a great potential for healing on all levels: body, energy, emotions, thoughts, and spirit. There is a great deal of information contained in our feelings, both bodily sensations and emotional states. When we are mindful of the purpose and messages of our feelings we can understand how to prevent the things that lead to painful, disruptive, or confused tensions and emotions. Mindful awareness—relaxation and mastery of the story we tell ourselves—is a powerful tool for emotional balance. As the mind settles, issues that were below the surface are revealed in the same way that we can see into deep waters when the surface is smooth and still.

Mindfulness aids emotional balance through awareness and personal responsibility. Even though we are programmed to attribute our internal emotional state to external happenings, mindfulness reveals how our own beliefs and perceptions color situations and create emotional drama. We tend to lay blame for our own feelings on others. Mindful attention gives us the chance to take responsibility for our feelings instead. Although this ownership may be difficult at first, ultimately it empowers us to master our emotional state and choose to remain uplifted and confident in the face of pain or challenge—in other words, to respond to life rather than react. Mindfulness meditation trains us to shift from an automatic reaction to a clear, measured response to any given feeling. In a reactive situation we fall back on our programming and emotional habits, repeating problematic feelings and beliefs of the past with little control of ourselves or the current situation. With mindfulness, however, we develop the ability to mentally take a step back, pause, and witness the feelings and their messages. In this gap of space we are able to measure a response and determine our own best path of clear action, rather than react automatically in a repetitive and often unhelpful pattern.

EXERCISE: **Response versus Reaction**

Think of your feelings as having two components: physical sensations and mental thoughts. For most of us, these sensations and thoughts operate beyond our consciousness awareness. Mindfulness helps us become aware of these underlying sensations and thoughts as well as revealing the subtle relationship between them. This exercise gives you a chance to witness the relationship between sensations and thoughts as they happen. Notice what arises within you throughout the process without needing to judge, explain, or change anything about your personal experience.

1: Read the following situations one at a time and then pause. For each one, notice the various sensations and thoughts that arise:

• • • • • • • •

- Relaxing on a warm day
- Missing an important deadline
- Holding an infant
- Spotting a deer
- Hurting someone's feelings
- Cooking a good meal
- Cleaning the toilet
- Floating in the ocean

2: Ask yourself, "How much of my reaction to the situations was based on past experience?" Become curious about the source of your reactions. Re-read the list of situations with greater interest in your own mind's activities rather than the situations themselves.

Many people will have similar reactions to each of these situations; however, the subtleties of their experiences are unique. At first, become mindful of your reactions, sensations, and thoughts. In time, as you understand yourself better and become accustomed to observing your internal processes, you can move away from the automatic reactions. Instead of operating on reflex, you may become more curious about your internal habits and their origins and outcomes. In his book *Meditation for Your Life*, Robert Butera recommends a four-step process to limit reactivity. This practice can be easily remembered by the mnemonic STAR:

Stop

Take a breath

Attend to bodily sensations

Respond rather than react

The response you choose may be to do nothing, to speak with awareness, or to employ mindful action. The capacity to respond mindfully strengthens each time we interrupt an automatic reaction. Mindfulness teaches us to allow feelings to be as they are and supports us in navigating life's upsets with grace and insight. In addition, you can support your mindfulness practice through journaling, talking to spiritually minded friends or a meditation mentor, and seeking counseling for problematic memories and feelings. This curiosity and the opportunity to process your emotions allows you greater emotional freedom and opens you to the possibilities of each moment. As we change the way we focus our attention, breathe, relax, and relate to our feelings, we actually change our neural pathways, quality of connections, and the shape of our brains.

· · · · · · · ·

Mindfulness and the Brain

Studies have shown that various forms of meditation, including mindfulness, change the structure and function of the brain. These alterations to the brain's pathways and shape are known as neuroplasticity and come from changes in behavior, thoughts, feelings, activities, or one's external or internal environment. Neuroplasticity, or the brain's ability to reorganize itself and form new connections, holds great implications for our ability to transform our emotional, mental, and behavioral patterns and improve all areas of our lives. If we can change the shape and function of our brains, we can change our emotional world, life circumstances, automatic reactions, and even levels of physical and emotional pain. Mindfulness can be a key practice in establishing these changes.

Mindfulness practice activates many areas of the brain at the same time; thus, the neural effects of mindfulness are complex. During the last few decades our ability to look into the brain has improved. We use various technologies to see what happens in our brains when we meditate, reflect, observe, or receive sensory information. We can even see how our brains change shape and function when we change our thinking, either after a single session of mindfulness or over a longer period of time. All these studies have altered our former belief that the brain cannot modify or develop after a certain age. We now know that the brain has the potential to never stop developing as long as we continue to introduce new information or variety into our thinking and activities. Mindfulness and variety create new pathways in the brain. Then again, if we don't change our thinking and activities, the old pathways get stronger. If we keep thinking and doing the same things, the results of these thoughts and actions will also be the same—not only in our external lives but internally as well! Although the brain is plastic—in other words, able to change shape—it will not do so if we do not offer it new experiences.

Mindfulness can be seen as a way to bring variety to the brain: a newness in perspective or an interruption of our usual way of thinking and being. Mindfulness offers us the opportunity to experience reality as it happens. Every moment is a renewal. Our thoughts, feelings, and interactions with the world around us are constantly changing. When we attune to these changes and witness the myriad internal effects they bring, this mindfulness introduces a change in the shape and function of the brain.

Many recent studies have related mindfulness to the neuroplasticity of cognitive areas of the brain. In other words, mindfulness helps with thinking. Experienced meditators have a thicker cortex than nonmeditators. The areas of the brain associated with decision-making, reason, and focused attention tend to be more developed, with greater connections between neurons and more intricately developed pathways. What this means is that if you practice mindfulness, there is evidence that you will be able to think more readily, formulate theories, recall information and abilities, come up with new ideas, and concentrate better in everyday life. Some studies suggest

• • • • • • • •

it may even protect against the loss of gray matter that was thought to be a part of the natural aging process! Mindfulness helps the thinking brain.

In addition to these cognitive benefits, mindfulness is also related to more stable emotional processing. The hippocampus and amygdala, which are associated with emotional regulation, among other functions, change via mindfulness. This is consistent with reports from mindfulness practitioners that they experience greater emotional awareness and are better able to witness their emotions without reacting. Furthermore, evidence of increased density in parts of the brain stem could relate to practitioners' ability to respond rather than react to stressful situations. Mindfulness meditators report that they are less emotionally charged, even in extreme circumstances. By incorporating mindfulness and remaining the conscious director of our thoughts and feelings, the areas of the brain that fire during worried thinking, anxiety, and even pain responses begin to alter.

Mindfulness practice is shown to have neuroplastic effects. These profound changes in the shape and function of the brain improve our cognitive and emotional processes as well as protect us against some of the neurological effects of aging. Additionally, studies consistently reveal that the longer subjects have been practicing mindfulness, the more pronounced are the benefits. What this means for you is this: the longer you practice, the more elaborate the neuroplastic effects and the stronger your cognitive and emotional benefits. Even a few moments of mindfulness every day can rebuild your brain and support these healthy shifts. What is most important is that you continue to practice in some way, without succumbing to discouragement, laziness, or sabotage.

Self-Sabotage in Mindfulness Meditation

The mind has profound power to improve our mental and physical health, especially when it is harnessed through mindfulness meditation. However, the mind is also powerful enough to sabotage our efforts. Judgments, expectations, and old programming are key factors that can interrupt our steady mindfulness practice. How we handle self-criticism, our expectations, and the stories we tell ourselves are key factors in whether or not we persist with a mindfulness practice. Our own personal vision can serve to either inspire or sabotage our efforts toward mindful living. Here we will discuss the common sabotages of judgments, expectations, and programming and offer suggestions for circumventing them in order to stay true to your path of mindful living.

Is mindful living a good thing or a bad thing? Don't answer that; it's a trick question. Mindful living is one valid way among many ways of going through life. It is neither good nor bad. From an early age we are taught to categorize our decisions, and as we grow up this process of judging things becomes more subtle and refined, even automatic. We get so accustomed to judgment that we consider it a normal part of life. As an experiment to watch your judgment habit in action, endeavor to go a full day without thinking "should." "Should" is a strong indicator of an inner judge hard at work, telling us what is good for us and steering us away from what is judged as bad.

• • • • • • •

Imagine how challenging it is to impassively witness the human mind while holding onto ideas of good and bad. Minds naturally wander to all kinds of dark and inappropriate places. If we are not allowed to watch the movement of our minds into these so-called bad places, mindfulness practice becomes impossible. The act of steering the thoughts—judging them as good or bad and then moving them in the direction we think they should go—undercuts the benefits of the pure, nonjudgmental awareness mindfulness brings. Soon, judgments will interfere with the witnessing process so much that mindfulness practice will fail. When judgment comes into play, we lose our connection to reality because we prefer it to be different.

Wanting different thoughts and realities is actually some of the intrigue of mindfulness. We gain insight and capacity to respond mindfully when we witness, rather than judge, our complex and contradictory inner experiences. The capacity to respond mindfully strengthens each time we experience vivid feelings and let them simply be there, just as they are, without reacting. Gradually, we learn that effective mindfulness practice arises from acceptance and openness to whatever is happening within us; judgments have no place there. As we begin to accept ourselves we find that acceptance of others increases as well and that compassion for ourselves and others flows more readily and easily.

Rather than sabotage yourself with judgment, when errant thoughts arise during mindfulness practice simply name them—for example, "thinking about the meeting at work," "making a grocery list," "wondering about the children"—or categorize them, such as "plans," "lists," "fears," "memories," and so on. Once you have acknowledged the thought by naming or categorizing it, just let it go. The practice here is to notice what thoughts arise, acknowledge them, and then return to mindful attention. Judgment does not exist in this process. Free from judgment, we greet ourselves with greater calm because we do not struggle against our thoughts and feelings, wish things were different than they are, or have expectations about how things should be.

Once we are able to hold nonjudgmental awareness, our expectations of ourselves and mindfulness practice is the next potential factor that can sabotage our efforts. Expectations are sometimes called "planned disappointments." In other words, when we preconceive certain outcomes and those narrowly defined circumstances do not turn out, it is easy to feel let down. The effects of mindfulness on reducing stress, improving energy, deepening relationships, and boosting creativity are well known. The trouble is, focusing only on the benefits sets up high expectations, and it is common for us to be hurt or disappointed when our expectations are broken. A more truthful approach is to remember that we have control over the efforts we offer the situation but no control over the results of those efforts. You can avoid a potential let-down in your mindfulness practice by acknowledging that you have preconceived expectations. This acknowledgment strengthens your mindfulness efforts before they even begin. Harness the power of your awareness of the truth of the present moment. Rather than trying to control reality and predetermine outcomes, you can focus on where your control truly lies: in your actions and reactions to reality.

• • • • • • • •

EXERCISE: **Managing Expectations**

This exercise is intended to support you in side-stepping any potential future discouragement by becoming clear about your preconceived ideas around mindfulness practice. Record the answers to the following questions in your journal. Be honest with yourself, even if you notice that some of your thoughts are irrational, selfish, or contradictory. One of the key aspects of mindfulness is letting go of judgment. Now is a good time to practice that skill.

1: List why you are interested in becoming more mindful. What do you hope to get out of a mindfulness practice? Perhaps you are seeking freedom from stress, greater awareness in your relationships, improved athletic performance, or enlightenment. You may consider what led you to exploring mindfulness in the first place: life experiences, stories you have heard, others you know who practice, etc. Circle your top three desired outcomes from this list.

2: Review your list objectively and place an asterisk beside all the outcomes that you do not control. Underline all the outcomes you do control. It is normal in the beginning to be unsure about which is which; simply contemplate the question and trust your answer for now. If later on you realize you were mistaken, you may revisit this exercise and change your answers.

3: Going back to your top three desired outcomes, note for yourself how you will handle each of these if they do not come to pass. In other words, if you apply mindfulness practice and do not see your expectations fulfilled, what will keep you motivated to continue practicing mindfulness? (Note that many unexpected benefits arise from a mindfulness practice, and these are often more deeply motivating!)

Acknowledging your expectations before you begin takes their power away. Simply by becoming mindful of the fact that you are hoping for certain outcomes—outcomes that you cannot control—neutralizes those expectations. This process is akin to when someone is playfully hiding behind the door, waiting to jump out at you: when you hear them giggling, you know they are there. When they jump out, you may still startle a little but the jolt passes quickly and does not deeply affect you. Likewise, when we are aware of our expectations beforehand and they do not come to pass, we may feel a little disappointed, but it is not enough for us to stop our mindfulness practice and let go of all the possible unexpected benefits!

• • • • • • •

EXERCISE: **Mindfulness Intention**

Whether or not we get what we expect from a mindfulness practice, there are benefits. Once you are aware of your expectations, you can take those genuine desires and purify them into a highly motivating sense of guidance. Internal motivation is powerful, rather than relying on external benefits to inspire practice. The following exercise supports this process of establishing pure motivation from the beginning while staying free from the pressure of judgment and expectation.

1: What is your intention for practicing mindfulness? Note that this intention is not a reward that will come or an outcome that you are seeking. Intentionality exists at a deeper, more pure level. Some common intentions include self-awareness, slowing down, compassion, or insight. Notice how simple and broad these intentions are, and that each one has a specific spiritual quality.

2: Review your list of expectations from the previous exercise. You may also write a new list of what you expect or hope to get out of a mindfulness practice.

3: Re-read this list, close your eyes, and notice the effect of it in your body and mind. This, in itself, is a mindfulness practice as you bring your awareness to places of tension and relaxation, the thoughts that move through your mind, passing feelings, and your emotional state in relation to the list of expectations. Do not judge what flows through your awareness; simply observe it. After a minute or two, record your observations.

4: Now, re-read your intention from step 1 and repeat the brief mindfulness practice. Notice the effect of the intention on your body and mind: places of tension and relaxation; passing feelings, sensations, and thoughts; your emotional state in relation to the intention. Do not judge what flows through your awareness; simply observe it. After a minute or two of awareness, record your observations.

5: Review your observations of your expectations and intention. Was there a difference between the feeling you got from your expectations and the feeling of your intention? If so, what were the differences?

Often intention is a starting point that guides the direction of our efforts. If we stay true to our intention, then—no matter the outcome—we know that we followed the path that was best for us. Often the intention will refine itself as our understanding grows. Expectation, on the other hand, keeps us focused on the end result of an endeavor without honoring the lengthy process or the underlying call to action. Intention helps us stay clear, focused, and relaxed; expectation causes tension, attachment, and judgment.

· · · · · · · ·

Avoid the potential sabotage of expectation by doing your best to keep your intention in mind. Thus, you continue to move in the direction of what is important to you. Once freed from expectations, many unexpected gifts and surprise insights can arrive into your open mind. Sometimes old patterns and programming arise as well, and these are the third common sabotage in a mindfulness practice.

From before we can remember, we have been taught to distinguish right from wrong—who we want to be from who we don't. Family, teachers, and even society at large offer constant input on what is or is not okay to do, say, or think. Furthermore, our interpersonal wounds and painful life lessons carve deep beliefs into the mind. This programming often occurs through language and makes it a challenge to have a full experience of the mind. We often believe that our biased perceptions are an accurate representation of reality; however, just because we think something, that doesn't make it real.

Mindfulness practice brings the uncomfortable realization that our beliefs and programming are subject to change. At first it can be frightening to realize how much of our old patterning we project onto new situations; however, if you persist you will come to notice how freeing it is to allow each experience to be new, without the burden of old perceptual patterns. Passing thoughts and emotions are impermanent reflections of a broader reality, often charged with the language of our programming, perceptions, and experiences. For example, note the difference between saying "I'm upset!" and "I'm experiencing upset right now!" In the first example we identify that we are the emotional state; in the second, however, we create distance and objectivity. Programming imposes limits on our ability to experience the full reality of a situation.

Our reactive patterns cover up true awareness and objective reality. Instead of getting caught up on old emotional patterns, ask yourself: "What is the truth in this situation?" Seek the deeper truth within the patterned discomfort. Imagine understanding why you are programmed the way you are and then disengaging that program. Grumpy coworkers would no longer bother you, long lists would not feel threatening, your partner could have a bad day and it wouldn't be about you. Mindfulness helps us see the programming as it runs, then let go of our limiting beliefs and live with greater freedom and insight.

By surrendering judgment, releasing attachment to expectations, and becoming objective about old programming, we clear the path of mindfulness. These three main methods of self-sabotage make awareness painful. Now you know how to transcend them. Without them you are more objective, ready to experience your inner world as it is and reflect that pure experience into your life choices and behavior. Once free from sabotage, mindfulness practice is simply a matter of persisting.

• • • • • • •

Trevor's Story

Trevor is a schoolteacher who came to meditation to help cope with the stress of classroom discipline, pressure from the principal, and frustration with limiting academic policies. Trevor dreamt of being the kind of teacher who could change children's lives and make a difference in the world. Over the years, Trevor's dream became jaded and most work days were about going through the motions rather than bringing true inspiration to the classroom—for himself or the children.

Trevor signed up for a mindfulness training program and engaged in practice by watching the breath. This soon led to an unexpected emotional awareness: Trevor was sad about his career path and felt helpless to support the children in the ways they seemed to need it most. Trevor also noticed the thoughts that went along with those feelings: *These kids don't want to learn... What difference does it make?...The curriculum doesn't match the need...I just want to go home.* Before practicing mindfulness, Trevor had not been aware of these deeper emotions and thoughts. There was a sense of extreme stress but no clear source or path to ease. Indeed, through being mindful, Trevor could relate the stress to feelings of pointlessness and futile thoughts.

When Trevor spoke to his mindfulness mentor about the disturbing thoughts and feelings, the suggestion was to continue to watch them. "Everything changes," the mentor noted. "Witness the change."

Trevor did not want to indulge the hollowness. He had chosen a teaching career to inspire others. Through watching his thoughts, Trevor noticed there was a lot of focus on things he did not control, such as the children's situations at home, the principal's expectations and personality, and the curriculum. By relaxing even as the futile thoughts passed, and by witnessing the emotional pain without trying to change it, Trevor found himself making different choices throughout the day. Instead of getting frustrated when children weren't absorbing the lesson, Trevor switched to a new teaching style or way of interacting with the content. When there were outbreaks in the classroom, Trevor indulged the brief disruptions and truly connected to what the children needed. When a child approached him, Trevor was able to see the person before him and listen deeply to concerns, even if he was helpless to actually take action and change things. Trevor even taught the children some basic breathing exercises to do after lunch and recess, which led to greater focus and quietude. Each of these small changes made a difference not only to the quality of the teaching, but also to Trevor's desire to be a teacher and the sense that his work had meaning.

Through mindfulness, Trevor was able to slow down the internal stress and separate out its distinct pieces. From there he was more engaged in choosing his thoughts, feelings, and responses throughout the day. In time this led to a greater personal awareness and satisfaction. Ultimately, although there were still stressful times, Trevor was no longer plagued by a sense of hopelessness or a continual overwhelming stress about his work.

· · · · · · ·

Maintaining Mindfulness Practice

Once you have rid yourself of sabotage, there is still the challenge of continuing mindfulness practice. Every day is a new opportunity to commit to self-awareness. Coming back to the present moment is simple enough, but it requires continual effort. There are ways that you can learn to sustain focus, cope with sensory and emotional distractions, and hold yourself to the present moment. Through these efforts, in time, mindfulness will become a habit.

Sustaining mindful focus is one of the most challenging things you will learn to do. It is strange to think that holding our attention to what is going on within and around us would be so difficult, but it is. Despite all the accolades mainstream media offers about mindfulness and meditation—which tend to be true—the challenges are rarely discussed. For this reason, it is common for people to get down on themselves about interruptions in practice. People often say "my mind is too busy" or "I lose focus all the time." The truth is, that is part of the process! And every time you notice your busy mind or choose to bring your focus back to pure awareness, your mind and practice get stronger. In time you will come to notice that it is quieter in your mind. When it does get busy it will not wander as far or for as long before you are able to call it back to your mindfulness practice. You can even measure these improvements.

EXERCISE: **Prolonging Focus**

The following exercise can be performed weekly over a number of months to help you track personal shifts in your mindfulness practice. It seems like a simple exercise, but over the long term it is highly validating. We often underestimate how far we have come and undermine the power of our own efforts. True change happens via small, consistent alterations.

1: Set a timer for sixty seconds. During that minute, set your awareness to your breath. It is normal for your mind to wander, even as you focus on the quality of your inhales and exhales.

2: When your mind wanders, note to yourself how far it went. How many thoughts were attached to the original shift in focus? Did your mind wander to many different thoughts and topics or did it shift and then refocus? Could you still sense your breath while your mind called on different thoughts? Did your mind return to the breath before the timer rang again?

3: Record your observations in your mindfulness journal. It is recommended that you keep a separate section in your journal for this practice; that way, you can easily find your tracking records. Keep the principles of mindfulness with you, remembering to simply observe without judgment, commentary, or problem solving.

· · · · · · · ·

4: Repeat this exercise weekly. Do not re-read the previous week's observations. After six to twelve weeks, go back and read your first two or three entries, then read your last two or three. Write a summary of the changes you noticed in your ability to hold focus, and rest assured that your small, steady efforts are making a difference!

Distractions occur for any number of deeper reasons; our personality type and associated vulnerabilities usually dictate what it is that tends to distract us the most. External sensory input, especially noise, tends to interrupt mindfulness, as does internal emotional processing. You can train your mind to cope with sensory distractions by applying mindfulness to each of your senses in a systematic way. Common practices include listening to only one instrument in a piece of music, watching the space between leaves of trees, or not scratching when you have an itch. As you strengthen your ability to master your senses, you will turn away from them more easily when they interrupt your mindfulness practice.

Mindfulness helps you discover how your mind works and what situations, thoughts, or feelings seem to trigger stress. While quieting your mind may seem like a great idea, the journey to quietude takes you through some uncomfortable places in your own mind! The distracting emotional pain or mental negativity is enough to make many people turn away from mindfulness. Unpacking the particular reasons behind your own mental busyness might be challenging, but with patience and effort (and perhaps outside support) you will come to understand the roots of your emotional distractions and weed them out. Allow yourself time in a journal or with a friend, meditation mentor, or counselor to move beyond the surface distraction and relate it to overall patterns in your choices, behaviors, and emotions. Investigate the truth of a troubling situation and apply a spiritual concept to this learning process. For example, a bank teller who was very frightened by a robbery found her way out of the fear by having compassion for the thief's socioeconomic barriers; very few people actually want to be robbers. Via the virtue of compassion, the teller's repetitive distraction of fear gradually loosened, and she was better able to not only focus her mind in practice but also live life with greater awareness of others. The process of investigating the roots of emotional distractions, weeding them out, and replacing them with spiritual principles helps limit habitual emotional distractions and brings continual improvement to mindfulness practice.

As your mindfulness practice improves, you will find yourself more able to remain a present participant in your own life. Continual practice is the most important thing you can do to make mindfulness a habit. Determine one virtue, such as compassion, love, joy, acceptance, peace, or faith, that holds power for you, and then keep that virtue in mind. That virtue becomes an anchor to the present moment as you witness it in action through your breath, body, thoughts, emotions, and responses. You may also use external reminders to draw yourself back to mindful

• • • • • • • •

awareness throughout the day. Every time you see your favorite color, hear a phone ring, or shift activities, let it be a cue to check in with your own mind. Uncomfortable situations, heightened emotions, or a slip in well-being are also excellent opportunities to observe the workings of the mind. Through this commitment to improving practice, mindfulness becomes a habit.

As you commit to incorporating mindful awareness into your life, your connection to healthy breathing, physical well-being, and emotional balance likely will improve. Mindfulness practice is an opportunity for personal evolution. A spiritual intention gives deeper meaning and motivation to the practice of observing the breath, physical sensations, emotions, and mental processes, as well as their connections to our behavior and life choices. Consistent mindfulness practice can change the shape and function of our brains, leading to cognitive and emotional improvements. In order to gain these benefits, you can learn to circumvent the common saboteurs of judgments, expectations, and preconceived ideas and programming. By linking your mindfulness practice to a personally meaningful intention, you further secure your practice and imbue it with meaning and inspiration.

Erin Byron is a psychotherapist whose Master of Arts dissertation was on yoga for post-traumatic stress disorder. Erin is a senior creator of Comprehensive Yoga Therapist Training and co-author of *Yoga Therapy for Stress and Anxiety*. Her home base is Brantford, Ontario, Canada, where she trains yoga and meditation teachers and comprehensive yoga therapists. Erin enjoys traveling to teach these subjects as well as leading diverse groups such as university students, business professionals, and mental health practitioners on topics such as body psychology, transforming feelings, and yoga therapy for mental health.

Peter Arcari

• • • • • • •

Meditation
THE ULTIMATE WIRELESS CONNECTION

● ● ● ● ● ● ● ● ● ●

MICHAEL BERNARD BECKWITH

On this, modern science and ancient spiritual traditions agree: when worry, stress, self-doubt, or resistance to our present-moment experience arises, meditation metaphorically blows back our hair, revealing our Original Face. When we direct our attention from the outer to the inner, we won't find a business mogul, musician, inventor, husband, poet, therapist, beautician, politician, spiritual seeker, or spiritual teacher. We will not be able to point to a mind-defined self, a "me" driven by the fickle ego's whims and wants for name, fame, fortune, or false power. Once we move beyond the obscurations of the restless mind, what we will encounter is our center of beingness, the home of our fundamental goodness, compassion, loving kindness, equanimity, intelligence, intuition, and creativity. The ultimate wireless connection to our inherently enlightened state of being, meditation is the art of living in what the Buddha called witnessing awareness—mindfulness.

Regardless of how the outer world of phenomena spins round and round, revealing the ever-changing landscape of thoughts, events, emotions, and conditions, meditation trains us in realizing that mindfulness is always available to us. As we deepen our practice, it becomes an

● ● ● ● ● ● ●

assisting grace that shakes us free from the fearful ego's intrusion into our interactions with life. We begin to relate to our challenges as allies in the sense that they offer us rich, liberating material to work with, releasing our tendency to resist, bypass, control, or avoid the circumstances, feelings, events, or people—including ourselves—that we'd rather not face. Rather than react, meditation trains us to mindfully act from a state of awareness. It softens and opens the heart to oneself and others. We become empowered to be more fully present to whomever and whatever stands before us. As we more deeply embody the realization that we are individualized expressions of the unconditional love governing the universe, our self-centered priorities begin to shift, igniting a flame of tremendous love-energy that we long to express as our contribution to the creation of an enlightened society. And during those inevitable gaps of forgetfulness that occur, there is no need to feel guilty. Instead, we can be grateful that we became aware that we had forgotten to be aware. The good news is that with practice, the gaps of forgetfulness will begin to close.

Witnessing the Witness

Meditation escorts you into an impersonal, witnessing awareness. This can set off loud alarms within the mind, whose job description is to guard the protective armor of safety and security it has so deliberately constructed to defend the sense of being a self separate from the whole. When combined with non-dual teachings that challenge the existence of such a self, the path of meditation can begin to sound rather dry, as though all the juiciness has been squeezed out of our human existence. We might wonder if we will continue to enjoy a warm cup of tea, the delights of making love, our favorite movies and music, working out, watching a great basketball game, or laughing at a joke in quite the same way. The paradoxical truth is we are meant to live with gusto, passion, and juice while simultaneously realizing that we are made from the fabric of Pure Awareness that is aware of the individualized expression of itself that each of us is. The unifier of this polarity of our existence is meditation, which you may prove for yourself in the laboratory of your own consciousness.

Begin with the End in Mind

The starting point is to ask yourself why you want to take up meditation practice in the first place. Your honest response will reveal your motivation and inform you of the most effective meditation practice that aligns with your intention. For this, I recommend an abbreviated version of the Life Visioning Process, an inner technology I originated and applied when founding the Agape International Spiritual Center in 1986 and practice to this day. Five qualities set Life

Visioning in motion: intention, receptivity, trust in what is revealed, the self-discipline to take action on what is revealed, and gratitude that you already possess all that is required to take mindful action. So let us begin.

EXERCISE: **Life Visioning**

Find a quiet location and disengage from your phone and other externalities. For at least ten minutes, center yourself by observing your incoming and outgoing breath. Feel deeply into your heart, opening and sensitizing your intuitive faculty. When you feel ready, ask the first question: "Why do I want to begin a meditation practice? Is it to relax, to attain peace, poise, confidence, to awaken mindfulness?"

Simply keep your seat in the present moment, just observing without forcing a response or judging what does or does not arise.

Next, place this question before your intuitive faculty: "What meditation teacher, method, and community best support my intention to meditate?"

If you are reading this book, you probably have at least some knowledge of meditation centers, teachers, and books that are available to you. When the meditation method that is right for you at this stage in your development is discovered, it will click in your consciousness. Go with it—explore, experiment, play—and remain open.

Now move to the next question: "What must I adjust in my daily schedule to establish my meditation practice?"

In the language of your own heart, regardless of the completeness or incompleteness of responses you have received, give your sacred yes to trusting that more will be revealed.

Enter a state of gratitude for your wholehearted commitment to this vision and its fulfillment.

The Power of Questioning

Empowering questions support us in discovering fresh truths about our intentions and motivations. They cause us to become more flexible, confident, courageous, and vulnerable, preparing us for extraordinary adventures in consciousness. Proceed with full confidence that your wholeheartedness will continue to deepen your yearning to live each moment in openness to life's limitless possibilities. As the teachings of the Hopi encourage, "Know your garden and where is your water," which is a way of inspiring us to become intimate with the terrain of our consciousness and the practices that will nourish it into the full bloom of awakened awareness.

• • • • • • •

Michael Bernard Beckwith is the founder of Agape International Spiritual Center, a worldwide movement headquartered in Los Angeles. A sought-after speaker, he addressed the UN General Assembly during its 2012 World Interfaith Harmony Conference and annually speaks on behalf of the Gandhi King Season for Nonviolence. He has appeared on *The Dr. Oz Show*, *The Oprah Winfrey Show*, *OWN Help Desk*, *Tavis Smiley*, and *Larry King Live*. He is the author of *Life Visioning*, *Spiritual Liberation*, and *TranscenDance Expanded*. His KPFK radio show can be heard every Friday at 1:00 PM PST. For more information, visit www.agapelive.com.

MariaRangelPhotography.com

Starting Out with Breathwork, Awareness, and Concentration

William L. Mikulas, PhD

The novice level is where everyone begins. There is no problem with being a novice; on the contrary, it is great you are beginning a journey that will significantly improve your life. It's important to start here. Be honest with yourself, be patient, and have fun.

Time and Place

Eventually, the mental training you will learn can be done almost anywhere and anytime. But at first it is more effective to simplify the situation so you can devote all your attention to mental practice, minimizing distractions.

First, find a time of day for the practices. Your schedule permitting, it is usually best to do the practices at about the same time each day, at least five days a week. It should be a natural part of your daily routine. If, instead, each day you wait to see when the practice will fit in or when you are in the mood to do it, soon you won't be doing the practices at all. Find a good time and simply do it.

For some people the morning is a good practice time. Eventually you will be able to begin the day with a mind that is focused and clear and an open heart, which will be a great help in whatever you need to do each day. After getting up and going to the bathroom, you might do some type of exercise, such as walking or yoga. Relaxing during this time will help the mental practice.

For some people the early evening is a good practice time. It is a nice way to gradually relax and get free from the stresses of the day, and perhaps then be more fully present with others. So, after the work and chores of the day are largely over, and probably after the evening meal, is a good time.

Of course, you can practice any time of day that works for you, and more than once per day if possible and desirable. It is good to be relaxed but not too tired. Activities that help you relax, such as listening to music, breathwork, or smooth stretching exercises, help prepare you for mental practice. At first during mental practice you will have a tendency to fall asleep, so it is good if you are not too tired. Similarly, it is good not to be too full from a meal, as this may make you physically tired and mentally sluggish.

How long to practice each day will vary with what level you are at and the exercises you are doing that day. But you will be surprised that not much time is necessary for real accomplishments. At first, fifteen minutes a day will be good. During mental practice your sense of time will often change; sometimes time will seem to go very slow, sometimes very fast. If you need to be aware of when some time arrives, such as time to go to work or school or to walk the dog, you can periodically glance at a clock. For most people it is better to set a timer that alerts you with a gentle tone or music.

Having established a time for practice, you now need a place for practice. This practice area should be someplace where you won't be disturbed, such as the bedroom with the door closed. Make sure that people who live with you understand and respect this private time. Turn off all phones and perhaps put pets somewhere else. You can add props to your practice place; this is helpful to some people but not necessary. For example, you might have a robe to wear or a special cushion to sit on that you only use during mental practice. You might burn some incense or play some music, as long as the music is simple background music that does not attract your attention or involve you.

At first, for most people, practicing inside is usually best—there are fewer things to deal with and fewer distractions—but periodically practice outside if you wish. Nature can be very helpful in mental training. Try sitting in a garden, next to a tree, beside moving water, or at the shore of a lake or sea.

· · · · · · ·

Form

Form refers to what you do with your body during mental practice. Eventually form will be irrelevant; you can work with your mind no matter what your body is doing. But at first, particularly when training concentration and awareness, it is best to keep things simple; set the body down and focus on the mind.

For most people sitting is the best form. Sitting might be in a chair with feet flat on the floor or sitting on the floor on a cushion with legs crossed. In either case your back should be fairly straight up and you should not be leaning forward, backward, or to either side. Hands should be placed in your lap, and your head should be tilted slightly down to the front.

Although it is not necessary, you might want to be more specific about the form. This helps some people be more focused and grounded in the body. For others it is a way to encourage being more precise in what one does, and for others it helps balance the flow of energy in the body. Here are some possible ways to be more specific with your form. Place your hands, palms up, on top of each other, so fingers are on top of fingers and the thumb tips touch each other. Keep your arms slightly away from the sides of your body. Be sure your head is not turned to the side; your ears should be in line with your shoulders. Put the tip of your tongue gently on the roof of your mouth, which in Chinese medicine is understood to complete an energy circuit.

A second form for the body is lying down. This form is good as an occasional change from sitting or for people who can't sit very long, perhaps due to back problems. Whether sitting or lying, at first there will be a tendency to fall asleep. This tendency is more true for lying, which is why sitting is usually better. When lying, lie on your back with your arms by your sides and legs uncrossed.

For most people, the best form at first includes closing the eyes; this greatly reduces distractions. As an occasional variation or if you are anxious with your eyes closed, have your eyes slightly open but not actually looking at anything.

Breathwork

You have the time, place, and form; now you are ready to begin the mental training. Start by observing your breathing and becoming more aware of exactly how you breathe. This observing will help you breathe more effectively and increase the health of your body.

First, pay attention to your diaphragm, a muscular sheet between your chest cavity and your stomach cavity. When you breathe in, particularly with deep breaths, your diaphragm goes down, massaging the organs in your stomach cavity and pushing your stomach out. When you breathe out, your diaphragm rises and pushes air out of the bottom of your lungs.

Sitting or lying quietly, put your attention on the internal feelings of your diaphragm rising and falling. Try to be aware of the various sensations associated with this movement. Spend one

· · · · · · · ·

or two training sessions just observing the movement of the diaphragm. If you have trouble with this, don't be concerned. Just notice the effects of the moving diaphragm, particularly your stomach going in and out. To emphasize this you might, for a little while, pull your stomach in during exhalation and then relax it for inhalation.

Next, observe the complete breath. When breathing in it is usually best to breathe through the nose, as the nose cleans, warms, and humidifies the incoming air. Of course, sometimes—such as when one has a cold—nose breathing is difficult. Exhaling through the nose is not as important, and sometimes exhaling through the mouth is better, such as when doing deep breathing exercises.

A complete inbreath has four stages. First is inhaling, ideally through the nose. Second is the filling of the bottom of the lungs. During this time the diaphragm contracts and falls, the lower ribs slightly expand, and the stomach rises. Third, the middle of the lungs expand and there is outward chest movement. And then fourth, the top of the lungs fill, and the upper chest and shoulders might rise somewhat. During a complete exhale, everything is done in reverse. The top of the lungs empty, then the middle of the lungs as the chest contracts, and then the bottom of the lungs as the diaphragm rises.

Spend a week of practice time just quietly observing your breathing, noticing ever more subtle aspects to it. Sometimes follow the breath through all the stages listed in the previous paragraph. Sometimes stay focused on just one of the stages for a while, such as the chest movement as the middle of the lungs fill or empty. Encourage your complete breath to be smooth throughout. Notice any obstructions and relax or free them. Use this as a time to relax. Imagine that when you are breathing in you are bringing in relaxation. You might say "calm and relaxed" to yourself as you inhale.

Breathing too quickly can reduce oxygen to the body and cause dizziness, feelings of breathlessness, and lack of concentration. If this happens, stop what you are doing, relax, and recover. Then alter the exercise, such as breathing less deeply or less frequently, until you find a way to continue and not get dizzy or lightheaded. Also, if you have heart problems and notice that breathwork causes your heart to beat fast or irregularly, stop the breathwork until you consult with your heart specialist.

There are four common bad habits of breathing: mouth breathing, overbreathing, breath holding, and chest breathing. When observing your breathing, see if any of these apply to you. In mouth breathing one tends to breathe too much through the mouth. Periodically throughout the day check your breathing to see if you are mouth breathing or have someone point out to you when you are mouth breathing. In overbreathing the amount of time to inhale is greater than the time to exhale. This is opposite to the way it usually should be, with more time to exhale than to inhale. To check this out, count or time your inhalations and exhalations. If you

· · · · · · · ·

are overbreathing, try to shorten your inhalations. Many people overbreathe when they are distressed. In breath holding there is not a smooth transition from inhalation to exhalation. Rather, the person catches and holds his breath, perhaps with some struggle to initiate the exhalation. This is particularly common during exercise. Look for this; if it occurs, relax and smooth out the breathing. Sometimes relaxing the stomach after inhalation can help.

Particularly important is the difference between diaphragm breathing and chest breathing. Diaphragm breathing, also called deep breathing or yogic breathing, is the healthiest way to breathe. As described above, it involves the diaphragm to best empty and fill the lungs. Diaphragm breathing is very important, since 70 percent of the body's waste is expelled by the lungs! In chest breathing the diaphragm is not adequately used; rather, it is the chest muscles that are doing most of the work. This is the type of breathing that one does when one is frightened or angry. It is good for emergencies but not for overall breathing. Chest breathing does not work the lungs effectively and keeps the body stressed. Unfortunately, many people chest breathe far too much for the health of their body and mind, and most of these people are unaware of when they are chest breathing or when they have switched from diaphragm breathing.

By learning to observe your breathing, as described above, and then periodically observing your breathing throughout the day, you will learn to notice when you are chest breathing and diaphragm breathing. Particularly observe your breathing when you are under pressure, stressed, or emotionally upset. Whenever you notice you are chest breathing, switch to diaphragm breathing. Stop what you are doing, if possible; focus on your breathing and take a few deep breaths. This practice may be one of the best things you can do for the overall health of your body, mind, and spirit.

To check your breathing, lie on your back, with knees bent and feet apart and flat on the floor. Put your palms flat against your lower rib cage with the middle fingers just touching. Inhale deeply and see if your fingertips are forced apart. With good deep breathing they will separate, perhaps by an inch or two. Then put one hand on your stomach and one on your chest. Breathe deeply and notice when the hands move and whether one moves more than the other.

There is much to be learned about your breathing. Take your time and joyfully explore. Learn how to gradually improve your breathing, both during practice times and throughout the day.

Awareness

Let us consider what awareness is. Awareness refers to the conscious aspect of your mind. When your ears pick up a sound, you may be conscious of music or a voice. When your brain is planning how to respond to a situation, you may be conscious of a thought about your intentions. This awareness is very common and obvious. But what is not well-known is that you can learn how to be more aware. There are two related aspects to this. First is becoming aware of things you weren't aware of before. Second is your awareness becoming sharper and clearer: you perceive things more directly and accurately, with less distortion and confusion. You are sobering up the drunken monkey. In Buddhist psychology this type of awareness is called "mindfulness," and cultivation of mindfulness is the most important Buddhist practice.

Understanding what awareness is not is trickier. Awareness is not thinking, evaluating, or reacting; it is simply being aware. For example, the neighbor's dog starts barking when you are resting. Your mind identifies the sound and you have the thought, "There is that dog again!" This thought is not awareness; it is just a thought. The thought may lead to another thought, such as, "Why don't the neighbors keep that dog inside?" This reaction to the barking is not awareness; it is just a thought. Awareness is present to the extent that you are conscious of these thoughts, such as consciously noticing you are having thoughts about the barking dog. But all of this happens very quickly, and people are readily pulled into their thoughts, so the role of awareness is small. Later, as you become more aware, you will control your thoughts rather than them controlling you. But for now it is simply important to remember that thinking is not awareness, although you can be aware of thinking.

Similarly, you may emotionally react in some way to the dog's barking, such as getting mad. But any type of reaction is not awareness; awareness is being conscious of the reaction, such as noticing a change in breathing related to getting mad. The point is that awareness does not do anything; it simply notices what is happening. You notice the sights, sounds, and memories that come to you. You notice the feelings and thoughts that are brought forth, and you notice how you respond to these feelings and thoughts. Awareness is a passive observer, a neutral witness. It does not choose, think, or evaluate, but it does observe choosing, thinking, and evaluating.

EXERCISE: **Develop Awareness with Breathwork**

An excellent time to develop awareness is during breathwork, as you have just learned to do. For now just sit or lie quietly and put your attention on your breathing. Don't be concerned about how you are breathing at this time; rather, put your emphasis on gradually being more and more aware of the fine aspects of breathing. Just let breathing go naturally and observe it in greater and greater detail. Put your attention on the breath at the tip of the nose. Notice how the air swirls around your nose and lip as you breathe in and out through your nose. Notice how the air you breathe in is cooler than the air you breathe out.

After watching your breathing at the tip of the nose, switch your attention to the rising and falling of the diaphragm and the stomach, as you did during breathwork. Don't be concerned about how you are breathing now; rather, encourage yourself to gradually become more and more aware of feelings in this part of the body related to breathing. Minimize thinking here and just become more aware of your body.

• • • • • • • •

Next, switch your attention to following a whole cycle of breathing, as you did in breathwork. Feel the sensations in your body as the breath comes in through the nose, enters the throat, and goes into the lungs. Follow the breath back out as you exhale. Feel the sensations related to movement of your stomach, diaphragm, chest, and perhaps shoulders. Simply feel; don't think or evaluate. Notice positive feelings that accompany breathing, and notice any obstruction to breathing, pain, or stress. Don't be pleased or concerned about any of this at this time—just notice. When watching a complete cycle of breathing, notice there is a pause after inhaling before you begin exhaling and a pause after exhaling before inhaling. Be aware of these pauses and any feelings associated with them.

For a while, perhaps a couple of weeks, have separate times for breathwork and awareness of breathwork. During breathwork cultivate awareness, but emphasize correct breathing. During awareness training just let the breathing go naturally, and emphasize passive awareness. Then, in the future, these can be combined, and you will develop awareness and work on your breathing at the same time.

EXERCISE: **Body Scan Awareness Practice**

Another awareness practice is the body scan, a popular practice in yoga and in clinics for stress and pain. This is a simple practice that will help you become more aware of your body as well as relax and heal your body. The body scan can be done standing or sitting, but at first it is probably best done lying down. Very slowly let your awareness move through your body, beginning at the toes and moving to the head. Move your attention slowly and notice whatever you encounter. Don't try to force awareness; let it happen. One possible sequence through your body would be: right toes up to pelvis, left toes up to pelvis, pelvis to torso to shoulders, down right arm to fingers and back up, down left arm and back up, and then shoulders to neck to face to back of head to top of head. Devise a sequence that works best for you. Do a body scan at least once a day, five times a week, for a few weeks. After that, do it however often it is useful.

As an awareness practice, each time you do a body scan, encourage yourself to become more aware of your body, noticing subtler and subtler details. Notice any stress or discomfort in your body. Notice if there is any numbness in some parts of the body. Notice if it is easier to be aware of some parts of your body than others. Is it easier to be aware of the front of your body than the back? Are you aware of your heartbeat? Can you be aware of the cavity of your torso, the space within your body? Do any parts of your body seem alien to you—somehow not truly part of yourself?

Relaxing

Relaxing helps breathwork, awareness training, and concentration training, which is why it is helpful to relax before doing any of these. In turn, breathwork and awareness training will gradually help you to relax more. Switching from chest breathing to diaphragm breathing is a very powerful relaxation practice for some people. This practice involves learning to be aware of your breathing so you notice when you are chest breathing, and then having the skills to switch to diaphragm breathing. Periodically when doing breathwork imagine that with each inhalation you are breathing in relaxation, and with each exhalation you are breathing out stress and anxiety. You might visualize these with shapes and colors, such as breathing in soothing white light and exhaling a dark mist of tension.

After doing body scans for a while as awareness training, you can modify the scans to also make them a good way to relax your body. When you notice tension in some part of your body, relax and let the tension flow out. For each part of your body that you attend to, imagine that you are actively breathing into that body part, with the breath bringing in relaxation. Then passively let the breath flow back out and take tension with it. Let hardness dissolve into softness. In Chinese medicine it is understood that when you focus your awareness on some part of your body, as during a body scan, you are bringing life force (chi/qi) to this body part that will help energize and heal this area. Thus, spend extra time with any part of your body that needs such help. Places that want healing may draw your attention to them. You might imagine that you are sending energy, healing, or love into that body part. Such imagining will actually have a physical effect.

Muscle Relaxation Practice

In Western psychology one of the most powerful forms of relaxation is muscle relaxation, also called deep muscle relaxation and progressive muscle relaxation. In this practice you gradually go through your body, tensing and relaxing muscles. As a result of awareness training, during this time you gradually learn to be more aware of tension and relaxation in your body. Then, in real-life situations when you start to get tense or anxious, you will notice it and relax. Eventually your body will do this automatically, but first it is necessary to begin awareness of muscle tension.

During body scans you are actively looking for tension to relax. To help this we now add tensing and relaxing muscles to body scans. A detailed description of muscles to be tensed and how to tense them is found in the following exercise. For example, say during your body scan that you are currently focused on your right hand. What you would add at this point is making a tight fist with your right hand and then gradually opening your fist, letting the tension flow out and your hand relax. During this time you want to be very aware of exactly what the tension feels like.

· · · · · · · ·

Equally important, you want to be very aware of what it feels like when the tension changes to relaxation and what relaxation feels like.

This muscle-tensing practice should be done a number of times to improve awareness of the body. You may choose to do it more, particularly if you have a need to relax or are aware of a lot of tension in your body. If you do continue, begin with the individual muscle groups listed in the following exercise. This approach allows you to give specific attention to each muscle group, perhaps spending more time with muscles that your body scans suggest need additional work. After doing that many times, combine these groups so that you are tensing and relaxing groups of muscles, such as all the muscles in your right hand and arm. After a few times of doing that, see if you can relax the muscles without tensing them. Finally, throughout your day periodically notice any tension in your body and relax it.

Any type of relaxation practice can sometimes be improved by giving yourself relaxing suggestions. Make up your own or try a variation of one or more of the following: My breathing is slow and deep. Each breath relaxes me more and more. My legs (or other body part) are heavy and relaxed. My leg muscles are smooth and relaxed. Warmth is flowing into my legs. My whole body is relaxing more and more.

Relaxing your muscles is one of the most effective ways to relax your body, and relaxing your body helps to relax your mind. Here you will learn a set of exercises to relax your muscles. At first it will take some time to do these exercises, about a half hour each day. But after a couple of weeks you can do them in much less time, and then eventually you can relax just by willing it. Everyone can benefit from doing these exercises for a few weeks, even if now or later you have another way to relax, for these exercises will put you more in touch with your body and also give you a sense of what a relaxed body can or should feel like.

The exercises are usually best done in a lounge chair with your feet on the floor. However, they can be done in other positions such as lying on the floor. It is usually not good to do them lying in bed since you will have a tendency to fall asleep. Do the exercises at least once a day—twice a day if possible. Take your time when doing the exercises. For many people it takes thirty to forty-five minutes at this stage. In these exercises first you will tense a muscle for five to ten seconds and then relax the muscle for twenty to thirty seconds, releasing the tension as fast as possible. When tensing the muscle you should focus your attention on the feelings of tension. Feel the tension! When relaxing the muscle you should focus your attention on the change from tension to relaxation. Feel the tension flow out of the muscle. Feel the change from tension to relaxation. Feel the relaxation in the muscle.

Below is a list of muscles to go through with this procedure. Use this list for a while, as it has been well tested. If you have any special physical limitations such as a trick knee or spinal injury, be sure to check with your doctor before doing any of these exercises. If you have certain muscles

• • • • • • • •

that tend to get cramps, do not tense them as hard as other muscles. Feel free to spend extra time with those muscles of particular interest to you. For example, if you get tension headaches, spend some extra time with the muscles of the shoulders and neck. As you do these exercises you will become more and more aware of your body and the muscles you wish to work with. For example, you may find out over time that as you worry, you tense muscles in your stomach or jaw or forehead. Then you would want to do extra work with these muscles. Eventually, you may even devise whole sets of special exercises for yourself.

Sometimes when you relax your body you may experience unusual body feelings such as muscle twitches or the sensation of floating. These are common and nothing to worry about. Just let the feelings go, notice them, and continue to relax. Remember that in doing these exercises, you are always in control! For a few people, doing these exercises makes them more aroused rather than more relaxed. If this happens to you, decrease how hard you tense the muscles. Gradually and slowly tense until you feel the slightest increase in tension, then stop tensing.

EXERCISE: Relaxing Muscles

Now it is time to actually do the exercises. Close your eyes and do some deep breathing, then begin muscle relaxation using the muscle list below. Keep your eyes closed as much as possible. Go through the list one muscle group at a time, firmly tensing the muscles as described. (Alternative ways of tensing some of the muscles are given in parentheses. You may wish to try these alternatives later on.) Tense and relax each muscle group twice in a row, tensing and relaxing as described above, with your attention on the feelings of tension and relaxation. Each time after you have tensed and relaxed a muscle group twice, relax and give yourself suggestions to feel heavy, calm, and relaxed. Then move on to the next muscle group on the list. Each time you see "deep breathing" on the list, spend a couple of minutes doing deep breathing. Let yourself relax even more with each outbreath. Let each outbreath say "relax" to you.

When you complete the list, stay quiet and relaxed, with your eyes closed. Then slowly count from one to five, letting yourself relax even more with each count. Stay relaxed for a few minutes. After this, slowly count yourself back from five to one and slowly open your eyes. Get up slowly and pay attention to all your feelings. Remember, you are always in control.

You may find it useful to make an audio recording of you or someone else giving you all the above instructions to tense and to relax, which muscles to tense, and when to do deep breathing. This allows you to put full attention on your feelings, without thinking about what to do next. However, the counting from one to five and back to one you should always do yourself.

· · · · · · · ·

Muscle Relaxation List

Following is a list of muscle groups to be tensed and relaxed. For most people, tensing and relaxing each of the following twice in a row works best. Alternative ways of tensing are in parentheses.

right hand: make a fist (bend hand back at wrist)

right bicep: bend elbow and "make a muscle," tightening the large muscle in the upper part of the arm (press elbow against arm of chair)

right arm: push arm straight out in front with fingers spread (reach for sky or out to side or back over head or one after the other)

left hand: make a fist (bend hand back at wrist)

left bicep: bend elbow and "make a muscle," tightening the large muscle in the upper part of the arm (press elbow against arm of chair)

left arm: push arm straight out in front with fingers spread (reach for sky or out to side or back over head or one after the other)

deep breathing: take several deep breaths, focusing on your diaphragm or the breath at the tip of your nose

forehead: wrinkle forehead and raise eyebrows (lower eyebrows and make exaggerated frown)

eyes: close tight and wrinkle nose (open eyes as wide as possible)

mouth: pucker lips and then frown, push tongue against roof of mouth (open mouth as wide as possible or grin broadly)

jaws: bite teeth together and pull back corners of mouth

neck: rotate head in both directions, rolling the neck (push chin against chest or head against back of chair)

deep breathing: take several deep breaths, focusing on your diaphragm or the breath at the tip of your nose

shoulders: push shoulder blades back as if to touch, then shrug shoulders and pull head, lowering chin to chest

back: arch lower back, sticking out chest and stomach

chest: take a deep breath, force out chest, hold breath

stomach: tighten stomach muscles (pull stomach in and/or push stomach out)

• • • • • • •

deep breathing: take several deep breaths, focusing on your
diaphragm or the breath at the tip of your nose

legs: (a) push against the floor, first heels and then toes, or
(b) with legs straight out, first flex your feet, pulling toes
toward you, and then extend, pushing toes away from you
while turning the feet inward and curling the toes

deep breathing: take several deep breaths, focusing on your
diaphragm or the breath at the tip of your nose

1–5 count: to go deeper into relaxation

5–1 count: to bring you back

EXERCISE: **Relaxing Muscle Groups**

You should do the above exercises for about two to three weeks. Then you can start
to shorten the exercises by combining muscle groups and tensing several groups at
once, such as:

- both hands and arms together
- forehead, eyes, mouth, jaws, and neck together
- shoulders, back, chest, and stomach together

Here you will need to develop your own best way of combining the muscle groups
for tensing in a way that suits your needs and interests. With the exception of combining muscle groups, the rest of the practice should be the same, including keeping
your attention on tension and relaxation and the use of deep breathing.

After you have done the above exercises with combined muscle groups for at least
two to three weeks, you can move to the next stage. Here you should practice going
through the list of muscles and relaxing them *without* tensing them first. That is,
you do everything the same as at the beginning of these exercises but leave out the
tensing. Be sure to include giving yourself relaxation suggestions such as "calm and
relaxed" while relaxing the muscles. Then every couple of days do the exercises with
tensing. Continue to practice this until you can relax your muscles at will.

Finally, practice relaxing combinations of muscles without tensing them. Move
toward relaxing your whole body at one time.

Some people find that it helps their relaxation if they imagine a relaxing scene. The
imagined scene might be sitting on a sofa in front of a fire on a cold winter night,
lying on soft grass on a warm spring day and looking at the clouds floating by, lying
on the beach on a warm summer day, or lying in a tent listening to a light rain.

. . . .

Concentration

Concentration is the ability to keep the mind focused on one thing. Sometimes called one-pointedness, it involves getting the drunken monkey to stop running around so much and stay in one place. Here are some very common examples of lack of concentration: Jim is listening to music he enjoys, but much of the time he is not hearing the music; rather, his mind is jumping to various thoughts about music, plans for the day, and concerns about his girlfriend. Stan needs a good night's sleep for an important day tomorrow, but instead of sleeping he is kept awake by a mind running through the next day's events. Rod is studying for an exam and has just read through a page of text, but he has no idea of what is on that page because his mind was jumping around. Kaitlin and Josh are disagreeing about how to deal with their son Aaron, and when Kaitlin is talking, Josh is not fully listening; rather, he is reacting to what Kaitlin says and planning what he will say.

You will learn how to keep your mind focused, a skill that philosopher and psychologist William James considered the most important part of one's education. With this skill you will enjoy sensory pleasures much more, such as music, food, and sex. People who are trying to lose weight can eat less of some food yet have more pleasure from this food than before learning to concentrate. Students learn how to stay focused on their lessons and thus learn better in less time. People learn how to listen better to others, which improves their relationships. Athletes improve in their sports, such as being better able to keep their eyes on the ball or being less distracted by others. Artists learn how to get out of their way and immerse themselves in the creative act. This is a small sample of the benefits you can enjoy as you develop concentration.

Concentration training will begin by keeping your attention on your breath. Later you can practice with other things, such as listening to music. Most people find this fairly challenging at first because they have such little control over their minds. As a result, many people give up early, convinced they can't learn to focus their minds. Don't be concerned if you find this difficult at first; you are just beginning to get control over your mind. Be patient and don't upset yourself! If you simply do the practices as described below, you will gradually develop concentration, even if at times it doesn't seem to you that you are making progress. You are. If you regularly do the practices, after a few weeks you will gradually start noticing the differences in your life, such as the beginning of some of the benefits listed above.

At the novice level the goal is to begin developing basic focus of the mind: one-pointedness. Later on you will discover that as the mind stays focused and does not jump around as much, the mind relaxes and becomes more tranquil and quiet. As the mind relaxes, it causes the body to relax. So, if you choose, eventually you will possess the world's three most effective ways to relax body and mind: quieting the mind, muscle relaxation, and breathwork.

· · · · · · ·

You'll be ready to begin concentration practice after you have spent a couple of weeks doing the breathwork and awareness of breath exercises discussed above. Begin by relaxing and then sitting or lying, quietly observing your breathing. Next, put your attention on your breathing, either at the tip of your nose or the rising and falling of your diaphragm or stomach. Breathe naturally, and don't be concerned about how well you are breathing or how aware you are of the breathing; now it is time to emphasize concentration.

Mental labeling can be useful here. If you are focusing on the breath at the tip of the nose, very gently in the back of your mind say "in" when you breathe in and "out" when you breathe out. If you are focused on the rising and falling of the diaphragm or stomach, then gently say "rising" and "falling." Experiment with this labeling at different times. For some people it is helpful, for others it gets in the way.

Now focus your mind on your breathing. It probably won't stay there very long. Soon it will run off, as to a sound, feeling, or thought. As soon as you are aware that your attention has left your breathing, gently and firmly bring your attention back to your breath. Again it won't stay long, and again you gently and firmly bring it back. That is all you need to do! Don't try to hold your attention on your breath; that won't work. Just keep bringing it back. Don't try to block other things from coming into your mind or grabbing your attention; that won't work. Just notice where your mind goes and gently bring it back to the breath. Sometimes this will be easy, sometimes hard. Some days you will feel you made progress, some days you will feel you did poorly. None of this matters! All that is important is that you do the practice regularly, regardless of how you evaluate your progress. Do this practice at least ten to fifteen minutes a day, at least five days a week. Do it longer whenever you wish. Again, be patient here. If during a ten-minute practice session your mind is focused for just one minute, you will benefit.

At the novice level, breathwork, concentration, and much of awareness is focused on breathing. Hence, there is a lot of overlap in these practices. At first it is important to keep these separate, at least for a few weeks. Then you can combine them into one practice. You sit or lie watching your breathing, cultivating awareness and adjusting your breathing as appropriate. You don't stay focused on one aspect of breathing, such as at the tip of your nose. Rather, your focus will move from one breathing area to another. But wherever your focus is, whenever your mind leaves the breath, you gently and firmly bring it back. Some days or sometimes within a practice session you may emphasize awareness over concentration; other times you may emphasize concentration. Experiment with different things to do here. Be playful and have fun.

Attitude

Attitude is the mental set in which one approaches situations. For example, some people have a positive attitude toward the world, seeing it as fun and challenging. Others have a negative attitude, seeing the world as unpleasant and problematic. Obviously the person with a positive attitude will have a happier and more effective life than the person with a negative attitude. As you will see, attitude is a very important part of mental training—a part that is often overlooked.

Attitude includes moods, associations, expectations, and intentions. The importance of attitude is often underappreciated because almost everyone is very inaccurate about their own attitudes; people generally perceive their attitudes as being much more positive, supporting, loving, and so forth than they actually are. Don't overlook the importance by saying things such as "I already do that" or "that doesn't apply to me." Rather, really reflect on suggestions related to attitude, and realize that whatever your current attitude, it can be improved in ways that will help you. There is a lot of subtlety here, and much more can be learned than it first seems.

The two aspects of attitude are to act with intention and have fun. To act with intention means to take your time and actually do the exercises, not just read and think about them. Acting with intention means to do it now, no excuses or procrastination. If not now, when? Acting with intention means to accept where you are right now and get started, not wish you were somewhere else or things were different.

The second part of the attitude is to have fun. Relax into the journey and enjoy it. Don't make the exercises into serious or heavy tasks, just do them and enjoy what you encounter and learn. Approach the practices with playful curiosity and be an amused explorer of your own mind.

William L. Mikulas is a professor emeritus at the University of West Florida and the author of *Taming the Drunken Monkey* and numerous books and articles combining Western psychology with Eastern wisdom and health traditions. Mikulas has also conducted lectures and workshops around the world on Buddhist and Western psychology.

· · · · · · ·

Deep Breathing

ROBERT BUTERA, PHD

Breathing exercises have been implemented in the field of yoga for thousands of years as an aid to calming the mind. While in deep states of meditation, yogis realized that the breathing rate diminished. As the yogi would wish to re-enter the deep mental state, one of the first steps was to slow the breathing. Hence, when teaching meditation to students, the yogi began by showing students how to breathe deeply.

Once, at a group meditation, I sat next to an older man—he was probably as old as I am now, but this was twenty years ago! He was sitting on a church pew, slightly hunched. While he was not very big, in the slouched position his stomach expanded and blocked his diaphragm from moving. Consequently, his breathing was very rapid and shallow, meaning that only the upper respiratory cavity moved (clavicle breathing). In addition, he breathed very quickly—roughly one to two seconds in and one to two seconds out—and overall his breath was quite forced and audible.

Breath and the Mind

"As the breath goes, so does the mind," says the yogic oral tradition. The difficulty with breathing so rapidly is that the nervous system, as well as every other system of the body, is largely regulated by the breathing patterns. Breathe in a rapid fashion as if you are stressed, and your body will digest its food differently than if you breathe in a slow and deep fashion. The nervous system heightens when the breathing is shallow. You can play around with it on your own: breathe a few quick, shallow breaths and see if you can keep yourself from having an emotional reaction related to fear or anxiety!

As a younger graduate student at the time of observing this man, I was perplexed. He was a kind and deep-thinking person, yet his breath did not match his mind. I had no way of sharing this information, yet I still remember the event: this is how important deep breathing is. I was unable to help him, as unsolicited breathing advice is just not a culture norm; however, you can use this example to learn and reap all the benefits of deep breathing.

The moral of this short story is that the thoughts in our mind, which are so difficult to stop or slow down, are regulated by breathing patterns. While this book glosses over the hundreds of proven health benefits of deep breathing, the quieting of the mind is greatly enhanced by some deep breathing. I cannot prove this assertion scientifically without a large research study, but it is plausible that most of the physiological benefits resulting from meditation are related to the fact that breathing slows while meditating.

Students new to deep breathing often feel as though they are meditating for the first few weeks when performing the slower deep breathing exercises. During this chapter you are bound to slow down your thoughts and discover yet another key preparation for meditation—without which you would find it tough to quiet your mind.

A Few Key Reasons Why Deep Breathing Is So Effective for Meditation

Diaphragm (belly) breathing is most important to include in your daily breathing because the majority of the lungs' red blood cells are concentrated in the lowest areas of the lungs. This increases oxygen absorption, which leads to increased vitality and an altered mind. Meditation requires alertness in spite of it looking easy. Secondly, as the belly is moved by the diaphragm in and out, blood circulates throughout the body, and the heart relaxes. Try it: pull in the diaphragm as you exhale and expand the breath into the abdominal area for a few breaths to feel the circulatory effects.

While it may require time to maximize, breathing into the lateral area of the lungs by expanding the rib cage to the sides is an important part of a full breath. To be fully clear, this second facet of a deep breath is the sideways expansion of the lungs. The intercostals muscles, if not used on a regular basis, become stiff like any other muscle. As you open the lungs laterally, you further slow down the process of breathing. What may have been a quick two-second inhalation is immediately slowed by the diaphragm and intercostals movements. This slowing allows small balloon-shaped air sacs, the alveoli, to fully expand and thereby promote greater oxygen absorption. On an emotional level, the slow breath tells the nervous system that you are in a stable, safe environment. Breathing is paramount to the health of mind and body.

As the air travels from the bottom of the lungs upward, the final area to expand is the clavicle or upper chest area. While most people do breathe into this upper region, it is usually just the very front of the upper chest where your hand would rest comfortably on your breast plate. However, if you expand the upper chest area slowly and continue until you feel the air flow into the very top of the lungs, you will notice that rarely does anyone fill that top area. It may feel refreshing and it will take at least two seconds to completely expand this final region of the lungs. Remember, the alveoli sacs resemble balloons and they need to be given time to fully inflate, just like a real balloon.

Exhaling offers a host of benefits as well. First of all, a proper exhale allows there to be a more complete removal of carbon dioxide or "dead air" from the lungs and therefore the potential for a deep inhalation to follow. First squeeze the upper chest, followed by pulling in the rib cage and finally squeezing your stomach back toward the spine. Now you are energized naturally!

After some time of regular practice for five minutes twice daily, along with periodic breathing observations during the day, your breathing cycle will slowly become deeper automatically.

Breath, Mind, and Sanity

"In-spirit-action" or inspiration means both the act of bringing air into the lungs and divine influence. The act of breathing is at once physical, biological, and tactile. The very act of breathing is our most vital of all life lines; without breath, no creature would be alive. Breathing connects all living creatures with the environment. One way of summarizing human suffering is isolation from the larger universe. Meanwhile, breathing is absolute evidence that human beings are not only dependent upon nature for existence but are intimately connected to nature with every breath. So to savor, honor, and revere breathing is akin to respecting the spiritual aspect of all beings.

The word "inspiration" is one of the key principles for meditation. In moments of silent reflection the human being is able to step outside of the humdrum of anthropocentric thinking and step into a larger awareness that begets spiritual fulfillment, joy, and meaning.

EXERCISE: **Breathing Self-Evaluation**

It is important to know where you are when first learning an activity akin to deep breathing. If you are a long-term meditator and understand your breathing pattern, please learn from this exercise as if you were a beginner observing breathing for the first time. Breathing alters our stress level and our state of mind, and it is literally a lifelong lifeline. Proper deep breathing is essentially the most important health choice we can actively make, as without breath for just four minutes, the human body ceases life-supporting function. Paradoxically, for all they *do* instruct, schools do not teach proper deep breathing to young students.

To learn the effects of improper breathing on your physique and mind, sit in a slumping posture that you know is a personal habit of yours. If you are unaware of a slouching position, imagine that you are sitting in front of a computer keyboard with your shoulders and upper body rounded and curved forward. Even though you know that this posture is incorrect, remain in the position and consider the questions that follow. This exercise is safe to use with children or friends, as you are only learning from observation. In fact, all of the breathing exercises below are intentionally simple and available to all fitness levels.

- What part of your lungs moves while you are in your slouched position? The areas to consider are the diaphragm (belly), rib cage, and upper chest (clavicle) regions.
- Which parts of the lungs are restricted in this posture? Consider the same areas as above.
- How many seconds do you inhale? How many seconds do you exhale? Is there a pause after inhalation, exhalation, or both?
- If you notice a pause at any point, how long did it last? What is the quality of the breathing? Some examples are: choppy, in stages like an elevator, starts fast and slows, starts slow and increases. Be creative in describing your unique breath pattern—the goal is observation, after all!
- How do you feel emotionally in this breath?
- To assist in emotional understanding, use your arms and hands to exaggerate the feeling associated with this breathing pattern and observe any accompanying facial expression(s).
- Keep your notes from these observations as we navigate through a series of exercises that will help to improve the quality of your breathing.

Posture Is First

During my first meditation experience in Japan my legs felt as though they had fallen off of my body. Never had my legs been asleep for so long, and never before had I sat on a zafu meditation cushion (let alone knowing that the cushion was called a zafu)! Before even considering meditation you must make sure that you know how to sit and why. In order to be successful with breathing, the spine needs to be erect and the arms and legs comfortable. No matter who you arc, breathing begins with the physical positioning of the body. It is most important to keep in mind that if you feel any physical pain from sitting in meditation, reposition your body. Despite the common image of a monk sitting stone-still for hours in meditation, such rigid positioning not only shuts off body awareness but can also be detrimental to the cushioning mechanisms of your bones and muscles. Do not worry if others are in the room with you—the noise created by you moving is of little to no interference to them—but injured knees are a definite interference to your present and future practice.

Let this point be reiterated: *if you feel any physical pain from sitting in meditation, reposition your body!*

Key Principles

- Lying down is not suitable for meditation; in spite of what people may say, lying down (supine position) is for relaxation. In this position sleep occurs for almost all people, even the most experienced meditator, within eight to twelve minutes.

- Keep the spine erect and the core upright, as this allows maximum blood flow to the brain—therefore keeping you alert and aware in your practice. In addition, an erect spine permits proper breathing; even a slight lean forward can compress the lungs and diaphragm, reducing breathing capacity.

- It has been shown that having a slight smile on your face can help facilitate relaxation of the entire body. Such a "half-grin" also helps settle the shoulders and calm the mind.

- Find a position that makes your legs as comfortable as possible. Remember that pain is to be avoided—sitting in a chair is permitted, if necessary.

- Be careful of your tailbone and coccyx, for improper sitting will compress the area at the base of the spine.

- Keep your pelvis tilted slightly forward (but not the torso) to use the skeleton to support the upper body. When someone sits with a rounded low back due to a pelvis that is tilted backwards, the low back will begin to ache in very short order. Sitting in a chair is best if this happens to be the case.

- While seated with the legs crossed in some fashion offers the idea of stillness and acceptance of one's situation, the legs may be placed really in any comfortable position. Having the legs externally opened in a butterfly position or internally rotated in a kneeling position (with a blanket or bolster for support) are equally acceptable.

· · · · · · · ·

- If you do practice seated meditation, be sure to vary the posture so that you do not strain the body by sitting in one position all of the time.

- If you opt for using a cushion, sit close to the front edge of it and let your crossed legs rest on the floor in front of you. Make sure that you never sit way back on the cushion, as this will cause the front edge to press the underside of the thigh, cutting off circulation and leading you to a lot of leg pain.

- Be careful of the positioning and integrity of your knees in any seated posture. Be mindful of the position and compressive forces working on your lower back. Remember that you are always certainly permitted to meditate in a chair for better support and comfort.

Acceptable Poses for Meditation

The key principles above lend themselves to some of the most common postures suited for meditation. Please keep in mind that this is not an end-all list, and it is more important to listen to your own body than follow someone's direct commands regarding a comfortable meditative posture. Comfort is predominantly subjective—so long as muscles and joints are not compromised—so use your own body's intuition to find what works best for you. As the body can become stilled, so too will follow the mind. Finding your meditation pose (or poses) is the first step.

Easy Pose: Simply sit cross-legged on the floor. Use a pillow or a blanket to keep the pelvis tilted forward if necessary. Be careful of the positioning of the legs so that they do not put undue pressure on your ankles or knees. Please be aware that while this pose is named "easy," you may find it to be quite challenging at first!

Lotus Pose: From easy pose, move your feet up into your lap. While this position is historically "the" meditation pose, be aware that it requires a good deal of flexibility as well as particular joint construction in the hips. If your hip joint anatomically cannot fully rotate externally, this position can be unreachable. For those who can physically get into the posture, it can cause great pressure on the knees. Be sure not to remain in this position beyond a few minutes and to alternate which shin is in front.

Half-Lotus Pose: From easy pose, instead of bringing both feet into the lap, only one foot is elevated. This tends to be easier than a full lotus position, as less flexibility and extreme external rotation of the hip is required. Like the full lotus position, however, it is advisable not to remain in this posture for too long and to alternate which foot is placed in the lap.

• • • • • • • •

Adamant Pose: From a kneeling position, fold the legs and sit the bottom down onto the heels of the feet, keeping both the knees and feet together. This position requires an intense fold of the legs, which can be impeded by tight quadriceps or ankles. This position can also put excessive strain on the knee joint, so you may wish to use a meditation bench, bolster, or blanket to help support the thighs. Traditionally, the tops of the feet rest on the earth, but as mentioned above this can be difficult on the ankles. The toes can be flexed so that the ball of the foot rests on the earth instead. This can be taxing to the toes but also provides some elevation to ease the knees. With a support, this position usually can be held for a prolonged period of time, but without support it is not recommended to hold for too long.

Butterfly Pose: From being seated on the ground, bring the soles of the feet together and let the knees fall out and apart. Like the lotus pose, the ease of even getting into this posture is dependent on the structure of the hip joint and flexibility in the groin. The knees may never reach the ground even in the most flexible individual if the hip joint does not allow for full external rotation. The use of folded blankets or blocks beneath each knee can help alleviate any holding in the legs. Unlike the other seated positions, it is very easy to round the low back sitting in this manner. The placement of a blanket beneath your bottom can help facilitate an easy tilt of the pelvis forward, thus relieving undue compression in the low back.

Sitting in a Chair: As cannot be stressed enough, sitting on the floor may just not be good for you, so you are always permitted to use a chair instead. When choosing a chair, ensure that it has a level seat, a straight back, and no arms. It is best to situate yourself in such a way that your back does not lean against the chair's back. Also, it is very important that the front of the seat not dig into the underside of your thighs, as this can cut off circulation to your lower legs. Once situated on the chair seat, bring your legs together and place your feet flat on the floor to maintain a neutral pelvis.

Standing Prayer Pose: Believe it or not, you can meditate standing! There are inherent challenges with this position, namely falling over, so ensure that the area around you is safe and clear of items. Standing comfortably, bring the feet together; if your balance is weak, it is acceptable to place the feet a few inches apart. Bring your hands up to your heart with the palms together, letting the elbows relax. You are not so much pressing the hands strongly together (which would raise the elbows) as letting them rest on your chest so that the elbows are heavy with gravity. Keep your posture as upright as possible and slowly begin to close your eyes as you move toward quieting the mind.

· · · · · · · ·

Simple Breathing Exercises for Meditation

In this section you will learn a series of breathing exercises, of which only the last will be used as a preparation for even formal observance in meditation. The first three exercises are introduced merely to begin opening the lungs and gain awareness of your full respiratory potential. These exercises may be performed by anyone with any health condition except, of course, any injury that could impede the movement of the lungs. Please note that the purpose of these exercises is simply to develop a slow inhalation and exhalation. The amount of time for the breath will vary; however, each area of the lungs will be in operation with practice and attention.

The exercises to follow, though listed sequentially, are not exercises that are to be "mastered" before moving on to the next. This is not to say that I do not recommend following them in the order they are listed, moving on to the exercises to follow only when you feel comfortable with the current breathing activity. Recall the concept of beginner's mind—each of these exercises are just as powerful to the regular practitioner as they are to the novice for the awareness that can be applied and continually cultivated.

EXERCISE: **Diaphragm Breathing (Part 1 of 3)**

Breathing with the large diaphragm muscle in the center of your body is the first stage for the full yogic three-part deep breath. It is imperative to learn awareness and control of this essential muscle, for the fullest potential of your breath is impossible without utilizing it. This type of breath is also recommended for emotional control—especially anger—because it gives you the time and space to become quiet, increasing internal awareness and emotional integration.

1: Lie comfortably on your back (supine position) and pull the knees up, placing the feet near your buttocks.

2: Place your right hand on your abdomen and see if you can breathe only by moving the diaphragm up and down (your right hand should rise and fall with the breath).

3: Place your left hand on the upper chest area and see if you can keep the left hand from rising and falling as you continue to breathe. A neat fact: watch a baby sometime and you will see that they breathe in this fashion naturally! It is only with age that we forget this completely normal breath pattern.

4: Keep the breath to a steady rhythm, starting with a three-second count in and a three-second count out. You may increase the count as comfortable to a maximum of ten seconds in and out.

5: Perform ten rounds; one inhale and exhale cycle is considered a round.

• • • • • • • •

EXERCISE: **Intercostal Breathing (Part 2 of 3)**

Breathing laterally into the rib cage is perhaps the most difficult part of the breath to learn as it is quite challenging to isolate this region. In addition, the intercostal muscles that lie between the ribs are usually so unused that they tend to "lock" and further prevent conscious control. Using the following exercise, however, freedom of motion can be achieved. To begin to cultivate awareness of this region, we start with a simple preparatory exercise.

1: Sit comfortably on the floor or in a chair and lean forward with the torso ever so slightly.

2: Carefully arch the mid-back to engage the intercostals for support and opening of the lungs. As you breathe, be careful to avoid breathing into the upper lungs as this actually restricts lateral movement.

As you learn to notice these muscles, you can proceed to the formal exercise.

1: Sit or stand erect with your feet shoulder-width apart.

2: Place your hands on the lower portion of the rib cage, just below the chest.

3: As you inhale fully and expand laterally, try to use only your intercostal muscles. The hands should ever so slightly and slowly grow away from each other.

4: Exhale when inhalation is complete, relaxing the intercostals and letting the hands on your ribs come back toward the midline.

5: The emphasis is to try not to use the diaphragm or muscles of the upper chest but to concentrate solely on the lower rib cage area.

6: If you find yourself having trouble with this isolation, try this alternative:

- Sit comfortably, as you did in the preparatory exercise, and this time lean the torso slightly forward.
- Place the hands on the lower ribs, as we did above, and draw the chin comfortably into the chest.
- In this shape, the bent torso restricts the diaphragm while the chin-to-chest helps hold back the upper chest.

7: As you build awareness and are comfortable, start with a three-second count in and out, maintaining an equal breathing rhythm, and gradually increase to five to ten seconds.

8: Ten rounds (one round is one inhale and exhale cycle) is recommended.

· · · · · · · ·

EXERCISE: **Clavicle Breathing (Part 3 of 3)**

Most people these days are quite capable of breathing into the upper chest—in fact, for many that is the only area of the lungs they use! As you perform this exercise of isolating the upper chest region, note that this is still, in fact, one aspect of a deep breath. However, this region can have a far greater level of control when used slowly and deliberately as opposed to the automatic, rapid, and shallow breath most of us experience throughout the day. This exercise aims to isolate the set of muscles that controls the upper lungs for practice purposes only, and not to further the habit of only breathing in the upper chest.

1: Place one hand on your upper chest between your collarbones. Inhale by moving only the clavicle muscles of this region and keeping the intercostals and diaphragm still as best you can.

2: Concentrate on the area below the armpits while keeping an equal count of breaths in and out.

3: To deepen the magnitude of this breath, inhale slowly and when you feel full continue for 2 more seconds, giving the alveoli of the lungs time to expand. You should be able to feel the tops of the lungs (near the base of the throat and neck) completely fill.

4: Release the breath and exhale, breathing out a few seconds longer than you think you possibly can so that the clavicle area is concave and emptied. It may help to cough gently to expel the air.

5: As you mature in the practice, there should be no pauses between inhale and exhale, even with these deeper breaths.

6: Use a count of 2 seconds in and out at first, and gradually increase the count to 5–10 seconds over time.

7: Do ten rounds, again maintaining an equal count for inhalation and exhalation.

EXERCISE: **Three-Part Yogic Breathing**

For this exercise we simply use each of the three parts of the breathing process described above in a coordinated, fluid manner, using all the muscles of the lungs for a deep, rhythmic breath. Inhale first into the base of the lungs (diaphragm) and then fill the intercostals area to the sides, finishing with the upper clavicle area. Without pausing, exhale from the clavicle area first, then draw the intercostals in second, and finish by pulling the navel to the spine as the diaphragm expels the entirety of the breath.

• • • • • • • •

Once the rhythmic breath is achieved, begin to concentrate on a smooth transition from inhalation to exhalation and vice versa. Starting out, though it may be somewhat frightening at times, avoid the tendency to start each exchange quickly. Usually, a person breathes in too quickly for the first few seconds, as there is a desire to get the air in; likewise, when beginning to exhale there is a tendency to expel the air forcefully. Attempt to breathe to the best of your capability in a smooth, even fashion. In time and with practice, you may work up a count to help equalize the length of the inhalation and exhalation. This even, balanced breath is geared toward being the breathing pattern for meditation. A slow, steady breath keeps the thoughts slow and steady as well.

EXERCISE: **Equal Breathing**

Once established in the three-part yogic breathing, the next step is to work on lengthening the breath and controlling the smooth transition when the breath changes from inhalation to exhalation and vice versa. A helpful tool to facilitate this is counting the breath length.

1: Periodically time your breathing rhythm as you breathe in and out of the nose. Fill each of the three areas of the lungs for an equal number of seconds, keeping it the same for inhalation and exhalation.

For example: Someone might start working at a count of two; two seconds into the diaphragm, two seconds into the intercostals, and two seconds into the clavicle. The exhale would have the same pattern.

2: Over time you may begin to work toward breathing in five seconds per each area of the lungs. This gives a fifteen-second inhalation and then a fifteen-second exhalation. After six months of practice, this is the level recommended for each person.

Please note: Those with athletic or musical backgrounds may notice the breathing patterns reaching thirty seconds in and out. This is a natural side effect of these other talents, but the key is to eventually reach fifteen seconds.

While there are numerous health benefits to a slow, steady breath, there are also mind-quieting effects of slow breathing. This exercise may be practiced for the duration of your life! To make things even better, larger quantities of carbon dioxide waste are eliminated from the lungs. This improves diaphragmatic functioning and ventilation effectiveness, allowing for a deeper, more nourishing inbreath.

· · · · · · ·

Remember, smooth breathing is graceful. The lungs move in a fluid fashion while they slowly open. As the lungs expand, the atmosphere encourages air to enter the lungs. If the lungs move in a jerky or tense fashion, the air enters abruptly and not to the fullest capacity. Pay attention to the flow of air into the lungs as a first step, then notice the transition of air after the inhalation and exhalation. Some may hold the breath after inhaling while others may drop the chest and suddenly force the air out of the lungs. After exhaling, the abrupt tendencies are sudden inhalation and a pause followed by a gulping breath—both of which greatly decrease the efficiency of respiration.

EXERCISE: **Breathing in Daily Life**

Once you learn deep breathing via meditation, it is a helpful tool to use whenever you feel stressed. Simply pause to center, then begin expanding all of the areas of your lungs as you enjoy a deep breath. Simultaneously consider a new perspective in the time that you are breathing and discover a healthy way of dealing with the stressful situation.

You can even practice breathing while moving. As an exercise, practice walking very slowly while you concentrate on your breathing rhythm. Many meditation traditions perform meditative walking in between longer meditation sittings. Simply take very slow steps with keen awareness of your breath and each micro-movement you make on your walk. Remain very aware of your actions and breath, as well as the thoughts that arise. As you might imagine, you may apply this conscious approach to living to any activity in your daily life: cooking, walking, exercise, repetitive tasks… the list is really endless. Your breath is with you always, from the moment you exist until you take your last—and this very simple exercise allows you to use that to your advantage and growth.

Summary (and Meditative Humor)

Please continue to breathe!

Kristen Butera

Robert Butera, MDiv, PhD, has studied meditation and yoga since 1984. He founded the YogaLife Institute of Devon, Pennsylvania, where he trains yoga instructors and publishes *Yoga Living Magazine*. His advanced degrees are from the Yoga Institute of Mumbai, India; Earlham School of Religion; and California Institute of Integral Studies. YogaLife has trained over 1,000 yoga teachers in programs in Pennsylvania, New Hampshire, and Ontario. He is the author of *The Pure Heart of Yoga: Ten Essential Steps for Personal Transformation, Meditation for Your Life: Creating a Plan That Suits Your Style*, and *Yoga Therapy for Stress and Anxiety*. For more information, visit YogaLifeInstitute.com.

Paying Attention on Purpose

Amy B. Scher

When I first discovered Japanese scientist Dr. Masaru Emoto's book *The Hidden Messages in Water*, it wasn't by chance. It was by necessity. I was ambitiously trying to heal from a medical condition that doctors called "chronic" at best, but more realistically, incurable. Raised by liberal, spiritual parents, I certainly wasn't new to the idea of the mind being an important asset to overall well-being. However, just barely into my twenties, I didn't understand it at a level deep enough to use it for my own transformation—until I studied Dr. Emoto's work.

Dr. Emoto took the notion of positive thinking, which most of us understand only conceptually, and translated it into pictures that explain more than words could make possible. His work is based on photographs that depict how crystals that are formed in frozen water change when specific thoughts or intentions are directed toward them.

Dr. Emoto's findings, which he shared in his books, came from collecting various water samples from different environments. Under a microscope he observed how the samples reacted when different words (such as "love" and "hate"), music (from classical to heavy metal), pictures, and prayer were directed toward them. The varied focused intentions presented a clear difference in how the molecules reacted to violent music, loving words, and more. Through these experiments, Dr. Emoto discovered that samples retrieved from clear springs and water that has been exposed to loving words and soothing music created gorgeous snowflake-like formations.

In contrast, polluted water or water exposed to negative thoughts, words, and violent music formed muddied-looking asymmetrical patterns.

The results are astounding. The implications of this research create a tangible awareness that we can positively affect our own bodies and selves by creating positively focused intentions. Because the cells in our body are more than 50 percent water, this intel is important in using mindfulness as a tool for emotional well-being.

While some question the validity of Emoto's findings, there are others in the field who corroborate them, showing that our thoughts, words, and feelings most definitely have a direct impact on our reality. Dr. Bruce Lipton, biologist and author of the *New York Times* bestseller *Biology of Belief*, presents that the body's physiology has the ability to respond and adapt to thoughts and emotions. This means that our mind dictates many of the physical and chemical reactions in our bodies. And Dr. Candace Pert, author of *Molecules of Emotion*, confirms through her work that unexpressed emotion from experiences can get stuck in the body's cellular memory, thus affecting us long-term.

How is it possible to use a practice like mindfulness, where negative thoughts may surface, without ignoring how negative thoughts and emotions can unfavorably affect us?

Mindfulness is based on the idea of paying attention on purpose while being devoid of judgment about the present moment. Mindfulness requires both concentration and acceptance of "what is." This means that during practice, we consciously pay attention to thoughts and emotions, even negative ones, without judgment of them. We fully accept them for what they are.

Now, let's explore how to strike a balance of paying attention on purpose without allowing the negativity that can block our best selves from emerging.

The solution comes from being aware and accepting of present emotions and thoughts, which will pass much more easily and quickly than when we resist them or try to force drastic positive thinking. Fear that negativity is altogether bad can cause stress and unease—the opposite of what we are trying to accomplish with practices like mindfulness meditation. Negative emotions and thoughts are not bad or dangerous for us unless we hold onto them, causing long-term reactions in our bodies. Negative emotions and thoughts are naturally fleeting, but our resistance to them and intent to control them creates their longevity. The challenge in allowing negative feelings to be accepted, which is the first step in releasing them, happens because they are too painful or because we force ourselves to "think positive" in order to heal. While the direction of positive energy, thoughts, and emotions is, in fact, essential for emotional well-being, we cannot utilize the practice of positive thinking in a natural feeling way without first honoring the negativity or reality of where we currently are.

• • • • • • •

The following example will help demonstrate this concept. Let's imagine you are practicing your mindfulness by sitting quietly, purposefully paying attention to your thoughts. Before you know it, you are remembering an old conflict you had with a friend five years ago. You try to just let it be but then you begin to sink into the memory of that, feeling the pain. Even after this many years, you immediately tell yourself that "it's time to just get over it!" Upon your awareness of that internal self-talk, you get angry because you are not supposed to be judging yourself during this practice, but here you are, doing that old thing again. And so it goes...

This type of cycle creates a "sticking" of negativity, which then has an impact on your body similar to the way heavy metal music and words like "hate" affected water molecules in Emoto's experiments, creating less-appealing formations.

By using mindfulness practices, we can cultivate the skill of being present to our emotions. By learning to be present to our emotions instead of resisting them, we naturally move into a more comfortable and positive place. Positive thinking is the next organic step, and no drastic forcing is needed.

Three Mindfulness Practices for Being Present

The simple three-idea approach I'm going to share with you will help make this a reality. First, I'll show you how to set an intention for a positive mindfulness experience. Next, I'll teach you a trick for sitting with uncomfortable emotions. And lastly, I'll give you ideas on how to support yourself with affirmations about where you currently are. From there you will flow more naturally into a positive space when your body is ready.

EXERCISE: Setting Intention

Setting expectations of ourselves that are too high can create stress and negativity from the get-go. We have usually practiced judging ourselves for a long, long time. Trying to undo that is not usually a swift process.

Instead, set an intention of curiosity and exploration about your mindfulness practice. Make a list of things you'd like to learn about yourself during this process, to take the focus off what you want to accomplish. Know that you will not be perfect at practicing mindfulness at first or maybe ever. Be into doing it for the doing and learning, not for the result. In this, trust that you'll discover and receive all that you need. This perspective on your practice will take immense pressure off of you and immediately create a better experience.

· · · · · · · ·

EXERCISE: **Tap the Thymus Gland**

As we discussed earlier, because we tend to resist feeling negativity, emotional energy can get stuck inside of us, creating negative results in us just as in those water samples. In a state of resistance we hold difficult emotions just under the surface, unable to be released.

When we can find a way to comfortably be with our difficult feelings, we are able to look at them without judgment much more easily. One of my favorite techniques for this is tapping the thymus gland. The thymus gland is located behind the sternum and in front of the heart. The thymus gland is the master gland of your immune system, which when tapped or thumped can help you let go of anxiety and fear in addition to boosting immunity. Because of its location, it is also believed to be the link between the mind and the body.

Resisting and judging negative thoughts and feelings is often a natural response for us. This is, in part, because they are uncomfortable and we just want these thoughts and feelings to go away. However, you've likely already learned that it doesn't work. Honoring and acknowledging whatever comes up, though, does. By tapping just over the area of this gland, you will be able to be more present to difficult emotions. Tap firmly enough to create a thumping or tapping noise against the chest. Soreness can be a sign that there is stuck energy there, so it's okay to tap even if you feel slight discomfort. Being present to our emotional state while we calm and soothe the body encourages their passing with more ease.

EXERCISE: **Affirmations**

The idea behind affirmations is typically that you are affirming positive thoughts or images—things that you'd like to be true for you. However, sometimes we end up using this tool to push away negative emotions, which we know is not always healthy. What often happens when you focus on something positive that doesn't feel true to you, which is common for the practice of affirmations, is that the opposite thought or image comes up. This becomes counterproductive. Instead, we can use affirmations for helping us stay present during emotional discomfort. This will help you be better able to accept where you are and process emotions in a healthy way.

The most effective way to use affirmations for this purpose is to affirm something that is both positive and true for you now and something that encourages feeling safe in the space that you're currently in. You will want to focus on self-acceptance and compassion—important themes in mindfulness. Crafting your affirmations carefully is key. Here are a few affirmations that might resonate with you:

· · · · · · · ·

"I am willing to accept myself where I am in this moment."

"I can learn to be okay with myself."

"I am open to the idea of accepting all of my thoughts and emotions."

When you learn to sit with and accept difficult emotions, you will find it much easier to be mindful. As you work with your mindfulness, just remember: it's practice. And with all practices, they are far more effective and fulfilling when we don't fight to make them perfect. And in that, we often get the bonus of moving naturally toward better-feeling emotions.

Craig Vershaw

Amy B. Scher is an energy therapist, a leading voice in the field of mind-body healing, and the author of *How to Heal Yourself When No One Else Can* (Llewellyn, 2016). She believes that ultimate well-being is born not from self-help but self-love. Amy has been featured in publications such as *CNN, Curve* magazine, *Psych Central, Elephant Journal, The Good Men Project*, and the *San Francisco Book Review,* and she was named one of *Advocate's* "40 Under 40" for 2013. Most importantly, she lives by this self-created motto: "When life kicks your ass, kick back." You can find out more about Amy at www .amybscher.com.

• • • • • • •

Mindfulness and Insight
for Problem Solving

KEITH PARK, PhD

My dog, Baron, was a bright, energetic German Shepard who loved to play ball. Sometimes I would throw the ball with him to take my mind off my worries. Unfortunately, this didn't always work out the way I intended—not because Baron was an uncooperative companion but because I would often find myself back in my worries, mentally someplace else, and not fully there with Baron.

This human capacity to digress from immediate experience is unique from many other animals. Unlike dogs and other animals, we humans can conceive of things not directly present, and this capacity is both a gift and a curse of being human. It is a gift in that it has allowed us to conceive of alternate scenarios, create art and symbols, solve complex and abstract problems, plan for the future, and build civilization. But it is also a curse in that we sometimes don't know when to disengage from it and just be "out there," in the moment, like Baron.

Dogs live in the moment. They don't lose awareness of what they are doing and go someplace else in their head. They see a ball and run after it, and that is that. Because they are not caught up in their head with other things, they can experience more of what is around them, as well as greater peace.

Unfortunately, many of us can't disengage from thinking and get lost in it too much. We're so used to immersing in and identifying with thought that we don't know when we're lost in it and suffering because of it.

Worrying and ruminating are perfect examples. Worry and rumination's perceived hope is that if we engage in them, we will anticipate potential obstacles and work through to solutions. Unfortunately, what typically happens is that we work ourselves into a blind alley with no perceived way out, not fully realizing that our "worked-through solution" is not reality but only a limited caricature of it.

A person, for instance, may hear someone sneeze in public. The thought may enter awareness: "I wonder if he's sick?" Other thoughts stream through consciousness: "Can I get it?... Maybe I need to move away?...I can't afford to take any more time off from work...Now I've got a scratchy throat...Maybe I should get a flu shot or avoid public places altogether?"

If not fully paying attention, this person may find himself unknowingly slipping into this stream of narrowing thoughts, working himself into a corner, and losing sight of the bigger picture: he just heard a man sneeze, and that is all; there could be other reasons for this man's sneezing, such as allergies.

This tendency to consciously "fall asleep" and get lost in automatic thinking is like being in a narrow trance. We enter into the auto thoughts, lose awareness of our surroundings (and ourselves), and react only to these thoughts. Since we aren't aware of anything else while lost in them, these highlighted thoughts then seem like our only reality. The result is a very constricted state of awareness, a self-imposed illusory state that Hindus call *maya* and Buddhists call *avidya*.

It is because of the conditioned and automatic nature of most thought that we find thoughts coming to us quickly and seemingly out of nowhere. Rather than consciously choose what we think, most of our thinking tends to happen on its own, and we unknowingly slip into it. As a result, we may find ourselves caught up in one thought one moment and another the next, with changes in emotion soon to follow.

The Hindu text Bhagavad Gita likens the restless mind to a "wild wind." Buddhists refer to it as a "drunken monkey." We may liken it to a rushing river. As the conditioned mind flows here and there, rolling out thoughts and memories, hopes and fears, desires and aversions, plans and regrets, we may get carried away in its torrents.

The restless and illusory nature of mind has been known for thousands of years, possibly as a result of many observers over those years watching it at work in meditation. Hindus and Buddhists believe it is the core of all human suffering; liberating ourselves from it is the way to enlightenment, peace, and joy.

The English poet John Milton summed it up best: "The mind is its own place and in itself can make a heaven of hell—a hell of heaven."

• • • • • • • •

Cultivating Mindfulness

The key to staying out of the illusion of mind and the unnecessary suffering it produces is to learn to be mindful. Mindfulness is the act of being fully aware of what you are experiencing at each moment. When you are mindful you avoid getting caught up or censoring any aspect of your present experience. You accept, with detachment, all things in your experience, including your thoughts and inner experiences.

The cultivation of mindfulness as a daily practice originated with the first Buddha, Siddhartha Gautama, and is still practiced today by many Buddhists and meditative-conscious people around the world.

The goal of mindfulness (and, really, all meditation) is to awaken and liberate one's true Self from the illusion generated by conditioned thought (and the constant mental stream known as the ego). Within all of us is a pure awareness, witness, or observer that is our true Self (or true mind) and not the illusion (the ego or illusory mind) generated by our conditioned thoughts.

Suffering and a sense of limitation come when the true Self loses itself in the illusion of conditioned thought. When immersed in thought, the true Self may not be aware of the captivating spell it is under. But by learning to be mindful, the true Self may awaken from this spell. In the words of the ancient Hindu sage Patanjali, the true Self "dwells in its own nature" and not in the ever-changing "thought streams."

EXERCISE: Basic Mindfulness

The best way to learn mindfulness is to try it yourself. Below is an exercise that will help you get started experiencing it in your everyday life.

The next time you are doing a daily activity such as throwing a ball with your dog, brushing your teeth, driving to work, talking to a friend, or preparing a meal, don't just go through the activity as you normally do, which for most of us is typically being mentally someplace else as we do it.

Really pay attention to it this time. Focus completely on what you are doing and on each step in the process. Be aware of how your body is feeling during the activity and on the rich sensory details of it. If you are brushing your teeth, for instance, pay attention to the circular motion of the brush, the feel of it in your hand, the texture of the bristles against your teeth, and the sight of it in the mirror.

Also be aware of what is going on around you. Notice the room you're in, its temperature and light level, and any other activities going on in the room.

Be aware also of your thoughts and feelings as you do the activity, but do not get caught up in them. Simply note them with detached curiosity. If you find yourself getting caught up in a thought or feeling or any one thing, simply return to a broad,

· · · · · · · ·

detached focus. See if you can do the activity and be fully aware of everything going on outside and inside of you.

You might want to practice this simple exercise daily to cultivate your ability to be mindful. Keeping a journal is also helpful. It will help you keep track of your progress as you do this and the following exercises in this book.

Fostering Insight by Observing Thought

Cultivating mindfulness—the ability to stay out of our heads and simply be aware of direct experience—is the first step to resolving emotional and interpersonal problems. We simply learn to get out of conditioned thoughts that trigger problematic feelings and conflicts and stay present. This simple act can be very powerful for resolving most of what ails us.

However, sometimes we want to understand why we think and react in certain ways to loved ones and specific circumstances. When this is the case, mindfulness can be a very useful tool for fostering insight into these special cases and helping to find more helpful ways to respond.

As mentioned earlier, when the true or observing Self gets lost in and fused with thought, it reacts to thought as if it is the only reality; this can be problematic when these thoughts are erroneous or incomplete assumptions of reality. Unfortunately, a lot of our thoughts are of this nature. Therefore, it benefits us to look at these thoughts and see what we're thinking and saying about ourselves, others, and our life situations.

Detached observation is the key. In order to gain insight into our thoughts, we have to stand outside and observe them. Outside, we are no longer entranced by thought. We see who we really are: the observing presence, the background awareness from which thought arises, and not the illusion generated by thought, so we need not dwell in thought.

Personal insight then arises once we are out of our immersion in thought. As we "wake up" and start to take stock of all the thoughts we normally immerse in, overlook, and deny, we start to gather a greater picture of our situation.

In fact, the word *insight* literally means "seeing into a situation," and much has been developed to foster it. In Buddhist tradition, particularly in the Southeast Asia Theraveda tradition, mindfulness meditation has been used to stimulate personal and emotional insight and is called *vipassana* (roughly translated as "insight") meditation.

In this form of meditation, one does not concentrate on a single point of focus—such as the breath, a sound, or an object—and push out all other experiences, as is found in most forms of meditation. Rather, one sits still and accepts into awareness all experiences, including the many thoughts, images, feelings, and sensations that may arise related to an emotional issue.

After we observe thoughts in our open, detached awareness, we may see how they are linked to our troubling emotion or issue. (For this reason, mindfulness meditation is also called "open presence" by many Buddhists.)

• • • • • • • •

It is this broader, detached awareness that seems to stimulate insight, as noted by insight research starting with the first experiments conducted by the Gestalt psychologist Wolfgang Kohler in the early twentieth century and compiled in his 1917 book *The Mentality of Apes*.

Kohler performed a series of experiments on chimpanzees on Tenerife Island during World War I to see how they went about discovering insight into problem situations, such as figuring out how to obtain a banana hanging out of reach from a string attached to the roof of an enclosure. He discovered that the chimps did not obtain the banana through simple trial and error but through the sudden realization of the larger relationships in the situation, such as realizing that two sticks could be put together and boxes stacked to span the gap between them and the banana. According to Kohler, insight does not come from taking a narrow, step-by-step process (i.e., trying this, trying that). It comes from instantly reframing or "restructuring" the whole situation and seeing it in different light (i.e., from broadened awareness and seeing the bigger picture).

Other Gestalt psychologists studied insight discovery among people and found that they tend to get fixed in mindsets when they rely too much on using what worked in the past and when they look at a problem too narrowly. For instance, a fixed mindset often occurs during disagreements when parties continue to talk over each other even though the action proves futile.

Mindfulness avoids fixation and stimulates insight simply because it requires looking at things fresh and in perspective. One observes from an unbiased mental distance and watches where the mind goes and what favored thoughts it likes to engage in. In doing so, one may glean overall patterns between what one thinks and how one reacts, just as Kohler's chimps gleaned overall connections between the sticks, boxes, and banana.

Thoughts (our "theories" about the world) become favored and conditioned over time as a result of our trying to make sense of the world. Over time, these favored thoughts (or views) become subconscious and automatic, and color much of what we perceive. When they are not observed or updated, they can keep us stuck in fixed ways of seeing and reacting to the world.

For example, Sam, a highly accomplished business professional, may develop the belief "every person is an island" as a result of being left alone as a child. Over time, as this belief becomes subconscious, he may experience a persistent feeling of emptiness, even though his outer circumstances change, such as moving to a new location, getting an exciting job, and meeting interesting acquaintances. Though the outer circumstances are different, the inner belief is unchanged and continues to lead to inner discontent. These fixed thoughts or beliefs are the cause of most persistent emotional and interpersonal problems.

As mentioned earlier, mindfulness meditation rectifies this by training us to sit still and observe troubling emotions and conflicts in a detached and unbiased manner so that we may gain insight into the thoughts that trigger them. However, detached observation is not always an easy thing. Thoughts may flood our awareness, be lost from awareness, or be resisted by awareness.

· · · · · · ·

Only our willingness to sit and acknowledge what we normally dwell on, deny, and ignore, without losing ourselves in it or censoring any aspect of it, enables us to see what we normally would not—and then do something about it.

A helpful reminder is to remember that thoughts are not facts or the whole picture. They are just our ongoing versions of reality or one way of viewing reality. In fact, they may not represent what has happened, is happening, and will ever happen "out there." Therefore, we do not need to get too attached to any of them, resist any of them, or get worked up over any of them.

Once favored thoughts or views are seen in perspective, they don't seem so real and convincing anymore, and neither should we feel the need to react to them in our usual way. We may be able to get free from what is keeping us stuck, creating suffering, and making life hard.

Being immersed in thought is indeed like being in a trance. But as many of my clients have pointed out, observing thought is like awakening from a trance. They state that when they are caught up in rumination, they feel compelled by it, unable to resist it. But, once they start observing the thoughts stimulating their reaction, they feel free from these troubling thoughts and emotional reactions.

EXERCISE: **Observing Thought**

You can do the same. Let's practice a simple observing experience. Here, we're going to practice watching thoughts in a detached manner. As mentioned, detached observation can be difficult yet quite illuminating. For instance, my clients routinely say "that was so dumb of me" or something similar whenever they recount their decisions and responses to various life events. At the point when they do so, I often ask them to stop for a moment and really pay attention to what they are saying to themselves. Many times, a light bulb goes off and they exclaim that they can't believe how often they say these things to themselves and then agree to be more accurate about their self-statements.

In learning to observe their conditioned thinking in a mindful and detached manner, clients are in a better position to see what has been holding them back and do something about it, rather than allow these conditioned thoughts to run on autopilot.

To begin experiencing this yourself, try this: sit and notice right now the thoughts in your head, but as if you are hearing them for the first time (as some of them you probably are) or as if the words were generated by a computer or spoken by someone else. You might think of a situation troubling you and then observe the thoughts that come into awareness in regard to this issue. Don't censor any of your thoughts. Simply allow them to be there.

Also see if you can catch yourself being drawn away by any of them, and if so, return to simply observing the thoughts. Finally, notice any thoughts that seem to come up over and over again. Explore these thoughts with curiosity. Ask: "What are the reasons for these thoughts? Where do they come from? How are they related to what I am feeling?" Then see what you find.

Exercise: **Observing Versus Immersing**

Here's another exercise to get you used to the difference between immersing in thought and observing thought. As you do, notice how much your mood and mindset change between the two perspectives.

Close your eyes and think of a difficult situation you recently encountered. Choose a mild one so that you can practice the exercise without getting too upset. Some examples may be a recent argument, an unpleasant task at work, or an unexpected frustration.

Next, mentally place yourself back into the situation for a moment. Conjure up all the details about it. Where are you? Who is with you? What are you and others doing? Follow the events right up to when you get most caught up in your reaction, and then really pay attention to how you feel.

For example, you're at home with your spouse. Your spouse is not talking to you and appears to be ignoring you. You're annoyed because this happens often, so you say something and your spouse just sits there. It seems as if you are being brushed off, so you assert yourself further and rebuke the behavior. You feel angry.

Now replay the scenario, but this time step out of it and observe it from a broader perspective. Look at it curiously with fresh eyes—as if you were a space alien trying to understand the situation for the first time. Also observe where your mind and thoughts are going. What assumptions, conclusions, and judgments are you automatically drawn to? Think of how you could view the situation differently and change your usual response.

For example, you're at home with your spouse and your spouse is not talking to you. Your initial reaction is to feel annoyed because this happens often. But you realize your angry thoughts and let them go. You observe your spouse's silence without judging or trying to interpret it. You begin talking and your spouse continues to sit there. You're aware of your usual assumption that you are being brushed off and choose not to respond to it. Instead, you say louder but gently, "Hi. How is your day?" Your spouse stops what he or she is doing and says hi back. You observe your spouse's apparent surprise with curiosity. The two of you begin to talk. You feel heard and appreciated.

Notice in the first scenario that as you allowed yourself to enter into your usual way of viewing the situation and its associated thoughts, more and more thoughts became available until you were fully immersed in them. One thought triggered

• • • • • • • •

another, and before you knew it, you were fully caught up in it. And this fusion with the usual thoughts led to a negative reaction. Plus, once here, there was little room to consider other thoughts and views. It was like you hypnotized or entranced yourself to the view. Yet, when you stayed out of the thoughts, observing them from a distance, you did not experience this negative immersion. Instead, you had a very different experience. You discovered a new perspective and new options, and you had a different reaction.

Go back again and replay both scenarios. This time, as you do, notice that as you shift between immersing and observing the scenario, your awareness of yourself as the observer fades and strengthens. At one point, when you are immersed in the scenario, there are just the thoughts that seem as if they are automatically there or as if they came out of nowhere. You, the observer, are merged with the thoughts. It is almost as if you are asleep, and since you aren't really there, reaction is instant and irritation seems to happen to you.

Yet, when you are observing the scenario, you become aware of yourself as an observing presence or witness to the thoughts. There is a gap between you and your thoughts, so you have time to choose what thoughts and reactions you want, rather than let them happen to you.

Actually, the observing "you" is present during both experiences. It's always present. It is just that when you are lost or immersed in thought, the observing "you" temporarily goes asleep (or goes into trance or into the background, so to speak). But, when you are observing thought, the observing "you" moves into the foreground, and you become aware that you are awake. Awake, you have a conscious choice about how you think and feel, and this is true liberation.

This simple exercise shows how our thoughts and reactions are connected, and how simply stepping out of our usual (conditioned) thinking can change our view of and our response to a situation. The emphasis here is that each situation or event is not all bad or all good, and therefore can be viewed in different ways.

Insight Meditation Exercises

The following two exercises will show you how to use mindfulness in a formal meditation session in order to stimulate insight in regard to a troubling emotion and an interpersonal conflict.

Persistent emotions such as anxiety, depression, and grief tend to indicate underlying fixed views or beliefs that keep us stuck in the feeling. We may meditate mindfully on the troubling emotion to uncover the fixed view; this involves dispassionately observing the thoughts surrounding the emotion, and finding the underlying link or pattern between the emotion and the thoughts. Once discovered, we may then update these views so that we may no longer react in our usual manner.

We may also use this detached perspective to explore similar underlying views that keep us stuck in interpersonal conflicts. Most interpersonal conflicts stay in place because of fixed ways of seeing and reacting among partners. Exploring your and your partner's views on a persistent conflict may lead to insight into why each of you holds your respective view (even though you may not agree with your partner's view), and this insight may lead to common ground or a point of an agreement between the two of you.

EXERCISE: **Emotional Insight**

In this exercise we practice detaching from immersion in thoughts that give rise to a negative emotion and observing these thoughts from an objective position.

We begin by intentionally bringing to mind an emotion and accepting all our thoughts and sensations about this feeling.

To start, sit comfortably, close your eyes, and bring into awareness an unresolved emotion that has been lingering for a while. It could be fear, sadness, regret, frustration, anger, and so on. Allow the emotion to be there. Ask yourself: "What am I feeling right now?" Explore it with curiosity.

Then label it. Is it fear, sadness, frustration, regret, anger…? What is the worst of it? Try to find the right words to label the core of the experience and put your finger on it. This will help you keep a gap between you and the experience while bringing it fully into conscious awareness.

As you sit with this feeling, also notice your body. Your body reacts to what is in your mind and will give you signs in the form of physical sensations. Don't judge or try to change anything just yet. Simply notice.

Scan your body and pay attention to where in your body you feel these physical sensations (emotional signals). Is your heart beating fast? Do you have butterflies in your stomach? Is there tension in your neck?

If you want, narrate the experience as you scan and the sensations enter awareness. Example: "I feel tension in my lower back, slight butterflies in my stomach, my heart is beating fast, my breathing is shallow, and my neck and shoulders are tense. I also have a slight headache."

Note: By learning these signals ahead of time, you may be able to use them the next time you're about to experience the emotion, and then do something about the reaction before it takes hold, such as stop a panic attack before it gets out of control. You can use these signals as cues to know when to step out and observe what you're thinking and doing.

• • • • • • • •

As you sit with the feeling and the body sensations it produces, also allow thoughts and images to come to mind. These thoughts and images may be about the past, the present, or the future. Their content may reflect a specific event or events or involve just you or you and another person or persons.

Try to find the specific triggering scenario or context for the feeling. Did you experience a loss? Did you get into an argument with your spouse? Are you looking at yourself in the mirror? Did your car break down? Did your boss reprimand you? Do you have to speak in public? Did your partner tell you that he or she needs space? Did you realize you forgot to pay your car registration? Did someone criticize or ignore you?

Simply observe these thoughts and images from a distance. If you find yourself getting caught up in any of them—and picturing yourself in the middle of the situation, experiencing its full intensity, or as you originally experienced it—shift your attention to the present moment and relax your body. Realize that these thoughts and images are not real. You are only observing them in the theater of your mind.

If you like, imagine that you are observing them on a large movie screen in an empty theater. You, the observer, are sitting in a chair, watching the scene from a distance. Be aware that you are watching, so that you do not get fused with the thoughts and images. The "observing you" is outside the experience, watching the "participant you" in the experience, noticing your emotions and reactions from afar.

The normal reaction is to get caught up in the emotion of the experience. Instead, notice the thoughts generating the emotion. Really listen to what you are telling yourself as you experience this emotion. Ask yourself: "What am I telling myself that is making me feel so (fearful, sad, regretful, frustrated, angry…)?"

Sit quietly for a moment and see what thoughts arise in response to this question. Be on the lookout for all the reasons and "evidence" your mind has for why you feel this way (e.g., I'm feeling sad because I don't have anyone, nothing works out for me, I'm not smart enough, good-looking enough, rich enough, etc.), but be careful that you do not get caught up in any of these thoughts. Stay separate from them and continue to observe them objectively.

If thoughts come too fast or not at all, slow down and focus on the question again: "What am I telling myself to make me feel this way?" Then listen closer to what you are saying.

As thoughts come through, look for overall patterns. Play like a detective. Try to find the common link between the thoughts and the emotion. Ask yourself: "How do these thoughts relate to what I am feeling specifically? What particular thought or thoughts keep reoccurring? Which ones may be triggering this emotion? Where do

· · · · · · · ·

they come from? What are they based on? Do they reflect what is currently happening or are they about some event or events in the past?"

As you put these thoughts into perspective, you may begin to discover your personal theories about you and your world—just as Sam, the business professional in our earlier example, discovered that his feeling of emptiness stemmed from being left alone as a kid and theorizing that everyone must fend for themselves.

Next, consider what you do with the insight now that it is in conscious awareness. What would happen if you simply let go of this view or did not believe it so strongly? Would it be possible? If so, what would happen?

This is the easiest option. However, most of us are very attached to our personal theories. If we have invested in a view for some time, we are not likely to give it up so quickly or easily; to do so would mean that we would have to admit we were wrong about our perceptions of reality, and this is quite frightening for many.

If you can't let the belief go right away, consider how you might modify or update it. Is there another way to see things? Where can you allow room for revision or update? Ask yourself, "Is this the *only* way to see this or can I entertain other possibilities? If there were other views, what would they be?" Then see if you can find some possibilities that might modify your original viewpoint, and write them down. Think also how you might act on them.

Finally, do another quick body scan and assess how you feel. Has the tension left? Imagine breathing into the body and relaxing all the tense areas, and then open your eyes and come back to the room.

Exercise: Interpersonal Insight

In this exercise we learn to cultivate insight into the blocks to interpersonal relations. As mentioned, most interpersonal problems stem from a lack of communication and understanding. Each party has difficulty seeing the other's viewpoint on a disputed issue and communicating their needs. As a result, the two have difficulty finding common ground or a point of agreement.

A mindful exploration of the typical communication pattern may reveal insight into any fixed pattern of relating and help foster common ground.

Sit quietly now, close your eyes, and imagine a disagreement or dispute that you typically have between you and your partner—one that reoccurs on a regular basis.

Bring the situation to mind, but this time, step back and observe the situation from an outside observer perspective. Let it unfold as it normally does, but this time, watch how it unfolds. Look for how it typically begins and the course it typically takes. For

• • • • • • • •

example, does conflict begin to arise when certain topics are brought up or important issues are discussed? Do certain words, tones, or gestures trigger it?

Observe your usual words, issues, tone, and gestures. Make sure to also pay attention to your partner. Observe them like you would for the first time or as if you were a space alien newly arrived on earth. Try to see your partner without judgment or any preconceived assumptions or notions.

Imagine that you are resisting your usual urge to jump in and defend your position or counter your partner's position. Imagine instead that you are shifting your awareness and viewing the conflict from your partner's angle. See if you can imagine what the situation would look like through their eyes, from their perspective.

We can learn a lot about another by "walking a mile in their shoes," as they say. You don't have to agree with how they see it, but by seeing it from their angle, you might come to understand why they hold the position they do, and this may help you find common ground—a win-win for both of you.

Finally, look for the common ground and change your usual pattern. To create a win-win, see how you can meet your partner's needs in return for meeting your needs. Then imagine seeing yourself offering this agreement with a different tone and gesture. Practice this a little while before opening your eyes and returning to the room.

A relationship or partnership is like a system. Each part (partner) in the system is tied to the other part (partner). By changing one part of the system, you automatically change the other part of the system. Therefore, when you get out of autopilot and take the initiative to change your usual behavior, your partner can no longer relate to you in their usual manner. They are forced to change their behavior in order to meet the change in your behavior and, as such, they often begin to listen and work with you.

Your initiative to change creates the change. Your willingness to see your partner's viewpoint encourages your partner to see your viewpoint, leading not only to mutual cooperation but also to an end to the unproductive pattern of senseless bickering and the beginning of seeing and relating to each other in a new light.

Conclusion

Difficulty is inherent in life. No human in history has escaped their share of pain and loss. The key is not to deny or run from life's challenges but to find a way to live with and grow from them. Though we can't avoid pain, we can avoid extra suffering. How much we suffer depends on how we view things. Recall the quote by the Greek philosopher Epictetus: "People are disturbed not by things, but the view they take of them." Most of our suffering is the result of identifying too strongly with our thoughts, which are largely incomplete and conditioned ways of seeing reality, but they are not reality.

• • • • • • • •

By cultivating a mindful approach to life, we may begin to learn to wake up and separate ourselves from our thoughts and experience life not as we think it to be but as it truly is. Fully aware and with a broader, more balanced and impartial view of life, we may understand ourselves and our world better and react in wiser, more sober ways. Though not all pain and discomfort may go away, at least we are not adding suffering to ourselves. Rather than allow life experiences to happen to us, we choose to accept these experiences and see them in different light—and not in our typical conditioned and automatic ways.

Practicing the exercises in this book can help you attain this level of mindfulness, as can sitting down and taking the time to reflect on any insights you've gained from trying these exercises and recording them in a journal.

In addition, you may want to incorporate mindfulness meditation in your daily life. Set aside a time and a place to sit on a regular basis to observe dispassionately what arises in your inner experience, and see if you can notice patterns in your thinking and approach to people and important life issues.

Ultimately, what you discover from looking objectively at your typical views and approaches is the ego at work. Once you see this for what it is, you discover that what is left (after stripping out what is false interpretation) is your true Self—that pure awareness or presence that is always there in the background, complete and whole and eternally connected to everything and everyone. When you see this, you will be like the Buddha, who replied "I am awake" when asked why he looked so peaceful wandering in the wilderness after his enlightenment. Once you are truly awake, then earthly problems seem less like problems, and you find greater peace, joy, and freedom.

Sears Portrait Studio

Keith Park, PhD, is a licensed psychologist and the author of *The Serenity Solution: How to Use Quiet Contemplation to Solve Life's Problems.* He currently practices in Southern California, offering individual sessions to treat anxiety, depression, and grief, using the ideas and techniques of mindfulness-based cognitive therapy presented in this article. Visit him online at www.theserenitysolution.com.

· · · · · · ·

Identifying Stressful Behaviors

ROBERT BUTERA, PhD

The amount of daily stress that a person accrues and permits in their daily routine has a direct effect on that particular day's meditation session. What the veteran meditator is usually aware of is that the manner in which you live your life greatly affects the waves on the lake of your mind. Entering a meditation session with a balanced mindset gives you a head start!

To begin to foster this awareness of how your mind behaves, evaluate how much peace you experience in your daily life and routine. Hopefully there are moments of sanctuary: eating meals with the family, taking brief walks, during exercise. But what happens when you leave these environments? How does your mind react to waking up a bit late or to sitting in heavy traffic? How do you handle situations when things do not quite go as you planned at work or during other daily chores and activities? What about your relationships with those close to you?

As you consider these elements of your life, please be honest but avoid being judgmental—the intent is awareness, not condemnation.

EXERCISE: Listing Your Personal Stresses

As difficult as it may be, with awareness and compassion, make a list of the things throughout your day that bring you stress. Try to capture every little detail from the moment you wake up until you drift off to sleep in the evening. Again, the intention is awareness; cultivate an objective and nonjudgmental attitude as best you can.

The intention of this exercise is to bring awareness at least once daily to one of the items on the list you have generated. Noticing your breathing as you sit in traffic or when someone cuts in front of you at the store; observing your emotions during and after a difficult conversation with a loved one or coworker; pausing for just a moment before responding to someone else's criticism—these are all very simple yet profound actions that can dramatically start to alter how your mind processes daily events.

EXERCISE: Understanding the Essence of Stress

After cultivating compassionate awareness to some of the "little things" on your list, we will next choose two or three of the most stressful items for further introspection. It is quite possible that some of these items are very personal, so it is encouraged to perform these exercises in a private and comfortable setting for full honesty in your responses to the questions to follow. I find it helpful to jot each item on a piece of scrap paper to give me plenty of room to freely explore this exercise. Fully and honestly work through each of the following questions. To get started, here are some examples of "big stressors" that I have seen throughout the years:

- Overworked, too busy, rushed
- Technology overload
- Relationship difficulties (boss/coworkers or domestic/family)
- Constant worry
- Excessive behaviors (overeating, alcohol consumption, addictions)
- Insomnia or oversleeping

1: What time of day is your mind most disturbed, and what particularly is it disturbed by?

2: How do you react and play into the disturbances created in your mind?

- For example, do you react to them impulsively, dwell on them for a time but keep silent, ignore them and let them sink into your subconscious, or some other response? Be as specific as you can.

3: What would you describe as the underlying attitude associated with these responses to the stressor?

- This point is most important and most avoided. You may have to physically feel the stressful sensation to understand

• • • • • • • •

it and give it a name. I am not advocating increasing the stress or actively seeking it, as opposed to learning from it and moving toward transforming that feeling.

4: How do you feel in relationship to the stressor?

- For example, do you feel saddened, angered, frustrated, or anxious about it?

5: What is the corresponding psychological state fueling this feeling?

- These include fear, egoism, attachment, aversion, or a faulty expectation.

Focus on the Opposite

With a statement of the psychological fuel for your responses to stress, we move toward a practice that can help shift the misalignment in the stressful situation back toward a more peaceful balance. For each of the stressors you have chosen to analyze, contemplate and experiment with a virtue that you feel would completely restore the balance in those situations. For example, I have had many students who struggled with speaking in public, even in small meditation group sessions. Nervousness, anxiety, and agitation were the most-cited feelings and responses to the stressor, with fear being the primary psychological block. Courage can be a powerful opposing virtue, which can then flow over into other aspects of your life. Acceptance and wisdom have also been helpful for others: accepting your self-criticism (for your audience may not criticize you at all) and realizing that no speech or audience will ever be "perfect."

Virtue in hand (and in mind), the exercise concludes by focusing on that concept and how you can practically apply the concept to the stressful situation. Your virtue (or virtues) becomes the positive point for centering and healing even amidst the former stressor. As the situation arises in the future and you find yourself responding to it, you may find it helpful to journal those responses and see how they change.

Prioritizing and Time to Practice

There is no denying it: the modern world is moving at an alarming rate. Computers are faster than they were even five years ago and communication networks now expand almost across every inch of our country, not to mention much of the globe. While even a few years ago most people had cellular phones, now even children have portable Internet connections, and just about everyone is connected to everyone else every moment of the day. While many technological advances have allowed for huge breakthroughs in the way of living, quality of life, and speed of information transfer, each new gadget only encourages and tempts the mind to also speed up. Meditation is all about applying the brakes and slowing the mind down.

. . . .

With that in mind, ask yourself how often you unplug from the world and go without electronic devices. I mean any electronic device: no Internet, no television, no cell phone or personal handheld. It is so easy to be connected to others, information, and recreation that it is tempting to never pull the plug. But just like electronic devices, if you do not unplug you do not shut down, and thus is the fate of the modern mind. Regarding recreation, how much of your previous down time do you find is occupied by technology? Use nonjudgment and objectivism in your response, but please be honest. How about your work life? Does your job require the ceaseless use of technology or is it a more traditional vocation?

As meditation aims to slow the mind down despite technology's urge to speed it up without rest, see if you can challenge yourself to unplug as fully as you can for a few hours one day in the coming week (in some cases we must have some connection due to the potential for emergencies, so this is not advocating complete aloofness). Even if you can only get off of the grid for a few hours, be mindful of how you feel during and after the getaway.

Shifting away from technology's role in recreation, take some time to examine other activities you engage in when not pursuing technology. If you have children of your own or have close connections to children either through family or friends, examine how you interact, exercise, and just play with them They have much to teach us about simplicity, creative expression, and the joy of discovery. For most of us, our jobs or schooling keep us indoors much of the day. When the work day is over and we move on to other chores or leisure time, how much of that time do we find ourselves out in nature? Nature is perhaps the easiest way to slow down the mind. Barring weather, of course, getting outside for even thirty minutes a day can be enough to reset the mental circuits back in tune with nature's rhythm.

Humans are social creatures, and this last section encourages you to critically evaluate your relationships to others at any level. From acquaintances to family members, examine the types of people that you interact with on a daily basis. Perhaps more than in any other reflection, it is imperative that you practice nonjudgment in this inquiry. The intention is not to criticize, condemn, or compare yourself to people in your life. Being social creatures, we play off of the feelings and actions of others. Bringing awareness to how our interactions with others affect us can be eye-opening and show us areas where perhaps we need to be less reactive or more open.

EXERCISE: **Examining Your Priorities**

This last exercise hopes to facilitate a better understanding of your priorities as they are now. From there, those things that rank lower on the list, depending on their importance, may be slowly substituted for activities that lend to a mindset more fruitful to meditation. Begin by asking yourself what is the most important thing to you in life. This "thing" need not even be a material thing. While all of the facets of life are important, the perspective with which you hold priorities greatly affects your view of things. Which of your material pursuits most consume your time and energy? These pursuits may well be necessary, as we all need food, shelter, and clothing, but do we need gourmet food from high-class restaurants, two to three mortgages, and designer clothes?

1: Rank the following elements of modern life in order from greatest to least priority where you are in your life right now:

- Shelter
- Finances
- Food
- Family time
- Spiritual practice
- Personal time
- Recreation/exercise
- Work
- Other personal category

Though you may wish for one of these to be a higher priority, do your best to honestly list them as they are.

2: Make (if you do not have one) or evaluate (if you do) your daily to-do list.

- Do you find that you are overactive, lazy, or pretty balanced in what activities you take on? If you are having trouble deciding, here is a hint: most people in modern culture need to choose to do less!

3: Once the to-do list is finished for the day (how often does that happen!), begin to note the activities you perform in the time that remains of the waking hours.

- With whom do you interact; what sort of physical activity do you engage in? Do you have hobbies or special interests? Are you active in the larger community?

The task is to reflect on how important these activities really are. If you are one of many who do not believe they have the time to meditate, the journey to inner stillness begins with letting go of some activities that do not serve this purpose. In the beginning, meditation requires only ten to twenty minutes each day, so one option may be going to bed thirty minutes earlier so that you can awaken just a bit earlier and meditate before you get ready for the day.

• • • • • • • •

For those activities that are necessities, like working and caring for children or family members, just because we are obliged to them does not mean that we cannot still utilize them as empowering activities. Whenever you are working—be it at a job, around your home or apartment, or volunteering—concentrating on the task at hand, no matter how small, can have dramatic effects on the mind. In the coming week, do your best to stay completely focused on the task. You may find that as the mind fixes itself on a single point, the distractions and disturbances, though inevitable, have much less impact.

Robert Butera, MDiv, PhD, has studied meditation and yoga since 1984. He founded the YogaLife Institute of Devon, Pennsylvania, where he trains yoga instructors and publishes *Yoga Living Magazine*. His advanced degrees are from the Yoga Institute of Mumbai, India; Earlham School of Religion; and California Institute of Integral Studies. YogaLife has trained over 1,000 yoga teachers in programs in Pennsylvania, New Hampshire, and Ontario. He is the author of *The Pure Heart of Yoga: Ten Essential Steps for Personal Transformation*, *Meditation for Your Life: Creating a Plan That Suits Your Style*, and *Yoga Therapy for Stress and Anxiety*. For more information, visit YogaLifeInstitute.com.

For Your Health

There are many ways to apply mindfulness and meditation to your healthy lifestyle. This part inspires your well-being by teaching you to become more connected to your thoughts, feelings, needs, and authentic ways of revitalizing. Conscious relationships with your pets, the earth, and food improve your overall health. By becoming more present you replenish fundamental areas of health such as sleep, relaxation, digestion, allergies, and chronic pain.

The following chapters view your health in terms of your whole being as well as your relationship with the world around you. Danielle MacKinnon describes how your pets may be trying to tune you into a greater level of presence. Robert Butera and Erin Byron share mindful techniques to improve sleep. Angela Wix and Alexandra Chauran give you powerful grounding tools, which are key to living in the now. Rachel Avalon, Melissa Grabau, and Sarah Bowen each speak from their expertise on that tender topic of food relationships. Mindfulness can also help us cope with the extreme. Erin Byron offers techniques to assuage chronic health problems. Jeanne Van Bronkhorst will teach you the power of mindfulness regarding death and grief. Servet Hasan also shares a mindful approach to mourning. Read on for techniques on grounding, being more positive (in thought and habit), mindful eating, and coping with major stressors like illness, addiction, grief, and loss.

How Our Pets Help Us
Live in the Moment

Danielle MacKinnon

In my decade and a half as a professional animal communicator, I have been given many opportunities to work with all kinds of animals and their humans in all kinds of situations. These opportunities have allowed me to form a unique perspective about animals and their true purpose here on earth: they are here to help keep us front and center, attuned with our lives and the beauty around us.

When I first began my work as an animal communicator I spent a lot of time trying to fix, help, and rescue animals. I viewed animals as "beings in need" that were out of their element, victims of the evil human race. My intuitive communications with animals and their humans focused on making the animal comfortable. I would ask, "Do you like your food?" or "Does your right hip hurt?" or "Are you happy with your humans?" and the answers I received made sense. I would share with the animal's human the information I received about the animal's body aches, likes and dislikes, needs, and more—all perfectly aligned with my belief that animals were creatures in need that we, as the big bad human race, needed to save. I felt confident in my ability to psychically tap into an animal and find out what that animal wanted in order to be happy and healthy.

But the more that I connected with animals intuitively and the better I got to know them, the more confused I became. My communications started feeling wonky, and the answers ("I want a different food" or "It's too loud in the house," for example) stopped coming through. Instead, I was receiving information that I really didn't know what to do with. It seemed the animals were showing less and less concern about their own comfort and daily life and were instead much more interested in the lives of their humans. While at the time this was something I was completely unprepared for, it is now the backbone of my understanding of all animals here on earth with us. And it is the definitive reason that animals are so good at compelling humans to live in the present moment.

For many people, our pets are so dear to us that they become part of our hearts. When a bond like this between a human and an animal is formed, there is a great opportunity that arises—and one that many people miss—for learning, growing, understanding, and healing. How many times have you or a friend felt like you just couldn't go on because your beloved animal had just passed? How many times have you felt your heart breaking at even the thought of your pet—or possibly even any animal—being in danger or hurting in some way? When your heart is open in this way, there sits an enormous opportunity for shift.

Through my work as an animal communicator I've learned that animals know how to take full advantage of that, often by encouraging us back into living in the present. But what does living in the moment really look like? Sometimes, it's easiest to define something by looking at what it is not. Living in the moment is not worrying about your financial future, it is not gossiping with your friend about your other friend, it is not overreacting to a situation because you are so "over it." Instead, living in the moment is being able to be fully present with your current situation, emotion, or challenge. It is sitting in the knowledge that right now is where you are, right now you are safe, and right now you are loved and supported by the universe. But how often do we, as humans, really get to experience that type of presence and bliss? Luckily, that's where the animals come in—as long as we let them!

How Animals Use Physical Needs
to Help Us Live in the Moment

Let's start with the very physical job of having a relationship with your pet. Let's say, for example, that you have a dog in your life. There are many facets involved in caring for that dog. First, you must provide a home space, a place where you and your dog feel safe, do your sleeping, store your stuff, eat your meals, and more. If you have a horse, we need to add shoeing the horse, brushing him, and providing some method to keep the flies out of his eyes. If you have a cat, kitty litter maintenance becomes a major component to manage in the relationship. All of these examples are very basic needs to keep the animal in your life alive.

· · · · · · · ·

But there is another component to the physical level. It is the necessity of constant awareness. As you're feeding your dog, you have to keep an eye out for changes in her eating behavior. Has she been disinterested in food lately? Has she been throwing up a lot? Or as you care for your horse, you have to keep an eye on how he's using his body in the stall or notice whether his hips feel good despite the arthritis. As you're playing with your cat, you have to watch out for how he's using his body. Is he favoring that paw? Does he have a weight problem?

As you can see, maintaining the physical needs of an animal is an incredibly important piece to having a healthy animal, and to do it well requires quite a commitment.

But what happens when you are out of sync with this requirement? What happens when you are so worried about finding a job that you don't take the time to go to the barn to check on your horse?

Fear, worry, anxiety, depression, chaos, and even just plain being too busy are emotions that pull us away from our natural ability to be present with ourselves and what is required from us right now, today. When we give in to those emotions, we lose our sense of the current moment and of what is required of us. We tend to "miss" very obvious cues.

The animals in your life, however, are very aware of these obvious cues, and they will react accordingly. The horse whose human hasn't come by to ride him in two weeks will do everything in his power to bring his human back to him. But what does that mean? What is the horse's power to do this? At this level, it's pure physical need. Perhaps the horse will start rearing up every time someone else approaches his stall or perhaps he'll stop eating. That horse will find some way to get his human's attention to bring his human back to him, front and center. Cool, right?

Our pets use their physical bodies very purposefully to help create situations where we, as animal-loving humans, often feel like we have no choice but to pay attention. Perhaps they need a new leash or new cedar chips or perhaps they won't eat their normal food. In order to figure out the answer, you, as their human, must stop what you're doing and focus on the now. What is happening right now that is causing Sadie to tremble? What is happening right now that is making Wesley be so insistent that I pet him? When you don't slow down and take these things in, they tend to get bigger and bigger until you feel that you must.

As a novice animal communicator, I didn't believe this idea at first. I didn't want to believe it. I wanted the horse that was rearing up to be upset because his stall didn't have enough hay, not because his human was running on empty and needed to come back to center—because who wants to tell a human that?

In one session I worked with a cat named Rhonda who had almost completely stopped eating. Her human, John, a man in his mid-twenties, had brought her to me to figure out what was wrong. As Rhonda and I were intuitively conversing, she showed me a psychic video of what her home situation was like. In the image I saw Rhonda standing in the kitchen, facing a full bowl of cat food. She wasn't eating it. Instead, she was flinching, hiking her shoulders up, and her expression was intense and fearful. Next I heard "Bam! Bam! Bam!" and then "Ratt-a-tat-tat!" while in the image I saw Rhonda jump, startled. Whatever this was, she did not like it and did not want to eat while it was going on.

Now, as an animal communicator just starting out, I was looking for a simple answer. I wanted Rhonda to have a stomach problem or I hoped maybe she just didn't like the taste or texture of her food, because these are easy fixes. It would be much simpler to tell John to change food brands than to touch on something deeply personal that he may not have wanted to share with me, but as soon as I heard those loud sounds in the intuitive video Rhonda had shown me, I knew the communication was going in a different direction. I asked John about the sounds and he knew immediately what I was talking about. He played a lot of video games and said he was "kind of" addicted to a particular game, but that it was good for him because he had been feeling depressed lately about not being able to get a job.

Bingo!

Without realizing it, John was using the video games to completely disconnect himself from his entire life! I told him how Rhonda didn't like the sounds of the video game and did not want to eat, or really do anything else, while the game was on. At first John didn't believe me, but when I was able to use the intuitive information from Rhonda to reproduce the exact shooting sounds in the video game, he began to come around to what I was saying. For a two-week period, John agreed to give up the video game and instead would "hang out" with Rhonda in the kitchen during mealtimes. This inspired a feeling of camaraderie and reminded John how he was not alone because of Rhonda. They began walking around the backyard together before each meal, and John's former happiness started to return because he was reconnecting to himself. In Rhonda, the resulting calm and the lessening of John's depression allowed her to feel comfortable at mealtimes, and she began to flourish in her life with John. All this through Rhonda refusing to eat!

Animals are very comfortable using their physical needs to help their humans become aware of their present moment. When we slow down and pay attention to the needs of our beloved animals, we also naturally begin to pay attention to what is going on within us as well, and we more naturally find ourselves connected to the reality within our lives.

* * * * * * *

Lessons in Self-Acceptance and Unconditional Love

Another amazing thing I've learned about animals through my travels as an animal communicator is that animals—and by this I mean every single animal on the planet—have mastered unconditional love. Unconditional love is the ability to love oneself and all creatures great and small regardless of what benefit you may or may not get from that love. Clearly, based on the state of humanity right now, humans are still working on this lesson. So many people don't truly love and accept themselves for who they are, and that means they don't accept anyone around them either. Acceptance of this sort is one of the biggest requirements to achieving unconditional love!

Animals, on the other hand, accept themselves for who they are, regardless of their standing, stature, nature, profile, body type, intellect, and more. Unless affected by humans, it's uncommon to see a dog or a cat that doesn't have a naturally healthy sense of self. Animals innately believe in their ability to achieve and be successful at whatever they try. A coyote connects with his gut instinct to find the will and skill within to catch his prey. He doesn't question, "Am I good enough to get that squirrel?" He doesn't spend time worrying about how he failed the last three times he tried to catch a squirrel. He locks in, aligns with himself, and just goes.

Humans are a completely different story. Have you ever noticed that you can recall your mistakes more easily than your triumphs? Most people can. And while this may seem like a positive trait because it allows us to learn from our mistakes, it can also be very negative. Rather than gathering the lesson from a past failure, many people will beat themselves up until they are fully stuck in the past, unable to move forward. Luckily, our pets have found an amazing way to help us back to the current moment.

Animals Reveal When We're Stuck in the Past or Future

For the happiest, healthiest pet, you must be fully aware of your own self, your own life, and your own situation right now. People who live through their past rather than in the present moment tend to have a lot of needs in order to feel okay in their lives. They may need to ensure their income never dips below a certain level, they may need to keep themselves hidden in order to feel safe from the trials and tribulations of their past, or they may even need to be number one at whatever they do so that they never have to feel like a failure again. There are an unlimited number of ways that we, as humans, can allow our past to dictate our present moment, and none of those result in actual happiness. When our past creeps into our daily lives, we are evaluating our lives based on all the data that preceded this moment instead of evaluating our lives based on the data in front of us right here, right now.

Let's look at Tracey and her dog Belle to really understand how this plays out in the human-animal relationship. Tracey had been through a lot of pain in her life. Her father had abandoned her family when she was nine, and her mother didn't understand her sensitivity. Tracey often felt alone and unsupported in the world because of this, and much of her current situation reflected those feelings. Tracey wanted to avoid the pain from her past, so she did whatever she could to help the people around her avoid experiencing that type of pain themselves. Anyone who knew Tracey knew her to be a very kind, caring, giving, loving woman who would go to great lengths to help others.

Tracey adopted Belle, a small Tibetan terrier, from a local shelter. Belle's former family had abandoned her when they moved out of state. They heartlessly left Belle tied to a tree in the backyard with no food or water for two days until a neighbor figured out what had happened and rescued her. Despite her ordeal, Belle was a happy, loving, quiet dog who adored being petted and sitting in the laps of strangers. Tracey felt moved by Belle's story and knew that she wanted to help Belle feel all the love she had probably been missing out on her entire life. She eagerly made a huge space in her heart and in her home for Belle and began to get set up for a wonderful relationship with an amazing dog.

But Belle had other plans. By the time Tracey brought Belle to me, Belle was a nervous wreck. Within a few months of living with Tracey, Belle had begun shaking incessantly and was barking loudly at visitors, as well as whenever Tracey sat at her desk in her home office to work. Tracey wanted to know what had happened. She told me, "Poor Belle has been through so much in her life already. She was a victim of some really terrible circumstances and people. It's so unfair that she should have to go through this, too!"

When I psychically connected with Belle, her story was completely different from Tracey's. First, she didn't want to talk to me about her past abuse, what the family that abandoned her was like, or what those days living tied to a tree in the backyard were like. When I would intuitively try to push her in that direction, the information I received back was akin to, "Why go there? That's in the past!" It was as if she'd made her peace with the things she had been through. They felt intuitively to me like very distant memories. It reminded me of how I don't actually remember my eighth birthday party with my best friend, Jenny, but I clearly remember the photographs of going to the movie theater to see *Grease*. The memory is mostly there, but I don't have emotion around it because it is built through stories and old photographs more than emotional recall.

When I asked Belle to talk about her relationship with Tracey, however, the intuitive conversation changed in tone. Gone was the "eh…why go there?" energy, and in its place was now a concerned family member. Belle began sending me images, feelings, emotions, thoughts, words, and information dumps about Tracey. She clearly had a message she wanted to get through to me. She said that Tracey had a lot of nervous energy and was always worrying about at least five things at any given time. She showed me how Tracey never really sat still. Even when "relaxing"

· · · · · · ·

to watch TV, Tracey was on her phone or the computer or writing out a list of things to do. As I told Tracey this, she wholeheartedly agreed.

"Yes, I have trouble relaxing. I feel better if I'm busy, so I usually do a few things at once."

Hmmm… I thought to myself. *This is getting interesting!*

Next, Belle gave me a picture of Tracey holding Belle's face in her hands, her eyes filling with tears as they deeply searched Belle's. She said that Tracey spent a lot of time worrying that Belle was in pain and said that Tracey often emotionally felt the pain she perceived in Belle. Belle accompanied this information with a picture of a sagging, heavy, tired-looking heart. Belle then told me how Tracey would talk about the "ugly" people and tell her she never had to be around them again, and Tracey confirmed for me that the "ugly" people were what she called Belle's former family. When I explained to Tracey what her lovely dog was telling me, she laughed out loud and said, "Yes, I guess it's clear. I love her a lot! I just want her to be happy and love me!"

Can you guess what the solution to Belle's anxiety problems was? Tracey needed to learn to relax overall and slow down. Belle wanted Tracey to stop spending all of her time making to-do lists and instead invest energy in chilling out. Tracey spent so many hours planning for the future that she often missed the beautiful moments that were right in front of her. Belle wanted to be able to experience those moments with Tracey but couldn't begin to do so when Tracey was wound up and anxious all the time. If Tracey could, instead, calm down, look at her surroundings, and take pleasure in what was going on in her environment in this moment, Tracey's anxiety would begin to dissipate. This would make her a much more enjoyable person to be around, and Belle would no longer feed off that anxiety and experience it within herself.

Tracey perceived Belle as a nervous dog but was unable to see that Belle was really only reflecting Tracey's own nervous energy back to her. Basically, Belle was asking Tracey to be present with her in order to facilitate the best, most healthy relationship between the two!

Do as the Animals Do

Animals function perfectly in the wild. They try something out, evaluate whether or not it worked, and make their decisions on that moment. A wild elephant, for example, can smell fruit in a tree. She tries reaching up for the fruit, but that doesn't work because the branch is too high. Next, she'll try pulling on lower branches, and when that doesn't work, eventually she'll try pushing the tree over to get to the fruit.

If we, as humans, could always function this way, we would live in more success and happiness. Unfortunately, the way many people approach this situation doesn't lead to such a positive outcome. If a person were to want fruit from a high-up branch and found that they couldn't reach the branch, many people would start thinking they were failures or not good enough to get the fruit, or perhaps even wonder if they actually deserved the fruit. These thoughts would

• • • • • • •

stay lodged in their heads so that the next time a high-up piece of fruit presented itself, rather than just going for it, the person might say, "Well, high-up pieces of fruit never work for me. I've tried before to no avail…"

This is an example of living in the past. Just because it didn't work before doesn't mean it won't work this time. Animals understand this, but many humans don't. That elephant will try one method after another until she finally gets what she wants, while the human often doesn't even try because she remembers what happened the last time.

And this is what was going on with Tracey and Belle. Tracey knew about all of the pain in Belle's past, and it was Tracey who was holding on to it. For her, everything that Belle experienced in her present life came through the filter of her past. So, where Belle would be excited to meet another dog, Tracey would view it as a chance to finally overcome her abandonment. Where Belle would look at barking at the mailman as fun, Tracey would label it as fear from her past abuse.

The only way that Belle and Tracey were going to come to terms and live the happy life that Tracey had been dreaming of was going to be for Tracey to stop holding on to the past and to let go of her worry about the future—and that is exactly what this pair was able to do. Tracey began working on techniques to manage her anxiety and to help her release her attachment to Belle's past. And interestingly enough (and this is something I see every day with my clients), as Tracey began to let go of Belle's past, she also began to see the futility in holding on to her own past, which allowed Tracey to become a happier, healthier person and allowed Belle to live in a relaxed home where she was free to be her true self now.

Animals truly are masters at being present. After all, to survive in the wild they really have to be present to everything that is going on around them. Many people in close relationships with their pets forget this and instead worry about their pet's pending crossing or their animal's challenging past, but to have the happiest, healthiest pet, you must—as the animals will show you day in and day out—be fully aware of your own self, your own life, and your own situation *right now*.

Three Practices with Your Pet

Here are three exercises that you can do with your pet to stay fully present. Don't worry if you struggle. Your pet can get you back on track if you allow them to!

· · · · · · ·

EXERCISE: **Find Inner Calm for Outer Peace**

Try walking your dog or hanging out with your cat or visiting your horse (or just meeting up with your pet) without any distractions. Distractions include technology. This means no cell phone, no MP3 player, and no texting. It also means no mental list-writing, no composing conversations to your boss in your head, and no powering through just to check "taking care of my pet" off the list. The purpose of this exercise is to allow you to relax into the connection you have with your pet. Even though many of our pets may not behave as if they know what our emotional state is, they *do* know. All of them. Your cat will sense when you are fully present and bonding with him versus when you are just going through the motions, and he will behave according to your mental and emotional state. Your dog will bark more or pull on the leash or feel more afraid depending on how connected to her you are during your time together.

I work intuitively with animals every day and it's very easy—not because I am an amazing animal communicator, but because animals are amazing communicators. You can't fool a horse into thinking that you're calm and present just because you're acting calm and present. They know exactly what is going on on the inside. So, during this exercise, if you're able to eliminate all distractions and just fall into a loving groove with your pet, you'll feel a shift within you as well as your pet. If you don't feel a shift in either direction, then you didn't eliminate enough distractions, whether physical or mental, and you need to re-evaluate to figure out where you're still being pulled away from these precious moments with your pet.

EXERCISE: **Allow Your Pet to Call You Back**

When your pet isn't behaving or is clearly feeling scared or doesn't seem like himself, try this. You may want to carry a small pad of paper and pen around in your back pocket when you're spending time with your pet just so you can jot down notes, but this is not absolutely necessary (and I don't usually do it that way myself). The moment you notice that your pet isn't following the rules or is feeling upset or is destroying something or doing something out of the ordinary is the moment you want to begin. Notice exactly what you were doing, thinking, feeling, or who you were with at the time of the out-of-the-ordinary behavior. Most of the time when our pets "act up" they are doing so in order to re-focus our attention because acting up really only occurs when we're not fully present. If you're distractedly thinking about your job options or if you're a ball of emotion worrying about money, your pet will

• • • • • • • •

do anything in his power to try and get you to focus back in to the present moment with him. Perhaps he'll bark, neigh, growl, cry, whine, run away, or cower.

In order to correct this, you will have to do something different from what you were doing (after all, you can't bake a new flavor of pie with the same old ingredients). You must also determine why you had emotionally drifted away in the first place. You'll find that there is a pattern in your desire to leave the present moment. For example, you always drift off into anxiety whenever your mother talks about your prospects for a spouse. See if you can figure out what types of things promote you emotionally leaving the moment with your pet. Learning what takes you away from the present is just as important as catching it, and your pet helps you do both by reacting when you leave and then reacting as you return.

EXERCISE: See the World Through Your Pet's Eyes

Lie on the floor next to your pet (assuming this is possible). Look into your pet's eyes, as long as he will let you, not with force or purpose but with openness. Don't try to make your pet stare at you. For some animals this would be very uncomfortable and could even be viewed as confrontational. So, instead of being forceful with your stare, use your heart to look at your pet. Stay this way for several minutes, allowing your pet to move around as she wants. She may not want to lie on the ground with you or she may come and cuddle up with you. Whatever happens, allow it to happen. Your only purpose is to just look and observe. As you become comfortable in this new position on the floor, start to think about what life looks like from your pet's perspective. If you have a bunny, imagine hopping around in the kitchen, looking up at the countertop, for example. Imagine what it is like for your parakeet, who loves to sit on the edge of the cabinet by the refrigerator and chirp as he sings down into your hair…

Changing your perspective in this way has two benefits: first, it allows you to connect with your pet on her terms. This isn't something that we, as humans, so often do. We ask our cat to come sit in our lap, we ride our horses, we sit next to our dogs in our car—but these are all very human things. It also gives us a new perspective of our daily life with our pet and takes us out of our comfort zone. And when you're out of your comfort zone, it's much harder to drift away into the world of "ten ways to quit my job." Just looking at life from the point of view of your pet and throwing yourself out of your comfort zone is a wonderful way to keep you firmly focused on the now.

* * * * * * * *

So, do animals ever purposely think to themselves, "Hey, she's out of her head with worry; I've got to do something to bring her back to the present"? Not exactly, but their natural ability to push people into looking at the world differently, letting go of the past, and releasing worry about the future is one of the reasons the human-animal relationship is so powerful. In my family we constantly lie on the floor with our dog. In fact, sometimes it's my husband, my son, our dog, and me all in a big pile on the floor, just enjoying the moment with our hearts open. And when your heart is truly open, there is no room for fear, worry, anxiety, depression, or sadness—only love in the present moment.

Laura Wooster

Danielle MacKinnon has been recognized as one of the country's "Best Psychic Mediums" by psychic investigator Bob Olson and as one of the "Top 100 Astrologers and Psychics in America" by Paulette Cooper. As an intuitive and animal communicator, Danielle has helped people and animals around the globe live better, happier, healthier lives. Her work has been featured on TV, radio, and in magazines throughout the United States. Her book *Soul Contracts: Find Harmony and Unlock Your Brilliance* continues to assist thousands of people in breaking through their most difficult challenges. For more, please visit www.daniellemackinnon.com.

Mindfulness for Sleep
and Physical Relaxation

ROBERT BUTERA, PhD & ERIN BYRON, MA

Sleep is a necessary restorative process that affects all aspects of our functioning and well-being. Sleeplessness is a global epidemic that could be alleviated through mindfulness practices such as deep breathing, witnessing thoughts, gentle movement, relaxation, and daily routines. The body requires at least eight hours of sleep in a twenty-four-hour period in order for us to function optimally on all levels. The Centers for Disease Control and Prevention have tracked the phenomenon of sleep deprivation and found that the number of people sleeping less than six hours per night has steadily increased over the last few decades. This includes both sexes and people of all ages. While sleep is crucial to good health, a large proportion of the population has some type of sleep disorder.

Sleep deprivation significantly compromises our overall health. The consequences include an overall malaise, sense of tiredness, or lack of energy. As these feelings are prolonged, anxiety, depression, and chronic illness often arise. Even one night of inadequate sleep leads to irritability, memory issues, poor concentration, and decreased performance. It is common for sleep-deprived people to feel generally unwell, experience more aches and pains, and have emotional outbursts. All in all, when healthy sleep is not part of the daily routine, it steals health and joy from our lives!

Consequences of Sleep Deprivation

- Memory problems, including recall of known facts
- Trouble thinking clearly and making decisions
- Unable to consolidate information
- Difficulty focusing and maintaining attention
- Slow to learn new tasks
- More mistakes
- Tremors and muscular tension
- Increased sensitivity to pain
- Bodily aches
- Longer reaction times
- Decreased motivation
- Irritability and emotional outbursts
- Depression and anxiety
- Diabetes
- High blood pressure
- Obesity
- In extreme cases, problems with perception such as hallucinations or inability to perceive objective reality

You know you have had a good night's rest when you awaken feeling refreshed and motivated. The emotional and cognitive issues associated with sleep deprivation are eased, and we are physically better able to perform in life. On the other hand, not enough sleep makes rising painful and sets a tone of resistance and discomfort that can carry through the remainder of the day. Because so many people live as if eight hours' sleep per night were impossible, the idea of waking up feeling physically well and emotionally enthusiastic seems equally unfeasible. Sleep deprivation has become part of our cultural norm; feeling tired from day to day is a baseline experience for most people.

There are a number of ways we lose out on sleep. Insomnia is defined as the inability to fall or stay asleep. This can appear as trouble initiating sleep, staying asleep, moving into the restorative phase of sleep, or waking up too early. Sleep apnea (a profound interruption in breathing), sleep

• • • • • • • •

walking, sleep talking, and even sleep eating are also common sleep interruptions that some people experience regularly.

When asked about what is problematic for them about their sleep, people disclose a number of issues. Parents of young children found they slept far less than they did before their children were born, and spouses of people who snore have trouble staying asleep. Many people explained they wake up intermittently, toss and turn, look at the clock, go to the washroom, and lie awake worrying. Folks with a busy lifestyle or who work too much say there isn't enough time to sleep. It is common for people to turn to medication or substance use in order to help with sleep, but then they often don't feel rested. This is partially because substances interrupt our natural sleep cycles.

Common Reasons for Poor Sleep

- Erratic bedtime and wake time
- Disruptions from spouse
- Caring for children
- Poor sleep hygiene
- Not enough exercise
- Poor nutrition
- Not feeling safe
- Genetics
- Sleep disorders
- Busyness
- Overstimulation
- Antidepressants
- Steroids
- Decongestants
- Caffeine
- Coffee, tea, chocolate
- Alcohol
- Nicotine
- Stress

Healthy Sleep

Healthy sleep occurs in four stages, which are repeated in cycles throughout the night. Stage 1 is the transition into sleep, or the "getting comfortable" stage. Ideally, this is accounts for only 5 percent of the total sleep time; however, a common form of insomnia is the inability to fall asleep. Stage 2 is light sleep, where physiological changes such as a decrease in body temperature, muscular relaxation, and slowed heart rate occur. A whopping 50 percent of our sleep time is typically spent in stage 2 sleep. Stage 3 is deep sleep. During deep sleep the body repairs itself, fortifies the immune system, and regulates its chemistry to promote a sense of calm and well-being. Brain waves are slow. Stage 4 is an even deeper counterpart to stage 3, where the brain moves into delta waves. It is restful and restorative, aiding our immune and hormonal systems, improving healing, and offering a sense of rejuvenation when waking. Stages 3 and 4 account for 10–20 percent of our sleep time. These four stages are all considered non-rapid eye movement (NREM) sleep. Rapid eye movement (REM) sleep tends to begin after ninety minutes of sleep, once we have moved through the other four stages.

As the name indicates, REM sleep is characterized by rapid movements of the eyes, seen from the outside as a flickering of the eyelids as the eyeballs dart. Respiratory and heart rates, as well as brain activity, increase in REM sleep. Despite this mental and involuntary muscular activation, the voluntary muscles of the body—those that move you rather than perform bodily functions—are paralyzed. Ironically, during a time when the brain is most active, the body is most relaxed. Most of our dreams occur during REM sleep.

REM sleep is believed to help consolidate learning and memory, as well as keep the brain healthy and adaptable. When people do not get enough REM sleep, they are less able to think clearly and manage their emotions. Most REM-deprived people will have micro episodes of sleep during the day where they gaze off and their brainwaves shift into those consistent with a sleeping brain. After prolonged REM deprivation some people will hallucinate. Furthermore, the body will experience a "REM rebound" the following night, where more than the usual 20 percent of sleep time will go toward REM sleep. Despite its apparent necessity, REM sleep is not as restorative as stage 3 and stage 4 sleep.

Each night, sleep goes through a typical cycle. In the beginning we move sequentially through the first four stages of sleep into a REM cycle. Although REM sleep can last for up to ninety minutes, the first REM cycle is usually only about ten minutes long. Each time we move back into REM sleep we experience it for a longer period of time, which is why we require lengthy sleep times. Where most deep sleep (stages 3 and 4) happens in the first half of sleeping, most REM sleep occurs during the second half and alternates with stage 2 (light) sleep. It is easier to awaken from REM sleep and stage 2 sleep than it is from stages 3 or 4. The longest period of REM sleep is just before waking.

· · · · · · · ·

How well we sleep naturally shifts as we age. Although there is little understanding as to why, it is well-known that sleep becomes less efficient as we age. Babies spend two-thirds of their time sleeping, while adults spend less than one-third of their time asleep. Aging people experience a reduction in the depth, intensity, and continuity of sleep, including problems falling asleep and frequent awakenings. The older we get, the less REM sleep we experience. Also, we spend more time in stage 1 (transitional) sleep, so it is easier to awaken. This means that sleep is intermittent and not typically prolonged. As we age, the ability to sleep worsens while the need for sleep remains the same; thus, it is important for us to cultivate both good sleep hygiene routines and alternative strategies to rest the brain and body systems. In this way we can keep our restorative processes active and maintain good health despite greater sleep disruptions.

Sam's Noisy Apartment

Sam lives in a busy city and used to have a great deal of trouble falling and staying asleep. There was noise from the street and adjacent apartments and his own inner chatter all keeping him awake. Sam works a high-stress job and juggles so many responsibilities that he used to have trouble keeping track of everything. The middle of the night seemed like the only time he was able to review his list and prioritize all that was required of him. Needless to say, this impinged upon the quality of his sleep.

Despite his best efforts, the long, sleepless nights began to affect Sam's job performance to the point where his supervisors identified a problem. At first, this further contributed to Sam's stress and insomnia; in due course, he reached out for counseling. The first thing the counselor did was teach Sam deep breathing. She explained that by moving the diaphragm with the breath, his heart and digestive organs received a massage and his brain, endocrine, and nervous systems all felt safe and relaxed. To build on these benefits, the counselor taught Sam mindfulness techniques like how to witness his thoughts and emotions without becoming involved with them and how to relax the body through mental suggestions.

The counselor also recommended that Sam establish a bedtime routine in order to train his body into a proper sleep rhythm. She let him know that a walk after work or on his lunch break could go a long way in unwinding the stress he was carrying in his body and mind. Once he was established in a bedtime routine and daily walk, she had him add in a "review of the day" practice. This allowed Sam to mindfully witness his experiences of the day and be mindful of where there was an emotional charge. From that mindfulness, he was able to apply the deep breath and conscious relaxation they had practiced, essentially removing the stress from his system via exercise and reflection rather than waiting for bedtime to do so.

The next step was to cultivate a "preview of the next day" practice, where Sam would reflect upon his upcoming tasks and duties to notice where there was stress, fear, or uncertainty. In the

· · · · · · ·

cases where he noticed an emotional charge, Sam mindfully accepted the emotion and strategized about how to approach the situation. Sometimes there were actions he could take and other times the best he could do was remind himself to stay calm through deep breathing and mental suggestions when the situation arose.

Once Sam made deep breathing, relaxation, exercise, and mindfulness of his daily tasks part of his routine, he found it easy to establish a bedtime routine. He no longer procrastinated going to bed, fearing all the mental stress that awaited him there. Instead, Sam enjoyed settling in with his favorite jazz music and appreciated the relaxing comfort of his bed. Sam's bedtime routine became so effective that if he was ever out late with friends, his body would begin to fall asleep at the designated time! Sam's work and social lives improved as a result of his mindful lifestyle choices, and his overall health was reflected in the high quality of his new sleep regimen.

Sleep Hygiene

Like Sam, there are a number of habits you can create that will support your body in establishing a routine of restorative sleep. First off, don't spend an excessive amount of time in bed. Begin to think of your bed as sacred space. Do not read, work, or watch television in bed. You may want to consider extending this guideline to no relaxation or even napping in bed. Let your bed be a sacred nighttime space.

At the end of the day, when you get sleepy, get into bed! Trust the messages your body is sending you about when it is ready to transition into rest. You can amplify the power of your natural rhythms by creating a regular sleep/wake schedule: go to bed and rise at the same time every day. This programs the body to move into its sleep rhythms steadily, like a band following the rhythm of the drummer. The timing of your sleep can become automatic, and the body will follow the routine.

The comfort and quality of your mattress can go a long way in improving your overall rest. Ensure that the mattress is firm enough to support your spine so that the nervous system can relax; 72,000 nerves in your body are connected to the spine. When the back is comfortable, that comfort translates to the rest of the body. Be careful that the mattress is not too firm, which can impinge circulation so that you wake up due to the discomfort of pins and needles because your extremities have fallen asleep.

Everyday lifestyle routines also contribute to better sleep at night. Even a small amount of exercise during the day can lead to great improvements in sleep depth and quality overnight. Movement alleviates the stress we hold in our bodies by activating muscles and the cardiovascular system. It also provides an elevated contrast to the restful state we seek at night. Even a ten-minute walk each day can be a huge contributing factor toward better sleep at night.

· · · · · · ·

Proper nutritional intake, including a wealth of vegetables, supports the body in feeling healthy so that when it is time for sleep it has many of its other physical needs met. Do not, however, eat big meals before bed, as the body then spends its energy digesting rather than restoring. Also avoid caffeine, sugar, and nicotine at least four to six hours before going to bed. Many people cut off their caffeine intake by noon. Ensure that you are hydrated, otherwise dry mouth or the physiological stress of dehydration may awaken you in the night. Be careful not to drink too much before bedtime, though, as frequent trips to the bathroom are also disruptive!

Bedtime routines are a key piece in healthy sleep. Develop a bedtime routine that includes a relaxation period before bed. For most people, their bedtime routine includes turning off all electronics at least one hour before bed. Limit media interference like upsetting news programs and violent imagery. Blue screens and their flashing light, such as on monitors, televisions, and small, detailed screens like those on tablets and smartphones, activate the brain and nervous system. Thus, they disrupt the circadian rhythm and interfere with the relaxation and slowing down that would naturally occur near bedtime. For similar reasons, many people begin dimming the lights near bedtime to promote the release of melatonin, a hormone that helps regulate sleeping cycles. Physical hygiene like washing the face, brushing and flossing teeth, and a soothing bath are a welcome part of a bedtime routine. Many people drink herbal tea to further calm the nerves. It is recommended that we go to bed by 10 PM to gain a higher quality of rest.

Personal Reflection for Sleep Hygiene

A sleep journal can be an effective way of learning about your sleeping habits. Over time, it can bring to light factors that you were previously unaware of or had not considered to be damaging to your sleep. Note the variability in your bedtime, when you fall asleep, when you wake up (for the day as well as the number of intermittent awakenings through the night), the total time spent sleeping in that twenty-four-hour period, the quality of your sleep, your worries, and any of the lifestyle factors mentioned above such as routines, stress, substance use, nutrition, exercise, and so on.

By tracking your sleep habits and relating them to simple logs about your lifestyle and routines, you may identify contributing factors to your sleep problems. It also gives you a place to vent your worries so that they do not consume your mind once you go to bed. Writing down all of your worries—and any potential solutions—can alleviate underlying mental stress. This way, your worries are less likely to keep you awake or haunt your dreams.

To begin your sleep journal, you may ask yourself the following questions. After three or four weeks, repeat this line of questioning and relate it to any changes in your sleep routine and quality.

• • • • • • •

- What else do I do in my bedroom besides sleep? Are any of these activities disruptive to sleep? Do any of them support a better sleep at night?

- Do I tend to go to sleep and get up at the same time each day?

- Do I get any exercise or gentle movement during the day?

- How is my breathing throughout the day?

- Do I take anything to help me sleep, such as medication, alcohol, supplements, or the like?

- Do I take anything that might disrupt my sleep, such as nicotine, junk food, caffeine, or the like?

- Do I eat too much before bed?

- Do I turn off my electronics an hour or two before bedtime?

- Do I go to bed when I am tired? If no, why not?

- Do I have a semblance of a bedtime routine? What is it? What would an ideal bedtime routine look like?

- Thinking about these answers, what is one thing I can easily adapt right now that may help improve my sleep?

There may be other questions you have for yourself about your sleep and lifestyle habits. Allow your sleep journal to follow your curiosity. Use it as a chance to become more mindful and learn about yourself. As insights arise, you can make small, everyday adaptations to your routines and choices that will go a long way in supporting your improved sleep.

Mindful Yoga Postures for Healthy Sleep

Movement is a routine that greatly improves sleep. If possible, spend five to ten minutes practicing a few light yoga postures as part of your bedtime routine. By spending time paying attention to the shape your body is making, as well as how it feels to stretch and relax, you are soothing your mind. When practiced at bedtime, these simple, mindful movements can attune you to your sleepiness and affirm the body's need for rest. By the end of the sequence, if your mind stays focused on the breath and the postures, you may be well on your way to dreamland.

The following sample sequence promotes full-body relaxation. It is designed to quiet the nervous system in order to prepare the body to fall into a deep, restful sleep more easily. It will work best if you make it part of your bedtime routine. Consistent daily experiences are very comforting for the mind.

You may perform each posture only once or repeat them each three to five times. You may also do the entire sequence from beginning to end, then repeat it and notice how much more

• • • • • • •

relaxed you are the second time through. It is best to do these postures on the floor in the bedroom, then move into the bed with little disruption once the postures are complete. You may follow the yoga postures with a mindful relaxation exercise in bed.

Upward Reaching Pose (*Urdhva Hastasana*): Stand up tall and straight. You may put your heels, seat, shoulders, and head against a wall to ensure a correct posture, which may feel strange at first, especially to computer users. Inhale and extend arms up to the sky, doing your best to keep biceps beside ears and shoulders relaxed as the lift comes from the underarm space. You may exaggerate the lift in the chest and elongate the abdomen while holding the lower back stable as you breathe deeply. Feel a sense of upliftedness.

Standing Side Bend: Place feet wider than hip-width apart and protect back by keeping hips square, not pushed out to the left or the right as you bend. On an exhale bend into the soft part of your waist, shortening the distance between the side of the lowest rib and hip while keeping the core muscles engaged. Feel the lifted side of your rib cage open, allowing a deeper breath. You may raise your top arm to increase the stretch. If you hold the posture, be sure that your breath is flowing deeply while the core remains engaged. Inhale back to center and repeat on the other side for the same length of time.

Restorative Forward Bend: Come to a seated position. Place the soles of the feet on the floor and bend the knees toward the chest so you are seated in what looks like a loose fetal position. Ensure that ankles, knees, and hips are in alignment with each other. Exhale and spread the front of the body over the front of the thighs, resting your forehead on the knees. You may fold your arms on the knees to create a pillow for the head; otherwise, rest them alongside the legs. Feel your entire body relaxing with each exhale. Hold for roughly five breaths to give the muscles and mind sufficient time to relax, then roll up gently with the help of your arms.

Bridge Pose (*Setu Bandhasana*): Lie down on the back with the lower body in the same position as in the previous posture: ankles and knees hip-width apart, with the feet planted close to the buttocks and the knees pointing into the air. Ensure that your feet and knees remain in line with the hips through the entire pose rather than collapsing them in or out. Inhale and roll the pelvis and lower back upward, rooting the posture into the strength of the core and legs. Hold for a comfortable time, breathing regularly, or roll up with each inhale and down with each exhale.

· · · · · · ·

Reclined Half Twist (*Supta Matsyendrasana*): Extend each arm to each side at shoulder height, hands in line with shoulders. To protect your back, keep feet on the floor at all times; otherwise, knees can go right into chest. Exhale the legs to the left and ensure that the feet are supported by the earth. If you are free from neck issues, turn your face lightly to the right (in the opposite direction of the knees). With practice, thighs may come to a right angle to the torso and both shoulders may rest on the floor. Surrender into the support of the ground. Postures that revolve the spine increase circulation there and help regulate the nervous system, thereby preparing the body for sleep. Relax the forehead and abdomen to amplify this effect. Repeat the posture on the other side.

The practice of these mindful movements helps soothe your body's systems and prepare you for deeper rest. You can amplify the benefits of the yoga postures if you follow them with a relaxation like the one below.

Mindful Relaxation

For most people the condition of the nervous system (fight-flight-or-freeze mode versus rest-and-digest mode) is predominantly unconscious. It is not a typical thing for folks to focus on regulating the nervous system unless they have realized it is causing them problems, for example in the cases of anxiety or insomnia. It is a straightforward thing to balance the nervous system but not always easy to remember or implement. Breath and movement are two of the simplest ways to bring about the relaxed alertness that is indicative of a regulated nervous system.

The most effective way of balancing the nervous system is via the breath. Rapid breathing focused in the upper chest wakes us up, usually to the point of feeling hyper-alert and agitated. Slow, deep breathing calms us. As the breath, so the mind. Movement is another means of balancing the nervous system. Vigorous exercise burns off excess stress and anger. Moderate movement and stretching is soothing yet enlivening.

After a day where deep breathing and some exercise have occurred, the body is more prepared for sleep. You can further this effect by mindfully relaxing the nervous system at bedtime. Whether you perform the yoga postures above or not (we recommend that you do), when you go to bed perform a mindful relaxation. This eases the nervous system and other bodily systems and relaxes the body and mind, preparing you for a deep, restful sleep.

Begin the mindful relaxation by slowly scanning your body from the toes to the top of your head (or head to feet), all the while observing a slow breath. This scanning is a process of bringing mindful, nonjudgmental, relaxed awareness to whatever part of the body you are paying attention to. Calmly bring a feeling of calm, heaviness, or lightness to each area as you become aware of it. If you are still awake after scanning the whole body, pause for a moment or two to

· · · · · · · ·

integrate and appreciate the feeling of being relaxed. If you are not feeling drowsy, you may repeat the scan. Witness the tense parts relaxing a bit more on each subsequent scan. You possess a deep potential for relaxation. The more mindful you are of it, the more natural deep sleep will feel. Furthermore, if you can't sleep, deep relaxation activates the body's restorative processes in a similar way.

Mindfulness Strategies for Rest

If you awaken too early or cannot fall asleep when you go to bed, remain mindful of the importance of rest. Simply closing your eyes and relaxing the body as in the previous exercise can compensate for most of the wakefulness. Do your best to accept the wakefulness rather than count the hours until you have to get up. Becoming upset, frustrated, or stressed increases tension and interferes not only with the potential sleep you could enjoy but also the present potential for rest. Your mindful acceptance of the situation removes the stress. Use the time to practice mindful breathing, relaxation, or prayer in the night. Quiet activities like reading spiritual or other inspirational materials, listening to relaxing music, or following a guided visualization can also help prepare the body and mind for sleep.

In the case where you have been lying awake for more than twenty minutes, it may be best to get out of bed, especially if you are becoming agitated by your wakefulness. Keep the lights dim in the house but leave the bedroom and perform a quiet, boring activity such as washing dishes or knitting. Avoid anything activating, fun, or stimulating. Watching television, surfing the Internet, and playing video games profoundly interfere with sleep, as the blue screens and flashing lights stimulate the brain and carry you further from rest. Instead, do something that conserves your energy and helps you feel drowsy.

After twenty minutes or so, return to bed. You may practice the mindful movements proposed earlier, very slowly and gently, or perform the mindful relaxation. You can try lying on your right side so the left nostril, whose dominance is associated with quietude, draws more air. Focus the mind on slow, deep breathing or a single uplifting thought to help drift off to sleep. If you become more wakeful while lying down in bed, repeat the process. In this way you are avoiding associating the bedroom with frustration and wakefulness. Ultimately, it is most important to remain mindful of a sense of rest during the hours that you are meant to be sleeping, whether you are actually asleep or not. Amanda's story below speaks to the dangers of avoiding rest.

Amanda's Sleep Recovery Story

For most of my early life I was a good sleeper; in fact, I slept so well and so often that my over-sleeping was discovered to be one of my biggest migraine headache triggers. Things changed sometime in my early thirties, and I started waking up in the middle of the night

• • • • • • • •

and was unable to fall back asleep. As would any type-A person, at first I welcomed the extra time to get things done. There was never enough time in the day; I was busy, busy, busy! This insomnia thing was a gift! Until one morning when driving to work at 70 mph on the highway, I thought I saw a polar bear (which didn't occur to me to be impossible because I was so tired) and swerved to avoid hitting it. Thankfully, there was no car in the lane next to me and I recovered from the swerve intact and with a keen awareness that I had a serious problem on my hands. I went to see my primary care doctor who (surprisingly) talked to me about good sleep hygiene and recommended meditation practice or guided relaxation CDs at bedtime. I thanked her very much and asked instead for prescription sleep medicine (I didn't have the patience for all of that other stuff). And so, because I essentially chose to mask the real problem, for the next eight years I continued to struggle with insomnia.

Fast-forward to more recent years. I took yoga lessons at home with a teacher who focused on connecting to the spiritual aspects. Although I was still struggling with insomnia most nights, I began to notice that after my weekly lessons, I was almost always able to fall right to sleep after the teacher left. I was intrigued by the impact of mindful yoga practice on my ability to sleep but didn't quite appreciate the deeper, broader significance for some time. As time went on, however, I became more curious about the spiritual aspects and made a commitment to myself to learn more.

For the last three months I have been learning about and exploring mindful yoga as a way of living. I've learned about the often problematic ego, about nonattachment and faith and true presence. I've learned that all of the turmoil that used to keep me wound up all day and up all night was just a story, a story that I had been told, a story that I had adopted. Now, I've started to watch the story rather than live it (sometimes with great amusement). I am learning to surrender and accept what is and to appreciate all of the gifts that are right in front of my eyes all day, every day. I didn't expect to have a daily yoga pose practice or to read scriptures before bed each night, but now I find this to be one of the most critical parts of my day. Sure enough, unexpectedly, I have started sleeping again...on my own. I haven't taken a single sleeping pill in over a month, which is by far the longest break I have had from them since I started taking them so many years ago. I sleep soundly. I have dreams again. I can get up to soothe my daughter after she has a nightmare and fall right back asleep, no problem. At times this shift has felt nothing short of magic, but when I settle in at night to poses, reading scriptures, or meditating and I more fully connect with my true self, I can see that it's not magic at all, it's just the truth.

As in Amanda's case, many of us forget how vital sleep is for a healthy body and mind. Few of us are mindful about cultivating efficient sleep. Many of us think that sleep is simply the absence of wakefulness, something easy and automatic, so we don't prepare for sleep the same way we

• • • • • • • •

do for other daily tasks. It is wise, instead, to relax physically and emotionally before trying to sleep rather than merely drifting off with a tense body and busy mind. The stress that pervades the mind and body during the day does not disappear when the head hits the pillow. Yoga's common-sense philosophy says that relaxation, meditation, and deep breathing are essential for deep sleep. But by the time you work, exercise, eat well, and socialize, it may seem like there is not much time for mindfulness practices. You can, however, pick one centering routine that you enjoy before sleeping. Whether you reflect on the day, read a spiritual book, or meditate, perform this activity with a prayerful attitude and breathe deeply at that time. By clearing your mind, you transform stress at its root cause in the mind. View this relaxation time as a special gift to your soul.

When living a mindful lifestyle, we approach every activity with purpose. It is vital that we take a pure approach to sleep, focusing on concentration and intention. When the breath is deep, the body is fully relaxed, and the mind is calm and focused, the physiological actions of restorative sleep proceed unhindered.

For Robert Butera's biography, see page 55.

For Erin Byron's biography, see page 22.

Finding Wellness Through Mindful Earth Connection

Healthy living can be a challenge. Even if we have a long lifespan, that doesn't mean that good health automatically comes with it. Stress and inflammation have become epidemic issues that underlie many modern health conditions, and we face countless obstacles to our quality of life goals. Perhaps you've been making changes to positively affect your health and the health of those you love. This might include eliminating contact with products you know to be hazardous, eating more unprocessed foods, drinking water in place of sugary beverages, exercising more often, and making time for stress-reduction practices that you enjoy. These are the kinds of things we usually think of when we look for tangible lifestyle adjustments. But what if there were one more way to help tip the scales of health in a positive direction? What if it were easy? Even better, what if it were *free*?

If you're struggling with insomnia, chronic pain, allergies, headaches, low energy, or attention issues, connecting to the earth may be what you need to help these concerns and more. This practice, known as earthing or grounding, is as simple as placing your bare feet on the earth. That's it! In doing so you are helping to rebalance the natural electrical system of your body with free-flowing energy. According to recent observation and research, grounding appears to have a wide range of positive effects, including the following benefits:[1]

- Improves inflammation-related disorders
- Reduces or eliminates chronic pain
- Improves sleep quality and time it takes to fall asleep
- Increases energy
- Lowers stress and promotes calmness by cooling down the nervous system and stress hormones
- Thins blood and improves blood pressure and flow
- Relieves muscle tension and headaches
- Lessens hormonal and menstrual symptoms
- Normalizes the body's biological rhythms
- Speeds healing, including recovery from athletic activity

As humans evolved we've always held some form of connection with the earth, most often through our feet. In fact, your feet house some of the largest pores and contain more sweat glands than any other area on your body. This is one reason why it's recommended to put essential oils on the bottom of the feet and why detox foot baths are so prevalent; it's an excellent location to absorb what is most beneficial and to release what's not wanted. Our feet contain the highest concentration of sensitive nerve endings as well.[2] Perhaps this was all part of a design for optimum energy exchange through an area we most often would have in contact with the earth, but for many of us this isn't a natural occurrence any longer. With modern travel practices, plastic and rubber-soled shoes, and an affinity for the indoors, we're constantly insulated and removed from the surface of the earth. If we want to make a connection, we need to make a conscious effort to do so.

How Does Earthing/Grounding Work?

Before we dive into the fun of the practice, it will be helpful to have a more technical understanding of why and how earthing works. If you care about your cable hook-up or the safety of your electronics, you have a good starting point for appreciating what grounding is all about. In fact, Clint Ober (the pioneer behind our current earthing movement) actually discovered the

---

1   "The Benefits of Earthing," *Going Barefoot: Stories of Health & Happiness by Reconnecting to the Earth* Vol. 1, No. 1 (Palm Springs, CA: Going Organic Publishing Company, 2013), 8.

2   Canadian Federation of Podiatric Medicine, "Feet Facts," www.podiatryinfocanada.ca/public/Facts.

• • • • • • • •

benefits of connecting our bodies to the free energy of the earth because of his years in the cable industry.

We've learned quite a lot about the importance of grounding since we started using electricity in our homes more than 100 years ago. To begin, let's look at the basics of electricity, which show that energy is always trying to find the most efficient way to the ground. This is why we're cautioned about lightning, power lines, and outlets. Our bodies act as easy conductors for this energy, helping it move from where it is to where it wants to go. Because of this we stay inside during storms, leave downed power lines to the professionals, and don't stick forks in wall sockets.

Notice the third hole at the bottom of your outlet. That "mouth" is the grounding port. It has nothing to do with accessing electricity and everything to do with grounding electrons; it moves out energy that wants to get back to the earth, whether it's from a lightning strike, static electricity, damaged electrical wires, or some other cause of a power surge. Wires that connect to these extra holes in your outlets run to "earth ground," a rod that is stuck into the earth.[3] If we didn't do this, that energy might overload and damage appliances that are plugged in, cause a fire, or shock you if you're nearby.

But what does this all have to do with the practice of earthing our bodies for well-being? As Martin Zucker explains in his article "Earthing: Healing Power Right Beneath Your Feet!":

> One major aspect of Earthing's effect on the physiology is to reduce inflammation and pain. The hypothesis put forward by scientists involved in Earthing research is that bare skin contact with the Earth allows the transfer into the body of large quantities of negatively charged electrons that are present in infinite numbers throughout the crust of the Earth. The electrons, it is believed, quench or neutralize positive-charged, electron-seeking free radicals that drive chronic inflammation activity at the core of many common diseases.[4]

Once you've made that earth connection, you are instantly at the same electric energy level as the earth (known as "equalizing"), and positively charged free radicals that build up as inflammation-causing energy in the body are thought to then be neutralized, as they are always seeking to pair up with electrons.

We can easily enact this process outdoors. When you connect your skin to the earth's surface you are immediately taking in electrons from the ground beneath you. We also have options for

---

3 Rimstar.org, "Hot Neutral and Ground: Our Funny Looking Household Electrical Socket," published 12 April 2012, https://www.youtube.com/watch?v=k3OHzKz0qNc.

4 Martin Zucker, "Earthing: Healing Power Right Beneath Your Feet!" *Going Barefoot: Stories of Health & Happiness By Reconnecting to the Earth* Vol. 1, No. 1 (Palm Springs, CA: Going Organic Publishing Company, 2013), 7.

· · · · · · · ·

grounding indoors. This brings our discussion back to those grounding ports. Products like bed sheets, mats, bands, and patches are available that allow for grounding without directly touching the earth. In these cases, conductive materials attach to a cord that is plugged into the extra hole in your outlet. Alternatively, if you don't have a grounding outlet you can run a wire out your window and insert a connecting rod directly into the ground. A third option could also be running it to the copper pipes in your plumbing. From the earth ground, electrons from the earth's surface are free to run up the wire, reaching you in your home or work environment. You can confirm you've established a grounded connection by using a tester, available for purchase at your local hardware store or as part of a grounding kit.

More and more, people are paying attention to the science behind earthing and why it may be so important to reintroduce into our modern lifestyles. Various studies have shown a wide range of benefits from this simple practice. While well-known physicians like Dr. Sara Gottfried[5] and Dr. Andrew Weil[6] are paying attention and are intrigued, they and others like them agree additional studies are needed to better understand the full potential of this practice. From what we know so far, it appears that grounding

> doesn't cure you of any disease or condition. What it does is to reunite you with the natural electrical signals from the Earth that govern all organisms dwelling upon it. It restores your body's natural internal electrical stability and rhythms, which in turn promote normal functioning of body systems, including the cardiovascular, respiratory, digestive, and immune systems. It remedies an electron deficiency to reduce inflammation—the common cause of disease. It shifts the nervous system from a stress-dominated mode to one of calmness and you sleep better. By reconnecting, you enable your body to return to its normal electrical state, better able to self-regulate and self-heal.[7]

Electromagnetic Frequencies (EMFs) and Our Disrupted Energy

The realization of such a simple and readily available resource for well-being is exciting! But before you go frolicking away along your clover-lined path, we need to talk about the extra energy we've added into the mix. These are electromagnetic fields and frequencies, or EMFs, caused by our increasing technology usage.

---

5 Sara Gottfried, MD, "The Earth Beneath Your Feet (Part 2, The Science): Why Going Barefoot May Boost Your Health and Beauty," http://www.saragottfriedmd.com/the-earth-beneath-your-feet-part-2-the-science-why-going-barefoot-may-boost-your-health-and-beauty/.

6 Andrew Weil, MD, "Is There Anything to 'Earthing'?" published 8 January 2013, http://www.drweil.com/drw/u/QAA401221/Is-There-Anything-to-Earthing.html.

7 Clinton Ober, Stephen T. Sinatra, and Martin Zucker, *Earthing: The Most Important Health Discovery Ever?* (Laguna Beach, CA: Basic Health Publications, Inc., 2010), 12.

· · · · · · · ·

There are natural and human-made sources of EMFs. Natural versions include electric charges that build in the atmosphere due to storms, or the magnetic field we use with compasses and animals use for their sense of navigation. Human-made frequencies include high-voltage power lines; electricity you find in your home, television, radio waves, cell phones, and cell phone towers; Wi-Fi networks; microwaves; etc. The World Health Organization has been studying the effects of EMFs in light of growing use around the world and concern for how this might be affecting us. They explain that the cause of concern is because our bodies are built to function on electrical currents:

> Low-frequency magnetic fields induce circulating currents within the human body. The strength of these currents depends on the intensity of the outside magnetic field. If sufficiently large, these currents could cause stimulation of nerves and muscles or affect other biological processes.[8]

Their research so far appears to show no harm or that the findings so far are inconclusive. However, many are convinced that electrical hypersensitivity is a real consequence and that symptoms like headaches, nausea, dizziness, fatigue, sleep disruption, and more are the result of EMFs. A friend recently shared with me the discovery of unfortunate health effects caused by EMFs for her and her husband:

> We got new computers a couple years ago and had them installed with Wi-Fi. After a few weeks we started getting headaches. I don't normally get headaches, but I was getting them every day! We finally broached the subject with each other and realized the only difference in our lives was the Wi-Fi. We had it removed, went to wired Internet, and the headaches went away.

Stories like this are cropping up more frequently. While they are often cast aside as coincidence or phantom issues, there are records as early as 1933 showing that scientists were aware of the fact that electromagnetic fields have an effect on the human nervous system.[9] Further studies from the mid-1950s and on have identified electrical hypersensitivity as a real occurrence and concern.[10]

8   World Health Organization, "What Are Electromagnetic Fields?" http://www.who.int/peh-emf/about/WhatisEMF/en/.

9   Christopher Dodge, "Clinical and Hygienic Aspects of Exposure to Electromagnetic Fields," Bioscience Division of US Navy, Washington, DC, 1969, http://www.magdahavas.com/wordpress/wp-content/uploads/2010/08/Dodge_1969.pdf.

10   Lloyd Burrell, guest post by Evelyn Savarin, "Electrical Hypersensitivity: Is It Real, Does It Exist?" http://www.electricsense.com/9479/electrical-hypersensitivity-real-exist/.

• • • • • • •

Essentially, we don't entirely know what all of this human-created energy is doing to us in the long-term since it's a relatively new phenomenon. If we want to be cautious or if we suspect EMFs may be influencing our health, we can try to eliminate the culprit. Limiting cell phone use, moving electronics out of the bedroom, or cutting off the Wi-Fi connection (if not all around, then at least during the time we sleep) are some options. But with the prevalence of this kind of energy, its subtle impact, and often impossible-to-trace sources, correcting the issue can be a real challenge. There are movements to push for more protective guidelines, including 190 scientists from 39 nations who appealed to the United Nations and World Health Organization in May 2015, but creating change can be a slow process.[11] Thankfully, it looks like earthing can be helpful in protecting the body against potentially health-disturbing EMFs, at least to a certain degree.

How Earthing Can Help Counter EMFs

In 2005 electrical engineer Roger Applewhite published a study suggesting that earthing actually acts as a barrier to EMFs and showing how grounding reduces electromagnetic fields on the body.[12] A summary from the *Journal of Environmental and Public Health* states,

> the study showed that when the body is grounded, its electrical potential becomes equalized with the Earth's electrical potential through a transfer of electrons from the Earth to the body…The study confirms the "umbrella" effect of earthing the body, explained by Nobel Prize winner Richard Feynman in his lectures on electromagnetism.[13] Feynman said that when the body potential is the same as the Earth's electric potential (and thus grounded), it becomes an extension of the Earth's gigantic electric system. The Earth's potential thus becomes the "working agent that cancels, reduces, or pushes away electric fields from the body"…This study demonstrates that grounding essentially eliminates the ambient voltage induced on the body from common electricity power sources.[14]

---

11   EMFscientist.org, "International Appeal: Scientists Call for Protection from Non-Ionizing Electromagnetic Field Exposure," http://www.emfscientist.org/index.php/emf-scientist-appeal.

12   Roger Applewhite, "The Effectiveness of a Conductive Patch and a Conductive Bed Pad in Reducing Induced Human Body Voltage via the Application of Earth Ground," *European Biology and Bioelectromagnetics* (2005) 1: 23–40.

13   As cited in *Journal of Environmental and Public Health*, R. Feynmann, R. Leighton, and M. Sands, *The Feynman Lectures on Physics*, vol. II (Boston, MA: Addison-Wesley, 1963).

14   Gaétan Chevalier, Stephen T. Sinatra, James L. Oschman, Karol Sokal, and Pawel Sokal, "Earthing: Health Implications of Reconnecting the Human Body to the Earth's Surface Electrons," *Journal of Environmental and Public Health*, published online 2012 Jan 12, doi: 10.1155/2012/291541.

· · · · · · ·

To be clear, this pertains to EMFs due to things like electrical wiring and appliances. It's still uncertain what the effect or benefit is when it comes to other sources. The Earthing Institute clarifies further, saying:

> There is no research indicating that Earthing will or will not protect a person from exposure to wireless technology like cell phone signals, microwave radiation, or radio frequencies. What we know is that Earthing reduces significantly the induced body voltages generated by simple exposure to common household 60 Hz EMFs continuously emitted by all plugged-in electrical cords (even if the appliance is off), internal wiring, and all ungrounded electrical devices in the home or office.[15]

Because of this unknown factor, some have concerns that grounding in high EMF environments like offices and dense cities might create more harm than good by causing you to become a part of the electrical circuit. The thought is that by earthing, you may become an antenna that attracts and grounds electrical pollution.[16] However, according to Applewhite's findings, this is not the case when it comes to those common electricity power sources.

Even with the uncertainty of the effect of other forms of EMFs, I believe it's worthwhile to try grounding for yourself and see how it personally influences you. In addition, you can try eliminating possible EMF sources and also test levels in the areas you ground by using an EMF or voltage meter, with the goal of grounding in low EMF locations. In my case, I haven't gone so far as to test those levels, but I do try to influence lower levels by turning off the Wi-Fi at night, and I pay attention to how my body is responding in the moment. Since earthing is shown to improve the overall function of healing, it certainly seems that grounding would be a boost to those who suspect they are sensitive to EMFs.

A Return to Sacred Earth

Outside of the science behind grounding, there exists the long history of energy practices and sacred earth connection that has been handed down in many traditions. From *ki* in Japanese tradition, *qi* in Chinese culture, or *prana* in Indian medicine, the concept of energy and its impact on life is nothing new. Each of these examples equates to some form of natural living energy or life force that is sustaining. Elsewhere it is described as a mothering power found through sacred earth connection.

---

15   The Earthing Institute, "Earthing Basics," http://www.earthinginstitute.net/?qa_faqs= %E2%80%A2-can-earthing-protect-me-from-cell-phone-frequencies-%E2%80%A8.

16   Lloyd Burrell, "Is Grounding Really the Greatest Health Discovery of All Time?" http://www.electricsense.com/7130/grounding-health-emf-protection/.

• • • • • • • •

Tess Whitehurst discusses this in her book *Holistic Energy Magic*, saying that

> the soles of our feet are extremely receptive to the energy of Mother Earth and imbibe spiritual wisdom and nourishment that brings great benefits on all levels…a hundred years ago, the famous Sioux chief Luther Standing Bear said, "The old people came literally to love the soil, and they sat or reclined on the ground with a feeling of being close to a mothering power. It was good for the skin to touch the earth and [they] liked to remove their moccasins and walk barefoot on the sacred earth.[17]

Standing Bear continues, saying that

> the soil was soothing, strengthening, cleansing, and healing. This is why [they] still sit upon the earth instead of propping [themselves] up and away from its life-giving forces. For [them], to sit or lie upon the ground is to be able to think more deeply and to feel more keenly; [they] can see more clearly into the mysteries of life and come closer in kinship to other lives about [them].[18]

This rings true to the sense of well-being, personal insights received, and deep sense of connection to a larger whole that many report from their earthing experiences. Another way you might think of it is to consider your earthing time as a spa or healing therapy event. I note this partly because of the physical and mental benefits we receive from these experiences, but also because of the sacredness that can be found there. Perhaps the word "sacred" seems out of place when you think of getting a massage, but it is entirely accurate to me. When I first started practicing as an energy worker and massage therapist I was somewhat surprised by this. I would walk into the room with my client lying quietly under their covers and I was always humbled. They had paused from their hectic day and were honoring their own needs. Their eyes were closed, mind softly drifting somewhere else. Because of their action for self-respect I had an opportunity to impart healing, and the sense of kinship and blessing was so strong that it often brought me near tears. It hummed like energy vibrating the air around us. No matter how busy my days were, these sessions always felt sacred.

I get the same feeling from earthing when I take the time to put away the distractions and truly tune into the energy that is being passed along. But in these instances I am now the one coming for healing and Mother Earth is the one sharing a uniting force.

My Introduction to Earthing

When I first started earthing I'd been suffering through an extended period of poor sleep. On top of that, since it had been an extra wet season, mold was thriving. This is an environmental

---

17 Tess Whitehurst, *Holistic Energy Magic* (Woodbury, MN: Llewellyn Publications, 2015), 147–149.

18 Luther Standing Bear, *Land of the Spotted Eagle* (Lincoln, NE: Bison Books, 2006), 192.

• • • • • • • •

allergen that triggers the worst of my pain flares. Between inadequate sleep and the mold I was surrounded by, it had been a particularly painful spring. My body was not happy. The last thing I wanted to do was get closer to the culprit, but at my naturopath's counterintuitive recommendation, I went outside. She was determined it would help me, so I sat on the soggy ground with my dog curled up by my side for moral support.

Initially, the sensation of my bare feet on the grass felt threatening. I realized it was a sensation I'd subconsciously come to associate with negative conditions like allergies and chronic pain, issues that had progressively worsened since my teenage years. I tried to ignore my building anxiety, but the mildew smell of earth and sight of spring mold thriving here and there left me jittery. *What am I doing?* I wondered. I tried not to hold my breath or let my mind run along its incessant path of worry. I'd been attempting to avoid discomfort for years without success. I figured I might as well give this a real try, as backward as it seemed. *Maybe it's like yoga,* I thought, *moving gently into the discomfort in order to get through it.*

I worked to guide my thoughts back to the sensations I was feeling: the tingling in my feet on the earth, the eventual calming of my mind, and the blanket of relaxation that crept into my burning muscles. I lay down as my eyelids became heavy. For an hour I flowed in and out of a light nap as I maintained a grounded connection. My sleep improved some that night, so the next day I tried grounding outside for two hours instead of one. I slept even better the second night. After a week of daily grounding, I felt like my body craved earth time in the same way it called for a glass of water when it was thirsty. For the first time in a month I experienced a full night of deep, uninterrupted, and restful sleep. This, in turn, eased chronic pain and helped my body better handle allergies I'd been struggling with.

While I was surprised with the signs of improvement, I was still cautious with my enthusiasm. Was it just the soothing sight of nature that was affecting me? Or perhaps it was the extra vitamin D from spending more time outside? Ultimately, winter would be my truest test. I knew insomnia was worst for me during that time and indoor allergies were just as nagging, so I waited to see how things would play out. As autumn crept its way in, I broke out my therapy light to help counter the effects of seasonal depression (known as Seasonal Affective Disorder, or SAD) that affected me every year. Sadness is an obvious symptom of this condition, but insomnia was another that rooted deep for me, even with my use of the light box.

Knowing I wouldn't be shoveling off the snow to stand barefoot on frozen ground to earth outside, I decided to buy a grounding sheet that I could put on my bed. This device would allow me to maintain a connection with the earth while indoors. The months ticked by without all those sunny rays and good vibes from nature. As we hit the depths of January and then moved into February, my yearly dose of insomnia didn't come with it. I was astonished. No sleeping pills, no valerian root sleeping tea, not even calming essential oils were needed to coerce me into slumber.

· · · · · · · ·

I now fall asleep much faster and wake up less frequently throughout the night. When I do wake I fall back to sleep easily instead of counting sheep until the sun rises. While I can't say this was a magic pill that cured all that ails me, I can certainly say I've found benefit, and it's always worth having another tool in your wellness tool belt. Why don't you give it a try? I'm going to challenge you to ground yourself as you continue reading the rest of this chapter. We'll get into how you can go about doing this now.

Your Reconnection to the Earth

Grounding is simple. All you need to do is connect your skin directly with the earth. Take off your shoes and weave those tootsies into some cool grass or take a barefoot stroll on an open path. Sit down to rest your palms on the bare earth or actively dig them into the soil as you garden. Pay attention to the surface you're on. Grass, sand, gravel, and unpainted/unsealed concrete are all conductive surfaces that allow energy to move freely. Insulating surfaces like wood, asphalt, plastic, and rubber do not. Now make yourself comfortable and settle in for some good grounding time.

Various Ways to Ground

When I first began telling others about this newfound earthing practice, my dad joked that the next time he came to visit he was sure to find me popping my head up from a hole I'd dug in the yard, like a groundhog. While comical, this actually isn't too far-fetched. Some people do take it to that level, going deeper into the earth with the hopes of making an even richer connection. If you garden, you can probably relate to some degree. It can be extremely soothing and calming to dig in, get dirty, and really connect with the earth, but that's about as far as I'll go! I might not be digging holes in my yard to lie in, but I've certainly found some of my favorite ways to ground. Let's take a look at the different approaches you might try as well:

- Sit or walk outside and directly connect to the earth

- Garden

- Touch plants—they are rooted into the earth's energy. Dormant trees are still fair game in harsh winter climates.

- Go swimming in the oceans, lakes, and rivers

- Use a grounding sheet, mats, or blankets for indoors. These can be purchased online or made yourself based off of online tutorials and materials from your local hardware store. These items connect conductive material with a cord that you plug into a grounded outlet or from a rod that you insert into the earth, usually by running the cord out a window.

• • • • • • • •

- Use grounding shoes. These include shoes that have leather soles (like moccasins or cowboy/girl boots) and shoes that have conductive elements, such as copper conduits that energetically connect your body to the earth. There are also tutorials online showing how you can turn old shoes you already own into grounding shoes.

- Make use of your basement. If you have an unfinished area, you can earth there in the dirt. If your basement has a concrete floor, you'll be grounded so long as that concrete is not painted or sealed.

I practice many of these forms of grounding, but I think my favorite will always be going barefoot in the grass or on a beach. Take the time to explore these types. Test them out and see what works for you. If you don't want to spend money, you don't have to! Grab hold of the options that require zero spending. Find your favorite way to ground, whatever makes you feel most plugged in and imparts a sense of well-being.

How Long Should You Ground?

Any amount of time is better than none, so if you only have a few minutes to spare, go for it. If you have a bit more time, thirty minutes a day is a popular recommendation. I've found that at twenty to forty minutes something clicks and I reach a state of calmness. Beyond an hour of connection, there's a noticeable impact on my sleep quality, but it may be different for you. If you have even more time, all the better. This is one instance where you can't have too much of a good thing.

If you aren't in a hurry, let your body tell you when it's time to stop. Once I'm tuned into the connection, I often find it hard to let go. Like that sense of refreshment when you finally get a drink of water after you've been parched, you'll begin to recognize when your body's thirst has been quenched with earth energy. It's worth noting that benefits can diminish once you stop grounding for a period of time, so ideally you would make this a consistent practice.

What Is the Best Time to Ground?

Morning is a great time to practice earthing since there is still dew on the ground and moisture helps with conductivity, but don't worry if you're not a morning person. Really, anytime you think to ground is an ideal time. Moments of heightened symptoms can be good opportunities, in an attempt to help those pains subside. After traveling is beneficial as well, since earthing has been shown to help the body adjust to new time zones by resetting the body's circadian rhythm (body clock).[19] You may want to try grounding after (not during) a storm as well to see

---

19 Clinton Ober, Stephen T. Sinatra, and Martin Zucker, *Earthing: The Most Important Health Discovery Ever?* (Laguna Beach, CA: Basic Health Publications, Inc., 2010), 95.

if you notice a difference. Lightning is constantly transferring a negative charge to the ground via storms all over the earth. With the extra moisture, the sensation can be especially energetic.

If you suffer from allergies, it's good to be aware of when pollen levels are lowest and to ground at those opportune times. This is usually early morning, later in the evening, at night, and after rain has washed pollen from the air. Levels usually peak in the middle of the day. If it's windy, that will kick things up too, so take advantage of calmer weather.

Preparing for Your Earthing Session

As I noted before, if you're earthing on the fly there really isn't any amount of preparation needed. Connect your skin with the earth. Done! But if you have a bit more time, I've found some additional prep can make the experience more enjoyable. Think of it as a mini getaway or spa experience and pack a bag. Ensure you have what you'll need so you don't have to keep traipsing back inside. Some items you might gather include:

- Blanket(s)—I often bring one to lie on (extending my feet beyond the blanket edge) and one to cover up with

- Jacket or sweatshirt

- Hat

- Sunglasses

- Sunblock

- Bug net—when gnats, mosquitoes, and other flying pests love to harass, hanging a bug net beforehand can come in very handy

- Water

- Snack

- Journal and pen. In a relaxed state you might end up processing new insights to current or old problems. Writing them down in the moment can be very helpful in understanding and letting them go.

- Book, magazine, puzzle, and boardgames, if you want to make this more of an activity instead of a time for emotional processing.

Before we go even deeper into the details of this practice, I want to note some things worth keeping in mind. By taking some precautions you'll ensure your experience will be that much more enjoyable.

Take care outdoors: While grounding is a very safe and natural practice, there are some things you should pay attention to. Before you ground, take a second and be aware of what the weather is doing outside. Don't ground if there is any chance

· · · · · · · ·

of a storm. Should lightning strike, you don't want to become a conductor for that energy. Also, be cautious of any hazards you might make contact with, such as broken glass, pesticide-laden landscaping, animal waste, or pesky plants like poison ivy and thistle. Know your area and be aware of the potential for things like venomous snakes or ground nests for biting and stinging insects.

Listen to your body: When I first started earthing I went through a detox phase for about a week. My legs ached as though I had been exerting myself and overall I felt like I had a mild flu. Counter to the idea that I was taking in or balancing my energy, I felt generally wiped out. Sometimes things have to get a little messy before they tidy up. Apparently, this is simply part of the healing process for some people as you normalize the body's electrical system.[20] If this happens you can stop for a day or two or simply cut down on the amount of time per day that you spend grounding.

About medical conditions: Earthing should not be practiced in place of your therapy or medical treatments; always check with your medical professional for health concerns. While there are no known medical reasons not to practice grounding, there have been instances where symptoms improve and medication dosage has needed to be altered in response to those changes. For example, grounding has been shown to thin inflamed blood, improving flow. So if you are on a medication like Coumadin, which thins the blood, it would be a good idea to practice grounding gradually and monitor any possible changes with your doctor.[21]

Make It Mindful

Earthing is a passive practice. It doesn't take effort on your part. Once you've made a skin-to-earth connection there's nothing more you need to do. However, I think it is beneficial to incorporate mindfulness and visualization into the mix for even more benefit (we'll get to a visualization practice at the end of the chapter).

More and more we have become a distracted society. Our attention spans continue to shorten and it is increasingly difficult to hold ourselves in awareness. As you ground, you could easily be doing other activities like reading or any number of distractions we find with our phones like talking, playing games, or mindlessly searching the Internet. Instead of surfing through a preoccupied mind, try to tune into the process.

---

20   The Earthing Institute, "Getting Started," http://www.earthinginstitute.net/?qa_faqs=%E2%80%A2-i-just-started-sleeping-grounded-and-feel-a-bit-strange-what-could-that-be-from.

21   Clinton Ober, Stephen T. Sinatra, and Martin Zucker, *Earthing: The Most Important Health Discovery Ever?* (Laguna Beach, CA: Basic Health Publications, Inc., 2010), 114–115.

Become aware of the sensations in your body and what is going on around you. Feel the sun warming you or the breeze brushing against your skin. Notice the look of the open sky or watch the clouds floating above. Connect to the noises around you. Do you hear a bird? Try to trace the sound back to the one that you hear singing. Can you find it? Really listen to the song and call. Do you hear a response from another bird somewhere in the distance? Maybe there's a chirping cricket, the soft bubbling of a stream nearby, or grass and leaves rustling in the wind. Tune in and enjoy those soothing sounds.

If you hear noises that feel less than calming—perhaps a yelling neighbor, a dog barking, airplanes moving overhead, or traffic passing in a steady torrent—try to focus on tuning within. Really feel the connection to the earth where your skin is making contact with the ground. What does it feel like? Is it cool or warm? Do you feel any sense of energy movement—perhaps a tingling or itching sensation in your feet or running up into your legs? Has your breathing slowed and deepened? Are there any other signs that you're relaxing?

By becoming aware of what is occurring in and around you in these ways, you will benefit even more. You will be working in alignment with your earthing practice to reconnect with yourself, as well as calm the mind and body.

Feeling the Energy

As part of making your grounding practice a mindful experience, you've now paid attention to how the energy feels to you. Did you feel anything? It's okay if you didn't. Some people are more sensitive to energy than others, but with guided focus you may be able to connect with those sensations even more. We'll do an exercise in a bit to help you out, but first I'll share with you what this feels like to me. From this example you might recognize things you are currently overlooking.

When I first started grounding I would feel a tingling in my feet and up my shins. This is a common experience for many people, along with warmth. After a while I would feel that same tingling in my hands as well. With a background in energy medicine and Reiki, I found the vibrating sensation was very similar to when I would provide healing sessions for clients. It's much like when your foot falls asleep and you move it to allow the blood to rush back in. You're sensing a real movement, subtle but true.

When I grounded, this feeling was persistent enough that I would actually have to sit and stare at my legs because it felt like ants were moving along my feet or mosquitoes were targeting my shins and calves. It was that kind of obvious yet subtle combo, not physically irritating but enough to make a bug-hater like me a little skittish. I itched and tingled and vibrated as the sensation ran up and down. Only by seeing that there weren't actually any bugs on my skin could I be convinced it was the energy that I was feeling.

• • • • • • • •

Earthing indoors with a grounding sheet was a different story. While I didn't feel the same tingling in my feet as I did when I grounded outdoors, I did notice that my feet felt very warm. This is pretty significant since my feet are ice-cold throughout the winter months, as my husband can attest! The cause of this warmth is apparently due to improved circulation while you're grounded.[22] Now that I've been earthing consistently for hours at a time every night and day, I usually don't feel the energy movement or heat sensations as strongly as I used to. I assume this is because my electrical energy system has acclimated, and now connection with the earth is just a normal occurrence instead of something noticeable. Be aware of this and watch how your sensations of the energy might change over time as well.

EXERCISE: **Visualization to Enhance Your Earthing Practice**

As you near the end of your earthing session today (if you took the invitation I gave you earlier), let's tune into that energy once more. Visualize what you're feeling, or if you don't feel anything, try picturing this in your mind: imagine the vibration from your feet moving through your soles and up your legs, jostling around and shaking loose any stagnant energy. Search your body now for any discomfort. Perhaps you have a tight hip, shoulder pain, irritated sinuses, or a throbbing headache. Visualize these areas as fuzzy, dark orbs. This energy weighs you down, restricting the flow of nutrients, oxygen, and life. Now see earth energy as little beads of light, like sparkling dewdrops or fireflies. It scuttles around, absorbing tension, pain, and inflammation. Like a magnet, it's attracted to those dark areas of distress. It moves in and attaches to the shadows until they lighten, neutralize, and dissolve. Imagine any remaining dust being swept with the light as it all moves back down your body and into the earth, where new beads of light are ready to circulate back in.

You can continue with the exercise by imagining the earth, perhaps as a loving and motherly figure, waiting to take the ashes from you. Feel the love emanating from her heart and the burden being lifted away as she scoops up what you are ready to let go of. Know that you aren't burdening her. Like a phoenix, she's ready to transform the ashes into something new, composting the cast-offs into richness that will again support life. In the places left vacant by what you've now discarded, see new light rising up into your body and filling those open spaces. Know this cycle of energy transfer will continue as long as you are grounded.

22 The Earthing Institute, "Getting Started," http://www.earthinginstitute.net/?qa_faqs=i-started-sleeping-on-an-earthing-sheet-and-noticed-that-i-feel-warmer-whats-going-on.

Finding Wellness Through Mindful Earth Connection

The modern disconnection we are now experiencing from the earth is anything but natural and appears to come with a loss of many benefits. For most of us it will take awareness of our disconnection and mindful action to change old ways and rediscover the positives of this practice. For me, earthing has most obviously helped relieve bouts of insomnia. This is especially important because deeper sleep is when the body has the chance to really heal, and in my case this means better management of chronic pain and allergies. For you it might be relief from headaches, an increase in energy, or an easing of stress levels, but you'll never know unless you try.

Perhaps today you did try and you have been earthing for much of the time we've been learning about this process. Hopefully you feel rested from it. It's likely you took the most obvious option and have your feet on the earth. Now you have plenty more options that you might prefer to try in the future. Maybe you'll want to be active instead of sitting still. Take a walk or try earthing while doing yoga. Create an environment in your yard that suites your relaxation needs or go to your favorite park. Get above the bugs and swing in a hammock with a grounding mat at your feet and a rod plunged into the ground. Do what you need to do!

As with any practice intended for your well-being, find what works for you and make it an enjoyable experience. Set your soles on the earth. See if you can feel the tingling energy that you've somehow ignored all your life and sense the sacredness of our connection. Experience the earth as a partner and support instead of something to be overcome or shielded from. Maybe you will discover a spiritual bond you didn't realize was missing or a new route to wellness that you never knew was available.

Angela Wix is the acquiring editor for body-mind-spirit titles at Llewellyn. She is an unending student of holistic practices and has certifications in massage therapy and energy medicine. Angela's writing has been featured in *Elephant Journal* and her artwork has appeared in hospitals and healing clinics as part of the Phipps Center for the Arts healing arts program. For more on her writing, art, and healing endeavors, visit http://AngelaAnn.Wix.com/arts.

Sharon Marx Photography

• • • • • • •

Indirect and Spiritual Forms of Grounding

. . . .

ALEXANDRA CHAURAN

It was Claire's first time vending at a psychic fair. She arrived early, set up a card table and two folding chairs, and carefully stacked her business cards neatly on top of an old scarf that she was using as a tablecloth. It didn't look very fancy next to the professional booths of the other psychics at the fair, but it would have to do. She stood back to proudly snap a photo of her first business setup and then wandered around to introduce herself to each of the other psychics at the fair. She was excited but a little nervous. What should she expect? Were the people there going to be nice or rude? Would she have fun or feel awkward?

"It's exhausting," a woman wearing a beautiful purple head scarf told her. "Don't be ashamed to leave early if it feels like too much. I love seeing new faces here, but it's so rare to have a new psychic come back after the first time. We have a really high turnover here." Claire was about to ask why, but the woman shrugged and turned to pull a bagel with cream cheese wrapped in plastic out of her purse.

Good idea, Claire thought. *Time to eat something grounding.* Claire was relieved that she had learned some grounding techniques that would keep her from feeling overwhelmed and exhausted during the long day at the psychic fair. She returned to her booth and retrieved some

. . . .

salted peanuts from her backpack. The salt would help her ground this jittery excess energy, as would making a connection with the earth, if even through the cement floor of the auditorium.

Claire kicked off her shoes underneath the card table and pressed her bare feet onto the cold floor. She was on the second floor of a building on a university campus, but she closed her eyes and imagined the whirling, chaotic energy in her body traveling through the floor, dripping down through the interior structure of the building, and seeping into the cold dirt beneath the foundation. She imagined the earth as if it were humming with energy. The entire planet was ripe with energy that she could consume as needed. She imagined it rising like sap in a tree, filling her body.

For a moment, Claire heard the bustling around her and wondered how many more minutes there were until the start of the fair. Refocusing on her breathing, she pushed all other thoughts from her mind. This moment was important. She could always sit with her eyes closed a few more minutes. She allowed her body to relax and tried to note any places of tension. She stretched her legs out underneath the table to allow the energy to freely flow. *How do I feel?* she asked herself. She felt relaxed, refreshed, and eager to begin her first psychic fair. Claire opened her eyes and was ready to work. She knew that any time she felt overwhelmed she could take a few minutes to repeat this process. It might be a little embarrassing to have to take a break, but no more embarrassing than running out of steam and having to leave early.

Grounding without Touching the Earth

As you've learned, grounding is the process of connecting with the earth to reach a state of energetic equilibrium—that is, you feel calm and relaxed, yet energized and alert. While there is a scientific basis for grounding through direct physical connection to the earth, there is also a very real result that can be achieved by grounding away from that direct contact. These kinds of practices may not involve contact with the earth, but they can still help us remotely balance our energy in a grounded way. Indirect and spiritual forms of grounding, as demonstrated in Claire's story, are what I will discuss here. These techniques can be used to add a connection to the earth into your daily life, no matter where you find yourself.

In order to notice the benefits of grounding, it's important to know what an excess or lack of energy feels like. Think of how it feels when you have too much energy. You may feel anxious and even jittery, like you've drunk too many cups of coffee. You might feel irritable and snap at people for saying or doing things that you would normally ignore. You might feel unable to sleep, troubled with insomnia or the feeling of being so overtired that you are awake. You might feel tense feelings in your body, such as knots in your shoulder muscles or eyelid twitches. I was always a hyperactive child, and I'm still that way as an adult, so when I have too much energy I often feel restless, fidgety, and will pace instead of being able to sit quietly. Think about your own nervous "tells." Everyone is different. What sorts of feelings in your body tell you that you

· · · · · · · ·

have too much energy? To what sorts of behaviors do you naturally resort when you're feeling an excess of nervous energy?

Now think of how it feels to have too little energy. Tiredness is one obvious sign. You might feel sleepy or you might simply feel a sense of inertia or mental exhaustion that stops you from enthusiastic action. Some people who have low energy will experience it emotionally as sadness. You'll feel a lack of motivation if you're low on energy. You might feel less likely to notice things because you're turned inward and paying attention to your feelings or, conversely, you might feel oversensitive because everyone else's energy is overwhelming. Think about what sorts of things you do when you start feeling low on energy. What sorts of physical or emotional feelings do you have when you're drained?

Now that you've thought about the energetic extremes, you can hopefully paint a picture of what your life is like when your energy is at the sweet spot, just perfect. Think back to a day when everything seemed to be going right, and you had the energy and motivation to tackle anything. Perhaps you were going for a walk in the beauty of nature or snuggling up on the couch with a cup of tea and a good book. You probably felt joyful yet peaceful, alert yet calm. When properly grounded, your mind neither races nor feels dulled.

Everybody grounds themselves naturally to reach this state. It's an automatic process that you possibly do without even noticing. However, if you find yourself frequently in either of the above states of unbalanced energy, it's important to consciously learn to ground yourself. Even people who are naturally great at grounding should learn proper grounding techniques to use during stressful situations in which one's natural grounding might be forgotten or inhibited. Before we get into common methods for grounding and the method behind how it works, think about how you try to naturally achieve this ideal energetic state. You might do this by sitting down and petting a cat, going for a walk outside, or lying down and taking a nap. Grounding makes the process into a skill that you can perform anywhere, at any time, without significant disruption to your life.

Grounding Mentally and Spiritually

There are many different techniques to perform grounding, but all of them have three steps in common, and the first and the last steps are to check in with your current energy levels. That's because you really have to fine-tune your knowledge of what is the perfectly grounded feeling for you before you make adjustments. In between those check-ins, you make a connection with the earth for a while until you suppose that you are at the right energy level. If you feel like you're wrong after you check in with yourself, then you can perform the grounding again. The way that grounding is done is through intention with your mind. You can do this by visualizing the energy exchange as a picture in your mind's eye or by feeling it moving in your body like a buzzing, a warmth, a pressure, or some other sensation.

· · · · · · · ·

EXERCISE: **Grounding Meditations**

Here is a very common visualization example for grounding. Visualize yourself as a tree. Your roots are extensions of your toes, and they bury themselves deep into the earth. Sometimes this can be aided during the grounding visualization by taking off your shoes before you close your eyes to visualize. As your tree roots reach deep into the earth, they release any "toxins" as excess energy that flows harmlessly into the earth. The roots can also draw in fresh energy from the earth, creeping up through the trunk of the tree like water or other nutrients. Some people choose to imagine the branches growing and connecting with the sky at this time.

Any visualization will do. You can imagine energy as a fluid in your body, like water or smoke. You can visualize columns of light or pools of darkness. However energy moves and works in your mind will be right. Practice your visualization until it seems like a real vision in your mind's eye. At first, it's okay if the process is slow. Take your time seeing every part of the process. Then, stop to check in with your body and energy level. Still too much or too little energy? Start over and see the whole visualization play itself out in your mind again.

The hardest part to practice is performing the grounding until you're at the perfect energy level. As a beginner, it's easy to quit before you're quite at the right place mentally or emotionally. Be patient with yourself. You may have to start paying attention to your natural energy levels in order to remember what being alert but relaxed really feels like. Try keeping a log for a day, writing down how you felt at each hour. If you're a morning person, perhaps you'll feel naturally grounded at that time. If you're a night owl, you might feel a rush of energy from the earth around midnight. Try practicing your grounding at different times in the day. Is it easier to ground at one time than another for you? Getting the feel for your energy levels is definitely the most challenging part about grounding, so be gentle with yourself as you're learning. Experience will make the process easier, quicker, and more effective.

The process of grounding itself, either by the visualization above or by sensing energy in your body in any other way, is an excellent way to be mindful of your connection with the earth. While you are performing the energy exchange you are like a child of Mother Earth, connected by an unbreakable spiritual umbilical cord. These grounding meditations can enhance a sense of significance and oneness with the divine. This can be especially needed if you usually go from home to car to office and back without time to spend out in nature.

Additional Grounding Ideas

Grounding can fit into your lifestyle however you choose. In this section I'd like to present you with a collection of ideas on how you might ground during moments when you don't have the option to physically connect to the earth. This is meant to be an array of choices rather than a list of rules that you have to follow. Choose what works for you and remember to practice grounding frequently; this is, hands down, the most important grounding tip I can offer. Practice is the only way that it becomes a honed tool that you can deploy at any time.

Food: Eating food is a classic grounding technique. Heavy food, especially salty food, is very effective for grounding. You can eat a big meal, but even a small saltine cracker will do. In a pinch, you can even put a bit of salt on the tip of your tongue for effective emergency grounding. Eating food can sometimes feel too grounding before meditation, especially trance meditation, so save this tip until afterwards so that you don't accidentally fall asleep when you're trying to meditate.

Sex: Any sexual activity is very grounding because it brings you into the here and now and connects you with your body. Sex with a partner can be mutually grounding, but self-pleasure is just as grounding for yourself on its own. Taking a shower, with or without sex before or during, can also be a grounding experience. Let yourself feel the water pouring over you and washing any excess energies down the drain, deep into the earth.

Bare Feet: A great passive grounding tip is to simply go barefoot whenever you can. Even if you're indoors, the act of sensing your bare feet directly on the floor can be especially grounding. Get in the habit of removing your shoes and socks before meditation time. Feel the soles of your feet on the floor as a tactile reminder of your connection to the earth.

Holding a Rock: Another passive grounding technique is to hold a rock in your hand. The rock acts as a symbol of the earth and may have properties that help absorb your energy. Some people choose rocks that are especially good at this, like hematite. However, any rock will do. This is a handy tool that you can keep with you in a pocket or a bag for when you need some subtle help.

Visualize Connection with Nature: Open a window. Listen to the sounds of nature, feel the breeze, and smell the fresh air. Even if you can't directly connect with nature, visualizing can be key. I even ground myself on airplanes that are thirty thousand feet off the ground by visualizing my connection with the earth.

• • • • • • • •

Indirect and Spiritual Forms of Grounding

I hope that this has helped you understand how grounding can be a resource in your everyday life and help you mindfully connect with the earth. Grounding can be in your metaphysical first-aid kit and your meditation tool belt, ready to be deployed at any time it is needed.

Alexandra Chauran is a second-generation fortuneteller, a third degree elder high priestess of British Traditional Wicca, and the queen of a coven. As a professional psychic intuitive for over a decade, she serves thousands of clients in the Seattle area and globally through her website. She is certified in tarot and has been interviewed on National Public Radio and other major media outlets. Alexandra is currently pursuing a doctoral degree, lives in Issaquah, Washington, and can be found online at SeePsychic.com.

Sarah O'Brien

• • • • • • •

The Connection Between Mindful Eating and Sustainable Living

RACHEL AVALON

Sometimes it's hard to envision your health or habits being radically different from where they are now, but as a holistic health coach of many years I've seen the transformation take place again and again. One of my favorite examples is a wonderful client named Debbie. When we first met she was smoking, overweight, stressed out, sedentary, and eating fast food regularly. She admitted she was quite nervous about doing my customized cleanse, but I lovingly encouraged her to take those first steps. After all, as Chinese philosopher Lao Tzu once said, "A journey of a thousand miles begins with a single step." Within two weeks Debbie was amazed at how mindful eating and sustainable living influenced her physical and emotional well-being. Her motivation continued to pay off as she quit smoking, lost twenty-five pounds, and shifted to a mostly organic, plant-based diet. She also began practicing yoga regularly and eventually found a better job. Like anyone, Debbie had doubts along the way, but she kept making small steps that added up to a beautiful new lifestyle.

What and how we eat not only has the power to fuel our mind and body, it also has the power to transform the world. In this chapter we'll explore a number of ways to infuse your journey of mindful eating and sustainable living with greater love and purpose. We'll start by laying the foundation with how you think, eat, and prioritize your time for healthy choices. Then we'll move into creating a more compassionate, sustainable diet that can minimize harm to yourself and others while increasing your vitality inside and out. A stronger immune system, an abundance of natural energy, and radiant skin, nails, and hair are common gifts often experienced with this peaceful way of life. Finally, we'll cover my top-ten list of empowering tips that will complement your eating habits in order to cultivate a mindful lifestyle all around.

Positive Thinking

You can eat all the superfoods under the sun, but if you're continually telling yourself that you're fat, ugly, unwanted, etc., your mind and metabolism will suffer. Most people understand the concept that negative self-talk will affect their emotional sense of wellness, but there are real biochemical consequences to hurtful mental clutter, too. For example, if you were to eat an avocado and say to yourself, "I can't believe I'm eating this whole thing; it's so much fat. I'm always going to be overweight," your hypothalamus would likely respond by activating your sympathetic nervous system and more or less shutting down your metabolic power. On the flipside, if you said to yourself, "Wow! I love avocados. They're so good for my skin and they taste amazing," your hypothalamus would respond with efficient digestion. So even though it's the exact same food, your thoughts act much like an on/off switch for your metabolism through the nervous system.[1]

Of course, improving your conversations around eating requires tuning into your inner dialogue throughout the day as well. Starting to really pay attention to the general narrative in your head is important and often surprising; you may have more negative commentaries than you're currently aware of.

Women and girls can be particularly bombarded by destructive messages stemming from both the media and social conditioning. Through magazine articles, shows, and day-to-day life, we're often taught to strive for unrealistic physical and fashion perfection. We're often groomed to be people pleasers with a sense of self-worth that's wrapped up in our looks and achievements. Of course, we logically recognize that we are more than our appearance and more than what we accomplish, but to really believe and feel that is a whole other thing.

Since I work with a lot of actresses, I see this struggle in a magnified way. One of my celebrity clients, let's say her name is Sarah, came to me to lose weight and boost her energy. She knew she needed some kind of an overhaul, but she couldn't quite put her finger on what that entailed. She had failed at various diets and health regimens and, not surprisingly, felt disempowered. After our initial coaching I assigned Sarah a certain amount of positive affirmations each

---

1   Marc David, *The Slow Down Diet: Eating for Pleasure, Energy & Weight Loss* (Vermont: Healing Arts Press, 2005).

· · · · · · · ·

day along with some other vital steps, many of which are included in this chapter. When she checked in with me after a couple weeks, she shared how she had experienced a powerful revelation about how negative and judgmental her "autopilot" thinking had been. She also shared how uplifted she felt when doing affirmations and how that was beginning to carry into what she wanted to eat, how she ate, her attitude toward acting, and her relationships. Sarah reached her goal of losing weight and boosting her energy, but she realized that those were actually secondary perks to the profound gifts she had gained from questioning her thought patterns and dedicating herself to mindful thinking and living.

EXERCISE: **Positive Thinking**

As you work to deconstruct any negative thoughts, be sure to counterbalance them with positive affirmations. For example, if you're aware that your self-esteem needs to be improved, try an affirmation such as "I am loved and loving." Chances are if your self-esteem is low, that will be expressed through your dietary habits in some way, so add in "I am choosing healthy foods and reaping all the rewards" as well. Spend five minutes in the morning and before bed saying these affirmations either on your own or with a prerecorded audio. There are many digital downloads to choose from that can guide you in positive thinking. Recording your own customized statements on your phone and then playing them back can also be transformative and fun. Just make sure that you are stating the desired condition as though it's already happening. Using "I am" is a powerful beginning to any affirmation, whereas "I will" perpetually puts the goal in the future and out of reach. I also recommend utilizing "I am enjoying…" because there are plenty of people who are considered thin and successful but feel totally unhappy. "I am enjoying being healthy and fit" or "I am enjoying mindful living" is a great way to set yourself up for real success.

Prioritizing Your Time for Mindful Eating

Many people want to improve their health but feel caught up rushing around, trying to meet basic responsibilities and still have some fun along the way. As a working mom I completely empathize. Of course, most people can still carve out some extra time if they really put in the effort. The trick is working through resistance and staying focused on the payoff.

EXERCISE: **Making Time**

Assess your daily and weekly schedule and ask yourself, "What do I need to do in order to practice mindful eating and living?" Perhaps you need to scale back on social or digital media to allow more time for food prep. Perhaps you need to shop for food

• • • • • • •

more often or set up a CSA delivery (local and seasonal food directly from a farmer) so you're not grabbing unhealthy food on the go. No matter what, be honest with yourself and find creative ways to allow more space in your routine so that you can unwind while eating. By prioritizing your time this way, you'll not only welcome in a deeper sense of peace, but you might be surprised at how many muses whisper in your ear when you're in this more relaxed mode.

Deep Breathing for Optimum Digestion

Oxygen is one the most miraculous nutrients. To put its role in perspective, we could go weeks without food and days without water but only minutes without air. Not surprisingly, oxygen is a key player with digestion and mindful eating. Here's the thing: it's very easy to feel perpetually stressed. Unfortunately, that often triggers your system to go into fight-or-flight mode and pump stress hormones such as cortisol and adrenaline throughout your body. When danger is perceived the blood moves away from the core and toward the extremities in order to prepare to fight or escape. Like the power of positive versus negative thinking, this reaction shuts down metabolic function because digesting that salad from lunch becomes a low priority compared to surviving an immediate threat. In contrast, when we take a few deep breaths before eating, not only do we become present, but we also send a signal throughout our nervous system that we're safe. By feeling calm, the proper amount of blood and energy is concentrated in the core and digestion is optimized.

Interestingly, of all the coaching tools I provide, deep breathing is almost always the one that's bypassed by new clients. People will improve their diet and hydration, do positive affirmations, take recommended herbs and supplements, but still forget about deep breathing. I think the main reasons are that deep breathing anchors us in the present moment and it really opens our hearts. Sometimes that feels uncomfortable. With the ego toiling away, we may want to linger in the past or project into the future. We may also want to keep our heart closed because we've been hurt before or because the craziness of the world can make us feel powerless. However, our true Self knows the difference and will always call us toward love, courage, and transformation.

My client Brian learned this in a profound way. In his mid-twenties he had been on anti-anxiety drugs and other pharmaceuticals for years. He had also seen a number of doctors and specialists for chronic pain he had been suffering. His goal was to get off all of the meds and to feel good again. I told him it would be essential for him to focus on going slow and steady and to do this under the supervision of his physician. I also told him that there was no "magic pill" for his health, but that if he took a holistic approach and integrated everything I suggested there was a good chance he could reach his goal. The first thing he was asked to prioritize was deep breathing. I wanted him to incorporate it like a supplement, and he did. I also helped him transition

• • • • • • • •

off of coffee[2] since it (and the caffeine in it) can often be an inflammatory,[3] calcium-depleting beverage.[4] We also increased organic greens and omega-3–rich seeds in his diet. I even taught him how he could combine deep breathing techniques with aromatherapy. Within months he was able to completely go off all of the drugs, and the chronic pain was reduced to an occasional flareup rather than a debilitating daily occurrence. The longer he stuck with deep breathing and mindful eating, the better he felt. His sense of joy from the transformation was palpable, and so was mine.

EXERCISE: **Deep Breathing**

Be sure to take three deep breaths anytime before you eat a meal or snack; this includes smoothies and fresh-pressed juices. If you'd like, you can incorporate organic or wildcrafted aromatherapy with this exercise. For example, lavender and lemon balm are very calming, peppermint is uplifting, and cedar is grounding.

When you're first developing this habit, go overboard with the reminders. Put them in your phone, kitchen, dining room, and anywhere else that will be helpful to you. If you find yourself halfway through a meal and realize you forgot to breath well beforehand, that's okay. Give yourself credit for remembering and just take three deep breaths before you continue eating. Like any new, healthy habit, the goal is progress, not perfection.

Chewing Your Food

Making time and deep breathing lead us into the next empowering strategy. Chewing your food is an easy access point to engage in mindful eating, and it brings an array of fantastic benefits. In addition to creating a sense of calm and centeredness, stabilizing hormones, and reducing gas, it also makes the most of where digestion truly begins: in the mouth. Even though we often think of the stomach as soon as we picture digestion, our teeth are designed to mechanically break down food and prompt a specific enzyme called amylase (*am-uh-leyz*). This important enzyme helps break down carbohydrates and lessens the workload of the small intestines. When we chew our food well we have more energy, a stronger digestive tract that isn't battling large pieces

---

2   There are definitely conflicting viewpoints on the risks and potential benefits of coffee. However, given the concerns I've come across and the critical studies I have read, I typically recommend that people seek out antioxidants through fruits and vegetables, which are much less controversial.

3   Antonis Zampelas, Demosthenes B. Panagiotakos, Christos Pitsavos, Christina Chrysohoou, and Christodoulos Stefanadis, "Associations Between Coffee Consumption and Inflammatory Markers in Healthy Persons," *The American Journal of Clinical Nutrition*, http://ajcn.nutrition.org/content/80/4/862.full.

4   DrHyman.com, "Ten Reasons to Quit Your Coffee," http://drhyman.com/blog/2012/06/13/ten-reasons-to-quit-your-coffee/#close.

• • • • • • •

of food (that can literally rot in our system), and we better utilize the nutrients we're taking in, which translates to greater vitality. It gets even better, though! Chewing our food well also helps reduce the likelihood of overeating. Since our brain and stomach need time to communicate with one another that the stomach is full—typically twenty minutes—chewing thoroughly slows down the intake and allows that valuable message to be received before we end up overdoing it.

EXERCISE: **Consciously Chewing Your Food**

To get started with this healthy habit and reinforce portions you can feel good about physically and emotionally, chew each mouthful of food twenty to forty times. At first it may seem laborious, but before you know it, it'll become second nature. Rather than counting, you'll simply notice that you finish each meal a few minutes after most people. Amazingly, that little amount of time can make a huge difference in the way you feel throughout the day. Plus, it'll free up your body to focus on healing and restoration while you sleep. Ultimately, like deep breathing, this simple practice can subtly inspire others to slow down and be present as well.

A Compassionate Diet

Mindful living embodies peace and compassion, qualities I'm sure we'd all like to see more of in the world. So how do we proactively cultivate them? Positive thinking, deep breathing, and other exercises go a long way. Additionally, we can practice peace and compassion through what we eat. From iconic scientists such as Einstein, Tesla, and da Vinci to beloved writers like Emerson and Shaw or political activists including Rosa Parks, Cesar Chavez, and Gandhi, nonviolence specifically through dietary choices has been explored and adopted by great leaders for thousands of years. As advocates of either a vegetarian or vegan diet, many of them pointed to our collective potential in creating a peaceful planet through our food choices. After all, history has demonstrated that the violence we condone in the world always has a way of circling back in some way.

A compassionate diet begins with awareness and a willingness to improve the status quo. Many are waking up to the fact that well over 90 percent[5] of animals consumed in the United States are raised in horrendous conditions. And more and more, we are facing the fact that the animals raised for food are not only like the dogs and cats we cherish and protect, but also very much like us. Of course, animal rights is still a foreign concept to many. Thankfully, though, there's a mindful shift occurring, and I invite you to welcome it with open arms. Perhaps for you this means enjoying a whole-foods, plant-based diet. Alternatively, it might mean supporting producers with better business practices and going veg one day a week while working toward fewer

5 FarmForward.com, "Ending Factory Farming," https://farmforward.com/ending-factory-farming/.

• • • • • • • •

and fewer animal-based meals. Whatever the case, your changes will move you in a direction that will have a larger impact beyond your personal health.

Major Benefits of a Compassionate Diet

- Rich in antioxidants to combat inflammation and disease
- Rich in fiber to improve elimination, weight management, and detoxification
- Rich in vitamins, minerals, and phytonutrients to increase natural energy and beauty
- An excellent source of clean protein that's heart-healthy
- An excellent source of complex carbs that are brain-healthy
- An excellent source of nature-approved fats that boost beauty, brain function, and energy
- Easier weight management

Major Disadvantages of Excessive Meat and Dairy

- Increased risk of heart disease and stroke
- Increased risk of type 2 diabetes
- Increased risk of various cancers including colon, breast, and prostate cancer
- Increased risk of obesity
- Increased risk of arthritis and osteoporosis
- Increased risk of acid reflux, constipation, and other digestive issues
- Increased risk of accelerated aging and low energy

Protein and Calcium Myths

There are two nutritional concerns that most people have when considering a compassionate, plant-based diet: where will they get their protein and how will they get enough calcium? Let's address protein first. The truth is amino acids are the building blocks of protein, and there's an abundance of them in plants. From greens to nuts, seeds, and legumes, our protein needs can easily be covered. In fact, not only are many professional vegan athletes demonstrating this in marathons, kickboxing, cycling, dance, and a number of other sports, but also many of the strongest animals on the planet thrive without meat protein, such as elephants, gorillas, oxen, horses, and giraffes. The average American consumes twice the protein they need. Since the body can't store it, it's converted and stored as fat instead. This process exhausts the kidneys and often results in unwanted weight gain.

• • • • • • •

When it comes to calcium, we've been told by the dairy industry for years that milk and other dairy products are good for our bones. Multimillion-dollar marketing has deeply ingrained the idea that dairy can help us be strong (and even successful, given all the celebrity endorsements). However, the countries that consume the most dairy have the highest rates of osteoporosis![6] Rather than fortify us with calcium, it can actually deplete us. That's because, like meat, it can overload our body with acids. In an attempt to neutralize the acids, calcium will be pulled from our bones to buffer them. The drawbacks don't stop there, though. Dairy consumption is also linked to acne, allergies, asthma, breast and prostate cancer, diabetes, excessive weight, heart disease, migraines, and other health challenges.[7] So, focus on calcium-rich plant sources instead, like kale, collard greens, other leafy greens, organic tempeh or organic soybeans, sesame seeds and tahini, almonds, and sea vegetables.

EXERCISE: **A Compassionate Diet**

Write down what you typically eat in a week. This is not a time to judge yourself at all; simply take stock of where you're at and where you might like to be. Once you have a clear picture, determine how you can include more wholesome, plant-based foods in your diet.

With any meat (including seafood), eggs, or dairy you choose to consume, be sure to seek out labels[8] such as these:

- Organic: Animals must have outdoor access and can't be given antibiotics or hormones. Selecting locally raised animals in combination with organically raised animals is a more sustainable step.
- Certified Humane: Animals are never confined in crates or cages, growth hormones are prohibited, antibiotics are only used as directed by a veterinarian, and slaughter must adhere to particular requirements designed to minimize suffering. Additionally, poultry aren't subjected to debeaking. However, access to pasture or range is not required by this certification.

---

6 *The American Journal of Clinical Nutrition*, "Should Dairy Be Recommended as Part of a Healthy Vegetarian Diet? Counterpoint 1, 2, 3," http://ajcn.nutrition.org/content/89/5/1638S.full.

7 T. Colin Campbell, "12 Frightening Facts About Milk," http://nutritionstudies.org/12-frightening-facts-milk/.

8 Environmental Working Group, "Decoding Meat and Dairy Product Labels," http://www.ewg.org/meateatersguide/decoding-meat-dairy-product-labels/.

· · · · · · · ·

- Wild Fish: These fish spawn, live, and are caught in the wild. In contrast, the "wild-caught" label indicates fish that may have spent some stage(s) of their life in a fish farm.

In general, it's a good idea to steer clear of businesses that subject animals (including farm-raised fish) to overcrowded conditions and large amounts of antibiotics. Factory-farmed animals are the most obvious example (the majority of meat and dairy sold in the United States). However, with clever marketing there's a lot of confusion over seemingly favorable labels and the conditions that come with them. Here are some distinctions to be aware of:

- Grass-fed: Ideally, this term refers to animals who only eat natural grass and other foraged food instead of grains and other unnatural ingredients fed on CAFOs (confined animal feeding operations, aka factory farms). Ironically, some cattle still spend part of their lives on feedlots or in pens even though they're marketed as USDA grass-fed. Investigate thoroughly before trusting this label on its own.

- Cage-free: Lacking a standardized legal definition, this label generally refers to hens that aren't raised in cages. However, they may not necessarily have outdoor access either, and debeaking is still permitted.

- Free-range: Only refers to poultry that is allowed outdoor access, but the duration, size of land, or quality has not been established by the USDA (United States Department of Agriculture). Debeaking is still permitted.

- Farmed fish: Half of the seafood in the United States is currently farmed, which often involves confinements that allow ocean water to flow through them and be contaminated with antibiotics, disease, and large amounts of fish waste. Usually this method of raising seafood is highly unsustainable.

If you're curious about the ethical reasons a growing number of people are prioritizing a compassionate diet, I recommend seeing the thought-provoking documentary called *Speciesism* or Melanie Joy's TEDx talk called "Beyond Carnism and Toward Rational, Authentic Food Choices."

Whether you feel motivated to make sweeping changes or weave in a few veggie dishes here and there, take advantage of the numerous websites, books, and apps designed to help you succeed with enjoying a more compassionate diet. Some popular and well-respected ones include VRG.org, The 21-Day Vegan Kickstart app, and The Blender Girl's site, healthyblenderrecipes.com.

· · · · · · · ·

A Sustainable Diet

One of the things I most love about my work is helping people connect the dots between their own health and the health of the planet. There are so many wonderful rewards with honoring this sacred connection! Although we're often raised with the impression that we are observers of nature, we are actually extensions of it, so whatever we do to the planet affects us one way or another. When we're in alignment with nature, being our true selves, we look and feel our best.

One of the most immediate ways to practice this alignment and mindfulness is by choosing a sustainable diet. That means eating foods that nurture our individual and planetary health while minimizing harm. Overall, a sustainable diet focuses on organically grown crops, a plant-based diet, responsible forms of food and beverage packaging, and minimal food waste. Let's take a look at the details.

Going Veg for the Planet

A plant-based diet goes well beyond being compassionate. It's actually the fastest and most effective way to take a stand for global health. In fact, the UN has encouraged us to adopt a vegan diet for years. That's because raising animals for food requires enormous amounts of water, feed, land, and fuel while creating staggering amounts of excrement and greenhouse gasses. For example, the amount of excrement generated by the entire human population is surpassed nearly 130 times by animals raised for food. Additionally, producing one pound of meat requires approximately 2,400 gallons of water. In contrast, only 25 gallons of water is required to produce a pound of wheat.[9]

So the ideal may be going veg, but what's the best solution for anyone who'd like to maintain meat in their diet besides supporting labels such as Certified Organic and Wild Fish? You might be surprised by the answer: entomophagy. More and more Westerners are eating insects as a replacement to traditional livestock for major health, ecological, and culinary reasons. Now I know eating bugs might sound strange or downright disgusting since it's not customary here, but did you know that 80 percent of the world's nations consume them?[10] They're also often higher in protein and B12, lower in saturated fats, and radically more sustainable than raising cows, pigs, chickens, etc. In fact, many food companies are already using cricket flour in health bars and protein powders, while gourmet chefs are serving various insects as delicacies. From gourmet burgers and baked goods to street tacos and spicy snacks, there are a myriad of possibilities. Of course, when it comes to water conservation there's no contest because 100 gallons

---

9   OneGreenPlanet.org, "Facts on Animal Farming and the Environment," http://www.onegreenplanet.org/animalsandnature/facts-on-animal-farming-and-the-environment/.

10 TheGuardian.com, "Insects Could Be the Key to Meeting Food Needs of Growing Global Population," http://www.theguardian.com/environment/2010/aug/01/insects-food-emissions.

• • • • • • • •

of water dedicated to crickets will help produce more than ten times the amount of protein gained from beef and nearly four times the amount in chicken.[11] Given those kinds of numbers, there are a lot of powerful people backing the rising trend of consuming insects in the United States. So if you want to include animal-based nutrients in your diet, think outside the box and discover for yourself why so many foodies, conservationists, and investors are talking about edible insects.

When it's all said and done, being mindful of how we manage resources goes hand in hand with nature's zero-waste policy. If we can better adopt that gentle way of life, then we will thrive—mind, body, and planet!

Supporting Organic

Pesticides are designed to kill, and as a result numerous species of birds, butterflies, bees, fish, and frogs continually have their health dramatically compromised through untargeted exposure. Bees, for example, who pollinate a significant amount of our food, are dying off in record numbers, while male frogs have been shown to lay eggs due to hormonal disruption. Additionally, vital water sources, microorganisms responsible for cultivating healthy soil, and the very air we breathe are under attack. With approximately 800 million pounds of these chemicals applied each year by the American agricultural system, we have to question how long these poisons can be relied on without causing irreversible damage to the planet.[12] The warning signs are everywhere. Not only are pesticides negatively affecting multiple ecosystems, cancer rates are on the rise. In fact, one in two men and one in three women are diagnosed with cancer[13] (compared to one in thirty-three people about one hundred years ago).[14] Although pesticides are not solely responsible for those numbers, it's important to note that they are a piece of the puzzle that can't be ignored. According to the comprehensive report from the President's Cancer Panel in 2010,

> Nearly 1,400 pesticides have been registered by the EPA for agricultural and non-agricultural use. Exposure to these chemicals has been linked to brain/central nervous system (CNS), breast, colon, lung, ovarian, pancreatic, kidney, testicular, and stomach cancers, as well as Hodgkin and non-Hodgkin lymphoma, multiple myeloma, and soft tissue sarcoma…Approximately 40 chemicals classified by the International

11 Chapul.com, "Grams of Protein per 100 Gallons of Water," http://chapul.com.

12 USDA Natural Resources Conservation Service, "Environmental Indicators of Pesticide Leaching and Runoff from Farms," http://www.nrcs.usda.gov/wps/portal/nrcs/detail/national/technical/?cid=nrcs143_014053.

13 The American Cancer Society, "Lifetime Risk of Developing or Dying from Cancer," http://www.cancer.org/cancer/cancerbasics/lifetime-probability-of-developing-or-dying-from-cancer.

14 Mauris L. Emeka, *Cancer's Best Medicine: A Self-Help and Wellness Guide* (Washington: Apollo Publishing, 2004), 5.

• • • • • • •

Agency for Research on Cancer (IARC) as known, probable, or possible human carcinogens, are used in EPA-registered pesticides now on the market.[15]

So if we want to better protect our own health and the planet as a whole, it's essential to prioritize organically grown food as often as possible. Apps like EWG's Shopping Guide to Pesticides in Produce lists the produce that has the most versus the least amount of contamination. Of course, the more you support organic farming, the more you reduce your toxic exposure and send a strong political message to the corporations and government agencies that still allow dangerous pesticides to be used.

On top of that, look for locally grown, seasonal food at farmers' markets and other stores to enjoy the freshest, most economical options. Naturally, the quality and prices will work to your advantage while the fossil fuel consumption for transportation will be cut dramatically too.

Packaging Waste

With the increasing interest in organic and plant-based foods comes the rise of conveniently packaged versions of those options. However, every plastic-wrapped packaged good (healthy or not) comes with a price, literally and figuratively. Bottled water is a perfect example. In addition to paying as much as 10,000 times the amount municipal water costs, the demand for petroleum is so high within this industry that it's equivalent to filling each plastic bottle a fourth of the way up with oil.[16]

Here are some tips to help you be as mindful as possible when it comes to sustainable packaging:

- Use reusable beverage containers made from glass or stainless steel.
  Whether you're headed to work, rehydrating while exercising,
  or picking up a drink at coffee or tea shop, avoiding disposables
  is a great way to decrease unnecessary waste. Klean Kanteen is
  one of my favorite brands for reusable beverage containers.

- Use reusable bags for any kind of shopping. Rather than limiting reusable
  bags for trips to the market, take them with you when you shop for clothes,
  home goods, office supplies, etc. This new habit takes a good amount of
  practice, but just put little reminders next to the front door or in your phone

---

15 2008–2009 Annual Report, President's Cancer Panel, "Reducing Environmental Cancer Risk: What We Can Do Now," http://deainfo.nci.nih.gov/advisory/pcp/annualReports/pcp08-09rpt/PCP_Report_08-09_508.pdf.

16 2013 Clean Our Oceans Refuge Coalition, "How Plastic Water Bottles Negatively Affect Our Environment," http://coorc.org/index.php/our-blog-more-media/blog-news/63-how-plastic-water-bottles-negatively-affect-our-environment.

• • • • • • • •

and you'll be in the swing of things before you know it. Also, be sure to take advantage of smaller organic cotton drawstring bags for bulk items such as nuts, seeds, grains, dried fruit, and legumes. These can easily be found online and last for years! I recommend simply transferring the goods into mason jars once you get home and tossing the bags in the wash. Speaking of buying in bulk, you'll not only reduce packaging waste, but you'll save a ton of money.

- Bring your own cutlery when you're out and about. There's something wonderfully satisfying and sophisticated about using silverware or bamboo cutlery instead of plastic. Companies such as To-Go Ware make this step easy by offering lightweight sets of bamboo forks, knives, spoons, and chopsticks in travel-friendly pouches. These also make memorable and economical gifts. From delis to picnics, vacations, and house parties, you will be amazed at how often you can bust out the reusables and skip the throwaways.

- Bring your own container for leftovers. Of all the eco habits I've adopted over the years, this one gets the most attention. As we all know, American restaurants (even a lot of healthy ones) have become notorious for large portions. So, rather than overeating or throwing away food, I recommend bringing a stainless steel container to pack your leftovers in. This way you'll cut down on what ends up in the trash and you'll bypass the Styrofoam, plastic, or petro-coated paper options that might leach questionable chemicals into your food. Clean Planetware is my top pick, with Lunchbots being another favorite.

- Request reusable glasses and dinnerware when eating out. Relying on disposables has become so common that some restaurants and cafés will automatically give you something to throw away even when a reusable is available, so be sure to ask. If reusables aren't an option at their establishment, then ask a manager to consider providing them. If enough people ask, they'll respond.

- Choose reusable sandwich and snack bags. If you're packing food for work or school, the financial and ecological benefits can add up really fast with this tip. There are many fun and sophisticated designs available for kids as well as adults. However, I recommend choosing clear bags with a strong zipper and FDA-approved food-grade materials such as xo(eco) by Blue Avocado. They're wonderfully resilient, and they make it easier to remember what's been packed and what needs to be unpacked at the end of the day.

· · · · · · · ·

- Look for the most sustainably packaged foods and beverages. Sometimes avoiding packaging can be a real challenge, but if we all support the best options available, the bar will be raised and the landfills will become smaller. Recycling glass, for instance, is cleaner and more efficient than recycling plastics, so choose glass whenever possible. Compostable containers that don't require special facilities to break down the material are also more favorable than those that state they do. Sometimes the best option is to cut down on the sheer volume. For example, you might see a large bag of chips and the same brand is offered as mini bags. Not only will you pay more per ounce for the small bags, but the amount of waste also goes up. So, pick the large bag instead and then divvy up appropriate portions in your reusable snack bags.

Food Waste

A mindful and sustainable diet makes the most of the food we grow and purchase. However, approximately 40 percent of the food in America is actually thrown away.[17] Think about all the water, fuel, and money that are thrown out with it! Most of us don't like throwing away food, but it can still happen for a number of reasons. In order to shrink that statistic down, here's what you can do:

- Get in the habit of assessing what's inside your fridge and pantry before buying more food.

- Consider weekly or daily food planning so you're making the most of your purchases.

- Display produce in your fridge so you can easily see it. Since fruits and veggies usually spoil faster, it's really helpful to store them in a way where all those vibrant colors are popping out at you. As a result, I recommend turning the humidity to the lowest setting and keeping breads, spreads, and nuts in the produce drawers and then stocking the refrigerator shelves with produce. Also, instead of loading up the door with excessive sauces, stock your favorites and then use the rest of the space for fruit. This way every time you open the fridge you'll be greeted and enticed by beautiful, fresh food.

- Put veggies such as broccoli, asparagus, and greens in a glass jar of water in the fridge. As with fresh-cut flowers, this will help them last much longer.

- Get creative with seemingly random food combinations instead of buying more food right away. For example, let's say you had a sweet potato, an

---

17 Natural Resources Defense Council, "Wasted: How America Is Losing up to 40 Percent of Its Food from Farm to Fork to Landfill," http://www.nrdc.org/food/wasted-food.asp.

· · · · · · · ·

avocado, and an orange in the fridge. I'd recommend peeling the sweet potato and grating it, chopping up the avocado, then putting them in a bowl and squeezing fresh orange juice over them for a simple, satisfying raw meal. You could also steam and mash the sweet potato and then top it with a dollop of creamy whipped avocado mixed with the orange juice. Really, there are so many possibilities. Search online for recipes using the food you have and see what kind of culinary magic unfolds!

Shopping with Intention

Mindful living often leads to mindful purchasing patterns, but not always. The consumerist-marketing machine, along with the demands of modern living, often pulls us toward convenience and fashion trends. If we step away from that norm (which is easier when avoiding ads) we can see there's a plethora of opportunities to radically transform and continually fine-tune how we shop for food, kitchenware, clothes, and other goods. All in all, our purchasing power is constantly shaping the world around us, whether positively or negatively. It's up to us to extend our activism and mindfulness and make every purchase count. Here are some ideas to help:

- Seek out integrity-based manufacturers. A quick Internet search can be quite useful in maneuvering around any PR spin and finding out if a company's reputation matches up with their branding. You can also discover who owns whom. For example, if you're aimed at boycotting a specific company that supports GMOs (genetically modified organisms) or water privatization, you can find out the extensive list of brands they own or are allied with.

- Use nontoxic cleaners. It's extremely alarming what companies are allowed to put in cleaning products and, unfortunately, many of the brands that seem to be natural contain questionable ingredients as well. That's why I highly recommend making your own to ensure the safest and most economical choice. If you're not feeling ready to take that step, though, then be sure to check out *EWG's Guide to Healthy Cleaning* online, which rates thousands of store-bought brands, at www.ewg.org.

- Ensure your wardrobe isn't supporting sweatshops and unnecessary pollution by attending clothes swap parties and buying secondhand whenever possible.

- Prioritize all-natural, certified organic cosmetics, which includes everything from shampoo to deodorant and mascara. There's no need for animal-based ingredients or buying from corporations that test on animals either.

- Seek out antique or secondhand furniture or sustainably made furniture.

- Take advantage of memorable e-cards or choose sustainably made cards.

• • • • • • • •

- Focus on sustainable office, school, and art supplies. Look for labels like FSC Certified and 100 Percent Recycled.

- Utilize clean energy through wind or solar options. There are three main options with this one right now. You can buy the equipment, lease it, or sign up for a green power program through your local utilities company.

- Choose transportation with the least emissions. Biking and public transportation are ideal. Of course, many communities and jobs still require a car. If you do drive, aim to buy an electric or hybrid vehicle.

- Make your parties green by purchasing a stash of reusable glassware and dinnerware. You can even lessen the cleanup load by asking guests to bring their own beverage container. I've been doing this for years and it's turned out to be a fun conversation starter for guests, especially when people are sipping on my famous vegan hot cocoa during my annual holiday party.

With your own awareness in mindful, authentic living, remember that each and every accomplishment is to be enjoyed and celebrated. Revel in the peace and cheer others on in doing the same. Together we can fill our hearts with so much gratitude and consciousness that the whole world will reflect it back to us. All in all, mindfulness is the golden key to a better life and a healthier planet, so let's enjoy the journey!

Rachel Avalon is a holistic health coach and eco expert who has transformed countless lives through coaching clients, multiple media outlets, and professional speaking engagements. Rachel has also been nationally honored as an innovative leader in conscious living and is the creator of the Avalon Cleanse. Additionally, she has served as an ambassador for nonprofits such as the Campaign for Safe Cosmetics as well as Healthy Child, Healthy World. She writes for the the *Huffington Post*, *The Kind Life*, and *The Green Girls*. Rachel lives in LA with her husband and son, and she loves sharing the benefits of a healthy, sustainable lifestyle beyond measure! Be inspired at www.RachelAvalon.com.

Haldane Morris Photography

Your Path to Mindful Eating

MELISSA GRABAU, PhD

Why do so many people struggle with changing their eating habits? At first blush it sounds ridiculously easy—akin to, say, changing your hair or skin care routine. Just choose new products, apply them according to prescribed directions, and enjoy the results. But as anyone who has started a new nutritional regime with determination and high hopes knows, it takes far more than dutifully following prescribed directions. Unlike your hair and skin, your insides have a lot to say about what you consume and when, and your insides often speak in coded, urgent language that can only be translated as "I WANT IT NOW OR ELSE!" In light of this, I propose that before changing your nutritional habits, you must first focus on establishing meaningful communication between your mind and body. *Food is both a form of communication with your body as well as a response to what your body communicates to you.* In other words, there is a dialectical relationship between you and your body, and food mediates this dialectic. In the following discussion I will provide you with some keys to mastering this dialectic in a proactive and intentional way.

Good communication depends far more upon listening than talking. Paying attention and getting interested are the cornerstones of effective listening. Mindful eating depends upon your receptivity to your body's messages. In other words, it is rooted in effective listening skills. In order to listen you must slow down, pay attention, and adopt a curious, even experimental, attitude. This, too, sounds easier than it actually is. Therefore, let us take some time to explore three things that interfere with receptivity to your body's messages and that, if unchecked, will thwart all your well-meaning efforts to respond more mindfully to your body's needs.

Stress

Stress is a concept that is thrown around so frequently now that it has become a shorthand explanation for everything from hangnails to heart attacks. But what exactly *is* stress? Stress is when the natural self-regulation of the body is sidelined to take care of the demands of the moment. Let me give an example from my earlier life, when I was working at an inpatient hospital and hell-bent on proving myself to be worthy of the title "Psychologist in Training." I kept long hours and barely had time for a lunch break. I was not aware of the impact on my body, but I was aware of urgency. Urgent hunger. Urgent phone calls. I quelled my hunger and met the needs of the moment as if my life depended on it. Physiologically, I might as well have been racing across the savanna with a hungry tiger on my heels. You see, the body knows no difference between a real physical threat and a psychological threat. The adrenaline, cortisol, and blood sugar release are all the same and wreak the same havoc inside the body as if you were truly running for your life. Fear of failure, the need to succeed professionally, the quest to be good enough—all exact their toll upon the body. You could say that we are blessed with the ability to ignore the body in order to get the job done. However, this ability to power through life and dissociate from the body leaves you without a home.

Stress is the great relationship disruptor, and it does this by impairing communication between your mind and body. It is an uncomfortable way to live and renders you clueless about how to respond intelligently to the needs of your body. Hunger, fatigue, and muscular tension become threatening sensations that you either try to ignore or are forced to medicate. Hunger and the act of eating itself can be experienced as sources of stress. The conflicting nutritional information you are inundated with and the number of choices you have for what and how to eat are overwhelming. If you are not in a healthy, communicative relationship with your own body, you have no ground from which to make intelligent choices that feel good. In the end, you may be left with a tired, hungering body and a nagging sense that something is just not right.

Habit

In yoga philosophy the word for your habits is *samskara*. The yogic concept of samskara goes much deeper than the ordinary concept of habit. Rather than being a pesky behavioral pattern that you wish you could stop, such as biting your nails, samskaras refer to the physical, energetic, and mental hold that your habitual patterns have upon you. Your behaviors function like seeds that you plant in a garden each time you do something. Actions that you repeat over time reproduce and create circumstances that influence what other seeds will find room in your garden. Weeds are negative behaviors that have taken root in your garden. Flowers and trees are the fruit of positive behaviors that you have repeated over time. Negative habits (weeds) that people commonly develop in relation to food are using it for anchoring or self-soothing, using it for energy, and getting caught up in momentum (otherwise known as appetite). In order to begin cultivating seeds that will flower into more mindful eating, it may be necessary to do some weeding first.

Anchoring/Self-Soothing

Are you someone who eats for comfort? If so, you may be dealing with an even deeper samskara of anxiety. If your body-mind has become habituated to stress, eating can provide you with a sense of grounding in your body and an anchor in the world. This does not mean that you actually enjoy your food. As discussed, food and eating themselves can act as stressors. But food can also simultaneously function as a way to mark time ("How long till dinner?") and to anchor yourself in the world ("I'm bored—what's there to eat?"). A lot of mental energy can go into thinking about the next meal as a reward or goal. Food becomes an unconscious and habitual way to soothe anxiety. It distracts. It feels good. It rewards. You can count on it when all else fails. The act of eating itself sometimes occurs in an almost a trancelike state, a hypnotic act of ritualistic soothing that you have attached to in order to provide scaffolding in your world. A psychological term for this is that it binds anxiety—meaning that food and eating give a structure and focus for your anxiety and give you a false sense of control over it.

Energy

The energy factor is another way you may habitually use food. Particularly if you are reliant upon simple carbohydrates for fuel, your body has developed a pattern (a samskara) of needing sugar for energy. Hence, every few hours you need more energy in the form of quick-acting glucose, regardless of whether your body actually needs sustenance. Since many of us live in overdrive without reliable means of rest, relaxation, and pleasure, it is easy to rely on food, particularly simple carbohydrates, as a reliable source of energy to get through the day. Coffee and a donut in the morning, snack at 10, lunch, snack at 2, munching before dinner—the body learns to run on quick sugars for energy, and you can easily develop the habit of interpreting fatigue as hunger.

Momentum

The habit of momentum refers to getting caught up in the primal pleasure of eating and allowing your back brain to take over. When you are eating and it tastes good, it is very easy to get carried along in the momentum of a meal and your brain's giddy response. Particularly when food is hyper-palatable—meaning that it is designed to captivate your taste buds and brain with fat, sugar, salt, and sumptuous mouthfeel—you may eat to the point of being over-full without even realizing it. Your attention is hijacked away from the more subtle cues of your body and

· · · · · · · ·

you lose touch with your internal sensations of satiety. If this becomes a habitual pattern for you, your body accommodates by enlarging your stomach and making other physiological shifts that lend this full feeling an aura of normalcy and perhaps even necessity.

Conditioning

Conditioning is the third and perhaps most important source of weeds in your garden. Your conditioning has deep roots that can be stubbornly entrenched. I use the metaphor with clients that your conditioning is analogous to the hard drive on your computer. This is where your deepest beliefs and patterns were laid down in early life, etched into the very fiber of your brain and nervous system. Think of your grasp of your native language; you did not have to study English (if that is your native tongue) to commit it to memory. It's part of you because it was downloaded on your hard drive before you were even consciously aware. Now consider how you were held, fed, and bathed in your early life. The rhythms of care you received gave you critical information about yourself and the world that you now live as being "true," but it is only what your caregivers communicated and is not "true" at all. The good news is that once you realize this, you can learn how to override your programming with new, updated information.

An example of how conditioning can influence your eating habits is growing up in an environment with two busy, distracted parents who did not have time for you (or themselves) and who unconsciously used food to soothe themselves (and you). Imagine yourself as a toddler who is fussing and then has a lollipop or a bottle inserted into your mouth. When this happens over and over again, your hardwiring develops around the experience that when things feel uncomfortable and not quite right in the world, you don't turn to other people for solace or holding; you put something in your mouth. The pernicious thing about this level of conditioning is that you live this out unconsciously. You don't consciously remember having lollipops placed in your mouth most times you fussed or the umpteen other times you witnessed food being used around you for comfort and distraction, let alone what you didn't learn—for example, the other joys of the senses, of music, laughter, touch, and togetherness. It is these aspects of life, and not what you put into your mouth, that make it worth living. If you were not exposed to and taught how to engage with the world in these ways, you literally don't know what you are missing. Finally, if you grew up in a home with less than healthy parents, you likely internalized patterns of tension and holding in your body that feel normal to you. You internalized the tension in the environment around you, which is now expressed in the way you move, breathe, and hold your shoulders and belly. Your body may be a very uncomfortable place to live, and you may not even realize this. The reliance on food as soothing is an ingrained way of coping with this uncomfortable body.

We have also been conditioned by our society to relate to our body primarily from the outside in and in terms of how it looks, measures, and appears to others. You likely spend a lot of time dressing and grooming, perhaps exercising, and of course fueling your body. But you may

· · · · · · · ·

secretly resent or distrust its needs. Okay, you have accepted the need to brush and floss your teeth, your bi-annual dental checkups, daily showers and deodorant, and, yes, the nightly skin routine, but enough already! Now the trip to the gym, next foraging through weeds for some wild greens and chewing each bite thirty times. Who has the time for all this? "I have to work, thank you very much!" I hear you retort. And adding to this conditioning to relate to your body as an object, consider the conflicting messages that you have been exposed to since you were a child. Eat thick, chewy, double-stuffed-crust pizza, and get a load of this pizza cookie topped with marshmallow, chocolate, and caramel goo, and how about this awesome pasta dish? Oh, and now take a look at this supermodel on this magazine sporting a sexy swimsuit, and check out this new diet with a fast track to losing forty or fifty pounds. It is enough to drive the most stable among us absolutely crazy!

Your Path to Mindful Eating

Considering these factors of stress, habit, and conditioning, I am hoping that you are now primed to engage with your own path toward mindful eating. Here are some guiding principles to help you as you move toward positive change.

What do you want to be healthy for? Examine your reasons for wanting to heal your relationship with food and your body. Perhaps you are tired of your energy being wasted in worry, not feeling well physically, or the drain on your self-esteem caused by eating habits that are not in alignment with your values about health. Think about a better channel for your energy. Where will that energy go? Health is a condition of mind and body that frees your energy toward something larger than yourself. Consider what that might be in your life.

Honestly listen for what is best for you. Rather than prescribing some draconian diet plan for yourself, I recommend making a few small, healthful changes, listening to your body and intuition. This is a long-term lifestyle, not a quick fix. This is the only way to create sustainable change. Trust yourself to know where to begin and when you are ready to build upon your changes. The point here is that you are consulting your intuitive sense of what is right for you rather than following a prescriptive plan from outside yourself.

Start a relaxation program. I am not suggesting that you need to start meditating an hour a day if you are new to it, but would you consider a period of sitting in silence, bringing attention inside, for five minutes in the morning? This creates a foundation of self-awareness upon which you can build over time, and it will translate to your relationship with food. Your body intelligence will grow as you pay more attention

· · · · · · · ·

to yourself beneath your skin. As your body intelligence grows, it is natural to want to support your body with what you eat.

Calm down before meals. Focus on deepening your breath before you begin to eat. You might need some sort of reminder to help you not surrender to the momentum of a meal and to stay present to the food. Putting your fork down between bites, chewing your food more carefully, and pausing for a few moments can all be very helpful practices. These tips sound very simple, but in my own experience they can be challenging to implement. Our ingrained responses to hunger are tricky to rewire. Have respect for this and try not to give yourself up for lost if you aren't successful with this at first. Instead, scale back your goals and perhaps just focus on becoming more aware of your patterns.

Have awareness of the influence food has on your body. Finally, at the risk of contradicting my suggestion to consult your intuition, some dietary tips that might be helpful are getting informed regarding the effects of both simple and complex carbohydrates on your blood sugar and gut health. The roles of inflammation, your microbial blueprint, and running on sugar as your primary source of fuel all influence mood, energy, and eating habits. The more you are balanced in this way, the easier it will be to act from a place of mindfulness.

I wish you well along your path to healing your relationship with food and your body. Remember, all is as it should be. You are exactly where you need to be. *Namaste.*

Melissa Grabau, PhD, is the author of *The Yoga of Food.* She received her doctorate in clinical psychology from Duquesne University in 1998. She became licensed as a psychologist in California in 2001 and has been in private practice since 2003. More recently she has broadened her existential/humanistic background in psychology to incorporate her long-standing interest in yoga and Eastern psychology. She is a certified yoga teacher and currently integrates mind-body techniques in her work with clients. Visit her at TheYogaofFood.net.

Bang Nguyen www.bokehstudio.net

• • • • • • •

Mindful Nonattachment to Cravings and Urges

Sarah Bowen, PhD

We bumble around trying to make ourselves happy. We try to feel good. We attempt to ensure love and outsmart rejection. We chase happiness and desperately want acceptance. We weave elaborate plots to avoid sadness and go to destructive lengths to avoid loneliness. We refuse to feel discomfort. We construct whole lifetimes around avoiding suffering. And we become, for the most part, pretty good at finding ways to feel better, find comfort, and have guaranteed relief at our fingertips. So what's the problem? We have many resources right at our fingertips, so why are even the most fortunate of us still suffering? Perhaps our solutions are misguided. Indeed, many of us are sadly inexpert at finding true respite and real nourishment—the things in our lives that will give us enduring and trustworthy happiness and refuge. Instead, we often trade immediate happiness or relief for longer-term suffering.

Nowhere are these tendencies and consequences more clearly illustrated than in the devastating cycles of addiction. Whether it's alcohol, cocaine, food, sex, money, or power, the immediate rewards and relief offered by these substances and experiences are inseparably linked to their shadows—the insatiability, the emptiness, and the destruction that inevitably follow.

Many, if not most, of us are not "addicts" as traditionally defined. We are not waking up in strange places or cycling in and out of rehab. But most of us have some substance or a behavior—food, alcohol, cigarettes, work, shopping—that causes harm to ourselves or others and that is causing problems in our life. At the very least, it is not delivering the happiness we'd hoped it would. For many, this is a process with which we are constantly embattled. For some, it becomes the go-to best friend and the worst enemy, and therein lies suffering.

The Buddha taught that suffering comes from attachment—clinging to what we have or craving what we don't have. This is addiction. The Buddha also explained our tendency to add another layer of suffering to our already painful experiences by shooting a "second arrow" of shame or blame to the initial arrow of pain. We punish ourselves by the thoughts and beliefs that accompany our behavior patterns, and we are punished, too, by our bodies' reactions or by those around us. However, let's consider our intentions before we are so quick to judge. There are also reasons we have engaged in this behavior that may quite simply come from a desire to be happy. So what if we at least forgo the added suffering of self-blame and judgment, stop pathologizing ourselves, and realize that this is part of being alive? It is inimitably challenging to be human, and we are doing our best. So let's start from there.

How? First, we need to be aware of our nature. We need to see the ways our minds and bodies behave, how we react when we feel triggered or threatened or uncomfortable. We need to understand the nature of conditioning—ways we have trained ourselves to react in these situations. We can view this with kindness and an understanding that this is part of being human. It is not our fault; it is how behavior works. We really are doing our best.

If there is a pattern in your life, something in which you repeatedly engage, there are probably things that you like about it or a function that it serves. Once we see these patterns and tendencies, we can also begin to see their true nature and how they may indeed provide immediate relief or pleasure, and how that is so quickly followed by further suffering.

What does this behavior or substance give you? How does it change or "fix" how you are feeling? What do you want from it? Does it help you feel more relaxed? Allow you to be more social?

Now let's look at the other side. What are the things it has cost you? What have you lost or how have things changed? Maybe these costs are financial, health-related, family, friends, or maybe your sense of self. Take a moment now to reflect on these, and list what comes to mind.

It can be helpful to acknowledge that there are reasons you've been engaging in this pattern. Maybe the problem isn't you. Maybe your intentions are very wholesome—you are trying to be happy. Maybe it's just the places you are looking for happiness or comfort are the problem: they aren't honest; they aren't working.

We also see that we can learn to pause at these decisional junctures. We can take time to notice what we are feeling, what the urges are, and learn to explore those with some curiosity

· · · · · · ·

and stay right there with them as they ebb and flow, rather than immediately react to them. We can find a more trustworthy, deeper happiness and freedom in this awareness and flexibility, even right in the midst of discomfort. This, of course, takes practice and kindness and patience, as we have been practicing other behavioral patterns for most of our lives.

When you find yourself in a situation in which you might be tempted to engage in a behavior that has been problematic for you, that might or has in the past caused you to act in a reactive manner or in a way that is not in line with how you want to be in your life, try pausing for a moment. We often tend to either fall into these cravings and urges or fight to resist them. What if instead we try exploring our experience, finding a balance, and just staying with and observing the experience without "automatically" reacting?

You might begin by noticing what physical sensations you experience at these moments. What sensations do you notice in your body? What emotions are arising? Notice, too, what is happening in your mind—maybe it's calm, blank, or racing. There might be specific thoughts you can observe.

What is it about this experience that feels intolerable? Can you stay with it and be gentle with yourself? Remember that we are practicing staying with this experience in a kind, curious way. We are making the choice to not act on any urges or cravings that are arising—just staying with them and observing, as best we can, what is happening in the body and mind, what a craving or an urge actually feels like. Just gently stay, as best you can, with this discomfort and unfamiliarity. See if you can be curious about what's here without tightening or resisting it, bringing a kindness to the experience.

You might ask yourself, too, what is it you truly need in this moment. Is there a longing for something? Maybe there is fear, anger, loneliness. Maybe relief or freedom. What is it you really need right now?

If a craving or urge becomes increasingly intense, you might imagine it is like an ocean wave. Imagine that you are a surfer riding that wave, using your breath to help you stay steady. Your job is to ride the wave from its beginning, as it grows, staying right with it through the peak of its intensity, keeping your balance while the wave rises and staying on top of it until it naturally begins to subside. You are riding this wave rather than succumbing to the urge and being wiped out by it, trusting that without any action on your part, all the waves of desire, like waves on the ocean, arise and fall and eventually fade away.

As you practice this, you may notice that you can simply stay present with this wave instead of immediately reacting to it, without having to make it go away.

Many people with addiction come to experience craving as the enemy. It is threatening, terrifying, the dreaded foretelling of the inevitable fall. But perhaps desire and wanting is not the problem; it's how all living things survive. But how does this drive to take care of ourselves, to

· · · · · · ·

feel better and be happy, lead to such tremendous suffering? What if it could actually be our best teacher—how to be with difficulty without reacting? To have choice, and thus find freedom, no matter what our circumstances. If we can learn to stay and explore our experience, we may even learn something about ourselves and what we truly value and what we really need. We can take these previously feared experiences and find, right there in the center of them, our wisdom and the flexibility and willingness that bring us freedom.

Sarah Bowen, PhD, is an assistant professor at Pacific University, OR. Her research and clinical work has focused primarily on integration of cognitive behavioral and mindfulness-based therapies for addictive behaviors. She has authored numerous related journal articles and book chapters, and is lead author of *Mindfulness-Based Relapse Prevention for Addictive Behaviors: A Clinician's Guide*. Dr. Bowen has facilitated mindfulness-based relapse prevention groups in private practice, VA medical centers, prisons, and treatment agencies, and she offers professional trainings to researchers and clinicians internationally. She has a particular interest in dually diagnosed and other underserved populations.

Mindfulness and Illness, Chronic Conditions, and Pain Relief

ERIN BYRON, MA

A member of our yoga school is popular with the other students because of his approach to disease. He endured chronic sinusitis and continually repeated, "Sinusitis is my greatest teacher." He inspires other students to shift their perspectives on health. He explains that if he sways from the path of healthy living for even a day, his sinusitis lets him know immediately. Were it not for this condition, he might not enjoy the level of health that he does to this day. Other students take this note and look for lessons from their own illnesses. Like a good teacher reminding us to stay on the healthy path, disease can be a teacher. When we are sick we tend not to be mindful of the many different perspectives our illness can bring. We think that being sick is wholly a bad thing.

When we don't feel healthy, whether because of chronic aches and pains, illness, or other health issues, it does not take long before we become desperate for a way out of discomfort. Being aware of all aspects and details of our experience seems like the opposite of how to cope with "dis-ease"! Typically, people do their best to avoid the pain, either through distraction or finding a diagnosis and treatment plan in hopes of making it better. It's hard to imagine how it would do any good to become mindful of physical discomfort, emotional pain, or the future implications of our health problems. It seems like focusing on the issues could make them worse. However, research in the field of mindfulness teaches us that the kind of attention we offer our chronic conditions—and a mindful approach to everyday life—can, in fact, alleviate our suffering.

Taking Control of Your Condition Through Mindfulness

When we are wounded or sick, the typical reaction is to try to escape. We think of ways to soothe the pain, distract ourselves from it, or get away from it however we can. This escapist approach sets up a mental trap where we perceive the pain as all or nothing—in other words, we are either in pain or we are not. In reality there is a vast range in the quality and intensity of pain. Our wish to be completely free from pain or illness often sets us into a helpless, agitated state. "Oh no, this really hurts," we think. "I need to make it stop!" Being ensnared in this polarized thinking sets up a problematic relationship between ourselves and the pain. Such an approach to reality can ultimately lead to despair.

When our response to pain or illness is the desire to get away from it, we are resisting reality. We set our goals and expectations around a future reality of freeing ourselves from current pain, hoping it will make our lives better later while diverting attention from what is happening now. When our goals fail or our expectations are not met, we compound mental and emotional letdown with the existing physical problems. This sets us up for disappointment and even hopelessness as we feel more helpless against our conditions. In other words, our approach to seeking wellness makes us sicker.

Avoiding current reality and hoping for a healthier future is a valuable intention to hold; however, it is a problematic approach. Rather than meeting pain or illness with the desire to escape or get better, what could happen if we focused on the current reality? According to research in the field of mindfulness and chronic pain or illness, we actually empower ourselves to feel better when we focus on reality. It may be counterintuitive, but science shows time and again that becoming aware of and accepting our current condition increases our sense of health. In this way, our approach to relating to illness opens the door to a sense of wellness.

Wellness ensues when we focus attention on what is currently happening. Rather than letting the mind stick on the pain and how bad it is, when it will get better, or what will make it better, apply a mindfulness practice. Step into the observer self and watch the sensations, breath, emotions, and thoughts pass by. Remember that you are in control of where your attention goes. In moments when the pain distracts you, pause and note in a clear fashion that this has happened, then ask yourself, "Where is it best to put my awareness right now?" If you are at work, focus on work. If you are at home, pay attention to your surroundings and your loved ones. If you are alone, do something you enjoy. Although you may not be able to control your discomfort, mindful awareness reminds you that you do control your responses to it and the actions you take to improve your life.

Mindfulness practice helps with misperceptions in how we evaluate the pain or illness itself. Through cultivating an inner objective witness, we disconnect the feeling of pain from the meaning we give it. We are less likely to evaluate the pain and create a scary story about what it means for our future. When we witness the discomfort and the thoughts and feelings that go along with it, it is not as alarming. Through objective awareness, we create a new story for ourselves. Since the mindful approach is free from judgment, as shifts in health occur, it is not a time to get down on yourself about your choices or the nature of your health issue. It is a time to notice. You are free from the usual emotional or lifestyle evaluations that your mind might typically make.

A simple way to employ mindfulness practice is to observe your sensations. Through this type of awareness practice, people notice that their discomfort changes almost continually throughout the day. It is no longer about the dichotomy of being in pain or pain-free, sick or well, but more about the distinctions of the experience and which direction they are moving in. This removes the despair as it becomes evident that there is a near-constant change in the intensity and interference of the pain. Hope, optimism, and empowerment arise from this realization. Furthermore, through this awareness practice you are able to relate your lifestyle choices to a worsening or improvement in your condition. Subtle habits such as when you go to bed, what you eat for lunch, or who you spend most of your time with can become the crux of your well-being, where before you didn't give them a second thought. By observing changes in sensation throughout the day, you become mindful of the spectrum of experience and how to make choices that move you in the direction of physical health or overall well-being.

Take the case of Carlos, who was diagnosed with a slow-acting cancer and told that he would live with it for somewhere between ten and forty years before it ultimately killed him. What would his quality of life be? It was difficult to predict: he could be healthy for a long time, then get sick and quickly deteriorate, or he could feel very unwell for the rest of his life. These vagaries were distressing to Carlos, who did not know if he could live with the fatigue and achiness that he felt most of the time.

For almost a year Carlos lamented the pain he felt throughout his body and wished for more energy. He feared that every ache was a sign that the end might be near, that every tired day was one in a string of worsening health. Concerned for his well-being, Carlos's family and friends encouraged him to listen to his doctors and perhaps seek counseling to help deal with the diagnosis. At first Carlos resisted, but soon he realized that living each day worried about his death, which might be decades away, was not how he wanted to spend his life.

The counselor supported Carlos's fears while exploring other perspectives on the diagnosis and potential for health in everyday life. Carlos's counselor taught him to objectively watch his

· · · · · · ·

thoughts about his aches and pains, as well as emotional upsets during the day. He also learned to witness his achiness and fatigue and notice how they intensified or decreased, not as a general pattern but as a constant ebb and flow throughout a short period of time. This mindfulness practice soon showed Carlos that there were variations in his health that he had previously not been aware of.

Armed with new perspectives on what was possible for him, as well as an established mindfulness practice, Carlos ended his course of counseling and continued his practice. He began to honor his fatigue and achiness, taking more time in the day to rest. He noticed that when he ate sugar or drank his usual after-work beers he felt weaker for the rest of the evening and even days after. Sometimes, when his symptoms worsened, Carlos focused on what he was grateful for in that day or something that had gone well for him. Even though it did not always change the intensity of the aches, he somehow felt better.

EXERCISE: **Mindful Attunement**

This exercise teaches you to apply mindfulness techniques in order to witness subtle shifts in your own pain or illness. It is recommended that you apply this practice briefly a number of times per day—even one minute of mindfulness is beneficial! The more you practice awareness, the greater your attunement to your inner world and potential for well-being, no matter your physical condition. Healing begins in the mind.

1: Center your mind on your breath. Notice how it flows in your body without trying to change its depth or rhythm. Your breath may deepen on its own when you focus on it, and that is fine if it is a natural thing.

2: Notice the sensations in your body—all through your body, not just in the areas of pain. You may name the quality of sensations, such as relaxed, warm, tense, achy, stinging, tingling, light, and so on. Alternatively, you may associate an image or other analogy with the various areas of your body. Notice the pain itself, its quality and intensity, and the way it moves and shifts.

3: Notice the thoughts and feelings that pass through your mind. These may be in relation to the pain or illness or they may be memories, plans, or worries. Simply watch the way your mind and feelings pass. You may relate your thoughts and feelings to your physical observations and vice versa, but do not dwell on analyses.

4: Journal or acknowledge key points of observation. If you notice any associations, jot them down. Over time, reflect back upon your writings and seek broader patterns. Affirm your efforts and the differences in your quality of discomfort on physical, emotional, and mental levels.

• • • • • • • •

This awareness practice attunes you to a more comprehensive truth of your situation. By practicing a little each day, every day, you will understand more about the nature of your condition and your mental and emotional response to it. By noticing shifts in its quality, you will also come to realize how various activities, amounts of rest, nutritional choices, and emotional states also have a direct impact on the quality and amount of pain and reaction of your chronic condition.

Despite the power you have over your choices, it is important to avoid a cycle of self-blame or creating stress around changing your lifestyle. We truly change our habits in slow, systematic ways. As you continue to witness your physical experiences, thoughts, and feelings, you will learn about yourself. You will discover which habits you can readily change and begin altering those. Every step in the direction of health is a worthy one, no matter how small it may seem in its doing. Stay positive about the potential role you play in your well-being and be gentle with yourself as you shift the elements of your lifestyle that affect your health. Through awareness you are empowered to choose what to change! The following story from Marion shares how she did that very thing.

Marion's Story

I start many days with a quiet time of gratitude. There is so much to be thankful for. Some days my mind focuses on the changes that the practice of mindfulness has brought into my life, mainly in relation to chronic pain. I was introduced to awareness through classical yoga. I attended my first yoga class about eight years ago. When I first visited the yoga studio my body was stiff and in a great deal of pain. The instructor gently encouraged me to try the therapeutic class, and I immediately experienced a change in my relation to pain. The atmosphere in the studio was soothing and relaxing. There was no demand for perfection as I moved into the poses. I was aware of how tension was released, and I witnessed my body's choices in how far it would stretch, bend, or twist. This freedom of choice let me enjoy my body and accept its limitations.

The class ended with the corpse pose, a posture of relaxation and surrender. I lay on the floor, feet fallen outward, breath long, and hands facing the sky. My whole body surrendered into the ground and I witnessed my mind letting go of striving for perfection and attachments to outcomes. I let myself be aware of the moment of comfort. There was no pain.

I am mindful of how my range of movement has increased over the years. I can bend over to tie my shoes. While driving I can turn my head to look over my shoulder. I also see the awareness in life's decisions and changes. Mindfulness put me in a place of surrender. I stopped resisting and remembered that I am not in control. My mind and body relax when I witness my inner experiences and life and let myself be surprised by the outcomes.

Lessons about lifestyle awareness from yoga classes have motivated me to look for ways to be kind to myself. I no longer drink coffee, for it is hard on my nervous system and does not allow me to sleep. I choose to eat organic, wholesome food and prefer to stay gluten-free. My slow cooker is my best friend, since I can prepare the meal during the morning when I have more energy and have delicious food ready at the end of the day when my energy is low. Walking in nature is my favorite activity. I try to do this every day for at least twenty minutes. Other activities I make space for are reading, writing, and playing board games with my husband. This awareness of non-harm has helped me approach life by alternating between effort and resting. When I become aware of an ache in my body, I cease toiling. I lie on the floor with my feet up the wall in a resting position. I am thankful for my body and witness it as it is always moving toward health.

Mindful awareness has taught me that remaining in a state of balance is a key component for my health. In yoga class I attempt balancing poses; concentrating on the task at hand, I forget all else and feel a calmness in mind and body. I am not tense and nothing hurts. This skill transfers to my daily efforts, where my intention is to achieve a balance between productivity and rest. Through mindfulness I know that when I am out of balance I most certainly will experience pain. Listening objectively to my body tells me when I have eaten foods that are not good for me, when my schedule is too full of serious activity, and when I have not had enough sleep. Because of mindfulness practice I am able to stay steady and balanced in life.

EXERCISE: **Mindful Body Scan**

In the story above, Marion used mindfulness, conscious movement, and relaxation to become aware of and improve her responses to pain. You can use the following practice as a baseline experience to see how your body feels. Throughout the day briefly return to this practice of carrying your mindful awareness all the way through your body. This will help you realize, as Marion did, where the pain actually lives, how it moves, and the ways in which it changes throughout the average day and over time. With regular practice of the body scan, you will receive all kinds of feedback about the discomfort and how your emotions and lifestyle choices aggravate or alleviate it.

Find a comfortable position: sitting with the head supported, reclined slightly, or lying down.

Practice the following body scan for two to ten minutes. Any shorter and you may not bring full awareness through the body; any longer and you may fall asleep. If you find yourself dozing off during the body scan, it is a clear sign that your body needs more sleep. Consider going to bed earlier or scheduling naps.

• • • • • • • •

Breathe slowly and deeply. Commit to watching thoughts and feelings pass through your mind without becoming attached to them, judging them as good or bad, or trying to change them.

Slowly bring mindful awareness through every part of your body. Do this in a systematic fashion, moving from the soles of your feet through your ankles, lower legs, knees, upper legs, hips, pelvis, lower belly, lower back, middle back, upper back, chest, hands, lower arms, elbows, upper arms, shoulders, neck, head, jaw, lips, tongue, eyes, and forehead. (You may also move from head to feet if that is better for you.)

Bring your full awareness to whatever part of the body you are paying attention to in that moment. In other words, if your pain tends to be in your back, do not focus on feet and back, then ankles and back, then lower legs and back. In the moments when you are scanning specific parts of the body, let as much attention as possible be on those parts. It is true that you may continue to notice the pain, but it drifts through your mind softly rather than you giving it clear attention. As much attention as possible is on the single area of the body you are scanning. In so doing, the feeling and sensations in those areas increase. This will clue you in to which muscles or joints are at ease and where tension may be hiding.

Continue to be a witness to your body, creating some distance by changing "my body parts" to "the body parts." For example, instead of saying "my shoulders are aching," say "the shoulders are aching." This small change in language simply acknowledges the existence of discomfort while removing you from the direct experience of it—in other words, you are no longer labeling yourself as the pain. Now you have more space to mindfully observe the body without getting caught up in the story about the pain. This language creates a more detached perspective that greatly assists in cultivating your mindful awareness of the truth of your pain.

When you have scanned the whole body, pause for a moment or two to integrate your observations and a higher level of relaxation.

Giving a mindful scan to the body naturally brings about relaxation. People often find that relaxation alleviates pain and brings a greater sense of overall well-being. Deeper physical relaxation, in turn, helps you remain an objective observer of your physical and mental experiences. Studies run on a variety of conditions including chronic pain, rheumatoid arthritis, fibromyalgia, type 2 diabetes, Parkinson's disease, chronic fatigue syndrome, cancer, and heart disease indicate that through the power of mindful observation, you can alleviate your experience of pain and illness.

• • • • • • •

The Science Behind Mindfulness and Chronic Conditions

Scientific investigations have found mindfulness to be highly beneficial to people with chronic pain and illness. Some of the many factors improved or altered by mindfulness practice are:

- The structure and function of the brain
- The degree and quality of pain people experience in a given moment
- How people limit movement and activity due to pain
- Sense of vitality
- Self-esteem
- Mood
- Social functioning
- Symptom clusters associated with various diseases
- Negative view of their own bodies in relation to their poor health
- Healthy lifestyle choices and coping skills
- Distressing psychological symptoms such as anxiety and depression

It is natural for pain and illness to disrupt our physical experiences, emotions, thoughts, and lifestyle. Studies show that mindfulness practice increases quality of life, people's overall sense of well-being, and can even improve objective measures of health. What a relief it is to know that there is a tool that can restore or even improve our relationship with ourselves, our pain and illness, and our lives!

Mindfulness studies reveal that the benefits of mindfulness are seen no matter what a person's age or gender. Mindfulness is just as effective whether it is taught one-on-one or in a group setting. Even the degree of pain people in the studies experienced did not change the amount of gain possible from a mindfulness practice. Those with extreme pain benefit as much as those who had moderate pain. Similarly, the deeper and clearer the awareness (usually associated with duration of practice over time), the greater the benefits to overall health and well-being. On the flipside, no negative effects have been revealed in any of the plethora of studies on mindfulness practice.

Some mindfulness researchers went back to their participants after a period of time to see if the benefits of awareness continued once the study was over. Results in numerous experiments have shown that as long as people continue their mindfulness practice, their chronic pain, illness, or emotional upset remained low over time. In other words, the awareness practice continued to alleviate their sense of suffering over the long term.

• • • • • • •

An interesting point arising from mindfulness research is that people with chronic conditions have a skewed relationship with their health issues. For example, we tend to misperceive pain. We give it greater attention and value than time without pain. This habit is so powerful that most folks in chronic pain believe it is constant every minute of every day. In reality, in most cases, chronic pain shifts and may even subside for periods of time throughout the day. It is normal for some days to be worse than others—and that is easier to be aware of—but even during the bad days there are periods of reprieve. Yet when we are feeling better or our body isn't giving us trouble, we tend not to focus on it. Thus, the moments of ease go unattended, and we only bring our minds back to the pain when it returns. The worst part of this kind of selective attention is that we feel as though the pain never left because we did not focus on its absence.

Rather than the blanket belief that "I am in pain all the time," studies of mindfulness indicate that awareness practice teaches people that the pain is constantly shifting. The changes people notice are intensifying and subsiding pain, growing from sharp to dull, peaking then dissipating, and so on. The awareness of these shifts in the intensity and quality of the pain can change your relationship to the pain as you realize, through direct experience, that it is not a steady state of misery that you have to deal with on a moment-to-moment basis. Discomfort actually changes continuously; therefore, when it is at its worst, it is about to get better.

Become mindful of your pain throughout the day and attune yourself to the shifts in its quality and intensity. By witnessing the pain, you separate the physical sense of hurting from the emotional evaluation of pain and the mental alarms that it sets off. Because mindfulness separates the physical experience from the mental and emotional ones, there is less of an experience of suffering. The sensation itself may not change, but the emotional reaction and beliefs about it do, which in turn transforms the overall experience of pain. This effect is similar for emotional patterns and other discomforts or health problems.

Scientific research has much to offer the field of mindfulness. As studies are published every month on the benefits of internal awareness and mental focus, we are increasingly able to see the benefits of quiet, personal reflection. Experiments that related mindfulness to myriad physical and psychological conditions all report benefits of the practice. One of the key pieces of mindfulness is its effect on our ability to alter our perception of a situation and choose where to put our focus.

EXERCISE: **Mindful Meaning**

The following exercise offers you the chance to play with mental and emotional perspectives, what is important to you, and the direction you wish to steer yourself.

1: List ten things that are most important to you. To make this exercise meaningful, you can imagine yourself on your deathbed, reflecting back

• • • • • • • •

upon your life. Keep it real—imagine a life where you lived with this chronic condition. During your last days, you will be less focused on your absence of health and more present with what truly mattered in your life. What were those things? Who was important to you? Where did you make an impact? What brought you joy? Keep these things in mind as you list the ten things that are most important to you now.

2: Select five of these items and contemplate how you can engage with them in some way. For example, if you said that volunteerism is important to you, find an agency that can use your help in a gentle way, such as spending time with hospitalized children or telephoning seniors who live alone to ensure their daily wellness. No doubt loved ones are on your list of important things. How can you truly share yourself with them? They don't need you to be active, to spend money on gifts or energy on cooking; truthfully, they just want to be with you. For each of the five items you chose, list one means of engaging them in a positive way.

3: Make a plan to take action on one of these items this week. Each week, commit to taking a meaningful action at least once. Be gentle with yourself; remember, these don't need to be grand gestures. The point is to stay connected to what gives you a sense of love, meaning, purpose, joy, and engagement in everyday life. Over time, revisit what is important to you and discover ways to draw this deep meaning into your life.

Pain and other chronic health conditions, although they can impact all areas of your life, need not be the most important thing in life. You were a whole person before this condition came upon you, and those dreams, desires, and enjoyments are as important as they ever were. Allow the results of this exercise to inspire a shift in your everyday focus. Continue to cultivate life on your terms, even if they are modified by your condition. Draw in the activities, hobbies, and people that mean something to you, and enjoy your mindful experience of them! The following story tells of the importance of finding joy in life despite the protests of the body.

Alicia's Story

Since I was fifteen I have been dealing with pain problems: pain in my joints, stomachaches, headaches, and more. I also had trouble recovering from injuries, cuts, and bruises. At the time it seemed like an inconvenience; it was getting in the way of my ability to participate in sports and stay active. Inconvenience turned into frustration and anger, which turned into depressive episodes. When people lose the ability to manage their own bodies, it is typical to go through a

• • • • • • • •

period of grief, which can either be motivating or a shroud of darkness. In my darkest places I felt like life wasn't worth living if I couldn't function without pain.

I did what any person would do. I went to see many doctors. I was passed from doctor to doctor as they tried to identify what was wrong with me. The process of identifying the issue is empowering, but for me it never happened. In fact, the lack of identification left me feeling more out of control. I didn't have control, my doctors didn't have control, and I was left spiraling.

I knew in the past yoga had helped me curb some of the pain in my body, so I sought out a deeper education. What I found was the support and foundation I needed to feel control over my life again. I learned some poses that I could repeat daily to strengthen the muscles around my achy joints. I started exploring the eight-fold path, which first and foremost introduced nonviolence to the self, something I had lost. I started practicing mindful breathing exercises. Mindful breathing allowed me to be aware of the relationship between my pain and my stress levels, similar to the relationship between a chicken and an egg. Then breathing brought me to meditation. Meditation became a tool that I use to quiet my mind to stop the stress-pain cycle in its tracks.

While it produces many benefits, the healthcare system of our generation is lacking when it disempowers the patient. The patient is told to manage their condition under the monitoring of their physician. Unless they take initiative, they never learn the hows and whys of their own bodies. Yoga has created a framework for me to practice mindful living. I have been empowered by getting inside my own body, noticing the things that affect me in both body and mind. I notice the negative relationships that can be created by things as tangible as foods and medications to things intangible like repetitive postures and thought patterns. And it doesn't feel like more work; it feels like I know myself. I know myself, I love myself where I am, and I accept what my body can do. By learning about awareness and utilizing it in my life, I have found a way to supersede feelings of grief and uselessness. It has helped me to feel empowered and regain meaning for my existence.

As Alicia's story reminds us, each person has an individual path to well-being. The way each of us perceives and responds to pain and illness will be slightly different. However, both research and countless stories from meditation students have shown us that no matter age, gender, illness, or intensity, mindfulness helps improve quality of life. The process of objectively steadying the mind on internal and external reality rather than judging it, avoiding it, or wishing it were different empowers us to understand. From that understanding we can consciously choose to build life in the direction of our own well-being. Mindfulness practice through physical and mental awareness also helps us discern nuances of pain, direct focus toward what is uplifting, and hold onto who we really are in spite of our physical condition.

· · · · · · · ·

Erin Byron is a psychotherapist whose Master of Arts dissertation was on yoga for post-traumatic stress disorder. Erin is a senior creator of Comprehensive Yoga Therapist Training and co-author of *Yoga Therapy for Stress and Anxiety*. Her home base is Brantford, Ontario, Canada, where she trains yoga and meditation teachers and comprehensive yoga therapists. Erin enjoys traveling to teach these subjects as well as leading diverse groups such as university students, business professionals, and mental health practitioners on topics such as body psychology, transforming feelings, and yoga therapy for mental health.

Peter Arcari

A Mindful Approach
to the End of Life

JEANNE VAN BRONKHORST, MA, MSW

Mindfulness is often defined as a contemplative, meditative practice of being self-aware in each moment. I like this definition of mindfulness, especially if I expand it to include being fully present and engaged with our emotions. Something quiets inside when we can allow ourselves to simply be present to our emotional lives. As David Gordon says in his book *Mindful Dreaming*, "The goal of mindfulness is awakened consciousness—after chipping away and releasing the chaotic, confusing thoughts and plans of our everyday ego, we discover the innate experience of well-being, peace, and unity with the world."[1] Mindfulness is remaining present and engaged with what is, whether that is joy, sorrow, love, or pain. When you allow yourself to be fully present to your emotions, you will find this presence brings an inner peace.

At no time is this practice of recognizing and accepting emotions more needed than at the end of life. For many years I have worked in hospice as a social worker, helping patients and their families find as peaceful an ending to life as possible. I have found that peace is more than the

---

1   David Gordon, *Mindful Dreaming: A Practical Guide for Emotional Healing Through Transformative Mythic Journeys* (New Jersey: New Page Books, 2007), 20.

absence of pain. People also need the spiritual and emotional peace that comes from their love, their sense of meaning and purpose, and knowing their place in the world.

Thomas Moore, author of the best-selling *Care of the Soul* and one of this book's contributors, speaks of serious illness as "a profound spiritual issue....It is a matter of meaning, emotion, relationship, and ongoing engagement with life."[2] We don't have to have a serious illness to contemplate how we find meaning or engage with life, but when time is shortened these themes feel more urgent.

A practice of mindfulness helps us become aware of our emotional lives, making it easier to find our life's meaning and connect with those we love. As psychologist Thomas Bien said, "When we are mindful, we see what needs to be done and left undone. We know what needs to be said and left unsaid. We are in touch with how work affects ourselves and others."[3]

As much as we know that only one person is actually dying, each death—each life—is connected to others who love and care for that person. From our first moments we are embedded in the lives of others, entangled with parents, grandparents, siblings, friends, and relatives. Throughout our lives we touch the world, move out into it, and change it through our relationships with others. Mindfulness of our emotions, then, helps us live more deeply in our relationships. Mindfulness can be an approach to a whole life—a way of connecting with each other and with our own deepest needs.

A Story About Mindful Living at the End of Life

Many years ago I met a woman named Diana, who lived with her husband Bryan in a small farming community.[4] She was not yet sixty years old, but she was dying of an aggressive degenerative muscle illness. She had lost the use of most of her muscles by the time she began my agency's hospice service. She could no longer sit up, and her voice was extremely weak. She couldn't swallow and was fed through a tube by Bryan twice a day. Bryan was an occupational therapist and had taken family leave to care for her the year before. When that leave ended he took an early retirement, and his two brothers and Diana's sister sent them money each month so he could to continue to care for her.

As I parked in front of their house the first time we met, I wondered how they were coping emotionally. I wondered if Bryan was struggling with caregiver burnout and how Diana was handling what I assumed would be anger and frustration at not being able to move. I also knew

---

2   Thomas Moore, *Care of the Soul in Medicine: Healing Guidance for Patients, Families, and the People Who Care for Them* (Carlsbad, California: Hay House, 2010), 234.

3   Thomas Bien, *Mindful Therapy: A Guide for Therapists and Helping Professionals* (Boston: Wisdom Publications, 2006), 182.

4   Diana and Bryan are not their real names. While this story is true, I have changed the identifying information to protect their confidentiality.

• • • • • • • •

that many people slowly become isolated by these great illnesses, as friends feel less useful and less sure of their welcome or get busy again with their own lives. After so many years of illness, I expected their house to be quiet.

But when I walked into their house, it was full of people. There were flowers, teddy bears, cards, and balloons everywhere, and Brian was talking to two former colleagues in the kitchen. He smiled easily as he welcomed me and introduced me around the room. Everyone seemed relaxed and at ease.

Diana was lying on a hospital bed and she smiled when I introduced myself, a tiny movement near the corners of her mouth and the thin lines at the corners of her eyes deepening. She held my gaze and somehow I understood she wanted me to come closer. I bent my ear toward her mouth and she breathed out two words: "Love you." I stood back up and looked at her, startled. She couldn't mean me, I thought; we had only just met. I glanced at her husband, who nodded. "She just wants to love us all," he said. "That's how she has spent her life, loving us all." She raised her eyebrows at him and he smiled. He reached over and brushed her cheek with a finger and said, "Love you, too."

I learned that Diana had been the secretary for the town's high school for nearly twenty-five years and in those years had been a source of encouragement and love to the students. Many remained in the town and continued to visit long after their graduations. During those same years she had volunteered at the local library as the Story Lady two Saturdays every month, and older children ran over to give her hugs when they spotted her in town years later. Now she and her husband welcomed dozens of former students, children, and colleagues into their home. When she could no longer give them hugs, she smiled at them. When she could no longer smile, she watched them and breathed out love. And they felt it, just as they had felt it when they were children

I found myself wondering what was it about Diana and Bryan's life that allowed them to love their visitors so extravagantly, when others in a situation like theirs struggled just to manage their own suffering.

I quickly discovered they talked to each other every day, sometimes about nothing but often about what was in their hearts. They practiced a form of mindfulness every time they attended to and accepted their inner lives, both the beautiful and the painful. Their emotional strength came from their willingness to accept and share their emotions. They didn't hide their emotions from each other or from themselves. When Diana became ill she didn't hide her condition or ask her visitors to ignore it. They were welcome to ask questions, which she answered until she could no longer talk easily. She was emotionally present to her young visitors and, by allowing her emotions to be less guarded, she invited her visitors to be less guarded and more emotionally present in return.

· · · · · · ·

I consider this a mindful practice, a willingness to be aware and accepting of deep emotions. Because of their practice, Bryan and Diana recognized early on their desire to consciously direct their love out into the world for as long as possible. Diana had come to understand early in her life that her particular gift was all about loving the world in whatever way she could, as much as she could, one young heart at a time. With everything she had left she was sending love to her former colleagues, students, and story listeners. Her life had meaning and purpose in the love she poured out, and now she was hearing every day how she would be remembered and honored by her family, her colleagues, and the children she had loved who were now all grown up.

As Diana and Bryan remained accepting of their emotions, they found themselves living through three great themes that people often face at the end of life: the themes of love, meaning, and legacy.

Love, Meaning, Legacy

After all these years in hospice I have come to see the three themes of love, meaning, and legacy as the essential questions or challenges of our lives. We all want to love and be loved. We want our life to mean something, if not to the world then to the people who know us best. And we all want to be remembered. Whether we have thirty years left to live or thirty minutes, these three themes seem to be woven into our souls.

Earlier this month I listened to a short talk by Matthew O'Reilly, emergency medical technician (EMT) on Long Island, New York, who rescues people from life-threatening accidents and sudden medical emergencies.[5] Occasionally he came upon people who were still conscious and who he knew would not survive. For a few years he told people they would be all right, fearing if they knew the truth they would die in agony. But when he got up the courage to tell them the truth, he found people responded with relief and a surprising acceptance. Rather than die fighting for their survival, which was what people did when O'Reilly falsely reassured them they could live, the people who heard the truth stopped fighting and turned their thoughts to loved ones. They thought about those who needed their forgiveness and the people they wished they could make amends with. They asked O'Reilly, "Did I do what I needed to do in this life? Did I make this life count?" And they asked him, "Will you remember me?"

I don't think it is a coincidence that O'Reilly found his patients most concerned with the same three questions that Diana and Bryan and Thomas Moore, earlier, held up as most important. I have heard variations on these same three themes from many people I've met in my hospice work. What feels most important at the end of life is who and how well they've loved, the meaning and purpose they found for their lives, and how they will be remembered. These three

---

5   Matthew O'Reilly, "'Am I Dying?' The Honest Answer," https://www.ted.com/talks/matthew_o_reilly_am_i_dying_the_honest_answer.

· · · · · · · ·

themes do not all have to be fully addressed before people can die in peace, but exploring them out loud with someone willing to listen helps people find peace. O'Reilly's patients went on this same search for love, their life's meaning, and how they would be remembered, made all the more intense by the short time they had left.

The strongest of these themes is love. Love doesn't contract at the end of life; sometimes it expands exponentially. All the people I have talked with over the years have expressed a need to find, strengthen, celebrate, and express the love they feel for each other—parents for their children, spouses for each other, brothers and sisters and in-laws, friends and friends of friends who hang back by the door, suddenly shy in the face of such nakedly open hearts.

It is a deep love that drives people to hang onto life for another day rather than abandon their spouses before their spouses are ready. They live for a grandchild's birth or graduation, or for one last anniversary. They hold each other as close as they can, only letting go when they must.

Diana showed me that her love was a powerful force for good, for all its breathy fragility. I am sure Diana and Bryan had their faults and arguments over the years, before Diana's illness made those faults pale into insignificance. I am sure they both went through moments of fear and anger and just wishing it was different. But I am convinced their patient awareness of their emotional lives gave them room to make a heroic choice at the end of Diana's life.

Diana made a conscious decision to spend her last months and then her final days sending her love out into the world, to her husband, friends, former students, and the people who came in to help provide her care. She could make this decision because she was already aware of her love and of her deep desire to be remembered for it. She could love the people around her with her whole heart and so she made an effort to do just that, as directly as possible. She told them she loved them, and when she could no longer say it out loud, she smiled at them.

I have thought often about Diana and her decision to love without reservation throughout her illness, and I feel at times I am still aiming my life toward her goal. I sometimes treat my heart as if it were too precious to share, as if showering love on someone else somehow diminishes my own power. Diana demonstrated that nothing could be further from the truth. I wonder at the lives of those who knew her well, who basked in her love and appreciation over the years. I like to imagine they each found a way to pass that love along, to shower it upon their own children and friends and spouses and colleagues. This is a great gift of a human life.

The second theme of meaning comes with the questions: What has my life been for? What was my reason for being here? What did I do with my life; what have I accomplished? These are questions of both meaning and purpose. Sometimes people sum up their lives in just a few words, with pride, regret, gratitude, wonder, acceptance, or understanding:

"I've raised my children to be good people."

"I worked too hard."

· · · · · · · ·

"I know I've made a difference."

"I wish I hadn't felt like I had to fight so much."

"I took care of my parents when no one else could."

"I've done things I wish I could take back."

"I gave to my community."

Some people define their work as their life's purpose and struggle to finish a final project. Others see work as a means to an end and are happy to retire and focus on what really matters. Diana consciously chose to focus on loving the people in her life, and her decision gave meaning to the end of her life that transcended her suffering.

The best part of my work in hospice is listening to people tell what they have learned in a lifetime. I have noticed how often the meaning of a good life is intimately entwined with the well-being of others. Meaning and purpose and love are often bound together through the care we provide and the sacrifices we make. Diana was not alone in wanting to center the great meaning for her life on the love she could pass along to the next generations.

The third theme, legacy, is all about how we will be remembered. People in hospice ask their families, "What am I leaving my family? What lessons have I passed on to the next generation?" Even people with only minutes to live asked the paramedic if he would remember them. We all want to know our lives mattered and will continue to matter to those who remain.

Legacies can be as simple as a sentimental object that gets handed down—a grandmother's ring, a writing desk that stood in a parent's study. The very rich put their names on buildings, museums, and hospital wings. Some people build their legacies through their careers, creating works of art, daring inventions, or scientific discoveries. Everyone, no matter their wealth or skills, can leave a legacy of memories, stories, and life lessons. I have helped people record their life stories to pass along to their children and grandchildren, and these stories nearly always contained words of wisdom, lessons learned, and how they hoped they would be remembered.

Diana's legacy was her value for and deep capacity for love. I met this remarkable woman only twice and here I am, nearly twenty years later, still feeling moved to live up to the beauty I saw in her eyes that day as she let them shine with a loving appreciation of the people before her.

How Talking Helps

These three great human concerns at the end of life—love, meaning, and legacy—are most often met and explored through conversation. Look at any book or article from an end-of-life expert and you will hear stories of people finding their way into a more peaceful death when they allow themselves to speak from their hearts. I have seen families talk for years after a loved one's death about the emotional power of those conversations. Saying the important things and listening to what matters most helps make a peaceful death more possible.

· · · · · · · ·

Some people speak only through actions, but most of us need words to make our inner lives known. It is one thing to love someone, but saying it out loud (or writing it down) helps us make sure they know we love them. It is one thing to feel sorry for harming another person, but our apology gains power if we can make our amends out loud, in person. The conversation, the connection, and the interaction make the amends real. We talk to sum up a life or pass along wisdom or carry forward important family stories. In both action and words we hold each other close by showing what is most important to us and reassuring each other of our love and belonging.

Maggie Callanan and Patricia Kelley's wonderful book *Final Gifts* is all about the gift of communication, of people making not just their physical needs known, but their hearts as well. They also noticed how often family and friends of the dying chose not to show their hearts but focused on idle chatter instead. Callanan and Kelley never doubted the love these people shared, but without the emotional space to acknowledge what was most important, the people who were dying often felt isolated, noting that "their chatter keeps the dying person from being able to speak intimately. When dying people aren't allowed to talk about what's happening to them, they become lonely, even amid loving, concerned people."[6]

Sharing what is most important at the end of life needs emotional room, a clearing in the middle of a forest of chatter or, in the case of O'Reilly, the paramedic, letting go of false hope. Only when O'Reilly acknowledged out loud that his patients were dying did his patients have room to begin setting their emotional affairs in order. The patients didn't need much time, but they needed the clearing away of what was false, no matter how difficult it was for O'Reilly to tell them the truth. And when O'Reilly did find the courage, he found these moments to be profoundly satisfying to the dying and to the families who later heard their loved one's final thoughts through him.

For those who are living with hospice services, professionals and volunteers use what we call "life review" questions to invite people into these deeper conversations, if they choose. Our questions circle around the themes of love, meaning, and legacy. We ask them about their life-defining moments and the choices they've made that led to who they are now. We ask about the people they loved, the work they chose, the places they settled into, and the places they've left. We ask about the decisions they've made when they didn't have enough information, the leaps of faith they took. When we get bold we ask what they are glad to have brought to the world, how they want to be remembered, and what they are proud to pass on. We ask these questions because we know the answers can be a source of peace at an otherwise painful time.

---

6   Maggie Callanan and Patricia Kelley, *Final Gifts: Understanding the Special Awareness, Needs, and Communications of the Dying* (New York: Bantam Books, 1997), 57.

The practice of mindfulness can help make these conversations more accessible for you. The important conversations are more likely to happen when we are aware of and accepting of our own emotional lives, which mindfulness makes possible. A practice of mindfulness will help you know when you have something real to say and when you are skating along with polite surface chatter. Mindfulness allows you to relax your polite facade long enough to show what you are really thinking or feeling. Mindfulness allows you to breathe into the discomfort of asking about someone else's emotional life.

The rewards are immense; one moment of heartfelt sharing can be powerful enough to last the rest of your life. I have heard people at the end of life talk about a new awareness of the beauty that surrounds them. Because time is short, each moment stands out more clearly as unique, expansive, and epic. Colors become vibrant or more diffuse. Taste changes, and a single piece of chilled watermelon becomes a revelation. Smells of dinner and the sound of dishes clinking in the sink might remind them of childhood. Their future is shortened into this present moment and to their intense surprise, the moment contains all of life—heartbreak, wonder, suffering, memory, joy. The moment feels like a gift, and to be able to share this experience with someone feels like a second gift.

How to Talk About Love, Meaning, and Legacy at the End of Life

I have tried to show the great beauty that can come from people being allowed to talk about who and how they love, what their life has meant to them, and how they want to be remembered. I also know from experience that getting to those conversations often feels impossible. There are so many other concerns—pain control, bathing, groceries, loss of independence—that asking about love and meaning and legacy seems out of place. Caregivers focus on what needs to be done and often fill the air with friendly chatter to ease past the loss of dignity and independence. They ask about physical comfort and symptom management because those are also important questions that need to be addressed.

Beyond all those important concerns, however, lies an unconscious fear. Families and care-givers are often afraid to bring up the questions of love, meaning, and legacy because in our collective imagination we have linked these conversations with the final act of dying. Our final goodbyes are so strongly linked with final messages and final gifts that sometimes it feels like talking about what is most important will signal that we think death is imminent. We fear if we bring up the subject our loved one will think we have given up on them, which will cause them to die sooner.

Diana and her husband showed me that opening these important conversations early can be a gift. They liked talking to each other about important things, so they didn't feel the need to wait until she was dying to share what they most wanted to say. Instead, after each new diagnosis and

. . . .

treatment they said to each other, "I think this is a good opportunity to talk." And it was. They talked throughout Diana's illness, which made every conversation they had less about dying and more about how they wanted to spend their lives together.

Because they didn't wait to speak until she was actively dying, the two of them had much less fear that such a conversation meant death was near. They successfully disentangled the most important conversations they needed to have from the act of dying, which took away one of the greatest fears we have: of mistakenly accepting the end too soon. Their big conversations could and did remain focused on what Diana's life was all about, how she wanted to be remembered, and the love she could still give to her family and friends. Her friends and family took their willingness to talk about such things as permission for themselves. They began telling Diana what they would remember of her and the lessons they had already begun passing on to their children.

Families and caregivers also sometimes fear the feeling of vulnerability that happens when we speak from our hearts. We don't like feeling uncomfortable, and we don't want to make our loved ones uncomfortable either. For people who are seriously ill, however, the discomfort of emotional conversations often fades—not always, but often. It is one of the reasons people at the end of life feel lonely in the presence of well-intentioned chatter. They are facing the most profound event in their lives, and many—even those who never spoke openly of their emotions before—find themselves wanting to talk about it with someone who can listen.

EXERCISE: **Opening Important Conversations at the End of Life**
Mindfulness helps in opening these conversations sooner. When you pay attention to your own heart and emotional needs, it is easier to know what questions still need to be addressed. Here are three steps you can take to open these conversations.

Step 1: What are you missing?
Figure out what you, yourself, still need to hear from or say to your loved one. Sit in a quiet place and take an emotional inventory of your relationship. Have you said everything you want to say? Is there anything left you haven't told them that you want them to know—any life lessons or family stories you want to pass along? Anything you are still wishing could be resolved? Anything you resolved for yourself but haven't yet said aloud?

Sometimes I ask family members to imagine themselves in five years' time looking back at this moment. When they look back do they feel satisfied they have said everything they wanted to say? From this future vantage point, is there anything they wish they had said while they still had the chance, anything they regret not having said?

• • • • • • • •

Step 2: What are they missing?

The second step is just as direct, although it is harder to do. Find out what your loved one still wants to say to you or hear from you. Whether the ill person is you or a family member, in order to find out what is in the heart of your loved one, you have to ask and then listen closely to the answer.

Mindfulness will help. Practice letting go of the chatter and allowing a respectful silence to grow between you. Practice expressing what really matters to you, and then watch for how your loved one responds. Give your loved one time to think before they answer. If they are not able or willing to have these conversations, you will know. On the other hand, your invitation might be all they have been waiting for.

If you aren't sure what to ask, you can begin with a simple question: "How are you feeling today?" Asking about today makes the question more specifically about now and about them, rather than the polite question of greeting. It invites people to answer beyond the equally polite, single-word response, "Fine."

In my work I've often asked people, "How are your dreams these days?" which is just unusual enough to let them know I am interested in their inner lives as much as their physical comfort. I was surprised in the beginning how often people's dreams helped them talk more openly about who they loved, the meaning of their lives, and how they wanted to be remembered.

Some families offer to help their loved ones save their memories as a tangible legacy with memory albums, written memoirs, and recordings of them retelling their most memorable events. These projects help create a new, safe space for the important conversations.

Step 3: Practice and repeat.

Repeat the first two steps, asking and listening until you are satisfied that everything you need to say and hear has been said and heard. You will find the practice of these big conversations makes the smaller, shared moments of quiet more peaceful. When all that needs to be said has been said, you will find yourselves enjoying more the moments when nothing is said at all. Your loved one might tell you how they listen to you moving quietly about the room and know it means everything is all right.

How to Open Your Heart When It Seems Too Late

I have helped families gather around the bed of their dying loved ones in the last days and hours to share stories of what they have learned, what they will pass to their own children, and what they will remember. I think it is a generous and brave choice to tell someone who is at the very end of life, "This is how I remember you, this is what you've taught me, this is what I carry forward because it is important and is now inside me as a life lesson."

• • • • • • • •

I have also supported families who have gathered to say their goodbyes only to find their loved one no longer has the energy to respond to them. The very end of life often includes hours or days when the dying person can no longer talk or look around the room. How do families talk when it is unclear whether or not their loved one can hear them? How do they open their hearts when their loved one cannot respond, cannot give them the forgiveness or love they most need to hear? This is when families feel an acute crisis of grief. All they want is one more loving glance, one last word, or one last hug, and they realize it won't happen.

This is the most difficult time for many of us to remain emotionally present. Some families gather and say prayers, sing hymns, or read from holy scriptures, but many other family members feel helpless and anxious and restless. How to say what is in their heart if the person they love can't reply? How can they take the risk of saying anything out loud that might disturb the person they most want to see at peace? Some family members decide they can't talk to someone who can't respond to them. They fear it is too late and that they have missed their last opportunity, and they enter a new, deep well of suffering.

Even in these final hours, however, there are things families can say that might bring peace to their loved one. If it is too hard to speak your heart to someone who can no longer respond, then come with a friend and talk about your loved one in their presence. Doctors and nurses have long maintained people can hear even when they can no longer respond, so take this last chance. You won't be dishonoring them by pretending they are no longer present. On the contrary, you will be offering a kind of testimonial with the hope they can hear and understand everything you say. I learned this from my own father, who once told me the conversations he liked best were the ones between people he loved, when he could listen quietly and join in when it suited him.

If you aren't sure how to begin, use the life review questions to recount your own history with them: What is your first memory of them? Tell about the funniest thing that happened between you or the most angry you ever saw them. Tell your favorite memory, a story about one of their quirks or a moment when you realized their strength or wisdom. Tell a story about how they helped you, the lessons you learned, the lessons you will remember, and those you will be passing along to the next generation.

You will find yourself telling the stories that touch upon the three great questions of love, meaning, and legacy. If they can hear, they will hear in your stories that they were loved and forgiven and remembered, and their life had meaning and will continue to have meaning in you. You can give them this as your final gift to them.

You will find these moments of sharing—even if they feel casual or stilted at first—will hold you in your mourning for many years to come. They will help you find your own answers to the three great questions that so many people have asked: Who and how have I loved? What has my life been for? How do I want to be remembered?

· · · · · · ·

Thomas Bien writes, "Mindfulness is ultimately the art of living deeply and happily."[7] A practice of mindfulness that encourages our emotional selves to be more open and less guarded is a powerful tool and a profound gift at the end of life. Mindfulness helps us accept and appreciate our inner lives, which gives us the courage to speak from our hearts about what matters most. Our openness helps us appreciate and support the open hearts of others, and that is where the treasure of life waits for our discovery.

7   Thomas Bien, *Mindful Therapy: A Guide for Therapists and Helping Professionals* (Boston: Wisdom Publications, 2006), xv.

Jeanne Van Bronkhorst, MA, MSW, is the author of *Dreams at the Threshold: Guidance, Comfort and Healing at the End of Life* (Llewellyn, 2015). She has worked with people facing life-threatening illness for twenty years, including ten years as a hospice social worker and bereavement counselor in the United States and Canada. Her first book, *Premonitions in Daily Life: Working with Spontaneous Information When Rational Understanding Fails You* (Llewellyn, 2013), has been translated into four languages. She lives in Toronto and is now working on a research project with healthcare professionals about patient dreams.

Lisa Mininni/www.lisaphoto.ca

• • • • • • •

Mourning Mindfully
WORKING THROUGH
TIMES OF TRANSITION

SERVET HASAN

All of us will face challenges, whether we like it or not. It is the one thing that will bind us together as human beings. None of us can escape loss. Most of life's trials and tribulations are universal and eventually will find us. Whether we're moving to a new city, experiencing a divorce, or going through the recent passing of a loved one, having life throw a major curve ball our way can leave us longing for the way things used to be. Yes, there is often grief and pain associated with these sudden changes, especially the surprise attackers such as losing a job or discovering we have a serious, if not terminal, illness. But whether a life transition evolves slowly over time or is forced upon us by an unexpected event doesn't mean we have to plunge ourselves into purgatory. Instead, we can take a more compassionate and spiritual approach and turn heartache into wisdom and understanding. In this chapter I will describe a mindful way in which to process grief that will provide that distinction.

Mindfulness is not just a meditation practice. To me it is a way of life. Being mindful is about being fully aware and present. It is about experiencing each situation without analyzing it, judging it, and, more importantly, reacting to it. By walking a mindful path through your grief, you

. . . .

183

will not only learn to transform and heal but naturally learn to live your life more fully. Within the practices that follow you will experience what richness comes from asking deeper questions about loss that will give your life more purpose and meaning, and with the guidance of the exercises and meditation at the end of the chapter, be able to apply these principles to your daily life.

I don't believe that we have to sit quietly for long periods of time and empty our minds. I believe it's virtually impossible to clear your mind completely, especially if you are in a state of mourning over the loss of someone or something. Whatever turned your life upside down will probably continue to play on your thoughts. It's hard to avoid. But we can learn to transcend the mindless chatter and use it to our advantage. In other words, grieving mindfully allows us to accept the pain and redirect the emotions so they nurture our lives and help us grow as human beings.

Not too long ago I was tooling along, happy as a clam, and then one day the curveballs hit. But just when I thought my world had come crumbling down around me, I had a revelation. By looking at these outside circumstances mindfully, with a deeper sense of awareness, I understood the underlying meaning behind my tragic loss, and when I did, my feet landed on a much firmer foundation.

Rather than deny the circumstances, become a victim, or reach for whatever addiction I could find at the time, I actually embraced the pain. Mindfulness is the only way I know how to do this effectively, which I will explain in more detail below. The goal of mindfulness is not to cover up the pain, and it certainly isn't an instant fix, but what it can and will do is help us be okay with being who we are despite what we may be going through.

Growing spiritually is all about learning to leave people, places, events, and things behind us in order to become someone new. If we move through transitional periods mindfully, they can become some of the most exciting, creative, and even liberating times of our lives. Hard times can become catalysts for our personal evolution by forcing us to face every issue we have ever avoided facing, thereby uncovering the essential truth about who we really are.

A recurring theme of most spiritual practices is death and resurrection. We can look upon the challenge as an end or as a new beginning. But either way, to get through it we will have to die to who we used to be and become instead someone who is made anew. This is the gift. This is the miracle.

We move from place to place by going through a series of transitions: through a door to an exit, between the indoors and outdoors, and from the outside of our world to the inside of our souls. Rarely can we go anywhere without moving through some sort of transitional space and time as we know it. But this is when we can learn that it is the time *between* these times that is most important. It is during the moments when we are going through feelings such as grief, doubt, anxiety, depression, and confusion that we may be most vulnerable, yet most open to hearing that small, still voice inside of us.

• • • • • • • •

Following is an exploration of how a simple shift in consciousness through mindfulness can shed new light on concepts like unconditional acceptance, living in the moment, and shifting perspectives that will help you transcend the loss and receive the gift buried within. Mindfulness is about bringing attention to this moment in time without judging it. Then we learn the true meaning of what Shakespeare meant by his quote in *Hamlet* when he said, "There is nothing either good or bad, but thinking makes it so."[1]

How you confront your disappointments and despair, the sorrow and the sadness, is one of the major goals of mindfulness. It is awakening to the constant rhythm of the sacred gift buried within each loss. It is my intent to show you how to uncover this mindful, magical ability within yourself. We will explore the principles that can and will move you through the process, such as staying centered through mindfulness meditation and exercises that allow us to unclench our fists and let go of the pain and sorrow.

Grieving mindfully is the process of putting the pieces back together consciously. As each part of the puzzle fits into the next, you will come to see an entirely new and improved picture of yourself. You can then not only appreciate who or what you have lost, but who you are and who you want to be.

My hope is to help you open your heart and move you closer to the joy within, even if you are experiencing one of the most trying experiences of your life. You can and will survive, and you can and will come through on the other side. Changing will always be a challenge, but we can move through our challenges much easier if we mourn mindfully. Now, let's explore what that really means.

Mourning Mindfully

Mindfulness isn't about burying your thoughts but becoming consciously aware of them. So, as I stated earlier, this isn't about clearing your mind. If you become distracted when you meditate, then give yourself a pat on the back. I mean it. If you are aware of the distraction, then you are paying attention to what you are thinking. When you bring your mind back to the present moment, you are being mindful, whether you know it or not.

I practice mindfulness as much as I possibly can, especially when I am doing simple things such as walking, cooking, or cleaning. This is explained simply in an old Zen saying that goes, "When you drink just drink, when you walk just walk."[2] Any activity can be done in a meditative state, which then allows you to cultivate a state of calmness, which will ultimately lead to a state

---

1 David Bevington, *The Complete Works of Shakespeare,* 7th edition (New York: Longman Publishing Group, 2013).

2 David Schiller, *The Little Zen Companion* (New York: Workman Publishing Company, 1994).

• • • • • • • •

of peacefulness. Every action we engage in can become a state of meditation simply by slowing down and appreciating the task at hand.

Mindfulness practices may not actually take the pain away, but they can and will alleviate it. We stop struggling and start relaxing into the now, which can open us up to an almost childlike curiosity that many of us may not have experienced in a long time. Suddenly, the world is a magical place again. We can look at clouds and see symbols and faces or taste the juice from a fresh peach as if for the first time, and find wonder and joy in everything and everyone that connects us to life.

A client I once had was so distraught after losing a loved one that he searched for a sign of any kind to help guide him through it. I asked him what he enjoyed doing. He said he liked to sail his boat, but at this time in his life he didn't think he could. I suggested he take the boat out anyway and try to sail it mindfully. He took my suggestion and said as soon as he left the dock, the first boat he saw was named Serenity. He took it as the sign he needed and moved through his pain much quicker than I expected.

Will mourning mindfully make you feel better? It most certainly can. But there will be good days and bad days. The process of mindfulness is not a magic pill, but if done correctly it will guide you to a place within that makes you feel better about yourself. By practicing mindfulness breathing, mindfulness exercises, and mindfulness meditation, as you will find below, we can take control of our thoughts and feelings and, therefore, our destiny.

Sure, it can be a challenge, but if we develop the skills for being mindful it can be the most important step we can take to transitioning into a peaceful state of mind. The good news is it doesn't require years of practice or expensive training. We can be mindful right here, right now.

Mourning in the Moment

Philosopher Søren Kierkegaard once said, "Life can only be understood backwards, but it must be lived forwards."[3] Fear is always about the future, but the future does not exist. Really, it's just a product of our imagination. If you are feeling overwhelmed by something that has taken place, it's time to move into a new time zone. The pain you may be experiencing is likely fired up by your own fear of what happened in the past, and continues to burn inside from our fear of what may happen in the future. Living moment to moment will help you see everything with new eyes and allow you to experience life instead of simply getting through it.

When you stop stewing over the past and fretting about the future, you will suddenly find that your challenges are much more manageable. Instead of resisting the judgments you are making about the situation, focus on what you can do in the present moment each day, here and now. Stick with the familiar and don't try to change any other certainties in your life unless you have

---

3 Søren Kierkegaard, http://www.brainyquote.com/quotes/quotes/s/sorenkierk105030.html.

to. When chaos erupts, keeping things normal can help you stay grounded. Getting up, getting dressed, going to work, making dinner, walking the dog, or whatever you do as part of your daily routine can provide a stabilizing force and give you a sense of comfort. You are less likely to lose your footing when you stay on a recognizable path.

However, if you start to feel as if you are running on autopilot, stop and take hold of what's happening right here and right now. Otherwise, you're more likely to fall into the depths of despair. Try to make everyday life special by appreciating the moment, whatever that might be. Take time to smell the flowers, as they say. Slow down and really relish what you are eating, seeing, being, and doing. The problem is that most of us can't maintain this present-moment awareness without our thoughts and emotions running amuck. That's the key: to stay in the here and now as much as possible.

One thing that blocks us from doing this is wondering about the "what ifs." All this serves to do is intensify your anxiety and fear. If you allow your thoughts of the future to run off on their own, they will snowball into a gigantic boulder that will knock the senses right out of you. Then, to add insult to injury, we usually add another worst-case scenario to the factors just to get ourselves even more worked up. Stop. Stick to the specific situation at hand, and only deal with what you can at this moment in time. Focus on the known and leave the rest up to the universe. This is what mindfulness does. Instead of "what if," stick with what is.

Remember that if there is nothing you can do in the present moment that will change anything, then try to stop stressing over it. And if you do have to make a decision that will impact the future, remind yourself that the choices you make now can always be amended later. Do the best you can do with the information available to you at the time.

By practicing mindfulness, we are forced to live in the here and now, and by doing so we can experience grief as a meaningful journey instead of something to suffer through. The goal then is to allow the anxiety and distress to take on a positive role that can transform your life by accepting what is and not fighting it anymore.

Unconditional Acceptance

We grow up making sense of the world by judging people, places, things, and events as good or bad, right or wrong. We then hold onto our judgments and resist change, often to our own detriment. Any event or situation can be seen as right or good for some people, yet the same situation or event can be seen as wrong or bad by others. Not only that, but there are times when we experience a situation and think it's good or bad, but a week, month, or even years later we realize that that wasn't the case. I can't tell you how many times I've looked back in hindsight at devastating events I had no control over at the time and am now thankful that they happened to me.

• • • • • • •

When there is truly nothing you can do about the circumstances that occurred, you mindfully become aware of your powerlessness. Powerlessness. How does that word make you feel? Does it make you feel bereft, lost, or, if you're like me, slightly sick to your stomach? What I discovered by practicing awareness is that powerlessness is just a bad feeling. It is nothing more than a temporary and necessary part of my soul's evolution. The feelings will subside when you stop trying to figure out why it happened in the first place and simply accept that it did.

You can't change the past; all you can do is learn from it and move on. If you believe that nothing happens by accident, as I do, then it's much easier to acknowledge a situation just as it is and not as good or bad, right or wrong. By learning acceptance we can finally get off of an emotional roller coaster. No more judgments means no more resistance, and no more resistance means no more struggling. This is actually the easiest path through life. By releasing our judgments, emotional negativity, and resistance, we are free to surrender to the present moment.

This doesn't mean that we have thrown in the towel and cannot change the situation. Being mindfully accepting of a situation will give us the clarity to see the situation for what it is. It then becomes more manageable for us to take appropriate action if needed. Rather than avoidance, we then find acceptance, and in acceptance we find our freedom.

If we resist the reality of death, grief, or any unwelcome situation, we are also resisting being mindful. A lot of people feel that being present in the moment of our sadness will only bring more pain. Consequently, we resist even more, which of course deepens our pain and keeps us stuck in the problem, which I'd like to show you how to avoid.

Getting Unstuck

It is generally emotional obstacles that make us feel stuck. And if you feel stuck, you will be stuck. Thoughts are electric but feelings are magnetic, and whatever you feel you will think and then become. It's no big surprise that grief can provide you with the ideal environment to create emotional obstacles. Its intensity alone will usually bring on feelings of anger, pride, depression, worry, and jealousy, just to name a few.

We will never entirely eliminate these negative obstacles. Why? It's called being human. But let's take the human out of the equation for a moment and just focus on the being part. When we practice mindfulness we can consciously be aware of our emotions and what triggers them. Usually, they are based on something you fear you are lacking.

For instance, you may be acutely aware of the grief of losing someone you loved. Perhaps you miss their love and companionship. Instead of focusing on the loss, start to look for moments of love and companionship in the present moment. It doesn't necessarily have to be within the context of a romantic relationship. You can establish love and companionship with almost anyone. Notice and cherish these moments. It's likely that you give and receive these gifts all the time,

· · · · · · · ·

but you just weren't aware of them. Look around at your environment, your friends, and your family and pets with present-time awareness and you'll see what is really real. Let's explore what that means.

What Is Really Real?

A friend's marriage was ending. She had married a man who came from an upper-class family and she didn't. Unfortunately, he took every opportunity to rub that in her face as much as he could. Despite this, or perhaps because of it, she overcompensated when it came to taking care of his needs. She catered to him hand and foot. When the marriage ended, she felt lost. She felt powerless and vulnerable. She felt as if she didn't belong to anyone or anything. Her sense of identity had been completely shattered.

What she needed to realize was that she was elegant and attractive and sophisticated before she met him or he wouldn't have been drawn to her, and she was still elegant and attractive and sophisticated. I wanted her to remember who she was before she entered the relationship, and that even if she learned and grew along the way, she was essentially that person.

When something ends we sometimes think that who we thought we had become ends too. *He made me feel special/intelligent/creative/beautiful. My job made me feel important.* These are sentiments I hear over and over again. But the truth is if you felt that way, you are still that way. These were and are your characteristics; someone else was merely highlighting them for you. Ultimately, how we perceive ourselves is more important than how someone else perceives us. That's the only reality you need to concern yourself with: yours and yours alone. When you stay focused on this, chances are you'll find that you are stronger than you thought and you will push forward.

Pushing Forward

When we are in the throes of an upset it's easy to believe that it will never end, but it will. Take a minute to think back to a life-changing event that occurred in the past. Did you survive? Of course you did, or you wouldn't be reading this. Now take another few minutes to remember what you learned from the experience. In what ways did it better prepare you for the future? By recalling that you actually made it through something horrendous once, you reinforce the fact that you can and will do it again. The past has laid the foundation for you to face whatever lies ahead, so remove the fear and keep pushing forward.

Also, if you are not moving through a tough time, determine whether there isn't an underlying reason. Dig down inside and see if there isn't a payoff to staying where you are. I know a woman who really didn't want to get well because then she would have to go back to work and her son would stop taking care of her. I also knew a man who really didn't want to get another

· · · · · · ·

high-paying position at work because he was tired of supporting his relatives. I can't tell you how many times I have heard people tell me that they don't really want to move on into a new relationship because they fear they would lose their freedom again.

These attitudes are based on fear: a fear of having to give something up to progress to the next step. Mindfulness allows us the courage to see beyond this by shifting our perspective.

Shift Away

A shift in perspective can work miracles. I know it's easier said than done, but try to focus on the positive aspects of this life-changing situation.

I have worked with countless clients who go through similar situations, and it never ceases to amaze me how they choose to deal with it. One can lose a job and be ready to jump off a cliff, while another is ecstatic because it was never what they wanted to do in the first place and being fired gave them the opportunity to finally pursue their dream job. A woman's husband left her for a younger woman and she was devastated, while another in a similar situation was as happy as can be because she really wanted to be in a relationship where she could finally be her authentic self. It's all in how we choose to look at it.

Saying affirmations by rote won't help, but if you can find ones that resonate with you, stick with them. Some thoughts to help you through a troubled time may be "this too shall pass" or "I know things will get better" or "when life gives me pits, I plant them and grow cherry trees." Anything that helps you look at the bright side and move through the crisis is beneficial.

Being in a transition of any kind is a process. You can't walk around it or slide under or over it; you have to move through it. Accept and, if possible, embrace the changes you are encountering. They are all part of the body's natural healing process. And if you can't accept it, there's still hope. Just pretend you can.

Fake It Till You Make It

Pretend, you say? Exactly. Being mindful means that you no longer rely strictly upon your physical senses to experience life. It will help you get in touch with your own needs by gaining conscious control over them. In a way, you step outside of yourself. The word *ecstasy* comes from the Greek and means "to stand outside yourself." If you do this, then you simply observe yourself as an audience would as they watch a play. Just as an actor can be directed to play a part differently, so can you.

Not long ago, I had a friend who found herself divorced after twenty-five years of marriage. At some point she thought about dating but kept telling me she couldn't because she was too shy. I told her to act like she wasn't—to play the part for a few minutes and just see how it felt.

· · · · · · · ·

If that was too hard for her, I asked her to find someone who wasn't shy and go out with them. People rub off on you. She did, and it worked miracles in her life.

Your thoughts are the script of your life. Change the lines and you will change the way you feel and act. And if you do it long enough, it becomes second nature. Through mindfulness we can redirect our thoughts and reactions and let go of what kept us bound to our present reality.

This is explained further in the exercise and meditation that follows. If you practice letting go and calming your mind, you will find that you stop the mental momentum of emotional negativity and can then gradually transform your life.

Exercise: Letting Go of the Ties That Bind You

The ties that bind us to certain people, places, things, or events in our lives can be wrapped around us loosely with silk threads or they can cut through our flesh like barbed wire. Sometimes it's just plain easier to dwell on the negative and let the anger out, play the blame game, and become a victim. That would be the metal cutting into your flesh and slowly strangling you to death. So how do we loosen those ties and turn them into flimsy pieces of thread that easily can be broken apart? Well, for starters, you have to put your attention back on yourself. Your attention grows wherever you plant it.

If you are going through a transition of any kind, pause and take a deep breath. Before I embark on any spiritual practice or meditation, I always allow a few minutes to just "check in" with myself. Center and ground yourself. Be mindful of the moment's importance and realize that you are moving from your involvement with the outside world into the space of your own sacred sanctuary. Leave the challenges or any unfinished business behind you. Trust me, they aren't going anywhere.

Instead of becoming immersed in the unending stream of things we perceive as problems, venture inward and become aware of the gifts that accompany each one. Consider this: the depth of our pain of loss is also a measure of the amount of importance we have placed in what we've lost.

The goal of any mindfulness exercise is simply to experience your life as it is unfolding now. Stay present, and don't allow yourself to slip back into thinking and worrying about the past or the future. Focus on the moment and nothing more.

Find a comfortable place to sit. I suggest an upright chair that will support your spine. Make sure you have everything you need, such as a blanket or sweater and water. Sit straight, but don't make your back rigid. When you feel ready, let the following ideas run through your mind.

· · · · · · · ·

First, you must think of something that is symbolic of what you are trying to let go. If it is a person, a photograph will work wonders. The same thing applies if it is a place or an object. Events can be represented by anything that reminds you of that moment in time. Make it personal, because it is.

Whatever you decided upon will be your symbol of what you will now release. Next you must find the item or something that represents what you chose. Don't make this too difficult. If you are having a hard time, you can simply make a simple drawing of what you want to express.

When you have retrieved the perfect talisman, place the item across the table from you. Now focus on the space between it and you. What does it feel like? Is the energy between you and the object sticky and heavy, dark or light, thick or thin? Allow your intuition to guide you to what you believe stands between you and what you cannot let go of. Your intellect is how you process your challenges, but your intuition is how you will experience and ultimately walk through them. Knowledge can help you understand the pain, but it's your inner voice that will guide you toward the wisdom you will gain from it. No matter how subtle the changes and shifts you are going through may seem, you must sit quietly and listen intently to your gut reactions.

What does it feel like now? Explore every detail and allow yourself to experience what it symbolizes. Usually, when you sit with your feelings, you'll likely see that none of the sensations or images associated with the person, place, or thing were as daunting as you once thought. By experiencing them now, you'll usually find that it was not as devastating as it may have seemed in the past. It could be that it is more about the unexamined beliefs about the situation than the reality itself.

Once you get a clear sense of what's there, allow it to slowly dissipate. Wipe the space between you and the object clean. Imagine that there is nothing there anymore. Feel how clear and clean it is. It may sound simplistic, and it is. By cleaning out and clearing the space between you and whatever you feel has blocked you from moving forward, you have created new space. The universe universe detests a vacuum and will fill it immediately.

EXERCISE: Meditation for Calming an Emotional Storm

Whenever we are in the throes of rough emotional weather, a continued daily mindful meditation practice is imperative. Many profound inner changes will occur, which will naturally bring about greater emotional equilibrium and well-being. These changes occur on three specific levels: spiritual, mental, and physical. If we want to heal any emotional turmoil, all three levels must be addressed.

· · · · · · · ·

First of all, meditation will connect us directly to our inner spirit, our source, our core—the very essence of who and what we are. This is where you are perfect exactly the way you are and you live in a state of perpetual peace and bliss. It's like the eye at the center of a hurricane. No matter what happens out there, you are safe and sound in the center of your own being.

Mentally, your mind is constantly interpreting and judging the circumstances of your life. If it perceives something as upsetting, it then signals your emotional body, triggering a related emotional response, usually anger or depression. By mindfully clearing your mind, you should be able to look at the events as they truly are, free from the negative perceptions that color our outlook. Greater clarity means less emotional turmoil and less emotionally triggered signals that can literally make your physical body ill.

As the meditation is clearing the energy blocks from your mind and body, placing you closer to your center, it is also healing and dissolving old emotional wounds. As you become more mindful, negative feelings will decrease. Simply bringing conscious awareness to dark states of mind will heal them.

A quick note before we begin: this meditation is designed to provide relief from grief, pain, sorrow, and any other emotional challenges, so the last thing I think anyone should do is worry about whether they are doing it correctly. Just go with the flow and allow yourself to sail off into calmer waters.

Now get into a meditative position. The room should be relatively quiet, and you should make yourself comfortable. It doesn't matter if you sit or lie down, as long as your spine remains straight.

When you are settled, begin by focusing on your breathing. Breathe naturally, allowing your stomach to expand with the "in" breath and letting your breath spill out of you with little or no effort. When exhaling, pull the pelvic muscles in and lift them up until you feel as if your bones are coming closer together. What you are doing is actually supporting your lower back, which naturally lengthens the spine upward.

Continue breathing and simply observe your breath coming in, filling up your lungs, and falling out of you. Then follow your breath into your body and feel it moving in and out. Feel your chest and your stomach expand as the air flows in and contract as the air flows out. Become fully aware of the life force moving through you, the give and take of allowing new life in and the old life dying. If you are truly focused on your breathing in the present moment, then you are being mindful.

· · · · · · · ·

When you feel calm and comfortable, slowly allow your body to relax. Gently bring awareness to one area at a time. Start with your entire face, your neck, your shoulders, and then move down into your heart and lungs. Rest in awareness here for a while, letting your heart open and relax until you feel a sense of peace. Now move down both arms and to your stomach and hips, and slowly move down both legs all the way to your feet and each and every toe.

Once you are completely relaxed, focus on your emotions. It doesn't matter if the pain feels like a fire-breathing dragon in your gut that just wants to burn you up from the inside out. Do not try to analyze the emotions or fix them, and whatever you do, don't try to push them away. Just lovingly give yourself permission to feel them exactly the way they are. Don't be afraid to experience the full force of your emotions.

Next, visualize what you would like to do. Perhaps you would like to scream or hit something. No, you are not actually going to do it—just think about it as if you are doing it. As you continue to focus all your energies on this irritation or issue, you are beginning to release your negativity and your emotional obstacles. You will find that after a while you will actually be straining to maintain your original momentum and level of emotions. The emotions will dim all by themselves. There is no need to resist.

Now, think of someone who doesn't cause you any pain. Someone you love, or who is kind, caring, and compassionate. It doesn't necessarily have to be someone you know. It could be someone you have never met. Perhaps it is Mother Theresa or Mother Mary. It's entirely up to you who you choose; see their face radiating in your mind.

Talk to this person about how you were just feeling. You don't necessarily have to do this out loud, although you can. But just explain how you were feeling and why. Give your loving being as much of an explanation as you can. Then, when you are done, offer the emotions to this person. Give them up completely and ask the person to take them away. You are turning the emotions over lovingly, without judgment, guilt, or criticism. You are simply asking that this person kindly transform and heal them within your heart.

When you are ready, thank them for all that they have done for you. Bless them, and bless all the people in your life that have helped you move through your challenges. When you feel you are ready, take several deep breaths, breathing in joy and breathing out peace. Feel how you feel. Continue until you are centered and grounded within yourself once again. Then, when you are ready, you can slowly come back to your new reality.

• • • • • • • •

You can practice this meditation until you feel calm and peaceful about a certain situation in your life, but you can continue to practice it later for your general well-being. Mindfulness is a state in which we become aware, helping us to appreciate life as it is. Sharing where we are on our life path can only intensify our ability to experience it to its fullest, and there is no better way to do this than by sharing it with a spiritual presence. We appreciate life more during good times and bad when we remain aware of what is happening.

Paul Gregory

Servet Hasan is the award-winning author of *Life in Transition: An Intuitive Path to New Beginnings*, as well as *The Intuitive Heart of Romance: Finding Your Own Path to Lasting Love*, and *Tune Him In, Turn Him On* (Llewellyn). A student of the mystic masters of the Far East, Hasan is also a renowned motivational speaker who inspires others to attain their full potential through her television and radio appearances, live seminars, and workshops. Born into a psychically gifted family in Pakistan, she is also a citizen of England, Canada, and the United States. She considers herself a spiritual ambassador of the world.

• • • • • • •

Dreams in Times of Grief

JEANNE VAN BRONKHORST, MA, MSW

Nearly twenty years ago my mother died in an accident, and my entire family was thrown into a state of shock and grief. I was lucky in a way, however. In the few months following her death I had two grief dreams of her that brought me an unexpected peace. In my first dream my mother rushed toward me, laughing and giddy, with her arms flung open wide, and I woke up feeling relieved to see her so happy and well. I still missed her and thought of her every day, but my dream softened my fears of her suffering.

Grief dreams like this one can bring enormous comfort when we remember them. In fact, grief dreams are the only dreams most people actually look for. People who haven't remembered a dream in decades will suddenly hope for a dream in which they can see and hold the person they love once again. And why wouldn't they want such dreams? My dreams of my mother gave me comfort in the midst of my grief that I might not have found otherwise.

Each night our dreams invite us into a world of color and humor, drama and pain, grief and love, and then they release us back to our waking lives, safe and sound. All we have to do is remember them. This is where a practice of mindfulness can help. Practicing mindfulness helps us hold on to even the most fleeting dream images when we awaken.

Mindfulness is a new word for the ancient practice of being fully present to our lives. Taking time to become more aware of our thoughts and emotions helps us appreciate better the fullness of each moment, especially the small moments of peace that inhabit everyday life.

When I practice mindfulness—when I pay attention to my inner life—I find that from the second I open my eyes each morning I am awash in feelings and thoughts carried over from my dreams. Simply by paying attention to what I am feeling, I begin to remember the dreams that inspired those feelings. A mindful approach to dreams in times of grief can help us all find a powerful source of healing.

How Dreams Help Grief

Grief dreams often act as companions, reflecting our fears, longings, and deepest love. In some grief dreams we get a chance to see our loved ones again. They smile and show us they are out of their suffering. They reassure us they will love and watch over us. Such dreams can help lessen the sharpest pains of grief. Occasionally our grief dreams are so vivid we wonder if our loved ones actually visited us. These dreams fill us with wonder.

Other grief dreams are painful because they remind us of our separation. We see our loved ones walking away and we call out, but they don't hear us. We reach for them, but we are held back by some insurmountable barrier. We cry and rant and then wake feeling overwhelmed by our loss once more.

These dreams can tear our hearts open, but even the most terrible grief dreams bring a promise of healing. Dreams allow us to safely act out our most explosive emotions—rage and hurt—with a freedom we seldom allow ourselves in waking life. When we face the hardest moments of our loss in dreams again and again, we begin to build a new emotional resilience in response to our loss.

Then slowly, over time, our grief dreams resolve. We dream less often of missing the person who died and dream more often about them as we knew them, with all their quirks and habits intact. Gradually our dreams turn their attention back to our own lives.

In my last grief dream of my mother I found her happily making pottery in the Arizona desert. She was glad to see me, but she was distracted by her new projects and had little attention for me. I was irritated at first, but then I realized I had to let her go. We said goodbye, and I woke up smiling, knowing she had moved into a new life that pleased her.

• • • • • • •

How to Practice Mindful Dreaming

Practicing mindfulness with your dreams doesn't require a lot of time. Like all mindfulness practice, your attention is all that is needed to bring your dreams back. If you remind yourself when you go to sleep that you want to remember your dreams, that thought alone will help train your waking mind to notice your dreams the next morning.

Practice being present to your thoughts and feelings as soon as you wake up. You will find your dreams lingering on the edges of your awareness. By paying attention to them, you will build a habit of awareness, a practice of observing your inner life.

I don't remember all of my dreams, but when I practice a mindfulness approach to dreams I remember many more of them. Before I get out of bed, I watch for the thoughts and feelings already running through my mind, and then I follow them back to my dreams.

If you want to learn more about dream interpretation, there are plenty of books available, but you will find most dreams—especially your grief dreams—are speaking to you in a language you already understand. You need only hold your dreams in your awareness and let them tell you their story. The path of mindfulness may be all you need to reacquaint yourself with this important inner ally.

Two simple questions can then help you build a conscious and engaged relationship with your dreams. Ask yourself:

- What am I feeling about the dream?
- What does the dream remind me of now?

Asking these two questions and listening for the answers is a path of mindfulness, of being present to your life in all its fullness and complexity. As you listen, you will find your dreams illuminate and support your waking days.

Your dreams offer useful commentary on your life, much like your thoughts and feelings. They might bring insights to problems, help you sort through hidden fears, or take you on new adventures. Their images can be profound or nonsensical, and their truths are as fluid and changeable as any emotional truth. As you practice your awareness of them, you will find your dreams can be trusted as the loyal friends they were always meant to be.

Grief dreams help us keep an emotional and spiritual balance through the hardest days imaginable. They help us strengthen our deepest life bonds with the people we love, and they gently lead us back, over and over, to the wonder of our hearts. All we have to do is give them our attention.

· · · · · · ·

Jeanne Van Bronkhorst, MA, MSW, is the author of *Dreams at the Threshold: Guidance, Comfort and Healing at the End of Life* (Llewellyn, 2015). She has worked with people facing life-threatening illness for twenty years, including ten years as a hospice social worker and bereavement counselor in the United States and Canada. Her first book, *Premonitions in Daily Life: Working With Spontaneous Information When Rational Understanding Fails You* (Llewellyn, 2013), has been translated into four languages. She lives in Toronto and is now working on a research project with healthcare professionals about patient dreams.

Lisa Mininni/www.lisaphoto.ca

• • • • • • •

For the Love of Your Body

Your body is the home of your soul. Our busy, mindless modern lives have us disconnected from our bodies or, worse, living in active distrust, dislike, and disregard of our physical selves. This section brings mindfulness and appreciation to your body through investigations of movement, self-perception, and sexuality. Rolf Gates shares wisdom and experience about the benefits of mindful movement, suggesting approaches for you to explore and giving you simple practices to begin right away. Melanie Klein builds awareness of your body image and how to cultivate self-appreciation. Mark A. Michaels and Patricia Johnson give you authentic perspectives on tantra and connecting your mind to the pleasurable potential of your body through fun, relaxing, meditative tools and techniques. By claiming a loving relationship with your body, you are brought to the present moment and mindful awareness.

Mindful Movement and Creating a Wellness Practice

ROLF GATES

I am a yoga teacher and love how this practice of mindful movement can cause even the busiest weekday to give way to spaciousness. As time fades to the background, we rediscover our capacity for connection to ourselves, to each other, and to our purpose. Through the movement of our bodies we can more easily let go of our trials and once again find the present moment.

I am fifty-one years old and have had an ordinary amount of challenges in my life. The ordinary nature of my life situations did not make my subjective experience of those challenges any less intense. The loss of a loved one, the loss of a job, the birth of a child, the day-to-day blessings of friendship, the ups and downs at work, the uncertainty, the hopes, and the fears may have all been very ordinary, but for me each was unprecedented. I have never had this day before. Each moment of my life has required me to learn new ways of being, and what has helped me most is mindful connection to my body. I have gone on to teach others to learn this way—to take the felt experience of their bodies and apply it to the broader experience of their lives. It's a skill we can all achieve so long as we pay attention.

· · · · · · · ·

Wellness and the Body

I began my career as a yoga teacher highly influenced by my own experiences as a yoga student with a fit body and a troubled inner life. It was not long, however, before it became clear to me that many of my students did not assume physical well-being. In fact, many of the students that came to my classes had long and difficult histories with their bodies, and yoga was offering them their first taste of true physical wellness and empowerment. I began to see how the practices I was teaching worked equally well for those with sound bodies and troubled inner lives and for those whose inner lives were troubled because their bodies were not sound. I began to see that the two things were really one thing, and that the common ground was our relationship to our bodies—a relationship that physical practices like yoga, exercise, and meditation are uniquely suited to heal.

Mindful Movement

One of the first exercises I put new teachers through is to make them stand in mountain pose and feel different states of mind. Mountain pose, for those of you who are new to yoga, looks a lot like just standing there—and you are, but you are standing on purpose. The steadiness and ease of the pose are in harmony, the breath is effortlessly complete, the heart is lifted and open, and the mind is a still forest pool that listens to the body and the breath in choiceless awareness. I have the students move into their mountain and come to rest upright with an open heart and a mind that is listening. Then I have them be in their mountain from a place of fear, then anger, then pride, then courage, then compassion, then kindness. It is a powerful exercise because many of the students come to a training to be taught how to be in a pose, and what this exercise points out is that the most important aspect of the pose is the way they are choosing to meet it. Mindful movement is moving and being from this understanding.

Mindfulness and Meditation

The reason most of us begin to learn mindfulness is that not paying attention has caused some sort of negative consequence. We are recovering from an injury or an addiction or an illness or a loss of some sort, and we don't feel like living the way we have been living anymore. We want a different result. Sitting still and watching is a great way to find out what is causing us to suffer. People have been doing this for thousands of years and report extremely positive results. In our time the empirical data supporting mindfulness meditation as a way out of suffering is becoming an avalanche of good news. In my own life the last decade has been a sitting-still-and-watching success story.

When we sit still and watch we are like a naturalist slowly getting a troop of gorillas used to our presence. Our inner life gets used to us and starts to reveal its patterns and secrets. Much of

· · · · · · ·

what we find is that most precious insights and understandings have been hiding in plain sight. We suffer more from our fear than from what we are afraid of. We think the impermanent is permanent. We think the unreliable is reliable. And we think that things that are not the self are the self. We suffer from the phenomenon of craving, the thirst for what we do not have, and the thirst to be rid of what we have. And it is all a misunderstanding. As we sit still and watch, we discover that everything is already okay and it always has been.

To sit still and watch is to include everything in the circle of our compassion and understanding. The meditator is studying the body and the breath along with everything else, learning to be still and to feel into this precious life. Who does not need this ability? The skills we develop in meditation have universal application and are only made richer when they are brought into movement. The person practicing mindful movement is just carrying a slightly different set of priorities. Where the meditator can safely allow the body to shift to the background as she allows her mental and emotional patterns to move to the foreground of her awareness, the person practicing mindful movement would probably sustain an injury if she were to do so. Mindful movement keeps the felt experience of the body and the breath in the foreground always. It is the quest to discover what is true, here and now, through the body.

What the Body Brings

When I began a mindful movement practice I had been training my body for twenty-two of my twenty-eight years. I had learned to concentrate, and I had learned to be patient, and I had learned physical courage, and I had learned trust, but I had not learned to listen. The difference between the work I was doing on my yoga mat and the work I had done on a wrestling mat was that on a wrestling mat the body was a means to an end; on my yoga mat the body was both the means and the end. The point of moving into a yoga pose was to listen to what the body had to say: what it was saying when I was moving into a pose, what it had to say when I held the pose, and what it had say as I moved out of the pose. I had been using my body for over twenty years. In yoga I learned to listen to it.

What I discovered is that the body brings us a message of peace from the rest of the natural world. Albert Einstein famously said that through an optical illusion of consciousness we feel ourselves to be separate from the natural world and that this sense of separateness forms a prison for us. The body brings us a message of belonging and freedom. Resting in the felt sense of the body and the breath is like moving into the most exquisite natural landscape. Consider your most sublime moment in nature and then imagine that this experience is available to us every second of the day—is available to us with each inbreath and with each outbreath. This is a message I need to hear as often as possible.

· · · · · · ·

Some Ideas for Movement Practice

Traditional Exercise: One of the kindest things we can do for ourselves is to continue to challenge the body. When challenged, the body responds superlatively and wellness happens. Perhaps the unkindest thing we can do to ourselves is to stop challenging ourselves when "aging" happens and difficulties mount quickly. The good news is that any form of movement such as walking, biking, or a more vigorous hike can be done with increased awareness, which brings the benefits of mindfulness. Even the most traditional fitness routine found in a gym can be turned into a mindful movement practice. The shift is, again, not what we are doing but how we are doing it. If we are lifting weights or doing an intensive cardio workout, we can still be asking ourselves, "Am I connected to my breath, am I grounded through my feet, where do I feel release, and where do I feel strain? Do I feel invigorated or is my body telling me to ease up?" The wellness you find in any of these more routine forms of exercise creates a high form of energy that can be channeled easily toward mindfulness in movement and in life.

Yoga: The easiest way to bring mindful movement into your life is to start going to a yoga class. Yoga teachers today have become adept at training beginners and offering new students a number of ways to get started. There are yoga classes for expectant mothers, yoga classes for addicts, yoga classes for people with chronic pain, yoga classes for victims of trauma, yoga classes for kids, yoga classes for runners, yoga classes on water, and yoga classes in prison. There will be a yoga class for you.

Tai Chi and Qigong: Yoga classes typically have a lot of getting up and down, making them less accessible to older students. For this reason I am a huge fan of tai chi and qigong as ways for an older student to develop a mindful movement practice. The mental and physical training of these classes is second to none, as are the methodologies and insights the classes express. They also serve as movement into the subtle for someone who has been in the habit of more intense forms of physical training and has begun to look for a form of movement that emphasizes meditation.

EXERCISE: A Simple Mindful Movement Practice: Touching the Earth

Whether you're at work typing or taking a walk, when you find your mind has wandered to the point that it is creating stress, take a moment to anchor yourself with this exercise. It is very simple, but it takes attention.

Wherever you are and whatever you are doing, feel the earth underneath your feet, and as you touch the earth, lift and open the heart. Allow the heart to find its natural radiance; as your heart begins to open, your mind begins to listen. Listening to the stillness of the body, listening to the gentle rhythm of the breath, you are listening to the stillness and rhythm of life itself. Take a deep breath in and a long breath out, and then carry this awareness back into the present moment.

As the message the body brings to us from the natural world starts to sink in, the pain and suffering we have caused trying to use the body to get somewhere start to make less and less sense to us. The perfect peace and assurance we feel by resting in the felt experience of the body and the breath call into question the efficacy of trying to get anywhere. Why not try out being here now?

In mindful movement everything becomes precious and sacred: the way the grass feels under our feet, the way food tastes on our tongue, the sound of the birds through our window, the colors of a cloud caught in sunset hues. The body is perceived to be an aspect of this precious, sacred now, and as this understanding starts to grow in our lives, we begin to treat the body with the tenderness and appreciation we are learning to offer everything in our world.

Arica Grafton

Rolf Gates, author of the acclaimed book on yogic philosophy *Meditations from the Mat: Daily Reflections on the Path of Yoga,* conducts yoga intensives, retreats, and teacher trainings throughout the United States, abroad, and online. A former social worker and US Airborne Ranger who has practiced meditation for over twenty years, Rolf brings his eclectic background to his practice and his teachings. Rolf is a cofounder of the Yoga Meditation and Recovery Conference, an advisory board member for the Veterans Yoga Project, and a contributor to the newly released anthology *Yoga and Body Image.* Learn more at rolfgates.com.

Body Image and Cultivating Self-Love

MELANIE KLEIN, MA

I remember standing in front of the mirror for what seemed like hours as a teen girl, unsure of what was being reflected back. I felt sassy in my cut-off shorts in one moment—and then felt like the fattest, ugliest person on the planet in the next moment. And because my self-worth was tied to how closely I could emulate the beauty standard of the time (think Pamela Andersen in *Baywatch*), I was terrified of gaining weight and being considered unattractive. I had learned early on that being thin was equated with beauty. Keeping the mounting hysteria at bay, I called to my best friend and asked him to please come in the bathroom. Compelled by the urgency in my voice, he bounded to my side, no doubt expecting to quell a physical emergency, not a crisis in self-esteem.

"Do I look like I've gained weight? I can't tell," I said, smoothing my hands on my upper thighs, searching for dimples or imperfections. He just stood there staring at me, mouth slightly agape as his eyes darted from my face to my thighs and back to my face in confusion and concern. He didn't know how to answer such a loaded question. "Do I look like I've gained weight?" I repeated, increasingly paranoid and agitated. I held my reflection in my gaze as I waited for an answer. My self-perception vacillated, like an accident victim moving in and out of consciousness. I honestly could not get a grip on what was "real" as I stood there locked with my reflection. My mood and the sense of self required an answer, so I could either "fix the problem" by any means necessary (and hide while I went about "fixing" it) or go about my day freely. I wasn't asking my best friend for an indirect compliment by wistfully fussing over my possible weight gain so that he could cheerfully tell me how fabulous and slim I looked. I truly could not objectively see the truth.

Exercise: **Mirror, Mirror**

What do you see when you look in the mirror?

What do you focus on?

What do you notice?

What kinds of conversations do you have with yourself?

Well, let's find out. Let's conduct an experiment in seeing! Park yourself in front of a full-length mirror and make sure you have the following: privacy, a timer, a notebook, and a writing instrument. Set the timer to thirty minutes and stand in front of the mirror. Don't pose by pouting your lips or flexing your muscles. Don't floss your teeth or tweeze your eyebrows. Don't pick at your face or fix your hair. Don't do anything.

Be with your reflection. Be with yourself. That may seem simple and mundane, but it's not. In a world where we're being pulled in a million directions simultaneously, absorbing thousands of images a day and tending to external concerns, it's rare to just be. It's even rarer to just be with ourselves. We're perpetually distracted. And, maybe, there's a part of us that welcomes the distraction as a way to avoid being with ourselves. But let's go there. Let's see ourselves in a new light. Let's be with ourselves with intention and see what we find out.

As the timer begins to tick down the thirty minutes, allow your breath to move in slowly and deeply. Let your hands softly dangle by your side. Allow your shoulders to fall. Try not to get caught up in your mental to-do list, what you need to buy at the grocery store, how many reps you're going to complete at the gym, or how desperately you feel compelled to wash the dishes sitting in the sink. And let the notebook and your pen rest beside you. You don't need them right now.

Hold your gaze softly in the mirror, scan the length of your body, and observe how you feel. Stay present with your reflection and notice the thoughts, stories, and memories that come to mind. If your mind wanders to thoughts of the dishes or what you're going to eat for dinner, come back to the experience. Continue to focus on the experience as best as you can. Again, notice the way you feel in the experience—the thoughts and stories that arise. When the timer goes off, write about that. Don't wait until later. Write it down now in a stream of uncensored consciousness.

· · · · · · · ·

Strip down. Take your clothes off and set the timer for another thirty minutes. Same as before: don't do anything. Try not to fidget or fuss. Try to stay focused and present with the experience of gazing at your reflection. Don't pose. Don't adjust your stance. Simply stand there and face forward. It may seem awkward or embarrassing to stand so long staring at one's self. That's normal. And, unless you have post-traumatic stress disorder (PTSD) and feel triggered by this experience, your discomfort should propel you to find out what's on the other side.

We tend to spend a significant amount of time doing something when we look at ourselves. Whether we're shaving, brushing our teeth, applying makeup, getting dressed, or putting in our contacts, we are busy doing and not necessarily truly paying attention to or remaining present with our reflection.

The two thirty-minute segments may seem indulgent. What a long time just staring at myself! But if you add up all the moments that we look at ourselves in reflective surfaces throughout a typical day, you'll find this experience doesn't amount to much more. In fact, this full hour may be a lot less!

The experience of viewing yourself nude may seem awkward or embarrassing. Your body may seem different than you usually experience your body or see other bodies. That's normal, too. Aside from medical diagrams, how often do we see nude bodies standing upright and squared forward? I know I'm culpable of posing, adjusting, or "fixing" something on my body when I look in the mirror. From raising my eyebrows to enlarge my eyes, smoothing my forehead to relax the lines or lifting my breasts so they appear perky, I rarely just stand there and look at the vessel I inhabit. It just feels strange, and my body usually doesn't measure up to my expectations or desires when I just stand there like that.

The bodies we see in advertisements, magazines, and social media are almost always posing in such a way as to enhance, accentuate, or hide a specific body part. Have you noticed the way models pose in print images and billboards? If you haven't, you'll notice after this experiment. Whether it's jutting out a chest, flexing a bicep, or sucking in a stomach, we and the public bodies we see on display in our culture are doing something, not just flatly standing there.

Seeing the Truth

I urge you to continue, and when the timer goes off a second time, write down your experience. How did you feel? What did you feel? What thoughts, stories, or memories poked through the surface? Write that down immediately. Be detailed and thorough. Even if the details are seemingly mundane, write them down. There may be some insight in these details you can't identify right now.

· · · · · · ·

Then reflect on the experience of gazing at your body clothed for thirty minutes followed by looking at your body nude for thirty minutes. Move beyond the facts of the experience. Move toward what you can learn from this experience in front of the mirror. What insight did you gain from the experience? What insight is revealed? How do you feel about the sensations, thoughts, and memories that you experienced during the experiment? This is an opportunity to dig below the surface, discover the truth of what you see, and see your authentic self.

I've been assigning this mirror assignment every semester for the last thirteen years. Approximately 1,600 students have turned in their written reflections to me during that period. Each time, the first observation that 97 percent of the students have is their fixation on their "flaws." Most of them spend at least some, if not all, of the assigned time in front of the mirror focusing on the parts of their body that need to be fixed or improved, the parts they have identified as problematic.

But what makes a body part flawed or problematic? How do we define a "flaw" and how do we determine what needs to be fixed or improved? We need a standard of comparison in order to identify a "flaw." Who or what do we compare ourselves against?

I certainly compared my body to the bodies of the women in my family. I was too tall and too heavy in a family that valued dainty and delicate outlines for the female form. I compared myself against my peers and chided myself for not being fit or thin enough. The bodies that were praised and coveted were perky, slender, smooth, and toned. I compared myself against the images in magazines and on television, images that had been carefully taken with the perfect lighting and heavily altered before publication.

Did you detect any "flaws" during the hour with your reflection? Were there any parts of your body that made you feel like you needed to do something to "fix" them? Were there parts of your body that made you unhappy or less than satisfied? If so, how much time did you spend in these thoughts during that hour? Write it down.

What standard of comparison did you use to determine these "flaws" on your body? And if you're one of the few people who did not feel disappointed with a body part and identify it as problematic or flawed, have you ever had thoughts like these? When you did, who and what did you compare yourself to in order to make this evaluation? Write it all down.

What are the consequences of comparing yourself to others? How has the tendency to make these comparisons impacted your sense of self? Your self-esteem? Your self-worth? How has the habit of making comparisons affected the way you see and evaluate others? Don't just ponder these questions; write down your honest answers. Yep, write it down!

There is nothing objective, arbitrary, or inherent about the way we evaluate and determine our body's "flaws" (or the "flaws" of other bodies). They're learned. Most times we are not

• • • • • • • •

seeing the reality of our reflection. It's filtered through a lifetime of experiences. We hear the comments our family members make about other people's bodies or we watch our parents make disparaging or negative comments about their own bodies. We are inundated with digitally altered images that covet and project one type of body above all others. What we define as attractive, beautiful, handsome, and desirable isn't "natural" or inevitable. What is considered a "good body" or a "bad body" isn't universal either. What we see reflected back is a combination of all this cultural input. It's subjective and variable.

We tend to be much more judgmental of ourselves than others are of us (or we are of others). It's because what we see in our reflection is not what others see when they see us. It's subjective, not objective. And our sense of our physical selves vacillates and varies—sometimes rather quickly. I know there have been days in the past when I woke up feeling absolutely fantastic in my body and a few hours later I felt dissatisfied and "ugly" (by the way, ugly is not a feeling). Could I truly have changed that much in a few hours? Sure, hormonal changes and water retention can cause a slight change in our bodies throughout the course of the day, but, for the most part, we can't go from attractive to unattractive in that time. What shifted?

When I stood in the mirror calling for my best friend, I wasn't looking for a compliment. I was looking for a reality check. I was looking for an anchor in the experience I was having because mine had gone adrift. What I saw reflected back had been informed by years of imposed (and failed) dieting followed by self-regulation through more (failed) dieting and compulsive exercise. My reflection held pain and an identity overwhelmed by low self-esteem. It reflected messages I had absorbed that my primary worth was measured by the numbers on the scale and on the tags in the inside of my clothes. What I saw at that moment was an understanding that my self-worth was based on external sources of validation. My reflection held experiences, stories, and memories that stretched over my lifetime. My reflection was not the truth of who I was.

Your reflection is not the truth of who you are.

Taking Shape

What many of us too often encounter in the mirror is not our real selves or the reality of what is being reflected back. What my teen self saw in the mirror was not who was actually staring back. What I saw reflected back actually existed inside me (and that internal image of self didn't match with what actually bounced back at me, an external reflection I was unable to see clearly). For the most part, the dissatisfaction, frustration, anger, and sadness my students described in identifying their list of flaws was impacted by their self-perception or body image, not the reality of their mirrored likeness.

Body image refers to an image of one's body. It's how you imagine you look. This psychological image of one's body is shaped from a lifetime of experiences, observations, and reactions from others—family members, peers, the media. Body image is not something someone has or doesn't have. It's not just girls and women or larger-bodied people who have a body image. Everyone has a body image or perception of themselves. Whether our body image is negative or positive is another matter. Social locations such as race and ethnicity, gender, sexual orientation, gender identity, size, age, socioeconomic status and class, as well as physical dis/ability also intersect significantly with and play a starring role in the formation of our body image.

I was nagged about my weight by family members and my pediatrician. I watched the women in my family diet, exercise, and scrutinize their bodies and the bodies of others. My peers talked about people who were fat in disparaging and negative ways. My peers who were considered attractive were praised and rewarded. I absorbed one-dimensional standards of beauty that informed the way I felt about myself and how I evaluated and assigned worth to others.

A student of mine wrote about the memory of her grandmother telling her that she'd get a boyfriend if she lost twenty pounds. Another mentioned being told that she should not wear a bikini unless she lost weight. Several others wrote about the pain and humiliation they felt after being teased for their bodies' lack of muscularity as teen boys.

Yes, it's possible to have a positive body image, to see yourself accurately and feel content and comfortable. But too often the reflection we see in the mirror is grossly distorted. As a result, much of our dissatisfaction (and disappointment) with our bodies is a result of an image grounded in a fleeting illusion, not reality.

EXERCISE: **Beyond the Illusion**

Take a few moments to contemplate the formation and current state of your body image. Grab your notebook again. Re-read the feelings, thoughts, and memories that came up during the reflection experiment. Pause. Take a breath. Let the inhale fill you completely; let the exhale linger. Sit with what came up during that hour.

And then write about your relationship with your body. There's power in words. There's power in mining your story. There's catharsis in discovering and proclaiming your truth, even if it's just to yourself on these pages. Allow yourself to dig deep and access memory and feeling.

Has your relationship with your body been overwhelmingly positive or negative throughout your life? Why? What informed your relationship with your body? Identify the experiences that helped mold your body image. Describe the standard of beauty that you learned to identify as desirable, worthwhile, and enviable. Did you measure up? Did you fail to achieve this standard? How did that impact you? What were the results? Describe your relationship with your body now.

• • • • • • • •

This practice of writing your story is an invaluable starting point in reshaping your relationship with your body into one that is more positive, loving, and compassionate. The current reality of our body image has been shaped, and it has the possibility of being reformed. Again, it's not something natural, static, or permanent. That's good news! In the same way that your body image was formed over the course of your life, it has the ability of being reformed with consciousness, care, and compassion. And it all starts with your story.

Once you've written down your story, take your time sitting with it. Our culture is constantly touting overnight solutions for what ails us. Instant gratification through quick fixes permeate advertisements for products and services promising happiness, success, and _____ (fill in the blank). But none of these products or services have the power to magically transform our body image overnight. It wasn't shaped overnight and it will not be reshaped overnight. Cultivating a healthy body image is a work in progress, and the process is a journey uniquely our own. All things meaningful and worthwhile require patience. Take your time.

Shifting to Gratitude

The other day my son told me that he had had the best day. In fact, he said, "Every day is the best day of my life. I'm so glad I'm not dead." The joy and gratitude in his voice was arresting and moving. It brought me back to a place of gratitude. First, I was grateful that he was alive, too, and that I could share that moment with him. And then I thought about all the things in my life I'm grateful for (and I'm not just talking about the big things). And then I reminded myself to start thinking about these things more often. Shifting to an attitude of gratitude is a practice and it can be powerful.

It doesn't mean we won't experience hardship, injustice, or disappointment. It does help allow the positive aspects of our life to shine more brightly and can make moving through challenges more fluid. And we can apply this attitude of gratitude to our relationship with our bodies. Focus on the parts of your body that work well, provide pleasure or joy, and help you do and be in the world. I may never have abs of steel, my belly has never and may never be flat, but my belly made room for me to carry my son. I find that incredible! My arms aren't ripped (they're not even toned), but they allow me to hug those I care for and love. Maybe your backside doesn't sit as high as you'd like. Maybe your pecs aren't as developed as the buff dudes on the cover of your fitness magazine. Maybe you have back pain, difficulty walking, or your ears can't hear. But I bet you can find gratitude for things about your body you like or appreciate. Start there.

Focus on the gratitude and make that a practice. Focusing on the gratitude you feel for your body will help to slowly let go of making comparisons. Write down what you're grateful for and repeat that to yourself. Come back to these things when you're feeling critical of your body, and your attitude of gratitude will continue to grow. It may feel forced and awkward at first. You're probably not used to looking at your body in this light. It may feel clichéd and trivial, but it's not. And, eventually, it will be like second nature. You're starting to reprogram the way you relate to and see your body.

Creating a Personal Mantra and the Power of Words

A mantra is something that is repeated frequently. In Hindu and Buddhist traditions this repeated phrase, word, or sound aids in meditation by focusing concentration. A mantra is also often viewed as sacred, with spiritual power.

We're all familiar with the power of words. Words identify and shape our reality. Language allows us to communicate and transmit ideas into a concrete reality. It helps us direct and align our energy. When you say "I," you are directly referencing and speaking about yourself. The words that follow define you to yourself and others. When you use "I am" you're directing your energy on a particular course and solidifying your sense of self.

Now think about how you communicate with and about yourself. Go back to the experiment in the mirror. What words did you use to communicate with your body? What did you say about your body and about yourself?

I can't begin to count the number of times I followed "I am" with negative, insulting, and disparaging words. Often those toxic comments were made in front of the mirror as I would fret over my "flaws" and compare myself to the "good bodies" of others, the ones I thought equaled a carefree happiness. If anyone could have heard those silent conversations I had with my body, they would have quickly labeled it a dysfunctional relationship, if not an abusive relationship.

Shifting to an attitude of gratitude is the foundation from which we can begin to use new words to speak to and about our bodies. Review your gratitude list, then think beyond your body. After all, we may inhabit our bodies, but we're more than that. And in a culture that places an excessive amount of value on our external being, it's important to focus on our inner being. It's always frustrating when the first compliment a person gives a little girl is that she's "pretty." It's not wrong to compliment people, including a little girls, on how they look, but isn't there more? Instead of telling a little girl she's "pretty," how about telling her she's "pretty smart" or "pretty talented"? How about doing the same for yourself? How about discovering all the other aspects of your being that are worthwhile? What other parts are worthy of praise, admiration, or simple recognition?

Can you craft a new mantra for yourself? Instead of saying "I am...(ugly, too fat, too thin, too short, too tall, dimply, etc.)," proclaim something new. Create a mantra that reflects your deeper truth and affirm that. Allow that to be your mantra for as long as you need it and speak it daily.

. . . .

Speak your mantra when you wake up and before you go to bed; repeat it silently as you wait for the tea you ordered. And, again, it may feel awkward (and a little hokey, perhaps) at first. That's okay. It may feel disingenuous or uncomfortable. The words may seem empty and silly, but they'll grow into reality. And, in time, the practice of speaking positively and powerfully about yourself will carry deep meaning and truth.

As we develop the practice of using kinder words in speaking to and about our bodies, we want to allow that practice to radiate outward. We may be our worst critics, but many of us don't stop there. We also tend to critique others, too. Too often body talk is a form of rapport-building among girls and women. It was definitely rampant in my household and, later, in my social circles. Comments about other women and their "thunder thighs" or "cottage cheese skin" was not uncommon. But let's face it: body snarking—the habit of rudely speaking about people's bodies or body parts—is commonplace in media culture at large, not just amongst girls and women.

Talking negatively about others by commenting on their "beer guts," "chicken legs," or stretch marks doesn't help improve personal self-esteem. We don't gain self-worth by diminishing others. In fact, it only perpetuates a body-centric culture that assigns more value to how we look than to what we contribute to society. It exacerbates a climate of negativity and insecurity (and increases sales revenue for the companies trying to "fix" our problem parts or fill the void).

By not engaging in negative body talk about others, we set a precedent and serve as role models for body positivity. When we refuse to body snark or make body-shaming comments about others, we decrease the negativity in our own life and the larger social climate. Not only can we choose to see ourselves in positive and fully dimensional ways, we can see others in a new light, too. We can decide to focus on the full humanity of others, not just select body parts. We can speak in kind and complimentary ways about people that don't objectify, humiliate, or harshly judge.

And if we can use kind and complimentary words about others, maybe we can accept compliments from others. If someone offers you kindness through words by complimenting you, don't push that gift away. Accept it. Believe it.

Practicing Mindfulness

Six years ago I looked in the mirror as I was pushing my son's stroller out the front door for a walk. As I caught my reflection, I stopped. My hair was up under a hat. My pants were too short and hovered a few inches above my ankles. I looked tired and worn. My belly was distended and soft. Had I caught this being reflected back at me ten or twenty years earlier, I would have probably felt distressed or embarrassed. I would have very likely stayed inside, feeling depressed and anxious. "Fat days" could easily ruin my mood and an entire day, if not months on end.

· · · · · · · ·

And while it was sometimes hard to recognize myself in my postpartum body and there were moments of discomfort and dissatisfaction, my reflection no longer had the power to determine my capacity for joy or love. I saw it for what it was: impermanent.

At that moment, my thirty-six-year-old postpartum body was the reality. And it would shift in the same way my twenty-six-year-old body was the reality when I was twenty-six (but no longer). Being fully present in that moment, I was able to recognize its impermanence as well as the recognition that I was not solely defined by it. I was able to accept the reality of my being in that moment without being defined by it.

Acceptance doesn't mean things don't change. Accepting your body doesn't mean it won't change either due to the aging process or as a result of dietary changes, exercise, or medical conditions. But if we can accept where we're at and recognize the impermanence of that state, we can move forward with increased gentleness, compassion, and forgiveness. And if we know that everything is impermanent and subject to change, maybe we can be more fully present and alive in each moment. Maybe we can cultivate a newfound appreciation for our state of being at any given time.

A meditation practice is a wonderful way to become more present. Because, after all, to recognize impermanence and become more accepting, we need to begin by increasing awareness, becoming present right now. In doing so, we can watch as things inevitably change.

There are lots of different ways to meditate. In fact, there are several different types of meditation in this book. You can turn your attitude of gratitude into a gratitude meditation that you practice at the end of each day.

A simple breathing meditation is a wonderful way to begin building awareness—awareness of breath. That awareness of breath helps create a focal point, and that focal point helps still the mind. And when you still the mind, you become present. By becoming present, you become more receptive.

Sitting in a comfortable position, close your eyes and focus on your breath. This need not be a forced or exaggerated breath. Natural breathing is just fine. Simply pay attention to the breath coming in and out your nose. Allow the focus on your breath to still your mind and calm the body. That's it. Now try it for five minutes a day. Work your way up to twenty to sixty minutes a day, if possible.

You'll find that not only does meditation allow you to become more present, aware, and receptive, it helps quell the judgments and negative self-talk. This simple breathing meditation reconnects the mind/body and re-establishes (or establishes) a relationship with the body, one that isn't based on our desire to have our body succumb to our wishes, desires, or expectations. It can help build a solid partnership built on respect, care, and love.

• • • • • • • •

Seated meditation and yoga *asanas,* or postures (what my teachers call "meditation in motion"), when done with a focus on the breath, can help us move more deeply into feeling. And when we feel beautiful, we are beautiful. Looking good too often becomes a stand-in for feeling good.

When we engage in seated or moving meditation, we're utilizing a tool that can help us move past the clutter, learn how to listen, and make authentic choices about how we see ourselves and move through the world.

Lowering Our Dose

Another critical practice for me in improving my body image was limiting the amount of media I consumed. I wasn't trying to make a political or intellectual statement when I decided to get rid of my television in college. I'd been a pop culture junkie since girlhood, and when I broke up with the TV I felt like my best friend and I had broken up. But I noticed something extraordinary (and almost entirely foreign) in a few short months. For the first time since I was eight years old, I felt good about myself. I wasn't regularly and meticulously evaluating and judging every inch of my body. It took me a few weeks to figure out how the usual "fat talk" had diminished.

I didn't completely cut media out of my life. I still enjoyed movies, read a weekly tabloid or two, and of course I continued to be subjected to the usual onslaught of media messages on virtu-ally every cultural space available: billboards, buses, check-out stands, the free "postcards" (ahem, ads) in restaurants, etc. But just that one effort to minimize my level of exposure had produced some important results: an increase in my self-esteem and a broader, more inclusive image of beauty—one that was less defined by unrealistic standards and Photoshop.

I'd always known that I didn't fit the cultural beauty ideal, but it certainly didn't keep me from making endless dangerous attempts to squeeze myself into that narrow definition. But it wasn't until I stopped watching television that I realized the monstrous amount of images I had been exposed to, their negative consequences, and the incredible difference between what is expected and what is real.

And we're subjected to a lot more images on more media platforms than ever before, even if we don't consciously choose to be. It's inescapable. So I'm not proposing that you eliminate all forms of media in your life; just lower your levels of media or how much you consume. Take a media detox for a week (or a month). Jump off your social media accounts for a while and see what happens, or just begin to be more conscious of how much media you consume. Once you lower your dose, you'll be less influenced by the streams of images that reinforce narrow and unrealistic standards of beauty. We may understand that these images aren't real because they are so severely enhanced through the power of digital alteration, but our brain still absorbs them subconsciously. And we take in so many of these images that the cumulative effect influences our perceptions of beauty and desirability. But don't take my word for it! Try it and see for yourself.

· · · · · · · ·

The Road to Freedom

The road ahead can get lonely, so it's important to have some company. Building a network of support through the development of a body-positive community is critical. We are able to rise and thrive when we're part of a larger group of like-minded individuals dedicated to the same goal.

And that goal is freedom—freedom from the tyranny of a dysfunctional body image. Because with that freedom we can become so much more than we are right now. Think about how much time, money, and energy has gone into finding displeasure with and attempting to "fix" your body so you can be happy.

Think about all the things you could have been doing, thinking about, or spending your money on if you weren't obsessing and agonizing over the parts of your body defined as wrong or unacceptable. When we are at peace with our bodies and have a healthy body image, we are able to become our fullest, most authentic expressions of ourselves.

Melanie Klein, MA, is a writer, speaker, and professor of sociology and women's studies. She is a contributing author in *21st Century Yoga: Culture, Politics and Practice* and is featured in *Conversations with Modern Yogis*. She is the co-editor of *Yoga and Body Image: 25 Personal Stories About Beauty, Bravery & Loving Your Body* and co-founder of the Yoga and Body Image Coalition.

Sarit Z. Rogers/Sarit Photography

· · · · · · ·

Mindful Sex

· · · · · · · · · · · · ·

MARK A. MICHAELS & PATRICIA JOHNSON

In American society, approaching sex mindfully is a radical act. Sex pervades our media, most often for marketing purposes; the Internet has given people access to greater quantities and ever-widening varieties of explicit sexual material. At the same time, our culture remains profoundly sex-negative—purity balls, abstinence-only education, and slut shaming are still commonplace—and a large segment of the population is against providing easy access to contraceptives or even opposes the use of birth control entirely.

Neither the overexposure to sexual material, whether for marketing or titillation, nor the censorious, sex-negative attitude that treats women who enjoy their sexuality as sluts and idealizes sexual "purity," is conducive to developing a mindful approach to sex. The former often leads to checking out and numbness. The latter partakes of a way of thinking that at once presumes sex is a natural function that we should be able to engage in without instruction (and perhaps without too much enjoyment) and also stigmatizes sexual pleasure and sexual self-awareness.

If women are often shamed for using birth control or openly embracing their sexuality, men are often subjected to a standard of masculinity or hypermasculinity that discourages consciousness around sexual activity. This has been a concern among twenty-something women we've met while traveling and lecturing on Tantra, relationships, and sexuality. One told us that she would have loved to share our book *Partners in Passion* with her fiancé but that doing so would

· · · · · · ·

have been received as an insult. Thinking that real men know how to satisfy women instinctively and that asking how to please a partner is somehow unmanly harms everyone involved.

We won't presume to argue that sexual mindlessness is the root of all social evil, but it's clear that the cultural pressure to be sexually unconscious has damaging effects. The moral panic over what's characterized as "the epidemic of porn addiction," the debate over consent on college campuses and elsewhere, and the association between risky sexual behavior and alcohol consumption are all symptoms that might be mitigated (if not eliminated) by a shift toward mindfulness in the sexual realm. At minimum, bringing more awareness to your own sexuality is likely to make you freer, bring you more pleasure, and help you feel more at home in your body and in the world.

Virtually everyone imbibes these wildly contradictory ideas about sexuality, beginning in childhood. Freeing oneself from them may take some effort, but bringing a more mindful approach to your sexuality and your erotic encounters will be beneficial. If you use one or more of the tools in this chapter, you should discover new pathways to pleasure. You may even find that becoming more erotically energized has unexpected positive effects in other areas of your life.

Tantra and the Inner Marriage of Masculine and Feminine

Our background is in Tantra, a tradition that has gotten a great deal of media hype over the last two decades but remains poorly understood. Our teacher, Dr. Jonn Mumford, defines Tantra as a "tool for expansion." We often say that Tantra is "an ancient Indian tradition that recognizes sexual energy as a source of personal and spiritual empowerment." In this context, sexual energy doesn't mean sexual activity (although it can). The core principle is that the more fully you can recognize, embrace, and work with your sexual energy, the more fulfilled you will be as a human being. To return to our teacher's definition, what you're expanding is your consciousness, and your tool is your physical body. From this perspective, any sexual encounter, and indeed any experience at all, can be an opportunity to expand yourself—if you approach it with the right mindset.

Tantra is often misrepresented as sexual yoga, sexual athleticism, sexual healing, or couples' therapy. It can be perceived as being too exotic, silly, or esoteric to be of interest or value for ordinary people. This is unfortunate because developing a Tantric approach to living can be beneficial regardless of your belief system. In fact, many of the techniques that are included under the "mindfulness" umbrella quite likely had their origins in Tantra, a tradition that influenced Hinduism and many branches of Buddhism, including the Tibetan, Chinese, and Japanese forms. Our mission here is to examine the core principles within a tradition that emerged in a very different time and in a very different culture and to find ways to apply them in a twenty-first-century American context.

· · · · · · · ·

In Tantric cosmology, the universe is perceived as an ongoing process of sexual union between the masculine principle Shiva and the feminine Shakti, and the classical sex ritual is a microcosmic reenactment of this macrocosmic concept. In the ritual, participants were typically cisgender (those for whom there's a match among the gender they were assigned at birth, their bodies, and their personal identities) and heterosexual, but the concepts can be useful for people of all genders and orientations. In Hindu Tantra, Shiva is inert consciousness and Shakti is energy. It is said that Shiva is *shava* (a corpse) without Shakti; this is reflected in Tantric imagery that shows a goddess (often Kali) having intercourse with a supine Shiva. The underlying concept is that energy without consciousness can be diffuse or destructive—think of manic states or being in a rage. Inert consciousness just sits there…

Thus, Shiva and Shakti are unrelated to cultural concepts about gender, gender roles, or one's anatomy. The underlying belief in Tantra is that everyone contains both Shiva and Shakti and that balancing these elements, creating an "inner marriage" between them, is central to leading a balanced life. These ideas exist in other traditions as well, and we find them to be useful as metaphors, as tools for deepening self-knowledge.

We'd like to take this a step further and suggest that the inner marriage is not so much the union of opposites as it is the development of an ability to move along a spectrum from passive and reflective to active and energetic, from being profoundly in touch with and in control of your body and its responses to surrendering completely to the erotic experience. It also means being focused on and acutely aware of your own mental state and emotions while also being able to tune into those of your partner(s) and to move fairly freely along the entire spectrum of interiority and exteriority.

Doing this requires a deep level of self-awareness. To the extent that there's such a thing as sexual mastery, it has little to do with techniques, ejaculatory control, or the "Singapore grip" (the ability to bring a partner to orgasm by pulsing the vaginal muscles). Instead, sexual mastery involves doing two apparently inconsistent things at once—maintaining focus and giving oneself over with abandon. This is a mental skill that can be developed and refined.

Witness Consciousness

The first, and in some ways most difficult, step is to cultivate what is called witness consciousness. Witness consciousness is the capacity to observe one's experiences without judging them. Try paying attention not only to what you feel during sex, whether partnered or solo, but also what happens whenever you feel aroused or have a fantasy. In addition to paying attention, keeping a journal is one of the most effective ways to hone your observational skills.

· · · · · · ·

Exercise: **Keep an Erotic Diary**

Keep a notebook next to your bed and record your dreams for a minimum of two weeks, focusing specifically on any erotic content. Also chronicle daytime events or thoughts that precede or accompany any feelings of arousal. This can help bring your attention to the current state of your unconscious and your current sexuality. Don't analyze or judge what you observe, but do your best to note any patterns or themes. If you can openly and honestly recognize your erotic triggers, you can work with them as a way to become more sexually self-aware.

Another way to think about witness consciousness is to draw on the idea that you are experimenter, experiment, and laboratory. The experiment can be anything you're doing. The laboratory is your mind-body complex, and the experimenter is the witness, the scientist whose job is to collect data. Generally speaking, data collection and interpretation are distinct processes that aren't done simultaneously. The same principle applies to self-observation because as soon as you start trying to "understand" what's happening or attach meaning to it, you're no longer in the experience; you're in story-telling mode. It's normal and human to want to attach stories to whatever happens to us, but there's more value in gathering the data first and attaching the meaning later. In our years of teaching, this concept has often been one of the most difficult to get across, so strong is the urge to interpret.

We have one very important caveat regarding witness consciousness. In certain respects, it resembles dissociation—the partial or total standing apart from an experience. Dissociation is often a by-product of abuse or other trauma, and in its severe forms it is recognized as a mental illness. Dissociation is not typically voluntary; it's a reflexive coping mechanism. By contrast, witness consciousness is something that you can choose to employ; it's a way to become more self-aware. If you have any problems with dissociation, especially if those issues are related to sexual abuse, we strongly encourage you to seek professional help before trying to use witness consciousness as a tool, particularly in a sexual context. While it's true that becoming aware of sensation and focusing on it moment to moment can be helpful in bringing people back into their bodies, enabling them to reclaim their sexuality, this reintegration has to be undertaken carefully, usually under the guidance of a trained sex therapist.

Awareness

Among spiritual seekers there's a fairly common belief that total awareness, a kind of omniscience, is an earmark of the enlightened state. But, in fact, total awareness would be unbearable for any of us, even for a few minutes. Imagine being aware of everything that's going around you and inside you—the noise from the street, the wind, the buzzing of the electric lights, the

· · · · · · · ·

feeling of your clothing on your skin, your digestion, and on and on. We need our filters; we need the ability to tune out, just as much as we need the ability to tune in.

As we see it, the central purpose of doing Tantric practices is to become facile with your awareness—in other words, to develop the ability to regulate your attention at will. Perhaps the greatest meditation manual ever written, the *Vijnanabhairava Tantra* (a seventh- or eighth-century Kashmiri text), describes a vast array of techniques for doing so, and we recommend it highly for anyone with an interest in developing a more mindful approach to living.

Technique 1: Eye Gazing

One of the most basic techniques is known as *tratak*, which means "to gaze without blinking." The purpose of tratak is to develop one-pointed concentration; it is often done on a candle flame. According to the *Vijnanabhairava*, "Having fixed his gaze without blinking on a gross object (and having directed all his attention inward), and thus making his mind free of all prop of thought-constructs, the aspirant acquires the state of Shiva without delay."[1] Eye gazing—looking into another's eyes in silence, a practice we describe in detail in *Great Sex Made Simple*—is also a form of tratak.[2] It differs insofar as the object of focus is another person, so it's a more layered experience, involving emotional and energetic exchange, even though the intellect is not engaged.

This technique may be challenging for some, or it may feel silly, or it may seem almost ridiculously simple, but over our many years of teaching, we've watched eye gazing at work in public and private settings, and the benefits are palpable. Couples sometimes arrive at our classes in obvious disharmony, due to being late or having experienced some other disruption. Almost without fail, people will be in each other's arms after just a few minutes of eye gazing. (There may even be a few bursts of laughter or giggling.)

Technique 2: Meditating on Sound

Another technique from the *Vijnananbhairava* may seem at first glance to be unrelated to sex. It involves meditating on sound: "If one listens with undivided attention to sounds of stringed and other musical instruments which, on account of their (uninterrupted) succession are prolonged, he will, at the end, be absorbed in the ether of consciousness…"[3] If you've ever heard tingshas (Tibetan cymbals), you'll likely recognize that their sustained chime has a similar quality. It's even possible to use mechanical sounds, such as passing cars or planes, in a similar way.

---

1 Jaideva Singh, ed., *The Yoga of Delight, Wonder, and Astonishment: A Translation of the Vijnana-bhairava* (Albany: State University of New York Press, 1991), 75.

2 Mark A. Michaels and Patricia Johnson, *Great Sex Made Simple: Tantric Tips to Deepen Intimacy and Heighten Pleasure* (Woodbury, MN: Llewellyn, 2012), 52–54.

3 Singh, 39.

• • • • • • • •

The basic practice involves listening intently to the prolonged and gradually fading sound, staying with it until it disappears and then withdrawing the consciousness as fully as is possible, snapping it back, in a sense, and mentally blocking out all external sounds and stimuli. Becoming adept at this technique is a way of playing with your awareness and becoming familiar with a very broad range of states—from fully exterior to fully withdrawn. As with the concept of Shiva and Shakti, this is about developing the ability to move along a spectrum of awareness.

And what is great sex anyway? We'd suggest that one of the keys to having it lies in developing this facility with your awareness, which is far more important than knowing all the right moves and positions. Being a skilled lover entails being both acutely aware of your own state and also being attuned to your partner's. Sometimes it's good to simultaneously have awareness of both, sometimes you really need to turn inward, and sometimes you will want to focus on your partner with one-pointed concentration. Becoming skilled in choosing how to direct your awareness and recognizing the appropriate times to shift your focus will make your sexual encounters more intense and more fulfilling. It may seem paradoxical, but developing and refining this exquisite self-control is actually the key to giving yourself over, to surrendering, to making love with abandon.

Our good friend and colleague Arabella Champaq describes her approach to balancing self-control and surrender and how this process has transformed her sexual experiences:

> One of the principles of Tantra I have explored in my sexual intimate encounters is the principle of the inner marriage of Shiva (consciousness) and Shakti (energy).
>
> I bring my full attention toward the Lover—my initial experience of that inner marriage. This is sometimes called mindfulness, sometimes called presence. In this attentive space, I turn my breath toward the Lover while they turn their breath toward me.
>
> But not me. Not the Lover. Soon in this exchange of breath, attention, and energy, there comes a place of merging. Of emergence. This place is the beginning of the engagement of Shiva and Shakti. Edges, the distinction of I and Thou, are blurred, one breath no longer independent of the other; the experience is of being breathed, not by the Lover but by breath itself.
>
> Energy follows the breath, is carried by the breath. The energy flowing through the channels in my body into the Lover's body, until the edges become indistinct.
>
> I invite the energy to be pleasure and the pleasure to move from my body to the Lover's. This requires my exquisite attention, as well as the balancing relaxation of my need to control the experience.
>
> Part of me is determined to get it right and is limited to the awareness of what has been right before. When I attempt to re-create what has been right before, my experience of the moment is limited. Even the presence, the attention, the mindfulness can become a cage against what is possible. This is an apparent paradox. In fact, if we set up the stage (presence, breath, pleasure) and then get out of the way, the inner marriage is realized. The best sex of our lives, every single time.

· · · · · · · ·

Strive to Be Here Now—Most of the Time

You may be familiar with the Buddhist dictum that "the path is the goal" or its Tantric and yogic equivalent, "be here now." As commonplace as these sayings have become in American society, they reflect an approach to living that is basically in opposition to the way people are raised and conditioned to be in the world. Our society is driven by very materialistic beliefs about success and failure. We're expected to plan our work, to work our plan, to build our careers, to put money aside for retirement. We're likely to think of ourselves as "failures" if we don't achieve the goals we've set for ourselves.

We also live in a society in which looking backward is valorized—something that's reflected in the popularity of memoir as a genre and in much psychotherapy, which seeks to understand present behavior through the lens of past experiences, especially childhood experiences. By contrast, there's an old Buddhist story about two celibate monks who encountered a prostitute near a flooded stream crossing. She asked them to help her across. One monk immediately took her on his back and carried her to safety. She thanked him and went on her way. The monks continued their journey in silence, with the one who did not lend a hand brooding over what had transpired. Finally, he spoke up and said, "Brother, our vows preclude us from having contact with any woman, let alone one like that. Why did you carry her across?" The first monk replied, "I put her down by the stream, but you've been carrying her all this time."

Thus, some of the fundamental characteristics of contemporary America are directly at odds with philosophies that see the future as unknowable and the past as having no more reality than a dream. Of course, these ideas have probably never applied to all aspects of life in any culture. Tantric and yogic texts, for example, include many references to various forms of magical practice designed to influence future outcomes, and even within the context of monasticism, reference is frequently made to ancestral teachers and teachings. The very concept of karma depends on the recognition that past events and actions continue to reverberate in the present.

There is great value in thinking about both past and future. The level of historical ignorance in twenty-first-century America is shocking and potentially dangerous, and contemporary society is, if anything, insufficiently concerned about the future. People in many other cultures view their time on earth as limited and are taught to consider their responsibilities to future generations. Today everyone on the planet would be wise to give far more consideration to the future.

But in individual terms, it's fairly safe to say that people have difficulty freeing themselves from ruminating on the past or fantasizing about the future and that individuals are conditioned to be focused on everything other than what's happening in the moment. This conditioning often has profoundly negative effects in the realm of sex, where developing the capacity to be present is so central.

· · · · · · ·

Avoid Making Orgasm a Goal

Let's talk about orgasm in this context. For cisgender males, there's typically a very visceral and visible series of associations around sex, from arousal to orgasm. There's erection, which is equated with being aroused; there's a buildup; there's the point of orgasmic inevitability (or no return), and there's ejaculation, which is typically deemed to be synonymous with orgasm. This is true even though ejaculation can occur with few or no orgasmic sensations and orgasms can happen without ejaculation and even without erection. In many instances, boys discover this series of associations in early adolescence and fall into a pattern of masturbating to ejaculatory orgasm as quickly as possible to avoid being caught at it.

We have little use for essentialism and think of gender as a spectrum, not a binary. Still, we recognize that the situation for cisgender females is more complicated for both cultural and biological reasons. Where boys have readily apparent and obvious indicators of arousal and orgasm, girls in general do not. In many parts of the United States, female masturbation and sexual self-knowledge remain taboo. There's still a widespread belief that the ideal (or perhaps only real) orgasm is experienced during penetrative sex. In addition, most of the available research indicates that female orgasmic response is more varied than male, involving a number of different neural pathways. All of these factors play a role in creating conditions in which "fewer than a third of women consistently have orgasms with sexual activity"[4] and an estimated 10 percent of women are anorgasmic.[5]

These cultural and biological factors help create a climate in which having an orgasm is treated as the goal in virtually every encounter. This idea is reflected in our everyday language. An orgasm is the Big O, the climax, a completion, a happy ending; it is something that must be reached or, even worse, achieved. Make no mistake, orgasms are great; they feel good, and they're good for you. There's nothing wrong with being orgasm-focused from time to time. The problem lies in the fact that when you're focused on achieving something, when you have an objective in mind, it's much harder to pay attention to what's happening in the moment. And for some, this goal orientation can actually interfere with the "achievement" of the desired result.

It's far better to relax and enjoy the journey. The Tantric approach to sex takes this idea to what some might consider an extreme, where orgasm is de-emphasized (and male ejaculatory orgasms are discouraged in some schools) and building and prolonging arousal are central. The primary reason for this approach is to produce an alteration of consciousness, something that many people experience in the orgasmic state. By prolonging arousal, we are creating the con-

---

4 MayoClinic.com Health Library, "Anorgasmia in Women," http://riversideonline.com/health_reference/Womens-Health/DS01051.cfm.

5 "Female Orgasm: Myths and Facts," http://sogc.org/publications/female-orgasms-myths-and-facts/.

ditions for this alteration of consciousness to begin during the excitement phase and to persist through orgasm and into resolution and beyond.

Sensate Focus: A Mindfulness Technique

The tendency to focus on orgasm at the expense of the rest of the sexual experience is so deeply ingrained that it can be difficult to break out of the habit. Working with witness consciousness is the key. Western sexologists and therapists have been aware of this since the era of Masters and Johnson, although they frame the process somewhat differently, emphasizing what they call "sensate focus" for people dealing with various types of sexual dysfunction. Sensate focus is, essentially, a mindfulness technique, and it's one worth exploring even if you're satisfied with your sex life. It's typically done in a partnered context, but you can also explore it as a solo practice, imagining that you are, in turn, the person touching and the person being touched.

> EXERCISE: **Basic Sensate Focus**
>
> Sensate focus was popularized by pioneering sexologists William Masters and Virginia Johnson as a method to address people's inability to relax during sex. Many sexual problems or dysfunctions are related to loss of focus, becoming overwhelmed by the need to perform, or anxiety about what a partner may be thinking. Sensate focus is a way to become present in the experience, and it can help people move beyond distraction and anxiety.
>
> During basic sensate focus, each partner takes a turn touching the other while concentrating on what is interesting in the experience of caressing, and without thinking about trying to please or create arousal. Set aside time, limit distractions, touch with or without clothes. Do not treat these sessions as foreplay, and avoid any overtly sexual contact.
>
> This practice helps to cultivate a sense of curiosity during intimacy and can also guide you to having an embodied understanding of agenda-free touch. At the same time, it is important for the person receiving to give feedback and set boundaries. As long as you stay within the bounds of your partner's wishes, then you can freely touch in ways that pique your interest.

Imagination, Fantasy, and Mindful Sex

The most recent scientific research suggests that orgasm begins in the brain. Functional magnetic resonance imaging (fMRI) reveals that when people think about having orgasms, the same brain regions light up as when they are actually having them. Our brains are incredibly malleable, and it's even possible for people with spinal injuries to train themselves to have orgasms

. . . .

when parts of the body that still have sensation are stimulated.[6] Similarly, some women have trained themselves to orgasm when performing oral sex. At the opposite end of the spectrum are some women who believe themselves to be anorgasmic but who are, in fact, not recognizing their orgasms for what they are (perhaps because they're looking for that Big O, bombs bursting, dams breaking, fireworks going off) and some men who are locked into the idea that ejaculation and orgasm cannot be separated.

Thus, mindful sex can also encompass an imaginative component. We don't advocate faking orgasm to please a partner or to bring a sex act to a close; however, the act of imagining that you're having an orgasm from having your toe sucked (or that you're having one in your heart or your thumb) can be the key to expanding your capacity for sexual pleasure. The act of imagining can begin to forge new neural pathways and instill you with the knowledge that orgasm is more than a genital phenomenon. Beyond that, merely recognizing that such things are possible is the first step toward making them attainable.

There's another dimension to the imaginative component of mindful sex. Some people argue against using fantasy during an encounter with another person because it's escapist, disconnected, a way of not being present. This can be true in some cases, especially if you feel compelled to keep the fantasy to yourself or become dependent on fantasizing about someone other than your partner while in the act. Nevertheless, the intentional use of fantasy can actually help you become more present. As we've observed, anxiety and distraction are two of the most important contributors to sexual dysfunction and can affect and even preclude becoming aroused, let alone reaching orgasm. Consciously and intentionally creating a fantasy scenario—whether mild, wild, silly, kinky, or an utter cliché—and playing it out can serve to get you out of your head and into your body.

If you dive fully into the fantasy or play the role with conviction, the chances that anxiety or intrusive thoughts will interfere may decrease, and if you can maintain witness consciousness, you won't have to worry about whether you're "checking out." If you've ever done any acting, you should recognize how playing a role produces a highly focused state. You may also see some parallels between certain method-acting and mindfulness techniques. This makes sense because good acting requires immersion in the role and the ability to be present, listen to the lines, and respond to them naturally. It's also worth pointing out that there's a performative aspect to role-play, even though the audience is small. If you haven't acted, think back to childhood and remember how immersed you could become in playing a role. In this sense, role-play is similar to repeating a mantra to quiet the mind and go into a meditative state. This approach may not

---

6   Sara C. Nelson, "Rafe Biggs, Quadriplegic Learns to Orgasm Through His Thumb," *Huffpost Lifestyle*, http://www.huffingtonpost.co.uk/2013/04/22/rafe-biggs-quadriplegic-orgasm-thumb-pictures_n_3130545.html.

• • • • • • • •

be for everyone, but if you fantasize, do so freely, fully, and use it as a tool for becoming more present. Above all, be playful about it!

Michelle H. enjoys fantasy and role-play as a tool for enriching her erotic experiences and for bringing herself more fully into her encounters. She had this to say about fantasy:

> *Using fantasy/role-play during sex is just an added dimension of discovery for me. If I'm with a long-term partner, the one thing I can literally never be again for them is "new," but with role-play as a part of our repertoire, we can reimagine who we are and what we know or don't know about this imagined scenario or couple.*
>
> *Conversely, if I'm in a casual relationship with someone but not in love (which tends to be the default context for most sex), role-play helps me to contextualize our sex in some alternate way that isn't predicated on being in love and the pressure inherent in feeling that way or not feeling that way. Role-play allows me to be* MORE *true to my actual feelings about a partner because I don't have to inflate or invent any feelings that aren't really there.*
>
> *It also reduces a lot of anxiety about floating new ideas in the bedroom, since you can just "be" your character. It's like improv comedy in that you sort of just work with whatever's there and don't take it too seriously.*

Mindful Exploration of Your Sexual Identity and Inner Taboos

Ours is a very strange society. We have unprecedented access to explicit sexual material and information about sexuality. The Internet enables us to research virtually any form of human sexual expression and to find a community of people who share that interest. At the same time, sexual words are still widely used as insults. Children are still taught that pregnancy and disease are punishments for engaging in sexual activity, and we as a culture worry a great deal about shielding our kids from being exposed to sexual material even as we are relatively unconcerned about their seeing gruesome and violent scenes. This attitude may be more prevalent in more conservative parts of the United States, but it is not limited to them. We live just outside New York City, and not long ago our gym removed a flyer for a local book-launch party because parents complained that the word "sex" appeared on it and they might have to answer questions from their children. Being open about sexuality in twenty-first-century America remains taboo.

We suspect that just about every person has at least one or two unconventional tastes or fantasies. If conventional sex is still taboo, unconventional sexuality is often treated as freakish or worse. This is true even though the therapeutic community has become more accepting of alternative expressions—from nonmonogamy to homo- and bisexuality to kink. This cultural climate affects us all no matter how open-minded or free we might think we are. Thus, it's safe to say that most of us have some measure of guilt and shame around our sexuality, especially those

· · · · · · ·

desires or acts that are not considered normal by others or that we may deem to be "abnormal" ourselves.

A mindful approach to sex is not limited to being mindful during sexual activity; it also involves becoming self-aware as a sexual being and conscious of your interests, desires, fantasies, and proclivities. This requires courage and a willingness to explore and ultimately to violate deeply held cultural taboos, at minimum the taboos against sexual self-knowledge and thinking about sexual expression as something intrinsically good or intrinsically spiritual.

One of the core components of Tantric practice is transgression. This aspect is often over-looked in popular Western renditions of the tradition, and it may not be fully appreciated by more conservative practitioners of Buddhist or Hindu Tantra. But we think it is central and that it can be valuable to apply in a contemporary American context, regardless of your belief system. While some claim that Tantra is several thousand years old, we think the argument that Tantra emerged in the early common era is more compelling, and while the early practitioners drew on concepts that were far older, it was in part a movement that resisted—indeed, deliberately violated—the prevailing social norms. Tantric rituals of all kinds were conducted in cremation grounds, places of both power and impurity. The renowned sexual ritual or *maithuna* involved the consumption of meat, fish, alcohol, a type of grain that was considered forbidden, and sexual intercourse in a ritual setting, with others present and sometimes across caste lines.

It appears that these early Tantric practitioners were focused on obtaining power, and that the power was transmitted from women to men through the sexual ritual and the consumption of combined sexual fluids. Over the next few hundred years Tantric ideas and practices were absorbed into more conventional Hindu and Buddhist contexts, and the emphasis on acquiring powers diminished. The focus shifted toward spirituality. Nonetheless, these transgressive aspects persisted.[7]

What's the purpose of violating taboos? First, doing so can create a shock to the system, wherein we discover that something we've always feared or condemned suddenly loses its grip on us. If we've always believed that we would be punished for doing something, and nothing bad happens as a result, we will be released from this limiting belief. On a more subtle level, it can help free us from conventional thinking and preconceptions that we have about ourselves. In other words, breaking taboos can help us become more fully human, provided the transgressive behavior is undertaken with awareness and for the purpose of learning and growth.

Contemporary American society is nothing like India two millennia ago, and it's not much like Indian society today. For the most part, it's pretty easy to find a bar where you can have a few drinks, eat a hamburger, and perhaps meet someone who's up for having a one-night stand.

7 David Gordon White, *Kiss of the Yogini: "Tantric Sex" in Its South Asian Contexts* (Chicago: University of Chicago Press, 2003). We think White's argument about the historical origins of Tantra is compelling..

Having sex in a cemetery might get you arrested for public indecency, but few of us believe that cemeteries are impure places where powerful and menacing spirits prowl. Classical Tantric transgressive behavior simply doesn't carry the same psychological weight in twenty-first-century America; however, breaking your own taboos can still be immensely valuable, especially when it comes to sexuality.

It's very easy to become attached to a specific identity around sexuality. Orientation is perhaps the most obvious example; bisexuality is still questioned by some who believe that people are either gay or straight. The truth is that orientation is considerably more fluid and complex, and interacting with a gender you're not attracted to can be a very interesting form of taboo-breaking and experimentation. Sexual identity involves more than orientation; it includes many other ideas about ourselves and what we like and what we don't. These ideas are often based on preconceptions rather than experience.

Mindful exploration of one's sexual identity and inner taboos coupled with a gentle pushing of one's boundaries is a way to become more integrated and in touch with your sexuality. Intentional experimentation may lead you to realize, for example, "No, I really don't like being spanked," but it might also lead you to discover that spanking someone else turns you on. This is an ongoing process because no one's sexuality is static. What was smoking hot for you at eighteen may leave you nearly indifferent at thirty-five. By the same token, you may discover that something you thought of as icky when you were forty is sexy when you're sixty. If you don't allow yourself the opportunity to explore, you'll never know.

Note that we are not advocating doing things to shock others or going to extremes. We're asking you to find your limits and push them gently. Mindfulness in this context also entails being aware of and sticking to safer-sex protocols, keeping your welfare and that of others in mind, and being sure that you're engaging in behavior that's enthusiastically consensual. There are some risks involved in pushing boundaries, so it's important to be clear, careful, and ethical when you do so. And as always, it's crucial to maintain the ability to observe yourself and how you respond.

To close out this chapter, we want to reiterate that bringing mindfulness to sex can be immensely rewarding regardless of your belief system. Our references to Tantra should not be understood as suggesting that you subscribe to any particular worldview or follow any teacher or set of teachings; however, we think that many aspects of the Tantric approach have value for people who have been conditioned to think of sex as something "filthy" and shameful (we all have, at least to some degree). Practitioners of various forms of "sacred sexuality" often speak of the need to reunite sex and spirit. The truth is that fertility rites are perhaps the most ancient form of human religious expression, so at the deepest level of human consciousness, there is no dichotomy between sex and spirit. Approaching sex with awareness and intention—and a healthy dose of humor—enables us to become more fully ourselves; when we're comfortable in our sexuality, we are far better able to share our light with the world.

Mark A. Michaels and Patricia Johnson, a devoted married couple, have been teaching and writing together since 1999. Internationally known and widely quoted as experts, Michaels and Johnson are the authors of *Designer Relationships* and *Partners in Passion* (Cleis Press), as well as *Great Sex Made Simple, Tantra for Erotic Empowerment,* and *The Essence of Tantric Sexuality* (Llewellyn). They are also the creators of the meditation CD set *Ananda Nidra: Blissful Sleep* (Llewellyn) and co-founders of Pleasure Salon in 2007 to support New York's sex- and pleasure-positive community. Visit www .MichaelsandJohnson.com.

Adrian Buckmaster

• • • • • • •

For Reaching Potential

As a spiritual being, you have infinite potential. Refine possibility by becoming mindful of your heart's desires and consciously taking action toward them while eliminating internal and external barriers. This section offers perspectives and procedures to release the beliefs and habits that hold you back. Ana Holub demonstrates how to free yourself through genuine acceptance and forgiveness. Guy Finley helps you access your true self via authentic awareness in relationships, and Servet Hasan shows you how a nurturing relationship with yourself manifests many of life's gifts. This vision and connection of beingness is honed through Jack Canfield and Deborah Sandella's visualization practice. Tess Whitehurst addresses how to learn from and remove clutter from your mental and physical realms, leaving space for comfortable, mindful living. Alexandra Chauran inspires you to elaborate your personal potential, giving simple, specific techniques to harness the power of community so that you can make a difference in lives beyond your own. Enjoy the following section as you become mindful of your past conditioning and shift into an awareness of loving acceptance of self and others. Gain a greater ability to change what you wish to shift and release the habits and beliefs that do not serve you as you flow through an authentic, mindful life.

· · · · · · · ·

The Mindful Path to Acceptance and Forgiveness

ANA HOLUB

Today, as I sit down to write you a love letter about the path to inner peace, I'm full of gratitude for my life as a teacher, counselor, and author. Yet you should know that before I became a successful forgiveness counselor and peace educator, I lived a full, exuberant, and distressing life. I grew up in New Jersey with a mother who suffered from cyclical depression. I moved across the country to go to university, dropped out and joined a small cult, changed my name, gave away everything I owned, had a baby with the cult leader, discovered I had to be both mom and dad for my child, and my mother committed suicide—all before I was twenty-four. As you can see, I had plenty of accepting and forgiving to do if I wanted inner peace.

Finding the expanded form of forgiveness I now teach turned out to be my ticket to sanity, and it can be yours as well. I'm passionate about my work because the simple, elegant tools of mindfulness, prayer, deep letting go, and reception of divine love will heal anyone who wants to try them. The way is not complicated or hard. What I have witnessed through my twenty-odd years of teaching peace is that with sincerity and dedication, every person can find happiness.

Mindfulness is the practice of becoming gently aware of life in this moment. When we relax into our breath, our bodies, and the natural flow of life as it moves through time and space, we arrive consciously into the present moment. We also become aware of any knots of constriction inside us. These knots show up as fears, compulsions, areas of physical discomfort, and anguish about past memories. When tight spots surface and gain our attention, we have several choices about what to do about them. We can push them away and deny the deep lessons they hold for us, we can fight against them and thereby perpetuate them, or we can release them with loving, compassionate forgiveness. Only if we choose the way of love will we receive the soul teachings that lie buried within even the worst events in our lives. The guided meditation at the end of this chapter will help you explore this intimate and powerful path of healing.

I love the gusto with which my clients reach past their fears and judgments. Like me, they contend with the sadness and pain of their past and use the path of forgiveness to heal their hearts. They learn to let go of guilt and shame, humiliation and jealousy, anger and regret, by diving deep into the vast ocean of divine love. Here they find support, rest, and sanctuary. I've found, through personal experience and my work with others, that this blessing is open to everyone, no matter what happened or when and no matter who was involved.

It seems that the epidemic of disease, addiction, and depression in our world stems from a feeling of being caught in something we can't escape. Feeling sick, trapped, helpless, and hopeless, we do our best to cope. We may reach for drugs, food, sex, and other thrills to help us ease the throbbing ache within but feel ever more depressed when our strategies fail again and again. Fortunately, there is a path of healing that is available to all. This path leads us from mindful acceptance to forgiveness and letting go, and it ends in soul satisfaction and abiding inner harmony. I call it our clear path to peace.

Acceptance

The first step on this path to peace is to take an honest look at what is actually going on inside our hearts and minds. Many of us live in fear of taking stock of "what is" because, to be honest, "what is" doesn't seem to be so great. If we make a "searching and fearless moral inventory" of our lives, as step four of the twelve-step addiction program invites (it's a great tool for everyone), we'll probably find a tall pile of pain. Being honest, most of us realize that we feel anxious and unmoored at least sometimes.

Whenever we're not at peace in the here and now, we're not at peace with ourselves, either. We've forgotten the truth. We've missed the uncomplicated fact that at all times we are completely merged with the whole of the universe and beyond. We've lost our way and stepped out on another trajectory altogether. The answer is to come back to our true reality. We accept, breathe, forgive the entire situation, and let go. In this way we can let the healing power of love into our hearts. Although many modalities and religions describe it differently, it turns out that this path (no matter what we name it) is the only way to peace.

· · · · · · · ·

You may be saying to yourself, "Yeah, easy for Ana to say. She has no idea of the hard-luck, hard-core, hard-time life I've had!" And you'd be right. I have no idea what you've gone through, just as you don't really know my story either. I've written about my difficult childhood and early adulthood in my book *Forgive and Be Free: A Step-by-Step Guide to Release, Healing, and Higher Consciousness.* I hope my story will help you know that you are not alone. We are together in our healing, always.

Yet Spirit doesn't make a separate set of rules for one person or group and another set for others. All of us are equal in our birthright and spiritual awakening, even if our worldly circumstances vary widely. When we accept this truth we get to move on, freeing ourselves from suffering.

Acceptance Can Happen Anywhere

I know that access to Spirit is constantly available everywhere because I watched it unfold one day when I was teaching peace education inside San Quentin Prison. A well-known Buddhist instructor was visiting the scene, and I looked forward to receiving his wisdom. About forty inmates and a few teachers gathered in a musty basement classroom somewhere inside the bowels of San Quentin. It was about as far from glamorous as you could imagine. The ancient, creaky heater thundered on, the chairs were rickety, the paint was peeling, and the whole place felt dilapidated and gray. Most of the guys in our circle had been incarcerated in various prisons for decades. To my disappointment, the famous Buddhist teacher wanted to hear the inmates speak, and he didn't do any teaching until the last ten minutes of the class, but this situation turned out to be immensely positive because the inmate directly across from me in the circle gave me a profound spiritual teaching about acceptance.

The man, I'll call him Mike, was tall, dignified, dark-skinned, and about forty years old. He was a sincere student who had learned a lot about peace education during his time in prison. When it was his turn to speak he explained to us that he'd recently tried to break up a prison brawl. He put his body on the line, doing his best to be a peacemaker in a vicious situation. As often happens in prison, the guards didn't care about his motives and threw him into solitary confinement to punish him for being a part of the melee.

Mike began speaking about his experience down in the prison dungeon. He told us that instead of spending time raging and lashing out, he became still. Instead of agonizing about how his fate was forever to be a victim, he breathed into the present moment. He let go of all recriminations and accepted his situation and surroundings without complaint, even though every excuse to rail against injustice clamored for attention in his mind. Like the wisest Buddhist sage, he suspended judgment about what the moment meant and simply experienced it as whole and complete. He chose to visit the holy instant of Now and experienced a wash of grace that cleansed him to his soul. Even while in solitary, he drank deeply of his liberation.

• • • • • • •

After he returned to day-to-day life, Mike retained the immense glory of that experience. His quiet power emanated magnificently, on par with any famous spiritual teacher. I could feel his presence shining throughout the room, enveloping us in divine love.

That day Mike showed me that anyone, anywhere, can taste spiritual freedom, no matter what the circumstances seem to be. He became a guide for me, showing me the way home with his loving clarity and insistence upon truth. It was a lesson I'll never forget.

If Mike can reach unity with the Infinite while deep in a den of brutality and injustice, then surely you and I can give it a try. We will find all sorts of illusions and made-up realities on our way to Now—but then we can go deeper, diving past them to find the sacredness that breathes eternally in each moment. Aiming for harmony, we'll need an expanded form of forgiveness to purify ourselves of past pain. With trust, we'll find our way to lasting peace.

Acceptance Is Not Apathy or Cynicism

In the industrialized world almost all of us share a collective pressure to fit in. We endure heavy expectations to succeed financially above all other successes, and media images constantly barrage us with messages to look young forever and be happy all the time. We seem to be controlled by institutions (such as government, corporations, religions, education, health care, military) and simultaneously forbidden to ask revolutionary questions. The strain of all of this shared illusion bears down on us like a tractor-trailer full of cement, driving full speed at our vulnerable little bodies. Inside our minds we can hear our stricken voice of fear stammering, "I just can't take it anymore!"

What to do? If we're like Mike, we accept this moment and enter into reverence. We become a beacon of light that shines in service to others. Or, if we don't have the necessary inner skills, we probably choose protection, cynicism, denial, and other forms of fear. Given our shared dismal scenario, we may sink into apathy. Perhaps you've done this yourself and not even realized it. Apathy is a feeling that you don't care about anything. It masks your pain and seems to make it bearable. Apathy often comes with depression, a state of feeling completely buried by despair, helpless to do anything about it. You may also feel overwhelmed and hopeless at times, like you just can't cope with what life is giving you.

You might think that if you don't care anymore, you've accepted the depressing situation. "I've accepted this" in this case really means "I don't know what to do, so I'm going to numb myself to escape the pain. Life's problems are inescapable, so why bother?" Alcohol and other addictive substances seem pretty alluring in this state of mind, yet apathy and depression are not the same as acceptance.

When we accept what is, it doesn't mean that we sink into cynicism and denial. True acceptance is different. Relaxing into the present moment, we notice that we've stopped fighting. With relief, we find instead that we've left the battlefield and opened our hearts to peace.

• • • • • • • •

Being Here Now

When we accept the present moment, we admit to ourselves the ups, downs, and awkward angles of our hearts' anguish and our minds' fear. We relax and trust instead of striving for what we wish was happening and cringing against what we wish was not, especially on a subconscious level. All that pushing for something different than what is *right now* takes a huge, exhausting toll on our health on all levels. It zaps our precious vitality and zest for life.

If we yearn for an experience of something that is not here right now, we automatically find ourselves either craving or avoiding. Our thoughts clamor, "I want that! Yes! Give me that!" or "I don't want that! No! Get that away from me!" This mental situation is the epitome of nonacceptance. We feel that this moment isn't good enough as it is, so we want something different. In fact, we've probably been taught that who we are isn't good enough, so therefore we should be different and better…somehow. I know I was taught this message in countless ways as a kid. Depending upon your family of origin, culture, race, religion, and socioeconomic status, you encountered many ways in which the idea "you should be different because you're not quite right the way you are" could affect your developing mind.

It doesn't matter how you learned the message. What matters is seeing and then deeply knowing that it simply isn't true.

Forgiveness

I've spent most of my life meditating upon the effects of human conflict on earth. I ask myself, "What can be done to save our collective sanity and preserve the health of our beautiful planet?" After much exploration, I've come to see that the path of forgiveness takes us into deeper clarity and redemption than any other inner choice. But what I'm talking about here is not traditional forgiveness. In casual conversation, forgiveness might be defined as a state of mind in which we try to let go of past injustices. We let time go by and let bygones be bygones. We relax our feelings of betrayal and injustice and make a decision to release the blame and anger we feel about the crime (be it large or small) that occurred.

While this kind of traditional forgiveness can be a healing thing to do, it's possible to go much deeper. I call the expanded version "ecstatic forgiveness" because it brings us to the bliss of our true nature. In it we recognize that we are not individuals living temporary, separate lives of pleasure and pain. Releasing all of our angry recriminations and giving them to Spirit, we are healed of hatred and despair. We discover that we are divine, innocent, and love-filled souls. We are all equal, eternal, and constantly in union with our sacred life force, even when we mistakenly act out as frail, angry, and fearful human beings.

With ecstatic forgiveness, we always reach to connect. Our commitment to forgiveness is world work. It spans our environment, family values, social activism, diversity of race and

• • • • • • •

culture, faith, generosity, and creativity. Because we clear our grievances on behalf of ourselves individually and the whole body of humankind, forgiveness is political as well as spiritual. It links us to everyone, everywhere, all the time.

The Benefits of a Forgiving Heart and Mind

Forgiveness will save your life. By this I don't mean it will increase the length of your life in terms of hours and minutes (although it will help you to be healthier, so perhaps you'll get more time as well). What I suggest is that forgiveness will enhance the quality of your life so much that you will feel saved from despair and heartache.

With forgiveness, we are given a healing taste of the light and truth that flow eternally, beaming joy and peace. Without forgiveness, there is no way to reach this state of consciousness on a sustained basis. You might get a flash now and then or a drug-induced taste, but you must unlayer your pain through deep surrender in order to consistently experience the inner peace that is your birthright. No matter what happened, no matter who was responsible for the trauma, and no matter how long ago it occurred, you can heal through this profound inner practice.

Medical research has found that the benefits of forgiving and letting go of grudges have far-reaching effects on our health. For instance, studies show increases in healthy relationships as well as greater spiritual and psychological well-being after participants make the choice to forgive. In addition, forgivers enjoy decreases in the more negative aspects of their emotional and physical life, such as less anxiety, stress, and hostility. Their blood pressure and depression symptoms go down while their heart health, immune response, and self-esteem go up.[1]

Scientific studies show us without question the benefits of traditional forgiveness. With ecstatic forgiveness, the spiritual blessings we receive are extraordinary.

What Is Different About This Kind of Forgiveness?

When you first learned about forgiveness, you were probably about four or five years old. At some point, with a sibling, at preschool or kindergarten, you were taught to say "I'm sorry" and its sister response, "It's okay." It's possible that you traveled all the way into your adult life without any further insight or instruction. You know there are social expectations that you "should" forgive—but what if you don't want to? What if you don't know how? And the clincher: what if you thought you'd already forgiven yourself or someone else for a terrible offense but discover there's so much more inner work to do, and you don't know where to begin?

I have good news: you are not alone! All of us must contend with difficult situations and the constant, omnipresent law of attraction, which pulls learning opportunities into our lives

---

1 "Forgiveness: Letting Go of Bitterness and Grudges," Mayo Clinic staff, http://www.mayoclinic.org/healthy-living/adult-health/in-depth/forgiveness/art-20047692.

• • • • • • • •

over and over again until we heal. Rather than attacking yourself or someone else by feeling that something's terribly wrong, especially because that huge personal issue with your mother/father/ex-partner/children/money/health/career/world event, etc., is still not healed, you can:

- breathe a few deep, relaxing breaths;
- take a mental step back, away from obsessing over the details, to get an overview;
- and accept this moment—this one. I mean THIS ONE.

Once we accept this moment and all that we are feeling, we become ready to employ the HOW method, using Honesty, Openness, and Willingness to proceed. As the twelve-step program recommends, we admit to ourselves that we have a problem. It may or may not include an obvious addiction, but we have a problem nonetheless. The gorilla on our back is an addiction to believing the lies of our ego—the aspect of mind that wants us to feel separate and alone at all costs.

Gradually, we take off our veils of suffering and illusion; see the guided meditation at the end of this chapter to help you do this. We come to realize that this world, which looks so concrete and substantial and seems so real, is actually an alternate reality. In it we take part in a shared yet illusionary realm where we dream together. We dream that bodies are what matters, and each of us is trapped in a separate body with a separate, private mind. By releasing our pain and fear through forgiveness, layer by upsetting layer, we feel lighter, more alive, and more connected to Spirit. We discover that our cherished illusions are completely untrue.

As the Buddha taught, we begin to see and feel the impermanence of each lifetime. We live on earth for only a microsecond, thinking this life is everything. We take it so seriously! As we unwind our sadness and pain, we understand that the whole point of this mysterious exercise is to return to our true essence, sometimes described as the Christ or the Light of God, in order to share the divine love that we are.

The Buddha teaches that everyone has been your mother at some place and time, and you have been everyone's mother…and lover, boss, nurse, child, grandparent, whore, and savior. We intersect constantly beyond the identities of name, time, place, and body. Once we realize this, our suffering takes on a new meaning. "What is this forgiveness opportunity doing in my life?" we may ask. "What themes, arising in so many different relationships, have I come here to heal? How can I clear all samskaras so that none remain?"

A Sanskrit term, samskaras are impressions we make with our thoughts upon our subconscious mind. They can be full of love or full of fear. When our fearful thoughts create separation, isolation, loneliness, and anger, the imprints left behind are hard knots of pain and misery. We recycle these constrictions, sometimes called obscurations, over and over until we release them and let them go. Samskaras of fear can be healed through forgiveness, prayer, meditation,

• • • • • • • •

and focus upon serving others. As Jesus asks in *A Course in Miracles*, "What can there be that stands between what is continuous?"[2]

Even though I'm inviting you to forgive your trespassers—and yourself—in this dynamic way, I also fully appreciate how crazy people can be. I'm sometimes overwhelmed with horror when I contemplate the ghastly violence, rape, and pillaging that humans perpetrate upon each other and the earth. I know that even people who love you can be unbalanced, angry, and vengeful. So please understand that I'm not suggesting you become best friends with someone you don't feel physically safe to be around. This forgiveness work lives inside you, inside your relationship to your Creator. You can forgive by releasing your sadness, anger, and fear, and simultaneously assert any worldly boundaries you feel you need for your safety.

We Can Forgive by Letting Go, Then Receiving Love

Every day I delve into the mystical teaching "let go and let God." If you've heard this saying before, it's easy to casually nod your head and think, "Oh, yeah, I get that." Or, if you don't believe in God, perhaps you cringe when you hear it. Yet what I'm discovering about radically letting go is that every time I think I've achieved it, another layer of reality shows up right beyond my current understanding, beckoning me to expand into it with an even deeper release into divine love.

Summoning our humble yet determined readiness to forgive, we call forth a tremendous wave of sincerity from deep within. We reach all the way, past the dramas of the outer world, to the willingness of our soul. We pray the most profound and life-changing prayer I know: the prayer of giving everything over to the God of our understanding.

EXERCISE: **Guided Meditation for Ecstatic Forgiveness**

The following process (along with real-life stories, suggestions, encouragement, and science about forgiveness) appears in my book *Forgive and Be Free*.

I call this process a prayer sandwich because it begins and ends with prayer (which is a form of conscious intention). In fact, sometimes I refer to it as a peanut butter and jelly sandwich. The prayers are the bread. The peanut butter is the sticky stuff that we decide to release, and jelly is the sweet reward of opening to grace. Reaching to feed ourselves with the prayer sandwich, we recognize that we have run out of options and that the only thing that will bring us peace is a journey within, into the spiritual world. Use this process anytime you feel an upwelling of distressing emotions you'd like to heal. It can be a quick clearing or an extended retreat into examining your life

---

2   *A Course in Miracles* (Mill Valley, CA: Foundation for Inner Peace, 1992), 460.

· · · · · · · ·

and its patterns. Either way, its simple elegance will help you to calm yourself, inquire within, and transform sadness into joy and pain into peace.

Step One: The Opening Prayer

Your prayer is best if it's spontaneous. Just talk to Spirit, using whatever name is comfortable for you, and ask for help. Slow down, breathe, and center yourself. This step reminds you to take your healing seriously, giving it respect. It also allows you to create a sacred space or, more accurately, to meet the sacred space that already exists. With prayer, you become conscious of what is holy, acknowledging the aliveness that creates and gives life. Ask for assistance and support, enlarging possibilities beyond your painful thoughts and emotions.

If you desire, welcome the assistance and presence of spiritual teachers, angels, masters, or saints. They are happy to help, if asked. Welcome them into a council circle convened just for you.

Step Two: Releasing

Now that you have entered a sacred space and your celestial team is in place, you are ready to release whatever is bothering you. Examine the story that is running in your mind. There may be a few or just one repeating drama that has lots of discordant emotions that go with it. Your thoughts, when you believe them, bring up the emotions that are now upsetting you. Take time to examine them with honesty and breathe with them. Be bold and courageous—feel the feelings! As you feel them, breathe them out of your body with an exhale. Focusing on the outbreath, keep releasing and learning about the contents of your mind. Certain places in your body may want your attention or memories may arise or you may have realizations about certain repeating thoughts and patterns. Keep breathing all thoughts, emotions, and sensations out of your body using HOW: Honesty, Openness, and Willingness.

For some people, a visualization helps at this point. Imagine a sacred altar, complete with candles, a white cloth, and flowers. Its energy is pure, eternal, perfect love. It is the altar of Spirit. Lay your burdens down before the altar, watching as they disappear immediately before the light. Another image that works well is to release all of your suffering into the vast pool of divine love, where you float in the sacred space of your prayer. Whether you use the altar or the pool of love or something else that helps you, the main purpose is to allow the suffering to arise without judgment. It comes for healing and to teach you about itself, then it is gone.

When you release, you will notice that the other people in the story don't seem as evil or scary anymore. You may perceive them as actors in a scenario that you created as a soul, here to help you learn and grow. Dropping all judgment, release all of your assumptions about them and focus on clearing out the cobwebs in your heart and mind. Remember that the other people are also perfect, innocent children of Spirit, just like you, equal in love and magnificence.

Step Three: Receiving

When you've let go of everything that is available to release in this moment, you will notice a natural shift. First there is an empty feeling, like a pause between the inbreath and outbreath. Then you will have an impulse to start breathing in. Use your inhale to begin drawing the grace, light, and love of the sacred space into your body. With each exhale, relax deeper into the process. Continue drinking this pure life force, letting it feed your body, your emotions, and your mind. It has a wisdom all its own.

Just say yes to it and let it do its work. This is the only true healing we can experience—one of gentle, compassionate love. Tune into the space above your head; opening up, invite this grace to come down into your body, letting it settle into your bones, muscles, nerves, cells, and the spaces between cells, and go out through your feet. Receive love and grounding as it rises up for you from the earth. Give special attention to any spots that you opened up during step two. Keep going until you feel completely saturated with love.

Step Four: The Closing Prayer

By now, you'll be feeling relaxed and peaceful. Your soul will feel satisfied that it did a great job in remembering Spirit as the source of all healing. Your body will be enlivened and your cells will be dancing with joy. This is a great time to give a prayer or intention of thanksgiving to life, to your helpers, and for the wisdom you received from this process. Love is overflowing from you now, so gather the power of your council circle and, together, give this love away to all of creation. After all, we do not awaken alone—we awaken together!

When you feel complete, say something to close the circle, such as *amen* or *so it is*. This grounds and completes the prayer sandwich, signaling to your mind that the session is over. Trust that the healing grace you welcomed into yourself will keep integrating in your life, giving you further understanding when the time is right.

This process is a simple, effective way to walk the path of ecstatic forgiveness. It turns every feeling of shame, guilt, anger, and misery over to Spirit while showing us the meaning of our life's purpose, which is to live in peace. It fills us with pure love and extends into all of creation, including every awakening soul on our beautiful planet. It brings joy where there was pain and wisdom where there was ignorance.

Practice the prayer sandwich. After you feel comfortable with the steps, this process can become your path to clarity, your way to connect with your deepest self, and a wonderful avenue for profound stillness in meditation. You will find that accessing your intuition becomes much easier as you clean your inner temple, and decisions about your life and service will come to you effortlessly.

Forgiveness Is Not About Pain—It's About Joy

Ecstatic forgiveness offers us our clear path to peace. We choose it not as an intellectual ploy but as a direct, prayerful experience. We do it because we fervently desire joy and soul communion, and we're willing to go through whatever cleansing it takes to receive it. No matter what seems to be blocking the path, we insist upon compassion and freedom. And we gladly give to Spirit not only the suffering of this world of duality but also all the blessings and small miracles that brighten our days.

There is no need for forgiveness once we're living full-time in union with the One, yet while we awaken from our sleepy dream it is necessary. The forgiveness path gives us tremendous support and points us in the direction of joy. It opens our intuitive abilities and aligns us with our positive work in the world. It energizes us with newfound determination to live in personal freedom as well as in service to others and our beautiful planet. Forgiveness saves us from eons of recycling our mistaken thoughts about life. Its constant invitation is simply this: step out of war and come home to love. What could be more poignant and essential right now than this?

Tina Bolling

Ana Holub is a forgiveness counselor, author, poet, and peace educator. She holds a BA in peace studies and an MA in dispute resolution from Pepperdine University School of Law. Ana is also a certified domestic violence counselor and radical forgiveness coach. Over the past twenty years she's worked with thousands of people, including teens, couples, inmates, at-risk families, nonprofits, businesses, and schools. Her latest book is called *Forgive and Be Free: A Step-by-Step Guide to Release, Healing, and Higher Consciousness*. For free downloads, books, CD, e-courses, and sessions, contact Ana at www.anaholub.com.

· · · · · · ·

Breaking Dependency to Live an Authentic Life

GUY FINLEY

Have you ever wondered why, with so many people talking about the need to make authentic change in their lives, real self-change remains so elusive? For those of us who have already started walking this path that leads to being a more authentic human being, one thing should be pretty obvious: while one part of us wants to part ways with who (and what) we know we can no longer be, another part of us clings tenaciously to the same! We feel stuck. We want to let go but find ourselves more or less addicted to our existing relationships, dependent on them for the familiar sense of self they lend to us. And, as it often happens with interior struggles of this order, we lose sight of our original aim so that, little by little, rather than working to free ourselves from our unseen dependency on people, possessions, and "powers" outside of us, we find ourselves blaming them for our unwanted circumstances. The truth is that it's impossible to make any real change in our lives as long as we remain convinced that what needs changing is:

- The person we live with
- The masses of uninformed people around us who just don't get it
- The conditions we see as being beyond our power to change

- The pain or regrets of the past that keep pulling us down
- All of the above (or you fill in the blank)

Do you know anyone, including yourself, who hasn't struggled to change the problem areas in their lives only to realize, when all is said and done, that not much has changed save for one's growing level of frustration? Yet, as strange as it seems for now, it is just this realization—of having failed to liberate ourselves—that is a required leg in our journey to becoming fully independent. There are good reasons why we must face this disappointment before we can be truly self-determining, but underlying them all is this: only by awakening to the ineffectiveness of our past actions—and to our present level of awareness that gives rise to the same—does it become possible for us to shatter the limitations inherent in who and what we have been up until now.

When we've directly known the futility of trying to change others, hating our own weaknesses, or the waste of railing against a world that won't stop wobbling, one simple truth shines out like the beam from a lighthouse that pierces the darkest of nights: nothing within or around us can possibly be made different until we see, without equivocation, that *we* are the world that must change.

If you've already come to this important realization, or even if you're just starting to suspect its truth, then the bright facts that follow will seem like a reunion with trusted old friends.

Freedom Is Your Destiny

One day as I sat in my house I became aware of an irritating buzzing sound. I soon realized that a fly had become trapped, and it was furiously trying to escape. This poor creature kept banging into the window, shaking its little fly head, and then flying into the window again. It kept battering itself against the window until I couldn't ignore the situation any longer.

As I observed this futile battle—between the fly's will and the unwilling window that it could neither break through nor understand—it occurred to me that this everyday event contained a kind of celestial message; in it was a lesson about the presence of higher forces at work within us whose very purpose in life is to help lift us above our present level of self. Let's look into this beautiful idea together.

First we must ask why this intrepid fly was beating itself into the window. Clearly, this tiny creature wanted to get outside. But why does a fly want to get outside?

It may sound silly (at first), but even a fly has a destiny, and much in the same manner as we are moved to complete ourselves, so too is it compelled to seek what it must. To what end? It wants to fulfill the purpose of its little fly life. It's fairly vital here for us to understand that this fly did not create its own purpose; we can't separate the reason for a creature's existence from its nature. And, as such, it can no more escape its will to be free than it can hope to fly without wings—which brings us to our next important insight.

· · · · · · · ·

The only way that any creature—from insects to sentient beings—can fulfill its life purpose is by being free to do so. Within all creatures is this longing to be free—an unyielding wish that is the expression of its need to do what it was put on earth to do.

You and I feel this exact same longing. Every heartbeat passing through us is attended by this silent need to be free, yet flying in the face of this longing is what feels like an inescapable fact of life: not a day goes by where we don't crash headlong into some invisible barrier that seems to stand between us and fulfilling our God-given destiny.

Even after knocking ourselves senseless with repeated run-ins with life's windowpanes—so that there are times when we're not even sure what we're doing anymore—this innermost cry for freedom still sounds out. Then something lifts us up from the floor, taking us into battle once more to challenge our sense of being captive. It would seem, intuitively, that some part of us is trying to get through to us with this distinct lesson: the only way we can fulfill our destiny is if we are free to do so. And we *are* free—we just don't know it yet!

Please ponder this next idea until you can see the liberating truth behind it: nothing in creation can keep us from fulfilling our highest of possibilities. How can we know this is true? By seeing that life itself has placed this longing within us and has, accordingly, already placed within us everything that we need to succeed.

This means that there can be only one thing (temporarily) in our way: an unseen complicity with unconscious parts of ourselves that keep tricking us, deceiving us into seeing ourselves as needing something that can set us free! Much like the Wizard of Oz made Dorothy and her friends tremble before his pretend powers—so that for this fear they would increasingly depend on the false powers he projected—so it's true of our lower nature: it too has a thousand tricks up its sleeve. First it convinces us of our captivity; then it promises us the power we need to escape it. But we need have no further fear of this interior trickster; after all, who sits in awe of some mysterious magician after seeing through his illusions? The moment we see the truth that nothing real stands between us and the freedom that we seek, the "windowpane" that once stood between us and our own highest possibilities just disappears.

Breaking the Unseen Chains of Being Codependent

If we're going to learn how to let go and outgrow our present limitations—the parts of us keeping us from making the positive changes in ourselves that we know we must—then this should be clear: our first task is to shed some much-needed light into wherever it may be that we're still in the dark about the nature of codependency. The more mindful we can be of its unseen presence within us and the invisible ways in which it keeps us in its grip, the sooner we will be set free from its captivity.

· · · · · · · ·

Generally speaking, codependency can be defined as follows: any form of unconscious conduct between ourselves and others that is in some way self-compromising, self-limiting, and ultimately self-destructive. This negative behavior also includes the ways in which we unknowingly enable the self-harming parts of others.

That said, we should also acknowledge various forms of what can be called "positive codependency"—a form of a beneficial symbiosis. For instance, in nature we can see there's a relationship between the flowers and the bees that serves to nourish both parties.

Higher up the scale of being, partners in life can be rightly codependent upon one another, but only as long as they work individually, using spiritual principles such as self-reliance and conscious selfless action to prevent themselves from becoming wrongly dependent upon each other. In fact, a beautiful and very natural codependency is intended to transpire between opposites such as male and female where, through the natural exchange of energies, everything from conception to consciousness may be brought to its next higher level of fruition. In this example we can see how positive codependency actually serves to develop individual possibilities, and that's good in every sense of the word.

But what we want to understand is negative codependency: a mutually destructive relationship in which the parties involved enable or otherwise strengthen certain characteristics in one another that either destroy or severely limit their own higher possibilities.

We should all be pretty familiar with the external forms of codependency. One example we're all familiar with is the woman who remains in a relationship with an abusive man. In the end her fear of being alone—of not knowing who she would be without alternatingly caring for or cursing him—allows his dark side to grow and eventually consume them both.

Or perhaps someone enables their best friend, who is an alcoholic, by not speaking up—never saying, unmistakably, "Your behavior is destroying both of us; either you start taking real steps to rise above your present condition or you leave me no choice: much as I care about you, I'll no longer be a part of your life!"

But there are other forms of codependency, largely unseen because they tend to be more internalized; they are far subtler in their appearance but no less sinister or destructive.

Imagine for a moment two friends who have gone to a club to share a few drinks. Each is busily putting on a show for the other across the table, working hard to appear as though he has the world on a string. This scene should be familiar enough to us. We have all been there.

Between drinks each portrays—and basically states to the other—"Everything is just great!" But if we were able to read between the lines, see through the stage performance, the following represents what isn't being said but is most clearly implied:

"I'm going to pretend that everything in my life is just great, and when you start talking I'm going to agree with you that everything is great for you too. That way—if you act as though you

· · · · · · · ·

believe me and I give you the same courtesy—then at least for the next hour, while we sit here drinking together, we can depend upon one another to feel good about ourselves and our lives."

Can you see the secret codependency playing itself out in this everyday scene? Even as each deceives, he is being deceived by the other so that in this unspoken agreement, they enable in one another parts of themselves that believe the appearance of being happy is the same as actually being happy.

Or perhaps, and just as likely, two women—long-time friends—sit together at lunch and complain about how upset or disappointed they are with their lives. What is the nature of their painful pact in this instance? How are they codependent? Here is what lies hidden within their unspoken and unconscious dependency on one another: "Okay, you can unload all of your unhappy thoughts and feelings on me, as long as we agree that when you're done it's my turn to dump my discontentment on you."

The dark sense of solace they find in each other is secretly the seed of further sorrow because it ensures that they will remain captives of the very limitations they lament. And what are these unseen, self-imposed limitations?

Each has agreed that the reasons for the negative condition of the one across from her are based in fact. This mutual deception has many far-reaching implications beyond what's seen with just the casual glance.

Whenever we get caught up in some pain and start complaining or crying about it, we actually believe (albeit totally unconsciously) that what we are telling others and ourselves is based in reality itself. In these same moments our stated belief—that we are somehow inescapably compromised or impossibly incomplete—is strengthened because someone is looking at us and sending along the unspoken message, "Oh yes, poor you!"

But if we wish to break free of any such codependent pattern, we must take a deliberate step back from our own practiced stage performance and choose instead to witness what's actually taking place as a result of our act.

For example, we must see that whenever we consent to or otherwise agree with anyone's dark assessment of their life, we are effectively telling this person, "Yes, that is true and, sad to say, what else can you do besides lament in the way you do?" Our actions and sentiment hide a secret message that silently says: "Sure…given your present conditions, I understand the prison you are in; it's only natural for you to feel like a captive!"

But the real reason we lend this willing ear to others (who depend upon us to believe in their story) isn't that we're really that concerned or otherwise compassionate. Truth be told, the underlying motive behind our appearance—dare we choose to see it—tells another story altogether.

We enable others in situations like these because we're afraid of how negatively they'll react if we don't agree with their side of the sad story. Implicit but never spoken in all such conversations between secret codependents is something like this:

"Look, what I am telling you now is true, so whatever else you may do, don't challenge this view I have of my life. And if you don't agree with my conclusions, then I will take your noncompliance as a threat and treat you accordingly."

Haven't we all been on both sides of uncomfortable moments such as these? How authentic are we being in these moments—to either our friend or ourselves—when we agree with what we know is wrong for everyone involved? Which sets the stage for the following key lesson: *the self that feels itself at risk in these times—the unsure self that not only looks for but attaches itself to codependent relationships—cannot possibly be the real you.*

Let's see why this has to be true.

Who you really are—your true self—quietly knows that you are here on this earth to grow, to realize through life's innumerable lessons your own highest possibilities. We all feel this constant nudge to know the truth of who and what we are in reality; it's a tireless longing for that touch of some greatness not yet known but never far from sight. And since the existence of this higher self-possibility is universally, timelessly acknowledged as being true, then it follows that your life is not and cannot be about agreeing to live with self-imposed limitations.

Taking this newest discovery to heart, can we see how all the pieces of the puzzle are starting to fit together? The following three points should help make the picture clear.

We've already realized (thanks to our earlier study) that our longing to be free is one and the same as our innermost wish to fulfill our true purpose—our highest possibility—in life.

We've also seen that whatever this higher intelligence wishes for us to know as true is always made possible by that same timeless wisdom.

Which means: the goodness of the whole universe stands behind us if we will put these truths before us.

Good odds, don't you think? Now, just to be sure we're seeing the big picture, let's bring in three additional insights to summarize our discoveries up to this point.

Any nature acting within you—by whatever name you call it—that tries to justify or otherwise explain to you why you need to ache or hate is dead-set against your wish to be independent and inwardly free.

Any part of you that has "good reasons" why you should feel bad isn't good for you and wants nothing good for you, regardless of its promises!

The level of self responsible for creating and sustaining any form of codependent relationship has no strength of its own; it wins its victory over you by tricking you into believing that the only solution there is to your weakness is to call upon the powers it says it will lend to you...after they're needed!

• • • • • • • •

Spiritually speaking, this condition is like just happening to find a friendly tow truck at the scene of your car accident—a wreck you don't know was also caused by the same tow truck driver cutting your brake line an hour before! You know the old expression "fool me once, shame on you; fool me twice, the shame is mine." This is why, throughout time, saints and sages have always prescribed the same cure for anyone seeking a real way out of what seems a recurring nightmare. "Wake up!" they cry in unison. "You're asleep in a dream that is not your own."

The suffering inherent in any painful or otherwise codependent relationship is due to one thing: it is the destructive effect of our having forgotten who we really are. Why else would we so anxiously seek the approval of others as the measure of our worth or, conversely, be so easily crushed by someone who withholds a smile from us? When we don't know who we are, we look to anyone and everyone to tell us; accordingly, we are defined and—without ever knowing what's happened to us—we find ourselves confined by our (unconscious) consent to see and to value ourselves through the eyes of others. Being mindful is the act of remembering—in the heat of any unwanted moment—that anything in yourself that is unforgiving or otherwise afraid of life is not and cannot be a part of your authentic self.

We have uncovered the root cause of codependency, whatever form it may take in one's life: our true self sleeps, which means we are left with only two possible choices if we wish to break the bonds of dependency. Either we do the interior work required to wake up and remember who we really are—that we might reclaim our innate independence—or we continue to create and then enter into false relationships that hold us as unwitting captives.

For the knowledge, insights, and encouragement we need to move ahead, let me retell an abbreviated but updated version of a short story as written in one of my earliest books, *The Secret of Letting Go*. Its surprise ending sheds important light on exactly what we need to see, then start doing, if our wish is to start living from our authentic self.

The Merchant Marine Who Woke Up and Found His Way Home

A World War II merchant marine vessel sailing somewhere off the coast of Africa gets blasted out of the water by an enemy torpedo. One sailor makes it to shore, where he finds himself in enemy-held territory. It's clear: at all costs he has to get out of that hot spot and reach home.

One late afternoon, this sailor, the hero of our story, finds himself hiding in a small harbor area when an enemy tanker slips in to be refueled. By its markings, he quickly realizes that here is his chance: the ship is heading to a distant port where he might be able to contact some underground friends. Knowing it would be much safer for him to reach this neutral port than to be left deep behind enemy lines, he creeps onto this ship under the cover of night. He soon discovers a safe hiding place, tucked into one of the lifeboats under a canvas cover.

Later that night the tanker sets sail, but soon it runs into a blockade. Peeking out from his hiding place, our hero can see his country's flag flying high on the helm of an approaching cruiser.

• • • • • • • •

A moment later, cannons roaring, the defending cruiser attacks the ship he's on, and soon the deck where he was hiding is all but destroyed. Not knowing what else to do, he leaps down a flight of stairs, seeking whatever shelter might be down there. But instead he finds himself in cold, swirling waters, which can only mean the ship must be on the verge of sinking!

That same moment the tanker takes another direct hit of some kind; its lights flicker and die out. People shouting in a foreign language seem to have him surrounded; as his panic sets in, he ducks into the first open cabin he can.

Suddenly, another larger blast rocks the tanker, knocking the stowaway sailor right off of his feet; his head hits the frame of a steel bunk bed, knocking him out cold. Moments later, as he slowly comes to, red emergency lights are blinking, klaxons are sounding, and a thick, heavy smoke fills the hallways.

Our hero struggles to make sense of where he is and what has happened, but he can't recall anything; everything is foggy. Taking stock of his situation as best he can given his temporary amnesia, the first thing he realizes is that his clothes are wet and ice-cold. "Better get into something dry," says one of his clearer thoughts. "Yes, that seems wise," he answers himself.

Opening one of the closets in the darkened cabin, he pulls out the first hanger of clothing he can get his hands on. He quickly climbs into the uniform, remarking to himself how well everything seems to fit. Meanwhile, all around him, in a growing crescendo—no translation needed—he can hear people shouting, "Abandon ship! Abandon ship!"

At that point the emergency generator kicks on and the red lights in his cabin flicker back to life. By instinct he turns to look in the mirror on the nearby wall and sees himself standing there in a captain's uniform! As he looks at himself, all decked out in his well-appointed suit, he completely forgets his desperate situation. But, less than a heartbeat later—in part because of the very image he had celebrated just a moment before—a flood of fearful thoughts runs right through him, washing away his pride.

"Oh, no!" he thinks to himself, shaking his head to clear his confusion, but a single thought keeps pushing itself into his consciousness. His heart sinks in the waves of his realization, along with its implicit responsibility: "I must be the captain of this ship, which means it's my sworn duty to go down with it!"

Fortunately, as he continues to look at himself in the mirror, his amnesia begins to clear; a moment later, everything about his situation comes back to him in a merciful flash. He remembers his true identity. What a relief! He isn't the captain of this doomed ship after all. Laughing out loud at his own folly, he thinks, "Thank the stars, this is not my ship!"

With his memory restored, he runs upstairs, gathers his strength, and leaps from the doomed vessel into the cold, dark Atlantic waters. Moments later he is rescued by his own countrymen, and in no time at all he is safely back home.

· · · · · · · ·

Remember Your True Identity and Realize Self-Liberation

The rescue of the man who forgot his true identity gives us a glimpse of a certain pivotal point— the appearance of a new possibility in our work to be free. This key moment in the story comes when our hero awakens to remember his true identity and (gladly) realizes that since he isn't the ship's captain, it isn't his responsibility to go down with it! Now, let's see if we can apply this same life-saving idea to those places in our lives where we suspect unseen codependence may be dragging us down.

What about that relation "ship" called remaining with an abusive partner, consenting to some compulsive habit, or otherwise justifying substance abuse? For that matter, and as part of any codependent pattern, perhaps something within has told you that's what "good captains" do... suffer the fate of their ship, regardless of the consequences to their soul. Well, here's the true story. Welcome it, for it has the power to shatter the chains of every codependent relationship— no matter how long you've believed otherwise.

That sinking sensation of being all alone, that dreaded feeling of inadequacy, those worried fearful thoughts...none of them, not a single one of them, is your ship! Yes, *the feel is real, but the why is a lie.* The only way anyone would ever agree to be defined by such dark thoughts is if he was suffering from a kind of amnesia, similar to what almost cost the merchant marine in our story his life. Living in this state of spiritual sleep is the same as unconsciously identifying with whatever "uniform" one finds oneself wearing in any given moment—for instance, the uniform of:

- The one who is a perpetual victim
- The one unable to get a break
- The one too weak to walk away from what is wrecking you
- The one who remains in a place clearly wrong for you, but who stays there for fear of finding yourself somewhere worse

Perhaps you can add other false identities to this list, but here's the main point: each codependent relationship in which we find ourselves also finds us decked out in the appropriate "uniform" for that role. And with each of these false identities comes the false sense of duty that one must be true to it, even though it may lead to one's destruction.

These familiar but totally unconscious roles we play—born from false images formed in us over time—outweigh even common good sense. Our original intelligence is buried beneath an alluring sense of self-importance, induced in us by having unconsciously identified with a fictitious sense of self. And once deceived as such, our story, including its inevitable outcome, is all but written for us. We're left with no other conclusion: "I am the captain, I must adhere to a captain's duty," and down we go with the ship!

We must do as the hero in our story did: he escaped a bad dream caused by the blow to his head when he remembered his true identity, his true self. For us this means—at the outset, anyway—working to become conscious of what amounts to a consensual relationship with what obviously compromises our best interests.

More than just being complicit in a destructive relationship with someone or caught in a vicious cycle of substance abuse, we must also agree to see how our fear of what others may think of us makes us fawn before them and how we think ourselves into some form of daily despair by constantly measuring ourselves against others who seem more successful or happy than we are.

The new and higher understanding we need—to leap from our present state of dependency to one of greater independence—is inseparable from an awareness of our true self. Only through this order of mindfulness are we empowered to see, remember, and act upon what we now know is true: any part of us that accepts as inevitable some punishing state is also its perpetrator, which means it is not the "friend in need" and protector it pretends to be! The light of this insight is the same as the power we need to see through and then let go of what is our "enemy in deed."

It may seem difficult at first, but to see that nothing real stands between you and your wish to be free is the first step toward winning the independence for which you long. The parts of you that "believe" in your inadequacy, in your inability to make meaningful changes in your life, are also the same ones that send you out looking for solutions to the very suffering they engender. It's time to stop believing in any nature that on one hand tells you there's no recourse other than to live in the cage of codependency it creates, while its other hand points to a "time when" conditions will be right and then you'll be free.

An Inner Exercise to Increase Your Higher Self-Awareness

The more we intend to uncover the parts of us complicit in creating codependent relationships, and how we're always dragged down by this unconscious proclivity, the more liberating discoveries we will make and the more we will be living our own authentic life. It's a law: ask to see the truth (of yourself), then do what you must to be granted that revelation, and all that has been hidden (from you) will be revealed. This same idea is stated in the New Testament: "Knock, and the door shall be opened to you." Revelation follows your intention to know the truth of yourself, as surely as morning light follows the darkest night. How can we be sure this principle has the power to help solve the mystery of our dependency, to bring an end to unconscious suffering? Because if being unaware of ourselves helps create and sustain our codependent relationships, then there can only be one true prescription to remediate this pain: we must become

• • • • • • •

aware. As Frank Herbert states so simply, so elegantly, in his classic book *Dune*: "The sleeper must awaken."

The problem is, none of us really believe that we are asleep, even though the evidence reflected by our continuing suffering tells a different story. The truth is—as told by all those who have awakened—we live in a world of dreams; we slumber in the subtle psycho/spiritual realms within us, seeing shadows and calling them real.

Sure, we are awake enough in the physical world; we have the awareness required to interact with everyday life—and even to learn challenging new skills—but this level of awareness holds no authority over what now holds us captive. To understand why this superficial level of awareness is powerless to release us from our present prison-like experience of life, we refer to one of the greatest and oldest spiritual maxims of all. When it comes to the secret forces responsible for creating our reality, the inner determines the outer.

Real spiritual exercises are designed to help awaken us to what's taking place within us as it's happening; they are designed to help shed light into the workings of our interior life. To this end, they serve a single purpose: to bring us into a higher level of self-awareness where—because of the intention established by that exercise being practiced—we're able to see what's unfolding within us as it takes place in that moment. Our new relationship with this higher awareness has the power to change everything.

For instance, where before we used to fall, by default, into unconscious agreement with habitual mechanical reactions—literally depending on them to define us and then tell us our possibilities—now, in our awakened state, we're able to detect and then negate this whole dark operation before it gets started!

Simply put, the more awake we are, the less we ache. The celestial intelligence within this higher self-awareness is all the power we need to be free because it's impossible for this wisdom to act against itself. Standing in its living light we cannot be deceived. We see that we are neither the weakness we feel, nor are we the one in contempt of ourselves for its power over us. Whatever our pain a moment before was just because we had been asleep to ourselves, that's all. And now we choose to be awake!

In that same instant old fears fall away. Doubts disappear. Pains born of past regrets lose their hold over us. This light shatters whatever had chained us, as surely as dawn dispels the fearful shadows cast by a full moon at night. Armed with this understanding, let's examine a powerful inner-life exercise beginning with the special knowledge we'll need to start seeing our world through new eyes.

An angel has two wings. On each of these wings—which represent what we need to rise above what is wrecking us—is written one of these two words: YES or NO. These two simple words represent special principles that are the wings of spiritual freedom.

· · · · · · · ·

We must learn to say yes to self-study, prayer, meditation, and contemplating the great restorative powers inherent in the living presence of the Divine. Can you think of other places where learning to say yes to life would help you go higher? For example, how about saying yes to those parts of you that know real effort is always rewarded or that anytime you say yes to your wish to outgrow some former limitation, you're that much closer to freedom from it.

And we must learn to say no to those unconscious parts of us that want us to believe the way our lives have gone so far is the only way they can go. We must say no to the lies this lower nature whispers in our ear whenever it tells us we can't learn something new. We must say no to any part of us that threatens us or that uses pain to make us act out its wishes. NO must be what we tell troubled thoughts that invite us to revisit something painful in our past.

There's really only one way to strengthen this grand spiritual *yes* in you: learn what it means to put truth first, last, and always in your life. For example, always say yes when it comes to being ruthlessly honest with yourself about yourself. And no matter where you are or what you are doing, no matter what you may have done, you can always say yes to starting life over. Say yes to the part of you that knows, regardless of what you see at work within you, there is no such thing as a bad fact. Daring to say yes to whatever is revealed within is like liquid gold. It enriches the right parts of you each time you're made aware of what has been wronging you.

But equally important to taking on this task of saying yes is our inner work of recognizing when and where to say no. We must never allow ourselves to forget that there are many sleeping parts of us that secretly feel good while they get us to do wrong!

Remember: no form of externalized codependent behavior can exist or exhibit itself without some unseen character at work within us providing the right conditions it needs to flourish. With this in mind, here are some common codependent areas where learning to say no sets the stage for our liberation.

Making "Peace" with People Who Would Punish Us

There are parts of us that would rather be punished by unkind people than have to spend one minute being alone, because the only way these same parts in us can exist is if they have someone to resent or fear. We remain in these ruinous relationships because the fear or emptiness we feel in even considering leaving them is felt to be too much to bear on our own. Here's the key to escaping this captivity: this fear that we experience does feel real, no doubt, but it belongs to an imagined self. Collecting and then consciously cultivating this new knowledge of ourselves points the way out if we will walk with its truth in our hand.

To begin, walk away from anyone who "helps" you feel that it is necessary to hurt; leave anyone who causes you pain "for your own good." Here's the rule to remember: never make peace outwardly—or inwardly—with anyone or any psychological state that punishes you. Say no and go! A whole new and independent life awaits you.

. . . .

Blaming Others

Whenever we allow angry parts of us to cast blame upon others for the conditions we find ourselves in, we enable the sleeping nature within us to stay in its dream that if it weren't for others doing us wrong, we would never be so upset and angry, defeated, or depressed.

The truth is there are unconscious parts of us that readily find fault with others in a misguided effort to remain infallible in their own eyes. Each time we blame someone else we agree to remain asleep in this misery-making mistaken identity. Saying no to this nature is saying goodbye to a host of imagined enemies this false self needs to remain itself, as well as to a war that can never be won.

Complaining About Your Life

The negative self that looks out at life—and complains about what it sees—can't see the following fact, but we can: if it weren't for its dependence on some false image of how things "should be"—sustained by a false sense of self created by fearfully clinging to this picture—it wouldn't have anything to complain about!

The more this nature compares what life isn't to its own idea of imagined happiness, the more it complains; and the more it complains, the more real it feels. Say no to this codependent negative nature by learning to choose consciousness over resentfulness.

To speed your journey to freedom from all forms of codependent relationships, it is very helpful to make a list of areas in your life where you find yourself aching for whatever reason. To get you started with this special self-study, I have made a short list of seven suspect places where we tend to fall into wrong relationship with those around us or with our own familiar thoughts and feelings.

We are in unconscious codependent relationships with others whenever we find ourselves:

- Meddling in the lives of others or allowing others to tinker with our troubles

- Gossiping about anything, but especially taking part in denigrating others we know and associate with

- Spreading any form of "gloom and doom," either in a casual conversation or in the confines of our own thoughts

- Agreeing with the hatred of anyone else for any other person, group, or condition

- Taking part in any form of dark inner dialogue with ourselves about some imagined enemy or unwanted circumstance

- Allowing others to make their problems our own so that we have to carry the weight of their discontentment

• • • • • • •

- Entertaining any thoughts from any source—either from within ourselves or from an outside source—telling us that our life is without meaning

Each time we strive to further understand ourselves through our willingness to see some yet-deeper truth about ourselves, then little by little we will attract to ourselves a higher strength that has no problem saying no to what has never cared for us. This new no is one and the same as saying yes to self-wholeness, the secret source of the happiness we had been seeking in all the wrong places.

Self-awakening spells the end of all addictive behaviors and the codependent relationships that attend them. No lie can live in the light of what is true.

Twelve Key Lessons for Mindfulness and Authentic Living

What follows are twelve special truths to serve as a grand summary of all that we have studied together. As you review these higher life lessons, remember the potential light hidden in any timeless truth is only as healing as is your willingness to see yourself in and through its lesson. A few of these insights you will no doubt recognize as "old friends" along the way; welcome them to live by your side, that you might borrow their light when things seem dark. As is true for any of the other right ideas that you've read in this chapter section, choose to ponder them until they agree to show you their light, which they always will. Soon you'll learn to see their authentic wisdom as being the foundation of an authentic life.

- As we discover more truth about ourselves, we gain insight into everyone else around us. Our higher psychology makes it possible to interact with others in ways formerly impossible to us, including being truthful without being hurtful.

- There is a big difference between making a mistake and thinking of oneself as being a mistake; any compulsive wish to be seen as perfect in the eyes of the world is a punishment that can never be a part of true peace and contentment.

- There is nothing we can say to a tornado to make it stop whirling. The same holds true for when and what we should say to people caught in negative states. Usually, if left alone, the storm they are in just fades away because it runs out of mechanical energy.

- The nature in us that sees any moment as a tunnel without a light at the end of it *is* the darkness that it sees.

- Not only is perfect awareness perfect protection, but in this order of mindfulness it is also the highest promise of ourselves fulfilled.

- It is impossible to resist something and learn from it at the same time.

• • • • • • •

- Fear is a lie; the same frightened self that seeks rescue secretly confirms its condition as being real with each of its plaintive calls for help.

- Anything in us that resists exploring the cause of a sorrow is itself part of the pain it prefers to keep unexposed.

- Never run from what you don't understand, as it will be waiting there for you when you stop.

- Our needless heartaches end as we see that the healing we hope for begins with letting go of our unseen relationship with those parts of us responsible for our self-hurting.

- The Divine loves those who do what is true in spite of the circumstances.

- Never forget that along the path to the truly authentic life, your true self cannot be confined by dark thoughts or feelings any more than sunlight can be held captive in a jar.

Mindi Morgan

Guy Finley is the author of *The Secret of Letting Go*, *The Secret of Your Immortal Self*, and more than forty other books and audio books on the subject of self-realization, several of which have become international bestsellers. Each week over 200,000 subscribers in 142 countries read his popular free newsletter. In addition to his writing and appearance schedule, Guy is the founding director of Life of Learning Foundation, a nonprofit center for self-study in Merlin, Oregon, where he speaks four times each week. Meetings are ongoing and open to the public. For more information about Guy and to receive five free downloadable gifts from his foundation, visit www.guyfinley.org.

Mindful Manifesting
FINDING LIFE PURPOSE AND FULFILLMENT

SERVET HASAN

Human nature is such that we have the ability to change ourselves for the better. It's simply a matter of taking the time to put into practice what we will discuss. The universe is extremely orderly: for every effect, there is a cause. I will explain how nothing "just happens." If we purify our motivation and find the cause, then we can control our destiny.

This chapter is all about finding our power from the inside out. By cultivating self-love, we will uncover the gifts and abilities that lie waiting within. I will share some of the tools that facilitate tapping into them, such as taking our power back by dropping our pretenses and self-perceptions. I will demonstrate how to stop living in fear and worrying about what has already happened or what will happen next, thus opening ourselves up to receive the abundance available to us in each and every moment.

As we learn to let go of our limiting beliefs, we move into co-creation with the universe. We do this by accessing the power that made us who we are in the first place. Through mindfulness practice we learn ways to train our attention, clarify our awareness, and develop skill sets that will allow us to be of service not only to others but to the person who matters most: you. When you love who you are, fulfillment will find you.

There are also exercises to help you get to that place inside of you where your personal freedom resides. You are what you believe yourself to be. You don't need to be a positive thinker and tell yourself that you're loved and strong and capable. You don't need to do that because you already are. The problem is that you doubt it, which probably tends to happen quite often.

This is when mindfulness is crucial. Mindfulness gives you direct access to tune into your inner being and develop an awareness of what you are right now. It is much easier to change and become something different from a place of awareness. And to get where you want to go, it is very important to start where you are. By following the practices and exercises, you can go within, know what you desire to be, and become exactly that.

Accepting Love

Somewhere around the age of fifty (yes, it took that long) I discovered that the gift that God/Creator/Universe gives us is being—not life, but being. I believe there's a big difference. Life is what you do about being, but being is just…well, being. That means we are already perfect. If we are made in the image and likeness of what created us, there's nothing more we need do except be who we are. What that translates into is the fact that we don't have to be what we think we should be—or, worse, what others think we should be. If we can be what we are, then we become love, and as a result, we bring about all that love is: happiness, joy, sharing, forgiveness, compassion, caring, and on and on.

Have you noticed that when you stop beating yourself up for all the things that you should be and just love yourself exactly as you are, things begin to flow? There's a reason for that. If you think you should be an artist, but are stuck working in corporate America and continually beat yourself up for that, then you are blocking the flow of the universe to give you what you want to be in the first place.

This works in all areas of your life. When two people are in a relationship of any kind, whether as a mother and daughter, parent and teacher, or romantically—especially romantically—you will find that if both parties accept each other exactly as they are, eccentricities and all, there will be love. When we accept ourselves and other people exactly as they are, that is the deepest expression of love, and a natural result of that is happiness.

Imagine that you are a container filled with the most precious substance on earth. Let's say the content is pure gold. It doesn't matter how beat-up the container gets, how dented or dirty or ugly or wrinkled or messed up. It's still filled with gold. What we are is not the container that we call a body. What we are is what's inside, and that can be described as nothing less than precious gold.

· · · · · · · ·

The real you within, your inner self, still remains perfect exactly the way it is. This is the truth, and this is why it says in the Bible, "And ye shall know the truth, and the truth shall make you free." You are love and you always will be, for all eternity. And when you give of your true self, which is that love, then all things become possible.

Self-love sounds easy, but for many of us it can be challenging. Remember, it's a process, a journey, and you know when you've arrived there because you no longer feel the need to arrive. Let's explore the path that leads you in the right direction.

Self-Love

If you have a problem seeing yourself as perfect, hang-ups, issues, and all, then think of all the people you know who are fine just the way they are with all those same hang-ups and issues that you think you may have. If you're overweight, then recognize all the people out there who are overweight and just fine, even successful because of it. If they can be, then you can be, too.

One of the basic tenets of most spiritual and religious doctrine is to learn to love everybody unconditionally. What we often don't take into account, however, is that this includes ourselves. After all, our capacity to love ourselves will account for exactly how much love we can give to others. The problem is this is easier said than done. Usually, this stems from the concept that loving ourselves makes us self-involved, arrogant, narcissistic creatures.

But it's not about being special or better than anyone else. It's about realizing that we are all divine beings; therefore, we are all special. Feeling less than anyone else is almost blasphemous in a way. If we are part of a greater source, then we honor that by expressing our authentic selves to the best of our ability. Being the best you that you can be, in your own unique way, is a blessing not only to yourself but to the world. That's why most sages agree that knowing who you are is the greatest knowledge of all.

So who are we really? If you feel you're not pretty enough or smart enough or whatever it is you perceive about yourself, is it really true? One of the most difficult things for people to do is to give up their self-perceptions, especially the negative ones, because they have become part of the story that we subconsciously need to justify our behavior. For instance, if you think you're not smart enough, then it may be okay to not push yourself to be competitive at work. Similarly, if you think you're not pretty enough, this may allow you to stay home and not date. In other words, we are giving ourselves permission to stay within our comfort zones.

Become conscious and mindful of how you observe yourself. More importantly, be cognizant of how much of that story you've been telling—not just to others but to yourself—is fictional. Through mindfulness you can crawl into those dark corners of your mind, wipe away the dust and cobwebs, and uncover the answers you seek. Contemplate your negative qualities. That

• • • • • • • •

means you're going to have to do a bit of honest soul-searching. Ask yourself if there are any underlying dynamics behind your self-perception. If there is a shortage of self-love in your life, this could be why.

We may be perfect spiritually, but on an earthly level none of us are. We all have a foible or two. Remembering this reminds us that self-love is mostly a matter of unconditional self-acceptance with a touch of compassion thrown in. Perhaps we are being hard on ourselves without realizing it. Often we give others much more leniency and support than we would offer ourselves. If someone were having the same difficulties as we are, we likely wouldn't beat them up emotionally the way we sometimes do to ourselves. Our minds can be real terrorists, convincing us that we must fulfill another condition in order to feel good about ourselves. Even if we do fulfill it, it will come up with another stipulation that must be attained before we can say, "Yes, I've accomplished that, and I am fine now." The exercise on page 279 entitled "What's Blocking You?" will help you uncover much of what's standing in your way.

Self-Confidence and Self-Talk

One thing I would like to make clear is that there is no such thing as lack of self-confidence. I can't find a single definition that describes the fact that one is lacking such a thing, and I now know why. It's because you can be just as self-confident that you are fat, ugly, and a complete failure as you can be about how beautiful, attractive, and successful you are.

So what is self-confidence? Well, if confidence is "a feeling or belief that you can do something well or succeed at something," which is the Merriam-Webster definition, then self-confidence would be your ability to tell yourself that you feel that way about yourself. The problem is, that's usually not what we are saying.

Do you hear yourself talking to yourself all day long? Well, guess what? That means you already have the ability to have tons of self-confidence. Now all you have to do is use it to your advantage. Okay, so you may say to me that you talk to yourself all day long about being successful, and you're not. This is why positive thinking alone doesn't work. Nothing ever happens to you that you haven't talked to yourself about first and feel you believe on a subconscious and unconscious level.

Fears and worries come from your subconscious mind. If you are affirming that you can't really get the job you want because you don't have enough education, then no matter what you say and do on a conscious level, you won't get it. The doubt itself is canceling out your ability to consciously perceive this.

Mindfulness will help you become aware of what causes the self-talk and the different states of being you are in. When you become consciously aware of what your subconscious mind and unconscious mind are actually saying, you can then change that reality. What you have in the physical world is the result of what you do in the mental and spiritual dimension. If you change how you think and feel, you will act differently and start talking to yourself in a more productive way. The most effective way to accomplish this is to be quiet and still in order to become aware of the experience of what it would feel like to be where and what you want to be. Imagine what you would act like—what you would be saying and doing and being—if you had what you wanted already. Chances are you wouldn't be acting and saying and thinking the things you are right now.

You don't have to do anything to be happy. If you've ever experienced a moment in your life when you were happy for no reason, you can then understand that at any moment in time you are capable of manifesting joy. If you want to be successful, feel successful. If you want to be an artist, go within and talk to yourself about it and then feel it. You become what you want to be by becoming aware of the things in life you deeply desire to be and then being those things in present time.

First and foremost, be gentle to yourself. I've included an exercise to help you be kind to the most deserving person in the world: you. You can't realize that through anything this world can bring to you. That realization is an inner experience in which you know that you are not only enough, you are already more than enough. Sometimes it's other people, especially those who claim to love us, telling us otherwise who stand in our way. This is also known as conditional love.

Conditional Love

I remember being about twelve years old and finally allowed to wear makeup. I got all dolled up to go to a party. When I got there, this young boy that I had a crush on told me I looked pretty. I think I almost fainted, but that's not the point. The point is that from then on, I somehow never felt pretty without my makeup on. I didn't realize it for years, but when I did, it really affected me.

So much of how we conceive ourselves is actually an accumulation of how others perceive us. Somewhere along the way, we made their ideas our own. The conditions people place on us can often become so ingrained within us that we're not certain if indeed that's how we felt in the first place. This is especially true when it comes to our parents.

If you got good grades and your parents told you how smart you were, or if the opposite were true, you believed them. If you were considered good because you did your chores, or if the opposite were true, you believed them. If you were labeled "well behaved," you believed them. And the list goes on and on. In essence, it seems that you are only as good as what you do, not who you are, which is a glorious soul having an earthly experience.

Consequently, as we get older we continue to strive to please everyone else before we can allow ourselves that same courtesy. We associate their responses to us as our own. In other words, we have a tendency to want them to love us before we can love ourselves. Unfortunately, this is highly unrealistic, as it's difficult to control everyone else's reactions.

As a result, if we are always striving to gain other people's approval of us, we become convinced that we aren't good enough without the blessings of those around us. This is a dangerous message to send to the universe, which is always going to say yes to any command it receives. The universe is really just a cosmic machine. It's your co-creator, your partner in crime, and if it hears you say that you are not worthy and don't deserve to succeed or shouldn't have a lasting, loving relationship, it will oblige. It is set up to fulfill your commands. The universe is made of love, so it can never purposely punish us, which is a good thing since a lot of us seem to do a remarkably good job of punishing ourselves.

One of the most effective ways to overcome this is by trying not to place as much importance on other people's opinions of you. If you have a healthy sense of self-love, you will find it much easier to love others, and it is much easier to accept the love of others if you detach from what they think of you.

When you love yourself, you feel deserving of the good things in life and the powerful support of the universe. This naturally opens the door for the manifestation of your spirit, which will always guide you to become who you were meant to be.

The Difference Between Becoming and Being

Two people I know wanted to be actors. They were both bartending at night, leaving most of their daytime hours free to take acting classes and go on auditions. One went on all of his auditions no matter what, regardless of the fact that he may have been fired any minute as a bartender. The other constantly worried about losing his job if he wasn't there when he was supposed to be, and consequently he missed a few auditions. Guess which one was successful? Should you do a good job? Yes, naturally, you should. But you can be at the job without being in the job. There is a big difference between a bartender who sometimes needs to bartend while he acts and a bartender who sometimes gets to act while he bartends. Thoughts that you dwell on for any length of time become your reality, whether you physically act them out or not.

Cause is a state of being. What you are being is what you think about yourself. If you don't know what you are being, then stop and listen to yourself, and you'll soon find out. Your decisions are the effect caused by that state of being, and when you act upon your decisions you have a result. Cause and effect will create a result. Therefore, nothing happens by accident. For instance, if you are aware of being sick all the time, you will remain ill, and you will probably visit a doctor. If you are certain that you make a great deal of money, you will. Change what you are being and you will automatically change the effect, and then naturally the result will be different.

It sounds easy, but what blocks most of us is fear. Part of what happens when we start to change is we get scared. We are moving out of a comfort zone that is very familiar to us, even if we don't like it. And, believe it or not, it's easier to go back to our old identity because it's most familiar to us. At some point you have to be willing to mentally and physically let go of whatever starts to disappear. If we grab for it back, then we never create the space to attract something new in our lives.

Antiques are not just objects in a store. Antiques can also be outdated ideas that we should have tossed out years ago. Upon closer inspection, most of these old attitudes are just junk, an accumulation of ideas forced upon us by advertisers, the media, and other social networks. Mindfully become aware of what you read and listen to. Society often dictates how ideals should be manifested in reality. For instance, if you are thin, then you must be beautiful. If you have money, you must be happy. Most of us know that's not true, yet we still try to attain the thing that we think will bring us happiness and joy. It is through mindfulness that we become aware of what we truly want and need, by making direct contact with our souls, the source of all knowledge.

Stop Worrying

Worry is the fear of something that will probably never happen. It sounds silly because it is. Yet, even though we know better, it can be hard to break the habit—but it is not impossible. In fact, people do it all the time, and it is absolutely within reach for anyone who has a desire to do so.

Mindfulness eliminates worry by making us aware that it is nothing more than nagging thoughts that keep bombarding our brain. It's the monkey mind that insists on dwelling upon worst-case scenarios and unrealistic predictions. The act of worrying itself is nothing more than that: a lot of obsessive chatter designed to drive us mad. Worrying serves no other purpose. All it really does in the end is suck the energy out of us by distracting us from the present moment. All that does is make most of us feel sick and tired.

When you take the mindfulness path, you will be less likely to get caught up in the ordeal. If there is a concern you truly should bring to your full attention, you will become aware of that and likely find solutions before it becomes a problem. Remind yourself that if there are no facts to substantiate your concern, then you must let it go. Nothing is certain in life, and one of the keys to happiness is being comfortable with uncertainty.

By spending time worrying about the Coulds, Woulds, and Maybes (ugly stepsisters of What If), you'll end up missing out on living in the present and enjoying the moment. Being mindfully aware of this will bring you back to the world of the living. I can't tell you how much of life I

· · · · · · ·

missed when I was younger because I was worried about the future. First I worried about finding my true love, then I worried about him leaving me. I never really relaxed and just enjoyed the relationship. The same thing happened with a job. It took a long time for me to see how much I missed because I was so caught up in worrying about what might happen tomorrow. I wasn't engaged in my own life.

In the end, the only thing worry does is create more of what you are worrying about. When we fear something that hasn't really happened, we are still giving it energy. And we often do that because we feel something is missing from our lives, usually a sense of security, which is really just a state of mind. Cravings can be useful if we don't become obsessive. Otherwise, all they do is agitate us into a state of frenzy.

Constant Cravings

Physical pleasures such as money, sex, and possessions are not inherently bad, and having them is not evil. They are a part of life and in many traditions are referred to as gifts from God. However, if we make these "things" our only source of joy, we become addicted to them, just as we would a drug. Addictive cravings will inevitably cause painful reactions, usually along the line of fear, anger, jealousy, and depression, because they are tied to a fatal attachment. We automatically suffer when there is a gap between what we crave and what we think we need.

Mindful happiness lies not in feeding and fueling our attachments but by reducing and relinquishing them. Buddha's Third Noble Truth states that "freedom from attachment brings freedom from suffering."

There is a way to feel completely fulfilled and satisfied. All you have to do is change your mind about what you think you need. There are many ingredients that contribute to a happy life. It's an even balance of work and play, of close friendships and intimate relationships, the financial freedom to do the things we love to do and the time to be able to do them.

It doesn't matter what you currently have now. The truth is that if you focus on not having what you want or not having enough, then you will continue to not have it. As I've stated earlier, the universe only responds in the affirmative. When we have a mentality of "not having enough," the universe will say, "Great. We'll just give you more lack."

One of the Sufis' favorite characters is the trickster Nasrudin. An ancient tale says that he often appeared to be a complete idiot but was actually a wise and cunning man whose tricks contained brilliant lessons about life.

One day Nasrudin was out walking and found a man sitting on the side of the road, crying.

"What's the matter, my friend?" asked Nasrudin. "Why are you crying?"

• • • • • • •

"I'm crying because I am so poor," wailed the man. "I have no money, and everything I own is in this little bag."

"Aha!" exclaimed Nasrudin, who immediately grabbed the bag and ran as fast as he could until he was out of sight.

"Now I have nothing at all," cried the poor man, weeping still harder as he trudged along the road in the direction Nasrudin had gone. A mile away he found his bag sitting in the middle of the road, and he immediately became ecstatic. "Thank God," he cried out. "I have all my possessions back. Thank you, thank you."

"How curious!" exclaimed Nasrudin, appearing out of the bushes by the side of road. "How curious that the same bag that made you weep now makes you ecstatic."

Countless sages agree. Some have argued that nonattachment is the greatest of all virtues. It is simply the difference between what we desire and what we have. That is why Gandhi, when asked to describe his philosophy of life, needed only three words: "Renounce and rejoice."

When you accept everything as good, true, and beautiful, you move into prosperity consciousness. And, in the end, it will truly awaken your power within you and stop you from being stuck where you don't want to be.

Getting Unstuck

What is it you want to do with your life? What gives you joy? When I ask most clients this, the answer consists of their heart's desire, followed by an explanation of why they can't have it. They often go to great lengths to explain their own limitations.

For example, I knew someone who loved animals but kept insisting that she couldn't possibly live on what she would make boarding cats and dogs in her home. I suggested she start a kennel and not only rescue animals but groom and train them as well. She now has a successful business. Keep your eye on the donut, not the hole. "What's the use" and "I'll never make it" are only ways to commit emotional suicide, since we become what we think and feel.

The trick is to stop looking at the problem and overanalyzing it and to instead start focusing on the answer. Everything you do should be directed at the answer and the results you want and not the need to be right and the fear of being wrong. The only time you have a problem is when you are not looking at the answer. It doesn't matter if you believe this or not; it works. Try it. Next time you have a problem, just say it's not really a problem and look for the answer instead. This frees your subconscious mind to stop believing in it and allows the universe to supply the answer that already existed all along, therefore allowing you to open your hands and receive what you are attracting into your life.

· · · · · · ·

Unclench Your Fists

We receive many blessings in our lives, but there is a fine line between allowing them into our lives and then wanting to possess and hold on to them forever. People, places, things, and events are all an integral part of who we think we are. Our personality uses these as place cards for our identity. Then we infuse them with memories that become deep attachments within our subconscious mind.

As we grow in mindfulness, we learn that on an existential level, we really can't "own" anything. Impermanence is an essential part of life, and the flow of life moves in and out of our hands.

A friend was once obsessed with *The Lord of the Rings*. I didn't mind, so long as she got the life lessons of holding on too tightly. There's a dark side to each of us that is so personified by J. R. R. Tolkien's character Gollum. He was once a free creature who became obsessed over the ring he lost. He goes in search of his precious ring, but in the end it destroys him.

As is the case with many of us, isn't it our fear that provokes us into clutching onto people and places and things? We all yearn to be secure. Usually, this revolves around a need to control our safety and well-being. I see this most often in people who have lost a position of power. I had a client who described his loss as the head of a corporation as if the earth had been pulled out from under him, even though he thought he lacked the ability to be able to pull it off in the first place. Yet this job was his life, and when he was asked to step down he not only lost his identity as a leader, but as a person.

Mindfulness gives us the gift of an opportunity to explore our fear-filled attachments. When we do, we can willingly unlock our fingers and release what we hold so tightly in our hands and hearts. Hold on to these things lightly, gracefully, and receive the lessons and blessings before relinquishing them. The Law of Circulation is that you always get back what you give away.

The Gift of Giving

A central teaching in most spiritual traditions is that what you wish to experience, you should provide for another. If you wish to experience more peace, provide peace for another. If you wish to know that you are safe, cause others to feel safe. If you wish to heal your own sadness or anger, seek to heal the sadness or anger of another.

I once had a teacher who would allow students to come to him with a problem once a week. I watched week after week as his only answer to any problem was to feed a hungry child. It didn't matter if the student had lost a loved one, had a spiritual conundrum that they wished to solve, or simply needed a direction in life. The answer was always the same: give to someone else first

· · · · · · · ·

and you will receive your heart's desire. Being of service to others will turn your life around and naturally guide you into the stream of the flow of the universe.

Getting Into the Flow

Most of us, even if it's subconscious, believe that we have to *have* something in order to *do* something in order to *be* something. We want to have it, then do it, in order to become it. It doesn't quite work that way. Actually, it works in the exact opposite direction. Now you may still get somewhere working the other way around, but it takes so much more effort and a lot longer, since you are paddling against the current. I believe that's called rowing your boat upstream.

So how does one turn that boat around and get in the flow? First, you stop struggling. Struggle is different than effort. Struggle is laced with negative emotion, and effort is not. If you are paddling against the current, you are also looking at the wrong end of the journey. It's almost as if you are fighting against yourself.

Another reason positive thinking doesn't work in and of itself is because you start from having and doing instead of being, and most likely you are subconsciously hanging onto the latter of the two. If you feel you need to start out having money to become rich, but subconsciously you believe that you are what you have, then you can't get it.

The reason you want whatever it is you want is so that you can be that. Let's take money. If you were rich, you think you would be happy, confident, and secure. But you don't need money to be any of those things. So if you were just being and feeling happy, confident, and secure, the universe would find a way to tell you what you need to do and then give you what you want to have as a result.

If you are truly free to accept yourself as you really are, then you realize you have no choice to make, especially not from your conscious ego. You allow the universe to make it for you and trust that you will be pointed in the right direction. Now, this does not mean that you sit on the couch watching bad television with a beer in one hand and the television remote in the other. What it means is that you allow yourself to be guided as to what to do next and follow through accordingly. Let your heart guide you. It generally knows what's best for you long before your brain does. When you live mindfully, from your heart, you cannot help but have this awakening: life really is a self-fulfilling prophecy.

With that realization, you can finally make peace with your life and everything in it.

• • • • • • •

Make Peace with Everything

Making peace with your fears, your anxieties, your problems—everything—can truly set you free. If you remember who you truly are, the real you, the part of you that is love, you cannot be fearful, anxious, or upset. These emotions will still arise in your life, but the difference is that you won't allow them to affect you by becoming caught up in things that are out of your control.

Making peace doesn't mean you deny it or stick your head in the sand, it just means that you can acknowledge it and let it go. So you aren't the president of the company. Okay. So what? Maybe that would stress you out and give you a heart attack. You're still doing a good job, and you're still a good person. Perhaps you aren't married. Okay. What's wrong with being single? You're still a good person.

If you understand that despite this fear you love yourself anyway, you will always be good enough. The real you is good enough. You are love, and by projecting that love into an issue or problem you can't help but melt it away.

If you simply are being your real self, loving yourself, you will manifest naturally. Following is an exercise and meditation that can help you become kinder and more accepting of yourself. As you practice these you will find that you are all right exactly as you are. No one can be physically or mentally perfect, but we are in spirit, in our souls. This surpasses the human condition, and to accept it fully is to create meaningful change in your life.

We start with a loving-kindness practice, as this is an essential aid in enriching your life and preparing you to create the life of your dreams. Do the following exercise and meditation for being kind to yourself before moving on to the exercise and meditation on manifesting. When we have genuine self-love, we can then tap into our source and co-create anything our heart desires.

Exercise and Meditation for Being Kind to Yourself

EXERCISE: Be Self-Indulgent

One of the ways in which you can truly honor yourself is to make a conscious decision to recognize what is pleasurable in your life and what you already feel good about. This doesn't need to be an extravagant idea. It can simply be listening to your favorite music or going somewhere close by that makes you feel at peace.

What I would like to suggest you do right now is to set aside an hour once a week where you do something you really love. What that will be is entirely up to you. It doesn't have to be time-consuming. It can be as simple as getting a massage, eating a decadent dessert, hiking on your favorite trail, or tossing a few rose petals in your

· · · · · · · ·

bath, as long as it is something you thoroughly enjoy. Personally, there is rarely a day that goes by where I do not put my loving dog on a leash and walk to where we can see the sunset. I haven't missed a day in months now because I don't feel right when I do. The times I have spent staring at the ribbons of color streaming across the sky will go down as some of the best memories of my life.

There is a caveat here: the reason my self-indulgence has so affected my life is because I do it mindfully. You must be conscious of what you are doing when you are doing it. In other words, you cannot watch the sunset and be on your cell phone complaining to your friend about how miserable your job is. No, no, no. You have to put all the electronics and gadgets and any other distractions away. (My dog doesn't count, as she is an excellent meditator.)

As you luxuriate in your chosen decadent behavior, stay mindful. Notice all of your thoughts and feelings, and keep them positive. You cannot relish the chocolate as it melts on your tongue if you are worried about gaining a pound or two. Appreciate the sensations you feel by engaging all of your senses. Consciously become aware of what you see, feel, touch, hear, think, imagine. Allow the experience to permeate your soul. Love it and love yourself for loving it.

Make a date to follow through on this experience, or one similar to it, in the next few days or once a week. It's up to you to fit it into your schedule and stick to it. Mark that event on a calendar and then keep track of it to see how many times in a day, a week, and a month you are nurturing yourself.

Also, you can carry this exercise one step further. Try to experience something pleasurable every single day. Find something in your everyday life that brings you joy. Begin each day by reminding yourself that you are going to find one thing today that is extraordinary. It's not as hard as you think. When you set the intention, something will arrive that makes your heart sing and blows your skirt up.

Exercise: "I Really Love Me" Meditation

This is a simple meditation that will allow you to accept and appreciate yourself exactly as you are. It is most effective because it isn't done from the perspective of your physical self, but rather from the unique perspective of your higher self. Your higher self is the non-judging observer within you. Your physical self—your body, mind, emotions, and personal traits—are part of a separate self that I refer to as your personality or your ego. The two coexist, and the goal of this meditation is to have the two unite and align. When they do, your lower ego self will actually cooperate with your higher self in attaining your goals.

• • • • • • • •

Find a comfortable place and close your eyes. Focus on the place where your body contacts the floor or chair and relax this area first. Simply feel your body and breathe deeply. Bring your attention to your lungs and your belly and allow them to rise and fall of their own volition. Be with each breath and acknowledge the pauses you experience between each one. Observing your breath can make the difference in how you feel. Breath is life energy. When we restrict it we diminish that energy. Deep breathing expands the lungs, which then send a direct message to your heart to relax. Relax your heart. Then bring attention to the rest of your body, from your head to your neck and arms to your stomach and legs, allowing each area to completely relax before moving on to the next.

When you feel comfortable, think about who you are. Your personality, your ego, is how you perceive yourself. Let it be who and what it wants to be. Without judging yourself, simply observe what your ego thinks you are. It may tell you that you are too fat or too thin, or too angry or upset. It doesn't matter where it goes, it's just important not to disagree. This is not an argument but rather a simple observation.

Next, imagine that your personality is your child. You would love this child as if she (or he) is your own, because she is. Accept your child as she is, regardless of her stage of evolution. Hug your child and give her words of encouragement and support. Look at your child with appreciation and compassion. Love your child with all of her faults and frailties. This child is your child, and you love her unconditionally. Pour that love out of your heart and into hers. Feel the love flowing into your own heart from your child.

As you love your inner child, think about how the Source loves you in the same way, and allow that divine energy to fill both you and your inner child with omnipotence. The vision is one of completeness; one where nothing is lacking and nothing ever will be. You are perfect, with a perfect body, perfect mind, perfect relationships, and abundant resources to fulfill your dreams. Source knows of nothing else.

Stay in this place as long as you like. When you feel ready, give your child hugs and kisses before you release her. Say goodbye with kindness. Relax and breathe deeply until you feel centered and grounded within yourself once again. Thank the universe for the experience before you slowly return to reality.

• • • • • • • •

Exercise and Meditation for Manifesting

EXERCISE: **What's Blocking You?**

The first thing you must do for this exercise is figure out what exactly it is you want to manifest. You must be really clear about this. As the Upanishads, among the oldest of India's spiritual texts, state, "You are what your deepest desire is. As your desire is, so is your intention. As your intention is, so is your will. As your will is, so is your deed. As is your deed, so is your destiny."

Now take out a piece of paper and state that desire clearly at the top of the page. Underneath that, I'd like you to create two columns. One will be titled "would be" and the other "wouldn't be."

Okay, so let's say that you would like to be a huge success in your career. Under the "would be" column you might write down something like *rich*. Perhaps some other things you would list would be things like *successful*, *independent*, and *happy*.

Once you've completed that column, balance it out by listing all the things you wouldn't be. You wouldn't be broke, you wouldn't be bogged down by menial chores, unrecognized, or doubting your career choice.

What this does is help you become aware of things that are blocking you from becoming what you want to be. If you believe rich people are dishonest and unhappy, then again you have a block. If you truly believe that being successful means losing your independence because your life isn't your own anymore, then you are stopping yourself.

Perhaps you have a desire to lose weight, but you also believe that thin people are more noticed and you would have to come out of your shell. Or let's say you wish to be more spiritual, but then you wouldn't be able to be rich; that is also a subconscious block.

Really absorb any blocks that you have so that you might release them. Simply digest what's on the list. Focus on the "would be" side first. If you are honest with yourself, you would see that you can be all those things now. Must you have money in order to be successful? No. There a lot of successful people out there who don't have a lot of money. Do you need to be successful to be relaxed, happy, confident, and at peace? Of course not.

It's likely that the reason you really wanted to be successful was so that you could be everything on your "would be" list—but exactly the opposite is true. That's like saying having money will make you happy. I know a lot of unhappy rich people, so that's not necessarily true.

· · · · · · · ·

Try the following meditation to help you feel exactly what you should be feeling.

EXERCISE: **"See It Happen" Meditation**

Begin by focusing on your breathing. Breathe in good health, abundance, and love while you breathe out fear, stress, and doubt. Next, imagine your blood flowing easily through every vein in your body, filling each and every organ with oxygen and energy. Relax your eyes, drop your jaw and your shoulders, and allow every part of your body to relax. Let your back and neck muscles become loose and limp, and then continue bringing awareness to your entire body all the way down to the tips of your toes.

When you feel completely relaxed, allow any worry, judgments, anxiety, stress, and tension to lift off your body and float away. See the negativity literally evaporate off your body; you'll actually start to feel lighter as you do this.

Now allow your mind to be filled with white light until it covers your entire inner vision. Within this light you will create a beautiful sanctuary, a place where you feel at peace. Take in the sights and sounds of your creation. It could be a beautiful garden, a golden temple, or the beach or forest. Whatever you have created is meant to be there. Relax and enjoy it. Now, in front of you, imagine a mirror. Notice all of the details of this mirror, and look at yourself as you are now, just as you appear today. Now think of something that you would like to have in your life, and imagine it appearing in the mirror.

Do you see it? Take a good look at it in the mirror. See yourself walking right into it. Whatever it may be, even if it's just a feeling, it is yours already. Feel the joy, excitement, and love for this thing you have created. How does it make you feel? What's around you? How has your life changed because of this dream that has materialized? It's important to feel as if this is a part of your life now, so soak it all in and allow it to become a part of who you are. Stay in this place for as long as you like. By experiencing the positive thoughts about the life you wish to have, you are coming into alignment with your true self, your higher self.

When you feel ready, slowly back away from the mirror until you see yourself in your present state once again. Ground and center yourself before returning to reality, and be grateful knowing exactly who and what you are about to become.

This meditation is a powerful force for manifestation. As you practice it, remind yourself to be careful what you wish for. Every thought we think is just like a pebble being tossed into the ocean of our life. The ripples will not only affect us, but everyone around us. That said, try to keep your manifestations centered around yourself and the endless possibilities the universe can provide.

· · · · · · · ·

Paul Gregory

Servet Hasan is the award-winning author of *Life in Transition: An Intuitive Path to New Beginnings*, as well as *The Intuitive Heart of Romance: Finding Your Own Path to Lasting Love*, and *Tune Him In, Turn Him On* (Llewellyn). A student of the mystic masters of the Far East, Hasan is also a renowned motivational speaker who inspires others to attain their full potential through her television and radio appearances, live seminars, and workshops. Born into a psychically gifted family in Pakistan, she is also a citizen of England, Canada and the United States. She considers herself a spiritual ambassador of the world.

Accessing Your Core Genius for Abundance and Success

JACK CANFIELD *&* DEBORAH SANDELLA, PhD

Each of us is born with a life purpose. Identifying, acknowledging, and honoring this purpose are perhaps the most important actions taken by successful people. They make time to understand what they're here to do—and then they pursue it with passion and enthusiasm.

For some people their life purpose is clear from early in their lives, and for others it's a bit elusive. Mozart, Benjamin Franklin, and the Buddha are examples of those who from youth persistently expanded their skills in the area of their genius. They demonstrate how your personal and spiritual growth is accelerated by moving in the direction of your "core genius"—some one thing that you love to do and you do so well you hardly feel like charging money for it. It's effortless and a whole lot of fun, and if you thought you could make money doing it, you'd make it your life's work.[1]

Once you identify your core genius, it's easy to focus your attention and time expanding and improving it. With this laser focus, you send out a clear message to the universe, those around

---

1 Jack Canfield and Deborah Sandella, *Awakening Power: Guided Visualizations and Meditations for Success,* 15.

you, and your brain's inner GPS to go in the direction of your purpose. In other words, when you know who you are and what you are here to do, the universe conspires to make it happen.

For seekers, the role between what we want and what the universe wants for us can be confusing; the struggle between human controlling and spiritual surrendering is at the core of our evolutionary journey as human beings. Our humanity organically seeks pleasure and avoids pain, while the spirit within intuitively perceives the naive joy and wisdom of life itself that's greater than earthly endeavors.

Both your humanity and your spirit are equally essential for a balanced and fulfilled life. The essential nature of life is to thrive. You are an expression of life and thus are organically urged to expand and prosper in your unique way. Meditation is a tool that helps you sense your core genius and gives you feedback as to what's needed to keep your humanity and spirit balanced. Sometimes we need more human action and sometimes greater spiritual connection.

In our home study program *Awakening Power*, guided meditations help you put into practice eleven success principles from the *Success Principles* book.[2] Below we share a brief version of the "core genius" meditation,[3] which is designed to help you own and invest in your gifts in a greater and more enthusiastic way. Enjoy!

EXERCISE: **Core Genius Meditation**

Find a private space and relax as you read each paragraph, and then with closed eyes experience it (or, if you prefer, record the whole script, pausing where there are three dots…and then listen to the recording with your eyes closed).

As you are ready, let your awareness shift to the very center of your being and imagine in your mind's eye…it's tomorrow morning and you are waking up in your own bed and thinking it's just another day…Easily you throw back the covers, swing your legs over the side, and walk across the bedroom floor to the bathroom as you feel the temperature and texture of the floor against your bare feet. Gazing into the bathroom mirror, you notice something feels different.

The surface of the mirror seems to waver and your index finger is drawn to the surface. Touching it…it responds like liquid and sends little ripples out to the edge. Your right leg weightlessly extends into the magical mirror, and seamlessly the surface opens to accept you. As you cross through…you feel yourself being drawn out of your human form to the other side of this magical mirror. Looking back over your

---

2 Jack Canfield and Janet Switzer, *Success Principles—10th Anniversary Edition: How to Get from Where You Are to Where You Want to Be* (New York: HarperCollins Publishers, 2015).

3 Jack Canfield and Deborah Sandella, "Staying Focused on Your Core Genius," *Awakening Power: Guided Visualizations and Meditations for Success*, part three, 3–4.

• • • • • • • •

shoulder, you sense your human form remaining before the bathroom mirror just as you left it.

Noticing your feelings as your spirit anticipates traveling into a new, mysterious land, you grow lighter and lighter, and before you know it, you are walking without touching the ground.

Noticing an uncontainable desire to play, run, and skip, you find yourself feeling complete freedom. The more you play, the happier you become, and the happier you feel, the lighter you grow. Before long, you find yourself feeling so light you can fly. Sailing on the breezes like a bird, you feel joy and excitement more than ever before!

Higher and higher you fly, until you notice you are floating weightlessly in outer space, seeing stars and planets twinkling in the near distance.

Before you even realize it, playmates have joined you in this wonderland. Glancing about, you note who is present.

Quite magically and without effort, you find the moon resting in your hands like a ball, and you play moon toss with your playmates and enjoy a wonderful party!

Lighthearted and bubbling over with joy, you glance down at Earth. From this lofty place, what do you notice about Earth?

Zooming in on Earth, you find your state…your town…your home…Observing your life from this perspective, what do you notice? (pause)

What do you sense in your life that makes you the most grateful?

From this perspective, you watch below how you engage in your core genius… What are you doing that expresses your talents without you even thinking about it? Take a minute…

Gently find yourself floating back to Earth, to your unique home. Touching down on the magical side of your bathroom mirror, you face your human on the other side, just as you left it…

With a loving, playful eye, notice your adult face.

Sensing the lines and textures of your skin, you can't help but see kindness and strength. As this face smiles, notice how the eyes twinkle. Receiving the radiant and loving smile, you find yourself speaking with great compassion to the image in the mirror: *What I really love about you is…*

Thanking your human self for all they've done for you, and for the world, look into these eyes and say:

I love you!

I trust you!

I know who you are!

. . . .

Stepping through the mirror, back into your human form, you hear these words and receive them as fully as possible…like energy flowing into your body.

I love you!

I trust you!

I know who you are!

Receiving the sentiment into your mind, heart, and body, you sense a wink of acknowledgment from your spirit.

Noticing the floor beneath your feet naturally anchors you back into your body. Each phrase has settled in a special place and you notice where each is now:

I love you!

I trust you!

I know who you are!

Sensing the vibration of these words in every cell…love vibrates…all the way down into the very strands of your DNA.

Sensing your being, you discover a different feeling than when you began this journey and you discern the shift now…

How might this shift affect your daily life?

As you are ready to bring this shift into your everyday life, your eyes spontaneously open and you return fully to your body.

Jack Canfield is the CEO of the Canfield Training Group and has conducted intensive personal development seminars for more than a million people around the world. He as appeared on over 1,000 radio and television shows including *Larry King Live*, *The Oprah Winfrey Show*, and *The Today Show*. He is the coauthor of *The Success Principles*, *Tapping into Ultimate Success*, *Coaching for Breakthrough Success*, *Dare to Win*, *The Aladdin Factor*, *The Power of Focus*, and the #1 *New York Times* bestselling Chicken Soup for the Soul series. Jack is also a featured teacher in the movie and book *The Secret*. Visit www.JackCanfield.com.

dereksmith.com

Doug Ellis Photography

Deborah Sandella, PhD, MS, RN, is an award-winning author, international speaker and originator of the RIM® Method, an unprecedented approach that has empowered thousands of people to dissolve hidden blocks and accelerate success, including emotional and physical healing. She's been honored as an outstanding clinician and excellent researcher, and her book/CD *Releasing the Inner Magicians* was named one of the "Best Personal Growth Books" of its time. As founder and CEO of the RIM Institute, she teaches others how to navigate the RIM of the mind-body barrier for better health, greater success, and improved productivity. Visit www.RIMinstitute.com.

• • • • • • •

Clearing and Creating
Space for Inner Peace

Tess Whitehurst

If you saw the movie *Field of Dreams*, you probably remember the moment when a disembodied voice whispers to a man in a cornfield, "If you build it, he will come." And while that Iowa farmer's dream happened to involve vintage baseball, whatever your goal happens to be, creating the space for it—not only in your home (or cornfield), but also in your mind, emotions, and life—is a most imperative prerequisite.

But even before we create the space for things (such as items we wish to own, accolades we wish to accumulate, or spectral baseball games we wish to observe), if we truly desire to live consciously, bravely, and fully, it's of primary importance that we create the space for space itself. We must create space in our home so that we can find what we're looking for easily and effortlessly and so that we can feel the empowerment and energy that comes from being the masters of our own domains. We must create space in our mind so that we have enough presence to appreciate each moment and notice the many blessings that surround us always. We must create space in our emotions so that our every thought, feeling, and action can be characterized by true passion and purpose. And, as a culmination of all these space-creating efforts, we naturally feel guided to create space in our life so that we can be open to opportunities, ideas, and blessings, and so that we can allow our activities to spiral into closer and closer alignment with our soul's most authentic flow.

Remember, after all, that everything is energy. Your current individual identity is a pattern of energy within the larger pattern of energy that we call the earth, which in turn is part of the pattern of energy that we call the entire unified field. The pattern of energy that we call "you" has a natural momentum and flow, and when you clear impediments to that flow—such as thoughts, habits, or items that don't serve you or contribute to your vitality—your vibration improves and you more organically and effortlessly draw positive feelings and conditions into your life experience. Clearing impediments to your personal flow is something like clearing stagnation and debris from a murky stream and transforming it in the process to its true identity as a fresh, clear, sparkling brook. Indeed, when it comes to self-help and conscious living, it's often not about adding something; rather, it's about clearing away anything that keeps you from being the fullest and most vital expression of who you naturally are.

As the stream example illustrates, when you are in your natural state, you are flowing and sparkling with clear spiritual energy, which propels you along a divine and beautiful course. This is not to say that you have no free will—it's just to say that when your field/pattern is open to divine flow, all your co-creation efforts (desires you express, conditions you choose, and actions you take) are infused and aligned with divine momentum and energy. Everything feels easier. You will still encounter challenges, as all humans do, but you will see clearly that everything that happens to you in this earthly existence is part of your soul's journey of learning and experiencing its true divine identity. Instead of obstacles and roadblocks, you will come to see challenges as opportunities to gain wisdom and experience varying aspects of the true oneness that underlies and animates all things.

Once you've let go of impediments and created the space for your most positive life momentum to flow, you might say that you're in a state of allowing. You are open to the flow of blessings that naturally wants to come into your life experience. In fact, you are one with it. You are no longer separate from it, disbelieving in it, or holding it at arm's length. While this momentum is vital and fresh, it is also characterized by relaxation. Relaxing your ego and your belief that you have to rush around or force things to happen all on your own, you allow yourself to merge with the Divine Spirit's vital and invigorating flow. It's similar to the effect of a serene natural setting: while it eases stress and relaxes your tension, it also fills you with an abundance of natural energy and vigor.

With all of this in mind, this chapter is about how you can let go of what no longer serves you, such as stress, clutter, unhealed issues, and limiting thoughts. It's also about how you can create space in your life for blessings of all varieties, beginning with the simplest and most coveted blessing of all (and the one that provides a fertile ground for all other blessings to blossom forth): inner peace.

· · · · · · · ·

Clearing Physical Clutter

I often say that if there's clutter to be cleared anywhere in your home or personal work area, then clearing it is your number-one priority: not meditating, not exercising, not journaling, not spending more quality time with the family, and not finishing your novel. Why would this be true when all of these other things are so incredibly important? Because there will be plenty more time—not to mention energy and clarity and joy—for all of these things (and more!) after you clear your clutter.

Of course, there are some things that you need to do even if there's clutter to be cleared, like brush your teeth, pick up the kids from soccer practice, or get to work on time. Fine! Do those things. But whenever you possibly can, chip away at that clutter and stop it from chipping away at you.

The renowned psychic Edgar Cayce was known to say, "Line by line, precept by precept."[1] In other words, if there is something you know needs to be done and it's right in front of you, just do that one thing and the next step automatically will be revealed. Indeed, the importance of freeing up the consciousness from the burden of perceiving and working around physical clutter in the home can't possibly be overemphasized. It sounds simple and mundane, but I have found clearing clutter to be the most immediate and potent method of clearing the mind and creating inner peace, and—as a result—activating health, success, abundance, and all number of positive things.

But I don't need to convince you of this, do I? Simply consider the palpable energy drain that you feel when you briefly glimpse a single item in your home that you don't love, use, or need, or the burst of vitality and joy that you feel when you open up a closet filled with only beloved and useful items—and you know exactly what I mean.

Clearly, whether you have a lot of junk or only a little, when it comes to releasing it, there's never been a better time than now. But where and how do you even begin? Here are some ideas.

Start Small

When I first became aware of the amazing benefits of clutter clearing, I worked outside the house a lot so I didn't often have large amounts of time to set aside to go through all my old junk. Instead, I looked at the clock and thought, "Well, I have an hour: what can I clear?" I found that simply clearing all the extras out of the fridge (or the medicine cabinet or my underwear drawer) filled me with so much motivation that I couldn't wait to get back to work clearing at my very next opportunity. Rather than draining me and taking energy from me, even creating harmony in that one tiny area revved me up, not just for clearing more clutter but also for every other aspect of my life. You'll find that clutter is frozen energy: when it's just sitting there, it's

---

1 Kevin J. Todeschi, *Edgar Cayce on the Akashic Records* (Virginia Beach: A.R.E. Press, 1998).

• • • • • • • •

heaviness and congestion. But when you get it moving, it transforms into lightness, inspiration, and fuel.

So what limited area do you have time to clear? Start there. After that, do like Edgar Cayce and take it "line by line, precept by precept."

Get Excited About Donating

Have you ever heard the metaphysical precept that states whatever you send out comes back to you, multiplied? What about the metaphysical precept (also a basis of quantum theory) that everything is energy? Combine these two precepts, and you realize that it's not about the superficial identity of what you send out but rather about the energy—the intentions and feelings—behind them. With this in mind, let's say you took what was clutter to you and then, with love and generosity, donated it in a way that brought blessings to others. From an energetic standpoint, then, you were not sending out junk—you were sending out treasure! By transferring what was indeed a bunch of junk (to you) to a place where it would be more needed and desired, you effectively shifted it into the energy of love. In the process, it became treasure and blessings to others. So you transformed your old junk into love, treasure, and blessings. And, because you sent it out into the world, what can all that positive energy possibly do but come back to you, multiplied?

EXERCISE: **Know Your Clutter**

Many people ask me, "How do you know if it's clutter?" Naturally, some things (like that moldy cheese or those saggy old shorts) will be obvious—others, not so much. So if you're not sure, you might try any of the following:

- Ask yourself, "If I were moving, would I take this along?" If not, it's clutter.
- Hold it in your hands and notice whether it fills you with positivity and joy or whether it drains you just a bit. If it drains you, it's clutter.
- If you haven't used it or worn it in a year, get really honest with yourself: will you ever really use it or wear it? Really, really? If the answer is no, it's clutter.
- Imagine your life without this item. Do you feel a little bit better, a little bit more free? If yes, it's clutter.
- Consider all of the things you have to do to hold onto this item: dust it, pay rent on the space it inhabits, give up space in your closet, etc. Is the price of your energy expenditure a little steep considering what it gives back to you? If yes, it's clutter.

• • • • • • • •

Remember That It's a Lifelong Process

It would be nice if you could get your teeth cleaned once, and then never have to go to the dentist again. But alas, that's not how it works. The same is true with clutter clearing: we are constantly in motion, and we're constantly bringing new things into our space and life. This means that—just like getting our teeth cleaned—we must periodically get in there and get the junk out. So, to prevent the need for a serious overhaul, get in the habit of regularly releasing the extras from every room and area. For example, if it's cleaning day and you realize that you haven't gone through the fridge in a few months, go ahead and do it. Or if you notice that you're wading through a bunch of odd socks in order to find a pristine pair, why wait? Go ahead and throw those suckers out.

Creating a Nourishing Space

Once your physical clutter is cleared, you're going to want to take it a step further by arranging your space to nourish you on every level: mind, body, spirit, and life. In other words, while clearing the space in the cornfield is an important first step, you mustn't stop there! You must lay the groundwork for what you want to experience. You must build the baseball diamond.

Here are some important keys to creating space in your home that will support a positive outlook and peaceful, relaxed, vibrant state of mind.

Choose Empowering Imagery

From ancient cave paintings that sustained the morale of the tribe to the modern-day Facebook photos that attract thousands of "likes" and "shares," we are quite clearly a species for whom imagery is no small matter. The images we see—especially those we see on a daily basis and that characterize such a personal space as our home—have a huge effect on our mindset. Indeed, the artwork in our homes conveys both conscious and subconscious messages that bring about subtle yet powerful shifts in vital life areas such as confidence, energy, relationships, and physical health.

This is why it is of utmost importance that the imagery we display empowers us rather than depletes or undermines us. So look at images (both literal and abstract) that you are currently displaying and ask yourself whether they add to your empowerment or subtract from it. Some answers will be obvious, like the warm-colored painting of the word "Love" (positive) or the lonely man sailing dejectedly away into the sunset (negative). But for others, you might need to look a bit more closely. For example, one of my feng shui clients once had a painting of a couple standing close together on a dance floor. That sounds like a good romantic image, right? But then I looked closely and noticed that one member of the couple was frowning and looking away, as if she were rejecting her partner on some level. Because we are so powerfully influenced by imagery on a subconscious level, even though my client didn't notice this consciously, it was affecting her relationship and helping hold challenging patterns in place.

It's a simple activity but such a powerful one for those who value spiritual expansion and psychological well-being: remove all imagery that doesn't empower you. And in the future, only choose imagery that does. Concentrate on the feelings behind the conditions that you'd like to experience in your life, and then choose artwork that gives you these feelings just by looking at them. Because of the unfailing law of attraction and the relentless regularity of seeing these images day in and day out, this will work on the subconscious level to effectively help magnetize these desired conditions into your life.

Honor Your Sleep

Every health practitioner of every variety agrees: sleep is good for you. And spiritual practitioners from time immemorial have honored dreamtime as sacred. Even if you don't consciously remember your dreams, they provide valuable guidance while helping you heal old wounds and release challenging patterns.

So, make sure your bedroom is restful! Keep clutter cleared and go for a more minimalist look in the bedroom than elsewhere in the house. Make sure your bed is comfortable and your bedding is clean. Also, some people sleep better with mirrors covered or removed, so if you have trouble sleeping you might try covering your mirrors and see if anything changes. (Mirrored closet doors sometimes look nice with curtains, which you can then open during the day as desired.)

Kill Your Television

Well, okay, you don't really have to kill it, but at least cover your television when it's not in use. This not only discourages excess TV watching, but it also reclaims the room from that dreadful black hole of a vibe-kill known as a blank television screen. It's just so unromantic—am I right? Seriously, who wants to live like that? So the next best thing to killing (or getting rid of) your television is placing it behind a closeable cupboard or covering it with an attractive cloth. I have also found that on certain occasions, some people prefer to pop in a DVD of an ambient view such as an ocean or a fireplace, which keeps the area pleasantly activated and is exponentially better for your morale and mindset than reality show bickering and catchy commercial jingles.

As an added bonus, if you're like me, this just might end all contentious discussions with your partner about whether or not the television should be on. Truly, mine hardly watches any TV now, when he used to switch that darn thing on all the time.

EXERCISE: Set Up an Altar

For those of us on the spiritual path, a home altar is a must. It breathes life into your spiritual path as well as your home. An altar is simply a focal point for your spiritual-

· · · · · · · ·

ity: a place where you honor the interconnection of form and spirit, seen and unseen, known and unknown. While you can get as fancy and elaborate as you'd like, all you really need is a single item (on a designated flat surface), as long as it evokes a feeling of transcendence in you: an awareness and honoring of Spirit.

It's great if your altar is in the same area where you meditate, but it doesn't have to be.

Here are some simple items that you might consider for your altar space:

- A small statue or framed picture that represents the Infinite in a powerful way for you
- Crystals and stones
- Flowers
- Other nature items such as apples, acorns, feathers, or leaves
- One or more candles
- An incense holder
- Written intentions and prayers

Releasing Mental Clutter

Next up on our creating-the-space agenda: clearing the way for positivity, focus, clarity, and calm. In the following sections we'll look at the different categories of mental clutter and the challenges they present, as well as how you can let go of them and effectively begin to clear them from your mental landscape.

Release Unhelpful Thought Loops

Our minds are interesting things and can get in unhelpful patterns or loops that run like background noise beneath our conscious awareness, siphoning off our clarity, vitality, and effectiveness. For example, in the past I have sometimes noticed myself getting into what you might call a "mirror loop." I would happen to glance in a mirror and begin a pattern that went sort of like, "Oh, there are dark circles under my eyes. My pores are really looking huge. I need to lose a few pounds. Wow, I'm really looking old…" Or I have also in the past had a "food loop," which would go, "I really shouldn't eat this but I'm going to anyway, even though it probably isn't good for me. Why don't I have any willpower?"

Truly, can you see any valid reason for sustaining thought loops like these? And—considering that our thoughts really and truly affect not only our bodies, but also the way we interact with and interpret every single aspect of our life experience—can you see how they would hold me back in a real and substantial way from experiencing all the joy and blessings that I profess to desire?

The good news is that an unhelpful loop is not that difficult to remedy. Think of something as innocuous as an annoying song running through your head. The best way to get an annoying song out of your head is often just to replace it with a different one. It might take a little while for the new grooves to form on your internal record, but with just a little diligence and repetition, you can form new and improved mental patterns and get your mind (and life) to begin playing a different tune.

Here's more specific guidance on how to do this. Using the examples above, you would begin by getting logical about it and asking: what's the point of this thought loop? Is it really serving me to berate my appearance or bemoan my eating habits? No, and as a matter of fact it's undermining my confidence and causing my digestion to become unsettled and my metabolism to tank.

Next, every time you notice the loop beginning, replace it with a more positive and helpful one. So the new mirror loop might be, "Wow, my skin is really glowing. I love my bodacious curves. I look great in this color. My eyes are so sparkly today…" And your new food loop might be, "I bless this food and give thanks for it. I am so fortunate to have this precious food to eat. It's so delicious and nourishing! I chew it fully and digest it perfectly…"

A word of warning: avoid the trap of getting into an I'm-not-thinking-positively-enough loop—it's too absurd! It's like the endless circular race in *Alice in Wonderland*. If you notice that an old negative loop has arisen, just gently smile at it and replace it with a positive one, without berating yourself. And if you notice a loop that goes something like, "Why do I still have the mirror loop after all these weeks? I shouldn't be thinking negative thoughts like this after all these books I've read. What kind of spiritual person am I, anyway?" you just have to laugh at yourself and let it go. Laughter—even internal laughter—dissolves and dissipates, lifting you up and out of the ridiculousness and into a saner and more positive perspective. Every time the loop comes back and you notice it (no matter how many times it happens), just laugh and lift yourself up and out of the madness. In time you'll create a new habit of lightness, and the old pattern will fall away.

Find and Shift Limiting Beliefs

Similarly, because our beliefs and expectations literally define the world as we know it (and they most definitely do, if you believe the quantum theorists), it can be a worthwhile pursuit to constantly be on the hunt for beliefs that you hold that aren't actually true or don't have to be true for you. Sometimes these can be easy to spot, like when you open a box of trophies and medals from childhood and then realize that you have been operating for some time under the belief that you "never win anything." Or when you notice that you're continually calling your awesome new job "crazy" and "too good to be true." Or when you hear yourself telling your best girlfriend that "men really suck," and then you realize that you're actually related to several

• • • • • • • •

quite wonderful men. In these cases, releasing these beliefs would make it more likely that you would win, that you would retain your splendid new job, and that you would meet delightful and trustworthy men, respectively.

Other times, though, discovering a limiting belief can take a little extra investigating. For example, as I read *Lean In* by Sheryl Sandburg[2], I realized that my culture had effectively trained me to associate successful women with bitchiness, and I therefore believed that if I was going to be successful in life, I had to be a "bitch." It suddenly hit me that for that reason I had been alternating between holding back from achieving all that I would have liked and unnecessarily bulldozing or snapping at people. Needless to say, releasing that belief made success a lot easier and more pleasant for me. But the point is that sometimes a belief can be so deeply embedded that you don't initially realize it's there.

Let Go of Non-Authentic Obligations

Do you do things that you don't really want to do or stay in situations that you don't really want to stay in because you believe you have to for the sake of someone else? Guess what? That's an exquisitely draining form of mental clutter I like to call a non-authentic obligation. "But," you might be thinking, "I really do have to do (this or that) for the sake of (this or that person or group of people)!" For just a moment, though, consider why you believe that you have to: that you have no choice in the matter, that it is absolutely not something you would choose if it were up to you.

Because I've got news for you: it *is* up to you! If you are doing it, you are choosing to do it for whatever reason, whether you're admitting it or not. But isn't it so much more empowering to admit this? Doesn't it feel so much better to say "I'm choosing to stay in this town because I love my children" instead of "I have to stay in this town because my children's father lives here"? And isn't it actually truer? Similarly, instead of thinking you have to work at a job you don't like in order to make money (which will cause you to run that loop over and over indefinitely), you can think that you're choosing to work at that job to support yourself as you explore other opportunities and possibilities (which will reframe the job as a useful stepping-stone to a more desirable situation).

What's more, once you release the erroneous belief that other people have power over you, you can also release the obligations that aren't things you would authentically choose. Acting out of obligation, after all, is not a healthy model to demonstrate to anyone, and healthy, loving friends and partners certainly don't wish such a fate upon you, nor do they truly and deeply benefit from being the recipients of your martyrdom.

---

2   Sheryl Sandburg, *Lean In: Women, Work, and the Will to Lead* (New York: Knopf, 2013).

• • • • • • •

There are many types of non-authentic obligations that you may benefit from releasing, but here are some examples to help you realize any you might have unknowingly adopted:

- Volunteering for activities that drain you rather than nourish you

- Believing that you're living somewhere you have to live

- Believing that you're in a job situation that you have to be in

- Doing housework or other chores with the attitude that you have no choice in the matter

- Saying things or behaving in ways that aren't authentic to you with the belief that you must do so in order to make other people happy or comfortable

- Telling yourself that you "should" do something that you're not actually doing, when, in reality, you are choosing not to do it

Just to reiterate, I'm not recommending that you quit your job or move to a new town immediately, but rather that you remember you are indeed always the one making the choices. Mentally reframing your daily activities to reflect your self-empowerment ("I'm choosing to work here because I'd prefer to pay rent this month" rather than "I have to work here because I have to pay rent") will help break you out of self-imposed ruts and continually pave the way to situations and conditions that clearly reflect that self-empowerment.

Streamlining the Mental Landscape

Just like with the physical environment, once you clear the clutter from your mental environment, you'll want to arrange it in a way that optimizes your life experience. Because, as we saw in the last section, your thoughts have everything to do with how you experience your life and even with what manifests into your life experience. That's why, in addition to letting go of thoughts and thought patterns that don't serve you, it can be extremely helpful to establish the habit of thinking thoughts that *do* serve you. Here you'll find a few ways to do just that.

EXERCISE: **Work with Affirmations**

When it comes to self-help, the practice of reciting affirmations (positive phrases such as "everything is perfectly unfolding") is an oldie but a goodie. That's because words are potent symbols, and when we repeat them over time, they act on our subconscious like a gentle yet powerful tonic that propels our inner dialogue—and consequently our outer reality—into a more positive momentum.

For example, I recently moved from Los Angeles to a country house in Missouri. While my partner drove a rented moving truck along with a trailer holding his car, I followed along in my car, which contained our cat and all his cat stuff in the back.

• • • • • • • •

While moving is stressful enough, as you can imagine, driving for three days straight and staying for two nights in a motel with an extremely spooked cat is not exactly the most mellow of situations. Not to mention the stress of watching that huge truck and trailer navigate two-lane highways, gas stations, and parking lots. So, when I noticed my mind veering into apprehension, I repeated the affirmation (adapted from the wonderful book *The Wisdom of Florence Scovel Shinn*[3]), "Infinite Intelligence goes before us, making clear, easy, and successful our way." This shifted my mindset from one of fear and the expectation of hassles to a mindset of joy and the expectation of ease. It was indeed an exercise in trusting and aligning with the Divine, and even if we had a few freaks-outs along the way, they were resolved as easily and quickly as could be expected, and we not only arrived as planned and in one piece, but also in miraculously high spirits.

Here's a more universal example: no matter how much money and resources we may currently have, most of us could benefit from getting into a more abundant mindset. Whether through our upbringing, schooling, or simply through the osmosis of cultural conditioning, most of us are in some capacity indoctrinated with the idea that there's not enough to go around, and that even if one has enough today, one might not have enough tomorrow. Of course, if we believe this to be true, it will absolutely be true for us. If, on the other hand, we believe that our resources are abundant and plentiful, and that they will continually flow to us in an unending, sparkling stream of luxurious wealth, that will be true for us instead.

The good news is that, just like with inner thought loops, while shifting longstanding beliefs and cultural paradigms can take a bit of time and effort, it is absolutely doable. And affirmations are an excellent way to reprogram your mind by replacing old beliefs with newer and more desirable ones. It's sort of like clearing a new trail through a forest: while effort is required in the beginning, once it's established and regularly used, the new foot traffic will keep it clear and useful for years to come.

First, choose or compose an affirmation that feels powerful and inspiring, and that puts you directly into the state of mind and reality that you'd like to create for yourself. For the example above, you might choose "my resources are abundant and plentiful, and they continually flow to me in an unending, sparkling stream of luxurious wealth." Here are some other ideas:

"I am loved and lovable."

"My mind is overflowing with creative ideas and inspiration."

3   Florence Scovel Shinn, *The Wisdom of Florence Scovel Shinn* (New York: Fireside, 1989).

• • • • • • • •

> *"I freely give and just as freely receive. I accept*
> *all the beautiful gifts that life has to offer."*

> *"Doors of opportunity are opening everywhere for me, now and always."*

> *"I am luck incarnate. I am blessed beyond my fondest dreams."*

Once you've chosen your affirmation, there are a number of ways that you may work with it. For example, you might try:

- Repeating it inwardly or aloud as you do something repetitive such as gardening, cleaning the house, or driving your car
- Lighting a candle, setting a timer for five minutes, and repeating the affirmation over and over again until the timer dings
- Writing a whole notebook page full of the repeated affirmation
- Creating an art or craft piece depicting the saying (such as a magnet or cross-stitch pattern) and displaying it somewhere where you will see it and read it frequently
- Putting it on your bathroom mirror with a sticky note or lipstick
- Singing or chanting it playfully as you walk or dance

Like exercise, one of the secrets to successfully working with affirmations is to do it regularly over time so that it can have a cumulative effect. In contrast to a quick fix, affirmations are about slowly, steadily, and purposefully creating longstanding positive change.

Exercise: Take Sea Salt and Baking Soda Baths

Mainstream thinking might lead us to conclude that a bath containing sea salt and baking soda couldn't possibly have anything to do with streamlining the mental landscape. However, if you've ever taken a nice luxurious bath, I'm betting that you have a pretty good idea of how a bath can actually do just that. Water is a conductor of energy, and warm water helps relax the body, relieve stress and stressful thought patterns, and get us into a receptive state of mind. Many people say they have their best ideas in the shower or bathtub, and indeed some of my best book ideas have seemed to arrive fully formed in my mind while I've been immersed in warm water.

But what about the salt and baking soda? Salt is extremely cleansing and can help absorb and transform challenging thought loops, while baking soda creates buoyancy and actually lifts your spirits. So, to get into a happier, healthier, more energized, and generally more positive mindset, draw a warm bath, add half a cup of sea salt and a

• • • • • • • •

tablespoon of baking soda, and soak for at least forty minutes, adding more hot water as necessary. Be sure to have plenty of drinking water on hand so that you don't dry out, and consider lighting a candle or adding essential oils to your bath to enhance your experience. Lavender is extremely relaxing and joy-inducing, peppermint is invigorating, and rosemary is clarifying and helps focus and energize the mind.

Align with What Is

When we fight what is—when we lament present conditions and inwardly wish that things weren't as they are—we create tension within us and within the situation, which lends energy to what we are fighting against and usually perpetuates it. On the other hand, perhaps counterintuitively, when we align with and accept what is, we stop feeding what we don't desire with energy and are consequently much more empowered to create and manifest what we do desire.

This will make more sense with an example. There was a brief period in my life when I had a real problem with blushing. It came out of nowhere at the most random times, like when a checker at the grocery store tried to make small talk with me or at family gatherings when everyone at the table stopped to listen to what I was saying. The funny thing was, when I really looked within, I discovered that it wasn't actually embarrassment: it was more that I started to worry that I would blush, and so I would. And then I would freak out that I was blushing, and I would blush more. This is a prime example of giving energy to what you don't want by fighting what is. It was only when I began to welcome blushing that it finally stopped. I actually played a game with myself during which I pretended with all my heart that I really, really wanted to blush. As soon as I did this, the blush went away, and in matter of days the problem was gone completely. Not only that, but look what a lesson it taught me in aligning with what is! What could be a more obvious and helpful example? All I had to do was pretend that it was a blessing, and it actually became a blessing!

If you'll notice, this is exactly the same lesson the princess learns when she kisses the frog. Yes, she would prefer that a prince had been standing before her, but the actual fact as it appeared was that there was a frog standing before her. If she had fought this reality—denied it or run from it—the frog would have continued to be a frog. On the other hand, when she aligned with the reality and embraced it by kissing the frog, the frog became what it truly was: not a curse but a blessing; not a frog but a prince.

If you choose to think of curses as curses, then that is what they will be. But if you choose to think of every single thing that happens as a blessing, or a blessing in disguise, guess what? Everything actually becomes a blessing. It's all up to you.

* * * * * * *

Getting the Emotions Moving

While our thoughts are the mountains, valleys, fields, and walkways of our inner landscape, our emotions are the lakes, streams, rivers, and oceans. Keeping them fresh and flowing allows us to be healthy, nourished, and connected, and to live our lives to the fullest. Here are some ideas for how to activate your emotions and get them moving.

EXERCISE: **Dance Like No One's Watching**

Dancing like no one's watching—in fact, dancing when no one's watching—is one of the best and most immediate ways to activate your emotional flow. It doesn't matter what kind of music you choose, as long as it's something that makes your body want to move. Even harsh or angry music can help you get your feelings out and might even be ideal if you have some pent-up rage or frustration that could benefit from an outlet. So create a playlist, set the lighting just right, and dance your little heart out. If time is limited, set a timer for ten or fifteen minutes. Otherwise, just dance for as long as you'd like. Really listen to the music and let it permeate your consciousness and actually shift you at the molecular level. You might feel silly at first, but stay with it until the music takes over, and then let your body do what it wants to do. Let it be an exercise in authenticity. That's really all there is to it! Try it. You'll find that it's very simple but also very effective.

Spend Time in Nature

We talk about "nature" like it's something inherently separate from humans, when in reality that's not the case. When you look at the big picture of human existence, our habit of spending so much time indoors is actually quite a recent development. Consider, for example, a wolf or a lion. Living indoors he would be safe and warm but would likely feel substantially disconnected from the fullness of his being. The same is true for us. So spending time outdoors regularly is an absolute must when it comes to feeling our feelings, connecting with our true inspiration, and being fueled by our emotional intelligence. Even if you live in a city, find an outdoor area where you can walk or spend time regularly, as weather permits.

Cry

Have you noticed that tears are saltwater, just like the oceans of the world? And saltwater, as we have seen, is extremely cleansing. But you already know that tears are cleansing because after a good cry you feel like your spirit has been opened up. You feel more connected, grounded, real, and open. Crying gets a bad rap in our culture, but it brings such relief and relaxation, and it helps us remember that this life is characterized by love as well as delicious heartache and emotional connection.

· · · · · · · ·

If you feel that you could use a good cry but one doesn't seem to be forthcoming, try watching a movie that has been deemed a "tear jerker." It's no coincidence that the earliest forms of theater were considered a form of spirituality and a means of healing through emotional catharsis. As author and professor Joseph Campbell taught in books such as *The Hero with a Thousand Faces*, we are a species that thrives on stories, and stories that move us deeply connect us to our humanity and fill us with a sense of meaning and purpose. Heartfelt music can also be an excellent tool for activating and unlocking your emotional flow.

Living with Passion and Purpose

Once your emotions are flowing, let them be powerful tides and undercurrents in all that you do. Find your passions: find the things that move you, anger you, excite you, open your heart, and bring tears to your eyes. And let these be the guiding forces in your life. You'll find that this will infuse you with the sense of nourishing satisfaction and purpose that we all crave.

Reclaiming Your Power and Living the Life You Want

Everything is energy, and you are the power in your own life. If you want to experience positive change, start on any level: the physical, mental, or emotional. Let go of what doesn't serve you, and adopt patterns and habits that do. You are never stuck. There is always something you can do to release conditions that you don't desire and help bring about conditions that you do. Like a snowball rolling down a hill, it's a matter of momentum, so begin anywhere. Keep up your effort and, in time, the positive momentum will take over, and you will find that you are rolling toward greater and greater levels of health, wealth, harmony, happiness, and success.

Ted Bruner

Tess Whitehurst is an award-winning author, feng shui consultant, speaker, and intuitive counselor who presents sacred and empowering wisdom in an extremely friendly and accessible way. Her books—which include *Magical Housekeeping*, *The Good Energy Book*, and *Holistic Energy Magic*—have been translated into nine languages, and her work has appeared in such places as *Writer's Digest*, *Whole Life Times*, and *Law of Attraction* magazine. She's appeared on morning news shows on both Fox and NBC, and her feng shui work was featured on the Bravo TV show *Flipping Out*. Discover her blog and YouTube channel at www .tesswhitehurst.com.

World Healing and Mindful Society

ALEXANDRA CHAURAN

Sarah was having a tough week, a tough month, and maybe even a tough year. She was in her early twenties, trying to live on her own for the first time. These were the sort of years during which she took pride in being tough enough to live on an absurd diet of cheap food while managing to work late into the night stocking shelves to pay for her schooling. She joked with her family about being a poor college student, but in reality her life felt lonely and bleak. Many days would go by without speaking aloud to another human soul.

Sarah felt herself becoming jaded about society in general as she watched protests at her university going on because of atrocities elsewhere in the world and unfairness and injustices right in her hometown. She began to even rethink her pre-med major, wondering if helping people was really the way to go. Then one Saturday, buried in a pile of homework, she shook her head out of a reverie and went for a walk about the town. Brazenly she watched the people around her, trying to remember the love for humanity that had drawn her to study for a medical career.

When she looked closely, Sarah really could see the beauty in these people. She saw mothers helping their children on the playground and a father soothing a toddler with a scraped knee. She saw a street artist painting a glorious seascape on the waterfront. She saw a man pick up a receipt a woman had dropped and chase her down half a block away to give it back to her.

At lunchtime, Sarah walked toward her favorite sandwich shop and spotted a penny heads-up on the ground. She stooped to pick it up and met eyes with a homeless man across the street. It seemed a strange coincidence that luck had given her a penny as she gazed upon the penniless. She went into the sandwich shop and emerged with two sandwiches.

Sarah walked across the street and greeted the man, handing him one of the sandwiches. As she unwrapped her own sandwich and leaned against the brick wall of the building, she listened to his life story. He had been a teacher for many years before suffering an illness and becoming permanently disabled. He had adult children that he was excited to visit for the holidays, and he pulled out a printed photograph of a baby grandson that had been born three weeks ago. Sarah pictured him caring for his children in the past and getting a chance to soothe a toddler in the future, should he get a scraped knee. She smiled, happy that this man was being fed for another day. It seemed as if the penny had been a message from the Divine and that her sandwich was an act of magic that brightened up the day for both of them.

As she bid the man goodbye and turned to walk away, he told her, "God bless." Just then, Sarah realized that she was indeed blessed. Before returning to her studies, instead of grumbling, she would recall this moment and this feeling that she had of doing something good in the world for someone who had less. She would think about the beautiful tapestry of society and the role that she played in it even when she was feeling lonely. And she would return to her work refreshed and with a renewed sense of purpose.

World healing, mindful society, and conscious communities are a collection of big topics. These are things we see activists and politicians struggling with in the news. But what can an individual do about such huge societal challenges? Realizing a conscious community, much less world healing, within one lifetime would be a monumental feat. However, every big change in the world begins with the mobilization of one person. Each person involved in a community or a society with high ideals must begin deep within the self. A quote attributed to Gandhi speaks this truth: "be the change you wish to see in the world." For those of us committed to mindful living, this is an essential metaphysical law. What we manifest within our own minds and consciousness can affect the exterior community, society, and world. We will take a look at each of these topics, starting with the broad world lens, zooming in to society, and finally narrowing to individual community. But first, let's look at the steps it takes to make a shift within each.

Three Steps Toward World Healing

There are three steps to making global change. Looking at the big picture, conscious communities can make up a mindful society, and a mindful society is an essential component needed for healing the world. So let's start small and build big; this is the ultimate grassroots effort. I've broken down the monumental task of world healing into three steps. First, start with your big vision

· · · · · · ·

for world healing. Decide what a healthy world would look like to you. Second, start building that mindful society with you as the first member of a conscious community. Finally, set those plans into motion and manifestation. Even a small ripple in society can cause something big.

Step 1: Define Your Manifesting Goal for the World

A healthy world begins within yourself. Look within your own heart and soul to decipher what you truly wish to manifest on this planet. What is your purpose? What draws you or guides you? If you don't know the answer, it may not yet be time for you to reach out and join a movement. If, however, you do have a good handle on your deepest values, you are ready for step two.

Step 2: Finding Community

Your next task is to find kindred spirits. There may already be a group in existence that promotes goals similar to your own. If so, excellent; join forces and begin to spread your work to a wider community. If not, you may have to start your own community. This is more challenging, but it is not impossible.

Step 3: Be a Good Influence

Once you have begun to grow a small community aligned with your goals, the next step is to be a good influence on society at large. Just as you, as an individual, might have had to inspire others to adopt your goals by leading a good example, the growing community you nurture will have to be a good example for society as a whole. The good news is that modern society is built around the desire to make positive change. You may be able to mobilize your local or even national government around a cause. You can spread your message on the Internet and through other media.

Don't get ahead of yourself, though. The biggest mistake that we change-makers tend to make is moving too fast. Trying to jump on a bandwagon that isn't feasible or sustainable will make for a short-lived movement. The world healing you wish to accomplish starts and ends within you. Always check in with yourself along your path. Keep true to your highest ideals. You may have to be flexible, but in order to be ethical you'll have to continuously ask yourself if you're doing the right thing and living each day with purpose. You're given a short time on earth during this lifetime. Bring forth those ideas that are uniquely yours and express the creativity that only you can express. I'm excited to help you get started.

World Healing

Prayer as a Tool to Make a Difference

The vast majority of humans are already good people, and we're all trying to find our way in the world. It can be easy to become cynical or jaded. Consider the case of a traffic jam on the way home from work. The natural impulse is to become angry and annoyed. Why are all

· · · · · · · ·

these people here? Why don't they all just go home! Well, the simple fact is that everybody is just trying to get home for dinner. The same may be the case with spiritual evolution. There are some religious traditions that believe nobody can reach spiritual perfection until everyone reaches spiritual perfection together. In that way, we're all in a sort of spiritual traffic jam on the way to world healing. The more that one reaches out and shows compassion to others on their journey, the more pleasant and even blissful one's individual journey can be.

Healing the world in the practical sense of things must be an act done by a mindful society. However, there are still things that a mere individual can do while doing some inner soul searching. As a metaphor, think of a loved one who is sick and in the emergency room. A team of professionals works quickly to stabilize the person who is sick and in need. Everything must work perfectly in concert. Each individual has a job. However, in the end, there is still a lot of luck involved. This is where spirit comes into play. When everything is done that can be physically done, the only thing left is to pray for healing. This healing prayer is a last resort in the emergency room, but it can be a first step for world healing.

Why is prayer such a powerful tool for world healing? Because prayer is a method of inner work that any individual can do. Prayer opens a line of communication with the divine and allows for guidance. The divine may be the thread that weaves all of us individuals together, making united mindfulness possible. If you're not yet sure what you can do specifically and practically to make a difference in the world, prayer is a good way to start that conversation. Ask the divine to guide you. Listen carefully in meditation for answers. Take action based on the inklings that you get in meditation and try to feel out your place in the world.

Mother Earth Connection: The Gaia Hypothesis

Some people choose to make a Mother Earth connection to world healing. This is because the earth is a personification of the source of divinity. There are those who believe that the earth itself is a living, sentient organism. The Gaia Hypothesis states that the planet itself is an organism, and we are some of the cells that make up her body. In this worldview, each of us are important parts of this organism. When you work to stop pollution or conserve energy, you are acting as the very hand of Mother Earth.

During your meditations, you can focus on becoming more aware of your place within Mother Earth and the duties you were made to perform. Sit in meditation and ponder your life's purpose within the context of a divine Mother Earth connection. Think about how you were made as part of her flesh and bone and body. Imagine that you were made to discover her, to love her, to serve her. You may serve a vital purpose in keeping her beating heart alive. You are a part of this divine life, and so is everyone around you.

Throughout the day you can add meditative acts of service to Mother Earth. For example, at sunrise or sunset, when the beauty of the earth is transitioning from night to day or day to night, you can take a moment to meditate as a way of acknowledging your place in this huge cosmic cycle. You can meditate while working in a garden and imagine yourself playing an important role in nurturing Mother Earth's plants. You can meditate before mealtimes as a way to thank the earth for providing you with nourishment for your body.

You can access this connection at any time and at any place. Nobody can take it from you or sever it. Connecting with Mother Earth in your meditation can be a powerful source of divine inspiration to keep your attitude elevated, even on the days when things go wrong. Remember that you have a purpose on this planet, and you can serve that purpose with less resentment or anguish. Dig deep to find faith that others are serving their purpose for Mother Earth, even if that purpose may at first seem destructive.

We know that each of the cells and organs in our bodies have different purposes. Some organs clean up wastes. Some cells build muscles. One is not lesser or more virtuous than the other. Each is needed in its own way. If you find yourself caring more about one aspect of world healing or mindful society than other people, acknowledge that this may be a unique purpose of yours, no more and no less important. Try to carry out your purpose without complaint. If every chore that you do is like a hymn to Mother Earth, then you can carry out your work here on our planet with joy even if your work is erased by another in the next minute. You do make a difference, even if making a difference in a large machine or organism doesn't seem very visible at times.

Sustainable Practice

Sustainable community and society practices are vital for mindful world healing. As we become more and more aware of how delicate the balance of life is on earth, we are each finding ways to improve our practices so that we don't harm each other or the planet. You can go as far as you like with the idea of sustainable practices. Look at the conscious communities that you're building to see if your group dynamics are sustainable for the long haul. Scrutinize your household for things you do that are or are not sustainable.

Let us start at the level of the individual or your household and note how you can make sustainable practices a little more spiritual. Reducing waste, reusing supplies, and recycling materials can be seen as spiritual acts if you do your part for Mother Earth. This can make even the act of grocery shopping an act of mindfulness. As you choose your groceries, look for reduced packaging options and select each food item with gratitude toward Mother Earth. Imagine that you are taking from the lifeblood of nature, only to give back to it with your good deeds and positive intentions.

• • • • • • • •

Even conserving energy can be spiritually meaningful. Think of the give and take of a mindful society when you turn off lights as you leave the room or make sure that you're not wasting water by leaving the faucet on while brushing your teeth. When you reuse items for sustainable practices, imagine that you are building on the sacred energy of that object with each use. A rustic table can be more meaningful if it was built with salvaged lumber from an old childhood clubhouse, for example.

And, of course, when you recycle something, you're leaving a little bit of your positive energy with that object as you release it back into circulation. Look near you for stores that sell recycled products and think about the energy of many sustainability-minded households that went into each object. A handcrafted license plate purse, a belt made out of recycled rubber, or a coat made out of recycled soda bottles takes on its own new life and new energetic meaning. These can make thoughtful gifts for sustainability-minded people in your community.

Reducing, reusing, and recycling are only some of many processes that you can make meaningful and sustainable in your community. Search for your own passions. For example, if you're into gardening, research the most sustainable ways to water, plant, harvest, and collect heirloom seeds. Consider joining an heirloom seed exchange in your local community. If you're a builder at heart, think of how you can sustainably create by using recycled materials or dyes and paints that you make yourself. If you like to cook, research the plants and foods that you cook to find out which are the most sustainable crops in your region, and focus on them when you're making dishes to bring to community potlucks. You can start a fad of sustainability in your community.

Mindful Society

Promoting a mindful society is a pretty lofty goal, but it's something that each of us can attempt to do as part of our own higher living goals. You've already done some meditation on earth healing and visualized others who are working toward that goal. It's time to mobilize those around you in society. However, it isn't as simple as grabbing five friends and doing some rabble-rousing. Certainly a community group can be one piece in the puzzle, but you should also explore other avenues of spreading mindfulness.

Think about what sorts of behaviors help you to be more mindful and how you can spread this throughout the world. These will be different for different people. Mindful behaviors can be as complex as making a planning list of random acts of kindness or as simple as smiling and making eye contact with every stranger you see today. It's easy to get full of hope and go straight to the government to try solving some problems. That's all well and good, and some people do link their spirituality with political action. You can pray over your ballot as you vote or even work in a prayer group or circle of like minds to try influencing the political world. However, political force may not be the only way to spread mindfulness and higher living. It may not even be the best way. Consider the idea that we're all working toward higher living together. Offering a helping hand along the way may be more important than barring all the "wrong ways" or telling everyone to rush and hurry along the "right way."

Think about what encourages you to your most mindful and highest self in your own relationships, in your workplace, and in your home. For example, in my house, if my husband and kids are complaining to me all day and acting very ungrateful, I will not be encouraged to be more mindful of their needs or to have the highest and best good of all in my mind. Instead, I will likely become cranky. However, if my family shows me gratitude and encourages me when they see me doing good things, I will be more mindful of their wants and needs in the future. Do this when interacting with people in the world. Catch people doing good deeds and thank them for that. Instead of campaigning against bad behaviors or bad politicians, find some actions and people that you can get behind.

A positive attitude is vital for promoting higher living. Be a good example for others to follow. Turn to your meditation to stabilize you when you feel provoked to negative words or actions. Building your meditative practice will do several things to help you be the voice of reason in our world. You will have a quiet place inside yourself to which you can retreat if you need to have a moment. Before speaking or writing a letter, you can turn to meditation to tap into your source of mindfulness about the higher good. You can also meditate before preparing to meet other people or walk around in the world. Instead of turning to relaxing meditation as a reaction after a hard day, you can soften your attitude with relaxing meditation beforehand. Use your own mindfulness as a touchstone before mindfully reaching out to help others.

EXERCISE: Be the Change You Wish to See in the World

Here's another meditation that you can perform by yourself in order to bring peace and a higher consciousness to the world. The object of this meditation is to stir up the feelings inside yourself through your own power and then radiate them outward to the world. This is different from praying to a specific divinity outside of yourself or from linking to others who are of similar mind. This is about bootstrapping your own personal power and creating a magical act of contagion that affects the world in a positive way.

This is a particularly useful exercise if you feel that you're not exactly the savior of the world; I would imagine that's all of us. Sometimes I feel down on myself because I'm not exactly living up to my expectations. Since I'm the mom of two young kids, sometimes I take off my mom cape and can get downright rude and mean. At times like these I remind myself that I can actually choose peace over other emotional states at any time. This is pretty empowering for me, and I hope it will be for you.

• • • • • • • •

Remember that you can always choose peace over anger, sadness, or any other maelstrom of emotion.

Begin this exercise by making sure that you have an especially peaceful environment in which to meditate. Double-check that your phone ringer and other notifications are off. Hang a sign on the door that reminds your housemates not to disturb you during this sacred time. Seat yourself or lie down in a comfortable position with blankets or pillows if necessary. Before you begin this exercise, make sure that you've attended to your basic needs. You shouldn't be hungry or tired or hot or cold or strained in any way, ideally.

Sit comfortably and turn your attention to the comfort of the moment. Even if life isn't perfect, there should be some things about this moment that are good. Bring to mind your life's blessings and think upon them until you can feel a sense of peace. Try to intensify those peaceful feelings with your thoughts and energy. For example, you might think of the memory of a camping trip by the lake or cuddling a favorite pet. Deep within yourself, find the well of peace from which you can draw at any time.

Next, visualize yourself sharing that peace with others in your community. Imagine yourself being able to pass this peaceful feeling along with every handshake or any time that you comfort somebody who is having a problem. Think about this web of peacefulness that is woven with every single human interaction. And finally, imagine yourself as a beacon of peace for society. Imagine your peaceful light radiating out to the rest of humanity, causing a ripple effect that affects the whole, then open your eyes and go about your day. You can recall this imagery each time that you interact with people and go out in public. You have the power to make small changes that trigger big changes the world over.

Conscious Communities

Nurturing conscious communities is hard work, let me tell you. Even when everybody in a given spiritual group you've gathered shares common goals, personality clashes and group dynamics can get in the way of things. Some people are simply not content unless there is discord in a group. Believe it or not, this can happen in spiritual communities based on peace and love. If you think about it, you're getting a group of change-makers together who want to make the world a better place, so it makes sense that they are going to force the group through periods of dynamic change. As a member of a conscious community, especially if you're a leader, you'll have to strike a balance between being welcoming to all and protecting the integrity of the group.

Never underestimate the importance of having a shared mission. If you have the opportunity of influencing a community, whether it's a community garden or a worship group, openly ask questions about everyone's eventual goals. What would everyone like to see in five years? Ten years? It may be a helpful exercise for the group to write an official mission statement, and then for each individual to meditate upon that mission statement. You might even turn your mission statement into an opening prayer, chant, or affirmation to start out your group meditation sessions.

When nurturing conscious communities it's important to have strong leadership. This might seem counterintuitive if you're hoping to build a utopia in which everybody agrees. Strong leadership doesn't necessarily hinder this process. Leaders provide a point of contact for people who may have interpersonal problems that require solutions. You can still advocate for consensus decision making, if you like. If you're committed to conscious communities, meditate upon the potential of becoming the leader of one. Remember, some of the best leaders are those who are not power hungry, so it's okay if you don't feel driven to be a leader. You can still be a good one if your skills match the opportunities in your community.

Finally, an important part of nurturing conscious communities is growth. If you're a member of a community that is intent on improving the world, chances are that one of the main goals is spreading the message and gaining new members. You'll want to be welcoming of diverse people who may have different value systems than you. That doesn't mean you have to accept people who seem to be working counter to your goals. This is another reason why writing out a clear mission statement can be incredibly helpful. People can decide whether they want to join your community with a clear idea of what the group wishes to promote. If some people break away, don't look at this as a failure. They may be working as an arm of your community, promoting some of your goals as a separate community. Diversity is a good thing, even if it means you can't work together directly. The more conscious communities we have in the world, the better.

EXERCISE: **Spiritual Community**

Here's a simple group exercise that you can use at the beginning of any sort of conscious community meeting. You can use this at your first meeting together to decide on a mission statement or you can use this format for every meeting in order to nurture a connection and make meditation your focus. For the meeting, you'll need a notebook to make an agenda and a talking stick (or something of that nature) to pass around so that everybody has an opportunity to contribute to the discussion.

Seat everyone in a circle. Begin with a prayer or affirmation that helps establish your goals of getting input from everyone without avarice. Here's an example prayer that you could use, and you can tweak it to suit your belief system if you like:

"Hail to the divine source; be with us today as we make important choices for our conscious community. Help each of us make a contribution to the whole. Help each of us relinquish individual ownership of ideas for the greater good of the group and make decisions free from bias. Blessed be."

Explain to the group that you will pass around the talking stick and have each person add something to talk about to the agenda. The agenda might address, for example, what to include in the group's mission statement, an activity that the group should plan together, or a problem that affects the group and needs to be addressed. Pass the stick around the circle and have one person write down agenda items as they are spoken, then have that person go through each agenda item and talk about it as necessary. If there's a problem to be solved or a group activity planned, pass the stick around again for a brainstorming session and have the ideas written down. When all the ideas are on the page, the group might choose to vote on an idea. If there's a problem that affects one person in the group, that person can choose one solution to try for a set period of time.

After the discussion it's time to meditate. The group can choose a meditative focus or simply allow time to sit in quiet and receptive meditation. Agree on an amount of time to meditate before you begin. For a new group, that might be just twenty minutes. For an established group, the meditation session might last an hour or more. After the meditation time is finished, allow time for people to share anything that may have come during the meditation, such as visions or messages or feelings and perceptions. Write down notes of any important things that come up in the meditation. Allow enough time for people to talk and stretch and return from a meditative state back to the real world. These sessions can be held weekly or once a month as a community-building exercise. When new people join, don't forget to explain the process so that they get to contribute to the group as well.

The Benefit of Group Meditation and Finding a Community

One of the most challenging parts of building conscious communities is coming together in person to do great spiritual things. If you're reading this book, it means that you're probably a thinker and an intellectual. That sort of person can easily become isolated through introspective practices like reading and meditation, but these spiritual practices don't have to be isolating. Introspection can be the very thing that draws us closer together.

Luckily, we live in a time when the Internet can bring us closer together with people who care about similar things. Try posting on message boards and online classifieds, group directories, and sites geared toward meeting up in person. Find a local public place where it's safe to meet people

• • • • • • • •

from the Internet. You may have a café or a store that sells recycled things or a library in your town that has a meeting area you can reserve for your group.

When you meet up in person, make sure that you have a way to keep in touch. You might choose to have an online site for communicating between meetings or you may simply collect contact information to let people know about future meetings. You can look at the community-building exercise earlier in this chapter for an example of how to structure your first meeting. Give everyone time to give input as to what the group should do.

Give time for group meditation as well. Group meditation can be a very useful exercise for several reasons. There are those who believe that the power of meditation—that is, its energetic benefits for individuals and the world—is multiplied in a group setting. In this belief system, when a circle of three or more people in the same room get together to meditate, it is much more constructive than when each individual person meditates on their own in their own time. Secondly, feeling each other's energy during a group meditation session adds to group cohesiveness. There's something special about sharing warmth, intention, and energy in a spiritual group context. It helps people bond. Also, those who are more skilled at meditating and manipulating energy act as models and mentors for those who are just beginners.

Finally, I find that group meditation is vital for my own life because I need accountability to remind myself to meditate frequently. I'm a pretty active person and don't need reminders to exercise. However, I do need reminders and accountability when it comes to sitting down and relaxing in meditation, otherwise I might let this important part of my spiritual life slide. When I have some buddies who come to my home once a week to meditate, it makes sure that I place meditation as a top priority on my calendar.

I hope that you will dive in wholeheartedly and become a mindful meditation leader in your community. You may feel awkward at first, especially if you're just a beginner yourself. It's okay to feel nervous. Everybody has to start somewhere, and chances are that others in your community will be overjoyed that somebody was first to gather a group of kindred spirits. There are definitely ups and downs to working with a group. Group dynamics seem to go in cycles. One month you may find people working together and excited about a goal, and then the next month you might find that barely anyone seems to care enough to come to a meeting. Have patience and be persistent. Just as it takes a while to learn how to meditate effectively, it takes a long time to establish a group and learn how to work together as a community effectively. People don't always see eye-to-eye. However, diverse opinions and skills are part of every mindful society.

So, be brave and break out of your shell. Help make meditation a part of every conscious community—something that we can join together and share, rather than something that is practiced only in private. Even if you live in a region that doesn't normally practice this sort of thing, you can be one of the people who plants a seed of change. You might be surprised at how many

• • • • • • •

kindred spirits come out of the woodwork and join you, thankful that somebody brought the conversation out into the open. You are now an ambassador for consciousness and mindfulness in your community. You may be the first, but you won't be the last. Go forth with my blessing and be the change that you want to see in the world.

Alexandra Chauran is a second-generation fortuneteller, a third degree elder high priestess of British Traditional Wicca, and the queen of a coven. As a professional psychic intuitive for over a decade, she serves thousands of clients in the Seattle area and globally through her website. She is certified in tarot and has been interviewed on National Public Radio and other major media outlets. Alexandra is currently pursuing a doctoral degree, lives in Issaquah, Washington, and can be found online at SeePsychic.com.

Sarah O'Brien

Peace in Our Hearts, Peace in Our World
A PRACTICE

SHAKTA KHALSA

As you read this practice or record it and listen to it, be in a meditative space. Treat it as a meditation or a time for prayer or contemplation. Go slowly, and let the feeling and ideas sink in. To stay present, it may be helpful to be aware of your breath. If you are reading this, close your eyes after each section. Give a pause to let the words sink in.

Since children are powerful, tuned-in creators, I've included wording in more childlike language after the adult sections of the practice. Feel free to improvise and adapt this for your personal use. After completing the exercise, allow space for children to talk about what they experienced. This is very subtle and sensitive work, so go slowly and focus on feeling the words resonate within you.

Sit down on the floor in a meditative position or sit straight in a chair. If you are doing the practice with children, sit side by side or across from each other.

1. **For adults:** "I let myself relax into a state of feeling for all who are suffering, and that feeling extends out to the whole world. I allow the pain. I sit with it and let it be as it is, in trust, simply because it is part of All That Is. After some time I find the pain has subtly transformed into something else: a compassionate healing, an accepting of the higher wisdom in this, as in all, actions."

   For children: "Let's close our eyes and allow whatever we feel, even if it is sad or angry or fearful. If pictures come to you—things that you've seen on TV, heard people talking about, whatever it is—just let it be. It cannot hurt you to let it be. Give yourself permission to feel, and just watch what happens if you don't block your feelings."

2. **For adults:** "I feel my prayer field, my energy field, extending out in front of me and all around me. It is a beacon of light that holds a space for a bright future, a world in which all conflict is resolved in the highest manner. I don't use my rational mind to think of strategies that would resolve it. Rather, I create a space—an emptiness that contains all possibilities—in which the universal wisdom can fully work. I trust humanity. I visualize us at our best, with full awareness of the consequences of our actions, using challenges as opportunities to propel our world into a new way of being. This does not mean that those who have hurt others are not called to account, but I see this happening in the miraculous ways of the universe rather than by ways that create more suffering and retaliation."

   For children: "Instead of trying to think about all the problems and solutions that are being talked about in our world right now, let's do something really different. Let's imagine a big, bright emptiness that stretches out in front of us and all around us and goes into the future. That big emptiness is a space of light in which anything is possible! Magical things, miraculous things, things no one ever thought about can all happen in this wonderful emptiness that we are allowing to be there."

3. **For adults:** "I have the courage to go into the mind and heart of someone who has hurt others. I feel the pain that can be translated into hatred and inflicting pain on others. I feel it pass through me, and I allow it as part of All That Is. I remember that when I accept what is, it cannot stay the same. My acceptance of it creates a kind of 'vibrational hug' around it, and it melts. I have a sense that these beings are brought into the fold of humanity through the transformation that happens through this compassionate act."

• • • • • • •

For children: "It takes courage to go into a place inside you where you allow yourself to feel the pain that is inside a person you don't like or who has hurt you, or someone else, in some way. Think of anyone who is like that for you. And now… allow them into your heart and feel their heart, too. The hate melts, and what is left is just a human being who didn't know how to handle their painful feelings."

4. **For adults:** "I trust that All That Is will unfold the events of the future that will match the vibratory frequency that I, and many others together, are holding and projecting—a sacred space where peace and truth prevail. In this deep space of trust and knowing, I feel the ecstasy that is my birthright, and I extend that birthright out to all of humanity."

For children: "Without even thinking, we trust that we will have another breath, and another and another, right? Now let's have that same kind of trust that something good is happening—something that is connecting us with everyone else on our planet. Feel the light of peace in your heart and connect it with everyone else: people you know and people you don't know. Let's grow peace so it stretches all around the world."

5. **Adults and children together, with hands at the heart center:** "And now, let's send a blessing to all the people, animals, and plants on our beautiful Mother Earth by saying together three times, 'Peace to All, Life to All, Love to All.'"

Edward Acker

Shakta Khalsa is a leading expert on children and yoga, having worked with both since the mid-1970s. She is a parent, Montessori educator, and yoga professional recognized by *Yoga Journal* magazine as one of the top five kundalini yoga teachers in the world. Shakta is the founder and director of Radiant Child Yoga, an internationally known training program for teaching children yoga and consciously working with and raising children. She has authored several yoga books, including her latest, *The Yoga Way to Radiance: How to Follow Your Inner Guidance and Nurture Children to Do the Same*. Visit www.childrensyoga.com and www.shaktawrites.com.

For Subtle Energy and Spirit

This final section offers you profound and subtle means of practicing mindfulness. Ultimately, a meditation practice fosters a strong relationship with your soul, or authentic self. Thomas Moore gives you a variety of perspectives on meditation and a concrete exercise so that you can connect to the depth of your own soul. Cyndi Dale simplifies perspectives on subtle energy and healing. She gives you plenty of techniques and practices for healing, inner power, personal guidance, and harnessing the authority of your chakras. Sherrie Dillard rounds out the section with key information on how you can be mindful of divine presence in your life, connecting to your spirit guides for healing and direction. Enjoy the process of applying the following techniques as you explore the subtle realms of mindfulness and meditation and deeply connect to your authentic self.

Meditation from the Deep Soul

THOMAS MOORE, PhD

From the time I was thirteen until I was twenty-six I lived in a Catholic mendicant order, where I learned to meditate in a monastic atmosphere. There it wasn't so easy to draw the line between meditating and living. I spent hours studying Latin and Greek and theology and philosophy, preparing music for the elaborate liturgies, walking quietly in the gardens, working inside or out in the orchard, and eating, for the most part, in silence. And there I learned that *laborare est orare*—to work is to pray.

I discovered that silence is not only a matter of sound and quiet but also a contemplative visual atmosphere. Those monastic arches and cloister walks and thick wood doors create an atmosphere of reflection so that just to walk the halls was a kind of meditation.

Today I would say that meditating in the priory was as much the work of the deep soul as the lofty spirit. The soul is the spirit's counterpart, a profound sense of self rising out of a world that is intimate, close, and sensual. The soul's meditating is based on a love of the world and its things, of nature and art and objects. If you value this deep soul, it matters where and under what circumstances you meditate. You don't try to get away from the world but rather more deeply into it. You look for the infinite and nameless that is deep within rather than far away.

In contrast to the spirit, the soul has its own values and preferences. It thrives on attachment to people, animals, places, and things. It progresses by means of pleasure rather than deprivation. It learns and expresses itself poetically rather than abstractly. It allows life to happen and follows what is given rather than pursuing what should be. Therefore, in formal meditating, the soul finds value in distracting thoughts and roaming images. These have significant meaning and should be embraced rather than avoided.

When you meditate from the soul, your guiding spirit is not Saturnine—distant, cool, abstract, goal-oriented; it could be Venusian—sensual, bodily, swamped by beauty. You may want to meditate while in the sea or walking through the woods or eating delicious food. When people ask me today how I meditate, I tell them I do it at the piano when, almost every day, I play some absorbing, sublime piece of classical music and get lost in the ether by means of my fingers and ears. I'm not speaking metaphorically or flippantly. For me this is a real and true soul way of meditating.

Some think, as I do, that our night dreams are the purest expression of the soul. They can be sensuous, whether delightful or disturbing, and bring the history of our ordinary lives into play with the eternal patterns of human life. For me, one value of dreams is the way they emerge from a well of unknown and bottomless images, memories, and emotions. I have no interest in controlling them and don't understand the continuing interest in lucid dreaming, the attempt to influence and shape them. To me, that would be like painting mustaches on the great painted men and women in art history.

Now imagine meditating in the style of dreaming, allowing images to rise and ripple across consciousness, mysterious and beguiling. What a sumptuous and meaningful way to meditate. You are the observer and receiver, not the controller, which reeks of the very ego many meditation teachers warn against. You allow the images to take their course and appreciate that they contain messages of real importance to you. You want them to appear of their own accord. Otherwise, you remain trapped in your current level and degree of awareness.

Such images are mysterious. Good. They challenge you. They stump you. They cause you to go deeper in your thoughts. They require some acquaintance with art and images and poetics. This is the language of the mysterious, which is the very stuff of the sacred and the spiritual. It's astounding that so many meditators buy into the modernist view that you should be in control, know what you're doing, and understand everything that appears before your eyes. Where is the spirituality in that? Rather, you could be skilled at responding creatively to mysteries without conquering them. Isn't that what religion, in the best sense, really is?

• • • • • • •

To work is to pray, but to do anything with such absorption that you lose yourself positively in what you're doing is to meditate. The whole point is to get lost, to lose your footing, to no longer know where you are and indeed who you are. Such lostness is an exquisite goal, and the world, with all its local particulars, can help you get there.

> EXERCISE: **Practices for Accepting the Distraction and Meditating from the Deep Soul**
>
> **1:** Sit quietly with your eyes closed, and pay attention to all the distracting outer sounds you hear, as though you were listening to music and to inner distracting thoughts and images, which no doubt have meaning for you.
>
> **2:** See your "soul meditation" as a movement deeper into life rather than away from it. Practice in a beautiful place, with visual art and music if appropriate. Include contemplation of the world and not just an inner drifting away from life.
>
> **3:** Use a tool for a world-centered meditating, such as a camera for thoughtful photographs or an easel for painting and drawing or a notebook for writing poetry or stories.
>
> **4:** Find a place that you find beautiful and that helps your contemplation. Go back to that place for special times of meditation, and connect your meditating with that place.
>
> **5:** Find or create a space that evokes contemplation. Choose the right materials— for example, raw wood or rocks or iron and textiles—and place helpful images so that they induce in you a spirit of meditation and contemplation.

I recommend that you try meditating from the deep soul in your own way. In the kernel of the soul lies a high degree of individuality. But you don't have to give up your spiritual forms. You can do both—soul and spirit. The only danger is to engage in one without the other. The two are equally valuable, even if in some ways they are radically different.

Humor, lightness, ease, and grace are the bright qualities of soul, but it has its shadow, too: irony, comedy, paradox, and absurdity are in there as well. You might also know that the soul often benefits more from loss than from gain. In the soul you don't have the payoff of feeling that you're getting somewhere or have achieved anything. Doing is its own reward.

· · · · · · ·

Thomas Moore, PhD, is the author of *Care of the Soul* and twenty other books on spirituality, sexuality, myth, religion, and depth psychology. He has taught religious studies and psychology and has been a psychotherapist for over thirty years. He often speaks at C. G. Jung societies and has done special work consulting at major medical centers with the idea of bringing soul to medicine. He also writes fiction and music and has a special relationship with Ireland, the land of his ancestors. He lives in New England.

Hari Kirin Khalsa

Enhancing Your Energetic Vibration

CYNDI DALE

As teenagers, my friends and I made our decisions based on "vibes." We ate food that gave off a "good vibe," dated people with the "same vibe," avoided situations that had a "bad vibe," and went to parties that would "raise our vibe." We didn't know it then, but we were tuned into one of the most important aspects of reality: vibration.

Vibration is one half of the formula that composes everything seen and unseen, or energy. Energy is information that vibrates, and everything and everyone is made of it, from flowers to thoughts. What makes a rose a rose, rather than a cupcake, is its unique imprint, or energetic code. Simplistically, a rose is an expression of its original formula, or code, as are humans.

If internal or external events are supportive of our original code, we'll be able to articulate our authentic, or true and genuine, self. The result is vitality and passion, clear thinking, beneficial emotions, a happy body, and the ability to flow from situation to situation with ease and grace. The opposite is also true. When inner or outer factors don't synchronize with this code, well, you can only imagine the results, including everything from poor health to disastrous relationships.

Many of us work hard to reinforce our authentic self and sustain its original code, even if we don't use these words. We diligently diet, read self-help books, and buy shoes that support our fallen arches. So how come all this busyness doesn't always leave us replenished or renewed?

There is a range of energy that is even more powerful than the everyday and concrete. It's called subtle energy, and the good news is that we're made of it as well as concrete physical energy.

Subtle energy is similar to physical in that it's composed of information and vibration. It's much less measurable, however, though that doesn't mean it's weak. In fact, it creates physical reality and constitutes the majority of our original code. Do you want to accentuate your authentic self? Change a harmful situation? You can leverage time and resources by focusing on your subtle energy, which, in turn, can transform physical energy.

Subtle energies emanate from and affect every part of our being—body, mind, and soul. Just as physical energies are housed in physical organs, subtle energies occupy their own subtle anatomy, a three-part structure that processes subtle and physical energy. You'll meet the three members of the subtle anatomy in this chapter, although I will mainly focus on two components: the subtle energy field and the chakras. Subtle energy fields serve a vital protective function, and the chakras—subtle energy bodies anchored in the material body—perform physical, psychological, and spiritual functions. As such, the latter are ideal vehicles for healing, manifesting, and enlightenment.

Not all subtle energies are created equally. Ultimately we want to attract, process, and emanate the subtle energies that match our authentic self and its supportive energetic code. We want to refrain from interacting with those that don't match our unique signature. When we hit the "right notes," physical reality follows suit and we begin "living the dream" instead of just "dreaming the dream." By "raising our vibration," or aligning our subtle and physical energies with our unique spiritual code, we literally change our reality.

How do we accomplish this goal? In this chapter I present vibrational healing techniques aimed at helping you do just that.

Before outlining these processes, which include playing with color and sound, performing a fun Tibetan finger healing exercise, and interacting directly with the chakras, I will acquaint you with the issues surrounding energetic vibrations. First, I discuss matters related to vibrational healing, the overview phrase describing the means for enhancing your energetic vibrations. Using anecdotal and scientific evidence, I explore the relationship between our original code and energy, specifically highlighting the vibrational component. I also include a quick description of the subtle energy anatomy, highlighting the chakras.

Our next step on the yellow brick road leading to Oz, the empowerment of our "good vibes," features ways to discern the difference between energies. How do we know when we are being positively or negatively affected by vibrational energies? A quick "cheat sheet" listing these factors will help you decide. At this point the chapter turns a corner and I lay out several easy and effective exercises, all designed to help you become the self that you really are. Once you've

• • • • • • • •

reached this stage, you'll be equipped with techniques you can use any time to raise your vibration or align with your true self. You'll be the star of your own dreams!

The Case for Vibrational Healing

A client, whom I'll call Kelly, set up an intuitively based energy session because everything in her life was going wrong. "I'm being audited—again. I'm underemployed, and I only meet unemployed or married men. Besides which," she sneezed, "I'm nearly always sick."

Kelly admitted she had an unenthusiastic attitude toward herself and the world. Then again, who would greet the world with a grin when it's usually raining on you?

Listening to her, I was reminded of an insight shared by an indigenous healer in Peru. When I complained about a malady I couldn't shake, he said something like this:

"If the clouds are always covering the sun, the problem could be the weather. Then again, it might be where you are standing."

My client was hardly going to move from Minnesota to China. That meant she needed to change something inside of her.

At first, Kelly refused this invitation to self-examination. "I want to eliminate the negative energy in people," she demanded. "Better yet, I never want to meet anyone nasty again." Apparently I was the magician with the magic wand who was supposed to help her accomplish these goals.

As I'm sure you've already learned, we can't control others. We can't rewrite tax codes or transform a toad into a prince or achieve a zero exposure to viruses. We can, however, alter our own energy and, by doing so, become our best selves. In turn, we make more effective decisions. Our intuition informs us who to trust or not. Our open heart might encourage kinder treatment from others. A new and improved attitude can influence the people and events around us. My goal was to help Kelly accomplish an internal energetic shift and learn to meet life like the adventure that it is.

Within a year, Kelly was a happier and healthier person. She was dating a great guy and hadn't been audited the prior year. She was also being treated more respectfully at work, a desire that hadn't made the initial list. Her health had also improved significantly, and she was enjoying the yoga class that was helping make the difference.

What did I help Kelly do? She used vibrational healing techniques to accentuate her authentic self and its signature energy. You'll be learning all about these concepts and techniques in the following pages.

Your Original Code and Vibrational Healing: The Formula for Increased Health and Happiness

As stated, I believe that we all have an "original code." This is our signature programming, and it upholds the essential elements of our genuine self. Most of this code is subtle, but that doesn't mean its goal is to assure a place in heaven. An enhanced energy code helps us open a little more heaven on earth.

There are three main subtle energetic structures that uphold this code. The chakras are subtle energy bodies; the meridians and nadis are subtle channels; and there are dozens if not hundreds of subtle energetic fields that surround and protect us.

The most famous subtle field is the aura, which extends from the chakras around our body, one layer atop the other. There are dozens if not hundreds of other subtle fields, which are distinct from but also married to our physical and measurable fields, such as our electrical, magnetic, and electromagnetic fields. How lovely if we could actually perceive ourselves as the beautiful assembly of complex and nonlinear energetic fields that we are. Combined, these fields create a cumulative biofield that coordinates all parts of our life, regulating our physiology as well as our ability to heal and manifest.[1]

I believe the auric fields are extensions of the chakras, in-body subtle energy centers that contribute toward our well-being. We have seven main in-body chakras, as well as several minor and out-of-body chakras. Each lies on a band of vibrating energy that determines the incoming and outgoing energy and governs physical, psychological, and spiritual functions. Person to person, our chakras share generic job responsibilities, just as do our physical organs, such as the liver and kidneys. Your chakras also resonate with memories, programs, and awareness unique to you. These special attributes contribute greatly to your original code. Because of this, your chakras are perfect vehicles for clearing issues and blocks and also activating your exceptional traits.

Following is a description of the seven main chakras. Included in this brief sketch is their Hindu name and bodily location, as well as the color that represents the vibrational wavelength running horizontally through and within a chakra. I've also provided a thumbnail description of their main job or task, which will help you apply vibrational techniques to the chakras later in this chapter.

---

1 Beverly Rubik, "Measurement of the Human Biofield and Other Energetic Instruments," Foundation for Alternative and Integrative Medicine, http://www.faim.org/energymedicine /measurement-human-biofield.html.

· · · · · · · ·

First Chakra: Muladhara

Color: Red

Location: Base of the spine

Mission: Security and survival

Second Chakra: Svadhisthana

Color: Orange

Location: Lower abdomen

Mission: Feelings and creativity

Third Chakra: Manipura

Color: Yellow

Location: Solar plexus

Mission: Mentality, power, and success

Fourth Chakra: Anahata

Color: Green

Location: Center of the chest, heart area

Mission: Relationships, healing, and love

Fifth Chakra: Vishuddha

Color: Blue

Location: Throat

Mission: Communication and guidance

Sixth Chakra: Ajña

Color: Purple

Location: Forehead, above and between eyebrows

Mission: Sight (insight, hindsight, future sight) and strategy

· · · · · · ·

Seventh Chakra: Sahasrara

Color: White

Location: Top of the head

Mission: Purpose and spirituality

Vibrational healing techniques are those that reinforce this original code, thus encouraging the expression of our genuine self. They do this by introducing vibrations into our physical and subtle system, frequently through our energetic fields, although they can also enter directly into the chakras. The vibrations that match our authentic self rebalance imbalanced energy, both physical and subtle. The correct vibrations will even linger long after a vibrational healing, continually adjusting our system. These "good vibes" counteract the vibrations we generate from negative thinking, emotional maladjustment, and unhealthy behaviors. They also counter-balance the destructive or harmful energy produced by others that is inherent in a world replete with toxins, loss, and war.

Vibrational tools are effective change agents because vibration affects all levels of our being. Of particular importance are our energetic boundaries, which is a term used to describe our subtle and physical energy fields. I believe the subtle fields are the most important, for when they operate in concert with our original code, they fulfill a vital protective role. They filter unnecessary information, alert us to danger, and communicate messages that augment our well-being. They also support, alter, and sustain our physical fields. Unfortunately, they can also operate on dysfunctional "software."

Negative programming stems from many taproots, including our soul, which carries issues from past lives, "family of origin" beliefs, the culture at large, and our reactions to life's events. This harmful programming causes "blocks" that inhibit our joy, health, and connectivity. Vibrational healing processes, especially those aimed at subtle energy, reinforce our positive programs and help clear the negative ones.

But, you might ask, do they really work?

Short of trying them, consider research from the Institute of HeartMath, which shows that certain vibrations are supportive to everyone. As well, certain vibrations are detrimental. For example, uplifting emotions, such as those equated with spiritual values, are beneficial on all levels. Concentrating positive feelings and attitudes in the heart results in increased energy, stronger cognitive abilities, psychological resiliency, and a bolstered immune system. Simplistically, positivity creates coherence, a state in which heart, mind, and emotions are balanced. In turn, all levels of our energetic self coordinate our immune, hormonal, and nervous systems. Conversely, negative emotions impair these same abilities, also reducing muscle mass, accelerating aging,

• • • • • • •

and even causing brain cell death.[2] Positive feelings, such as gratitude and joy, begin as subtle whispers and then instruct the physical fields. The heart is a powerful place for focus because it generates subtle energy and measurable energy. Its electrical field is about 60 times greater in amplitude than the equivalent activity in the brain. Its magnetic field is 5,000 times stronger than that produced by the brain.[3] Utilize subtle energies that match your innermost self and collective goodness and the rest will follow.

How Do You Know If You Are Harmonizing?

Sometimes it's easy to know if an energy matches your genuine self, therefore supporting your original code. Then again, sometimes it's not. How can you tell?

Healthy energy, which matches the true self, does the following:

- Boosts your physical energy without leaving you frazzled or frenetic
- Can also relax and encourage peace and calm, allowing for down time
- Smooths out and soothes emotions
- Kindles creativity and innovation
- Builds self-esteem and self-confidence
- Invites connection within self, others, and the Divine
- Enhances sharing of personal truths, accomplished with compassion and kindness
- Bolsters personal and professional vision
- Ignites energy to meet goals
- Opens the gateway to intuition and safe mystical encounters
- Promotes boundaries, the appropriate separation between self and other
- Raises your sense of self to an optimum level

In contrast, energy that doesn't vibrationally match our own can lead to the following:

- Loss of physical energy, sense of being drained, or illness
- Frantic or scattered feeling in body

---

2 Rollin McCraty, PhD, and Doc Childre, "The Appreciative Heart: The Psychophysiology of Positive Emotions and Optimal Functioning," http://www.metaphysics-for-life.com/support-files/heartmath-appreciative-heart.pdf.
Ed Decker, "Resilience: How to Build It, Maintain It, and Restore It," 12 December 2014, http://www.rewireme.com/wellness/resilience-build-maintain-restore/.

3 Linda Marks, "The Power of the Heart," www.healingheartpower.com/power-heart.html.

• • • • • • • •

- Illness, fatigue, or exhaustion

- Emotional challenges

- Muddled sense of self, goals, and desires

- Negative thinking, resulting in low self-esteem
  or, conversely, criticism of others

- "Can't do" attitude instead of "can do"

- Difficulty in sharing personal truth or hearing that of others

- Self-hatred or hatred of others

- Hypervigilant psychic activity or the opposite, which
  is the inability to receive spiritual guidance

- Poor energetic boundaries, either too loose or too rigid

- Lowers your sense of self to the worst common denominator

Noticing which situations, people, feelings, colors, sounds, events, and more create healthy rather than unhealthy reactions will help you know when you are imbalanced and need to rebalance, a task that can be made easier because of the next section's exercises.

Exercises to Enhance Your "Vibe"

The rest of this chapter is devoted to exercises that you can use anytime (and, with only a few exceptions, anywhere) to fortify your original code and genuine self. They can help rebalance you when you feel "off," as per the signs we discussed earlier. But you don't have to feel bad to make use of them. Even when you're doing great, why not step it up?

Some of the exercises refer to the Divine, the Higher Power that sustains us all. You can substitute any name you would like for this being, such as Creator, God, Allah, Greater Spirit, Kwan Yin, Mary, the Goddess, or even Higher Self. The name is less important than the concept of being wholly and completely embraced by a source of eternal goodness.

As you practice these exercises, make note of which ones seem most powerful and under what conditions. Feel free to alter them as you wish. After all, they have been developed to support your unique self and can be done in the way that is perfect for you.

EXERCISE: **Unlocking Your Intuition to Meet Your Authentic Self**
Most energetic techniques incorporate our intuitive gifts. As well, the good life is guided by intuition. We are all intuitive; we've only to envelop and apply our gifts to benefit from them.

· · · · · · · ·

The following exercise will help you access the basic intuitive gifts, which are visual, verbal, feeling empathy, and spiritual empathy. It will also assist you in applying your intuition to better understand and embrace your genuine self.

1: Take a few deep breaths. Affirm your spiritual nature and acknowledge that the Divine is fully present to guard, guide, teach, and empower you.

2: Set the intention for this exercise, which is to access your intuition to gain insight about your authentic self that generates and is supported by your original code.

3: Concentrate on your heart and ask that your authentic self step fully forward. It is you; many of us experience this self most fully through our heart.

4: Ask for visual clues to your authentic self. The visual intuitive gift presents images or pictures in your mind's eye. If you don't psychically see anything, use paper and pencil and draw whatever comes to you. All images constitute descriptions, symbols, or revelations about your authentic self. Know that your visual gift is available whenever you need it.

5: Request verbal messages about your genuine self. The verbal intuition gift is usually available through internally heard sounds, tones, words, or communication. If you don't hear anything, try writing, singing, humming, or talking. What messages do you express or tune into? What is important to this self? Acknowledge that your verbal gift is accessible whenever needed.

6: Breathe deeply into your body, which is the tool for your empathic feeling gifts. Your body speaks through feelings, smell, and touch, as well as sensations that could involve heaviness, flutters, twitches, pressure, and more. Link to your genuine self through the feeling gifts and get a sense of the emotions your authentic self resonates with or gravitates toward. Are there certain physical or emotional states preferred by your genuine self or, conversely, disliked? How does your authentic self alert you to people or situations that don't suit you? Affirm the ever-ready presence of your body's intuitive guidance.

7: Clear your body and ask what the Divine wants you to know through your spiritual empathic gifts, which instruct us through awareness, bursts of understanding, or streams of consciousness. In relation to your authentic self, embrace your full consciousness. When you focus on goodness, how does your body respond? Know that this gift is available to you at all times.

8: Now ask the Divine to merge the insights you've received through these four intuitive means—visual, verbal, feeling empathy, and spiritual empathy—into a

• • • • • • • •

complete whole. Request a final inspiration about your authentic self and what type of energies resonate with or repulse it.

9: Take a few more deep breaths and thank the Divine for assistance.

Finally, realize that you can trust inner capacities even if you can't categorize them by style. Sometimes we simply know what is true or not.

EXERCISE: **Meditation for Removing Blocks**

A block is any physical challenge, belief, feeling, or spiritual misunderstanding that prevents us from living fully in the moment and acting—or reacting—from our genuine nature.

The reason that blocks are so harmful is that their energy doesn't match our own. These impediments can therefore be said to degrade our natural expression, creating energetic and, therefore, physical, psychological, or spiritual disturbances.

There are two keys to releasing blocks or undesirable energy. The first is to do so with compassion and love. This allows us to gather the "pearl" from what was or is a destructive situation and move on, richer in knowledge and wisdom. The second is to substitute a new energy for the old, otherwise brand-new negative energy will refill the cleared area.

This second point is important enough that I want to underscore it with an example. I once worked with a woman who was fired from nearly every job, even though she had a PhD in her subject area and was friendly and warm. Previously, she had visited a healer who had removed a block from her family lineage. Both sets of my client's grandparents had barely survived the Depression. Her grandfathers had, in fact, lost job after job because of the economy. One of the results was a belief that inserted into the family, framed in this way: "No job is safe."

Certainly my client's grandparents were subjected to this reality, but once it entered the family energetics, it remained as a belief that kept asserting itself. In fact, my client's parents had also experienced several job losses.

The healer who first worked with my client had pinpointed the destructive belief but hadn't inserted a belief that would prevent a fallback. Because of this, my client's life hadn't changed. We spent a single session unearthing a more positive belief from her heart and asking the Divine to "spread" it vibrationally throughout her system. Consequently, my client has enjoyed the same job for several years.

The following guided meditation will allow you to accomplish the goals of releasing a block and opening to a more fulfilling energy.

• • • • • • • •

1: Take a few deep breaths and center yourself, resting your consciousness in the part of yourself in which you feel most at home.

2: Ask the Divine to help you pinpoint the most important block for you to work on. Your intuitive abilities will help you visually, verbally, or kinesthetically perceive this block.

3: Focus on the block and ask the Divine to show you what occurred to cause this disruption.

4: Ask the Divine to note the various negative ways this block has affected you. Then ask for insight about the gift inherent in the block. This gift is usually a teaching, understanding, or perception. Know that accepting a teaching isn't the same as validating abuse or undeserved trauma. Taking the silver lining out of the black cloud will, however, allow you to move out from under the cloud and bask in the sunlight.

5: Ask the Divine to cleanse you of the black or stagnant energy.

6: Request that the Divine expand the wisdom that you've gained and add additional supportive energy, thereby filling in the empty area left by the release process. Continue this activity until you feel more whole and complete.

7: Ask, too, if there are any additional activities that would enable you to continue moving forward.

8: Own the courage it took you to complete these steps. Feel gratitude toward yourself and the Divine for the healing process.

EXERCISE: **Prayers for Communing and Healing**

Most of us think of prayer as a single action, an outreach to the Divine. It is, but there are also numerous types of prayer, each of which accomplishes a different purpose, but all raise vibration and enable you to more clearly express your original self.

The following outline will familiarize you with five versions of prayers. After describing a prayer and its purpose, I present a "cheat sheet" that might help you construct your own prayer. These clues are presented as statements to address sequentially; some are fill-in-the-blanks.

Prayer of Decision: Getting Clear on Choices

Are you confused? The Prayer of Decision allows will help you summarize your need and gain clarity about choices leading to a decision. You can create your prayer by paying attention to these statements:

> *Divine, I would like clarity on the following decision: _____.*

• • • • • • • •

I am open to any revelation that would reveal the need this decision would meet.

*I would like to be shown the best possible choices and be supported in
selecting the one that will yield the highest possible outcome.*

Prayer of Petition: Asking for Higher Will

We often feel depleted or discouraged because we don't know how to make a dream come true. This prayer aligns your will with higher will through a request for divine help. We can focus the petition this way:

Divine, I ask your assistance in meeting this need: _____.

I understand that you will ultimately decide the best way for this desire to be met.

I am open to the intuitive guidance that will shape my attitudes and actions.

Prayer of Forgiveness: Freedom from the Past

Resentment and bitterness squelch joy and stop forward movement. I define resentment as the belief that someone else "should" have been different. Bitterness occurs when we think *we* should have been different. Forgiveness frees us from should-haves, would-haves, and could-haves, and creates a point of change. This fulcrum is the present, the only place from which we can step anew into the future.

An effective prayer of forgiveness includes these four ideas:

I have been holding a "should" for the following reason: _____.

I beseech assistance, for I want to realize that I cannot change what happened.

I ask to perceive the silver lining in the situation, which is this: _____.

Divine, I ask that you keep my heart door ajar for new insights so I can live in the present.

Prayer of Healing: Asking for Transformation

One of the main reasons we pray is for healing.

Healing is complicated. Sometimes we ask and receive exactly what we requested—a better attitude, a new job, a reduction in the size of a tumor. Then again, it can seem that the particulars we desire are completely ignored, or at least our time frame is overlooked. Maybe we find a super mechanic for our broken-down car—five years too late.

Healing is often paradoxical because the Divine gives us what we need, not necessarily what we want. As an example, I once worked with a client who had cancer. We prayed for healing. Over the next few days, her spine stretched and she grew two inches, which was not what we had requested. While she was eventually given a clean bill of health regarding the cancer, I can't take credit. She was also undergoing che-

· · · · · · · ·

motherapy. Maybe the Divine knew that she had that topic covered but was due for a new wardrobe or perhaps her spine needed to stretch to engage the healing properties in her body.

When we pray for healing, it's important to know that our human perspective regarding the desired cure and its distribution date is merely that—a human point of view. The prayer for healing aids us in setting aside our limited opinion so the Divine can fling open the doorway of our genuine self. Now we can receive the "special deliveries" that are required.

A beautiful way to ask for healing follows:

I am experiencing the following discomfort: _____.

I am willing to release all limited perspectives so I can be shown what I'm supposed to do, as well as what the Divine wants to provide for me.

Divine, I now ask you to connect me with the healing power of grace to create wholeness within and around me. I am willing to follow your plan in all ways.

Prayer of Intercession: Asking for Help for Another

Through intercessory prayer, you serve as a spiritual proxy for someone else, requesting assistance for someone who can't do so personally. I use it when seeking help for young people, animals, groups of people, the seriously ill, or even addicts.

Following is a lovely way to begin such a prayer:

From a place of compassion and surrender, I ask for assistance for _____.
I also request that I be shown anything I can do to personally provide aid.

EXERCISE: Color Your Energy

Remember when you were a kid and selected your crayons with concentrated precision, most likely furrowing your brow? You innately knew that a teddy bear colored red was a different animal than one that was brown.

One of the simplest ways to enhance your energetic vibration is to use color. Colors can be chosen as clothing, accessories, or environmental design items, such as pillows and blankets. I use colored eyeglasses to alter my mood and even eat off certain colored plates to control my eating. (Blue, by the way, reduces appetite.) The easiest way to use color, especially if you need a quick cleansing or boost of energy, is to employ visualization.

Visualization involves tapping into your visual intuition. I'll discuss a few ways to engage visualization for these purposes after presenting the ways the seven main chakra colors aid in cleansing and bolstering energy.

· · · · · · · ·

Color	Cleansing	Adding
Red	Burns out microbes, can clear causes of inflammation, reduces physical blockages and lethargy	Spices up life, stimulating passion and physical system; anchors you in present moment; empowers positive action
Orange	Washes away other's feelings, clears feelings you don't need anymore, erases blocks to creativity	Enhances feelings and your ability to share them, bolsters creativity, inspires appreciation of sensuality
Yellow	Dissipates negative thoughts and worries, dispels fears and prejudice	Sharpens mental acuity and ability to focus, raises self-esteem and confidence
Green	Disperses relationship confusion; cleanses body, relationships, and energetic field	Heightens healing powers, ability to love, and connection with self, others, and the Divine
Blue	Frees you from communication blocks, old messages, and interfering entities that keep you from stating your truth; can also reduce pain, inflammation, and heat	Activates inner truth and the ability to receive guidance, aids sharing of important thoughts, cools energies that are too hot
Purple	Dissipates causes of low self-image and confusion	Increases ability to clarify goals, attracts revelations, improves self-image
White	Purifies all levels of your being, exorcises negative entities and forces	Reinforces your sense of purpose and worthiness, enhances connections with higher guides and the Divine

For two easy ways to use this information, try the following:

Cleansing Blocks

Focus on the issue that is causing disruption and intuitively sense the color that will release the unwanted energy. Take a few breaths, visualize the color in your mind's eye, and imagine it washing through your body from the top down. Let this cascade of cleansing energy flow through your body and also through your energetic fields.

Boosting Vibration

Allow your intuition to select the color that will galvanize you. You can focus on the part of your body requiring a helping hand or, if your entire system requires rejuvenation, you can work in the heart chakra, which can carry energy throughout your system. Ask the Divine to expand the animating power and let it increase until you feel pepped up.

You can also access colors through your inbreath, your hands, or the earth at your feet. The latter process is a fantastic way to boost your physical well-being. Along the same vein, you can breathe in cleansing colors and then follow with a "chaser" of a bolstering color—a great way to gain instant empowerment.

EXERCISE: **Setting Energetic Boundaries with Shapes**

One of the easiest ways to enhance your vibration is to work with the energetic field, and shape is one of the secret ways to establish a field that's immune to others' negative thoughts and attitudes, challenging events, and even illness. It is also one of the keys in creating reality. As explained in an article by Meinard Kuhlmann in *Scientific American*, physicists have long believed that particles and force fields underlie reality; instead, these energies might actually themselves respond to bundles of properties, such as color and shape.[4]

Two Siberian shamans taught me how to use shape to change energy with two basic techniques:

1: Visualize a shape on or in the person or inserted into the energetic field.

2: Trace a shape with fingers or hands on the person, through the energetic field or in the air.

Their practice incorporated only three shapes—circles, squares, and triangles—creating a vibrational method accessible for anyone. In my description of these shapes, I also explain specific ways to cultivate their power.

Circle: Circles embody wholeness, completion, and beginnings. A circle pictured around your body will return you to a state of wholeness if you feel scattered or frenetic. Imagine a circle of light between yourself and anyone you feel disconnected from. A circle around the self will encourage self-reliance. Draw a circle around your body if you feel unsafe and want to affirm the protective power of the Divine.

Square: Squares provide protection and security. Perceive a square shape in your energetic field to protect yourself from a threat or if you need to hold your own in a challenging situation. Imagine yourself standing on a square pedestal

---

4   Meinard Kuhlmann, "What Is Real?" *Scientific American* 309, no. 2 (2013): 41–47.

when you must communicate with authority. Do you have a secret? Put it into a square inside of you; it's like hiding it in a pocket.

Triangle: Triangles symbolize change and wisdom. When problem solving, draw a triangle on paper and ask a question from each angle. The bottom right corner represents the masculine perspective; the bottom left corner accesses feminine insight; and the top of the pyramid shape is the eye of wisdom and assures a "big picture" point of view. Imagine a triangle or pyramidal shape in your energetic field to promote intelligence and quickness. If you seek intuitive answers, see a slowly spinning triangle around you. This triangle interconnects with various dimensions and planes of intelligence to deliver guidance.

EXERCISE: Tibetan Finger Healing

Sometimes we're in a quandary and need a quick energy fix—a sort of instant vitamin boost. There are also times we can't sit down and focus; maybe we're driving the car. And sometimes we're surrounded by other people and don't want them aware of our healing practice. Tibetan finger healing is fast, effective, and easily hidden.

In Tibetan finger healing, each of the five fingers is associated with an element and a color. Elements are the fundamental energies that create physical matter. The meanings of the colors are explained on page 340. I will share a few ways to perform Tibetan finger healing after outlining the relationship between the fingers, elements, and colors.

Thumb: Space (like ether)/white

Index: Wind (like air)/green

Middle finger: Fire/red

Ring finger: Water/blue

Little finger: Earth/yellow

The quickest way to bring instant (and secret) relief is to figure out which finger needs clearing and to wrap the fingers of one hand around the selected finger. Squeeze three to six times. Repeat on the opposite hand.

For instance, you might decide that your greatest challenge is your bitter relationship with a former partner. Consider your feelings. If you are bogged down with grief, sorrow, and sadness, the predominant issues are "wet." After all, tears are wet—and composed of water. You might focus on your ring finger. While holding the ring finger, focus on your sadness and fully own it. Then give permission to release these watery tears. Feel them flow out of your finger and back to the universe, restoring balance to your entire being.

· · · · · · · ·

On the other hand—pun intended—your predominate emotions might include anger, frustration, and rage. You can bring balance to yourself by selecting your middle finger, which manifests fire, the energy of passion and movement. When working with your middle fingers, first embrace your anger. You can even ask what message it can provide you. When you feel finished with the anger in each middle finger, release any leftover anger with the intention that it flows to a place in the universe that could use it.

Is there an energy you would like to activate or invoke? Select another finger and perform the same steps. Activating an energy is done in a similar way as releasing energy, but your intention is the opposite. Imagine that you feel bogged down mentally and need to clear your mind. What element best relates? Wind or air. Wind sweeps across the expanse, clearing whatever is in the way and delivering new energy. When you hold your index fingers, picture and feel the energy of wind wiping away your over-strained thoughts and delivering those that are clarifying. In general, the elements can be seen in this way:

Space: Relates to higher consciousness

Wind/Air: Refers to mentality and ideas

Fire: Pertains to passionate energies

Water: Reflects emotions and intuition

Earth: Relates to grounding and practical energies

You can also touch any part of your body with the finger that represents what you would like to clear. If you don't want anyone to notice what you are doing, simply touch the palms of both hands in the same way.

Working with One or More Chakras

There are many configurations of chakra work, chakras serving as ideal focal points for vibrational tools. You can work with all chakras at once, a chakra at a time, or a specific chakra. This section will show you how to accomplish these goals.

Sometimes we want to work on the entire chakra system all at once. Maybe we don't have much time; perhaps we can't figure out which chakra is most responsible for a specific need. You can accomplish this goal by focusing on your heart.

The fourth chakra is the meeting ground for the chakras underneath it, which are material in orientation, and the chakras above it, which represent spiritual energies. There is a reason that most spiritual systems suggest the heart as the center of the body, mind, and soul.

You can also engage the total system by moving from one chakra to another, which I will show you how to do in the "Relaxation Response and the Chakras" exercise. As well, you can use your chakras to create a healing mantra and conduct an interactive meditation.

• • • • • • • •

Exercise: **Relaxation Response and the Chakras**

This simple mindfulness exercise uses the chakras to compel a deep level of relaxation and, therefore, state of balance in body, mind, and soul. The first time you conduct this exercise, I suggest you conduct it with each chakra. This will familiarize you with every chakra. After that, you can work with the specific chakra that requires balancing. You can also set the intention to work with all the chakras simultaneously through your fourth chakra, which is the center of the energy system. What we do in the heart is shared throughout the chakra system. There are other configurations as well, such as working on two or three chakras. Follow your intuition and make the exercise your own.

1: Find a quiet and cozy place for meditation. Make sure you won't be disturbed or interrupted. Sit or lie in a comfortable position.

2: Take several deep breaths. The word for "breath" and "spirit" are one and the same in several languages. Acknowledge that every time you inhale, you draw the Divine deep within you, also affirming your own eternal spirit. Decide that every time you exhale, you invite the Divine and your own spirit to release you from all toxins, whether they are physical, psychological, or spiritual.

3: Focus on your first chakra, located in the lower genital area and coccyx. Breathe in and through the front and back sides of this chakra and allow each inbreath to fill it with the energy needed for security and safety. Every outbreath releases energies that have been causing insecurity or a lack of safety. As soon as this chakra feels balanced, you'll note a corresponding calm in your entire body.

4: Breathe into your second chakra, located in the abdomen area and lower back. With every inhalation, this chakra takes in emotional affirmations. On the exhalation, the breath unlocks repressed feelings and releases emotional energies you no longer need. When this chakra is cleansed and lit from within, feel the resulting boost of creative energy.

5: Sink into your third chakra, anchored in your solar plexus and mid-back. Every inhalation ushers in needed power and insight, and every exhalation releases data that no longer serves you. Acknowledge the resulting rise in your self-esteem and personal power, as well as increased clarity of mind.

6: Fall into your fourth chakra, located in the front and back of your chest. As you breathe into this chakra, revel in the unconditional love of the Divine. As you breathe out, release everything that opposes love. Settle into the peacefulness this process provides you.

• • • • • • • •

7: Focus on your fifth chakra, found in the front and back of your neck. As you inhale, receive all the spiritual guidance you need right now. Exhale to release negative thoughts and falsehoods. Accept the ensuing calm, which promotes the receptivity of spiritual guidance.

8: Through your sixth chakra, located in your forehead and directly across from it in the back of the head, breathe in the light of truth. Through your outbreath, release all shadows and darkness. You can now see yourself as the beautiful being that you are.

9: Sense your seventh chakra. The front side is on the top of your head and the back side is at the base of your neck. Your inhalation fills you with the spirit of the Divine; your outbreath frees you from any evils. Revel in the divine presence that is you.

10: Upon finishing this relaxation meditation, take a few minutes and enjoy the resulting pulsation of love and grace throughout your body. When ready, take a final breath and give permission for the Divine to continue to inspire you, even as you return to everyday life.

EXERCISE: **Making a Chakra Mantra**

A mantra is a tone, word, phrase, or even a wish that can be chanted, sung, or internally sounded over and over. When focused on, it serves as a prayer.

You can use any sound as a mantra, but it's especially powerful to employ the ancient Hindu chakra seed syllables, the sounds contained within and made by the energy bodies. Invoking these ancient sounds calls forth forces that have served the highest of intentions across time. After introducing you to the chakra seed syllables, I will show you how to use this information to personalize a chakra-based mantra.

CHAKRA	SEED SYLLABLE
First	Lam (*lum*)
Second	Vam (*vum*)
Third	Ram (*rum*)
Fourth	Yam (*yum*)
Fifth	Ham (*hum*)
Sixth	Om (long *O* sound)
Seventh	None (recommend silence)

To create a special chakra mantra, start by coming up with an intention. You might want to affirm a healing, the fulfillment of a wish, or opening to guidance. You can then proceed in one of these two ways:

1: Select a single chakra. Choose the chakra most likely to assist you in this effort. Chant the related sound repetitively, either aloud or internally. You can also mentally focus or physically touch the area managed by the chakra while affirming your intention.

2: Formulate a full-chakra mantra by selecting several of the chakras and assigning them an order of importance. Then string the chakra seed syllables together in sequential order. For instance, if you require money, select the first chakra, which promotes safety and security, and begin your mantra with its seed syllable sound. Do you believe that relationship issues are inhibiting your financial flow? These are related to the fourth chakra. Add the heart sound to your first chakra sound, and so forth.

Following is an example of a chakra mantra created for money. I have put the rationale for the sequence in parenthesis.

Lam (First chakra: to underline money as a security need)

Yam (Fourth chakra: to ask for healing of relational issues causing security issues)

Ham (Fifth chakra: to ask for guidance in earning money)

Om (Sixth chakra: to perceive a future including money)

Vam (Second chakra: to feel happy about receiving money)

Ram (Third chakra: to be empowered to stay on task)

Silence (To show gratitude to the greater Spirit for assistance)

Repeat *Lam, Yam, Ham, Om, Vam, Ram*, and silence, over and over.

Exercise: Interactive Meditation Through a Chakra

Mindfulness techniques often involve holding a focus so you can better understand and then heal a life issue. You can also obtain information from a chakra or galvanize it for manifesting purposes. Your intuition is a key tool in these endeavors.

The following exercise covers all these options.

1: Set your goal. What is it you would like to achieve through a mindful exploration of a specific chakra?

2: Select a chakra. Decide which chakra is most appropriate to work with.

• • • • • • • •

3: Relax in a comfortable and quiet place, and sit or lie down within it.

4: Breathe deeply into the selected chakra. With your goal in mind, relax into the chakra as if you were gently being lowered into its center.

5: Focus your intuition. Allow the wisdom of the chakra to communicate with you, sending feelings, awareness, sounds, or visions to help you figure out what you need to know.

6: Interact. What questions arise? Ask them of the chakra as if communicating with a person. Also ask if there is an activity to conduct to heal an issue, respond to an insight, or manifest a desire.

7: Gratitude. Send gratitude toward anybody on your mind—yourself, the Divine, even the person or people that might have created an issue within you. Gratitude for the lessons learned helps us open to the blessings from above.

8: Relax and release. Breathe deeply and return to full conscious awareness. Move slowly and be gentle with yourself for the next couple of hours.

As you practice these exercises, remember that they can be adapted to your own needs and style. Your genuine self knows exactly how to activate those "key codes" that define you. It also knows exactly how important "good vibes" are to your well-being. Ultimately, your authentic self also knows that the source of vibrational nourishment lies within an infinite wellspring of love that we've only to acknowledge in order to drink from.

Katie Cannon Photography

Cyndi Dale is an internationally renowned author, speaker, and healer. She is the author of eighteen spiritual books, including *The Subtle Body Encyclopedia*, which has garnered four publisher's awards, and her most recent book, *Llewellyn's Complete Book of Chakras*. Cyndi has conducted over 40,000 client sessions and presented training classes throughout Europe, Asia, and the Americas. Visit her at CyndiDale.com.

Awareness of Spirit

SHERRIE DILLARD

During my thirty-year career as a professional intuitive, medium, and pastoral counselor, I have been fortunate to observe and be a part of the evolving and mutually beneficial relationship that exists between mindfulness and the spirit realm. When we notice the world around us—the sun as it sinks into the horizon, the smile of a stranger, the soft touch of the breeze on our skin—we slip into the quiet essence of the moment. Becoming aware of our thoughts without judgment and attachment, allowing our emotions to move through us and noticing our reactions and habitual patterns—these move us deeper into the sublime inner quiet of self. It is here, in this inner sanctuary, that our intuitive senses awaken. In this present-time open awareness many experience sensations of loving warmth and feelings of connectedness to the unseen presence of spirit beings. Intuitively tuning into and communing with these nonphysical beings reinforces and supports mindful living.

Within the moment-to-moment awareness of mindfulness we often experience insight into the depth and magnitude of the wise and loving spirit within. Embodied within this expanded awareness, many sense a transcendent presence and realm of being that exists outside of the confines of physicality. Some are startled when this presence seems to reach out, interact, comfort, and offer guidance. Although you may not know what or who this presence may be, it likely invokes feelings of comfort, connection, and the sense of being known and loved.

· · · · · · · ·

For instance, have you ever suddenly felt that you were not alone? You may have felt as if something or someone was close, maybe even guiding and watching over you. Have you ever felt a warm touch on your shoulder or a tingling sensation quickly move up and down your spine? Some see the presence of spirit energy as soft, light-colored orbs or streaks of light, flashing in a room or when outdoors. Have you ever heard your name called, but there was no one physically present? Maybe a long-forgotten song suddenly pops into your head as you simultaneously feel the presence of a family member who is on the other side. Do you experience synchronicities? Have you ever received exactly what you desire or need in a surprising way or experienced a puzzling, yet beneficial, unlikely coincidence?

These are just some of the signs and experiences that can occur as you consciously become aware of the spirit realm. These experiences can be random and infrequent or they may be common and intensify without any effort or desire on your part. People often write to me wondering if they are imagining or making up these and other unfamiliar and surprising sensations and feelings. Despite not understanding the origin of these experiences, they also tell me that there is a comforting and alluring quality to them.

With increased understanding and awareness, you can begin to better trust your eternal alliance and interconnection with the spirit realm and even communicate with it. Perhaps the most common questions I am asked about the spirit realm are these: who is close to me and why, and how can I better communicate with them? The unseen nonphysical realm is vast and multidimensional. Saint Catherine said, "God opened the palm of his hand and existence ran in every direction."[1] Although the divine presence is within each one of us, the different expressions of this presence also embody a variety of nonphysical forms. The three types of spirit beings that most often come close to visit and assist us are our loved ones who have passed out of the physical body, angels and archangels, and spirit guides.

Learning more about these different spirit beings and tuning into their presence helps us to further experience our interconnectedness with all of life. This awareness enhances mindful living.

Loved Ones on the Other Side

Once our loved ones pass out of the physical body, they enter into the realm of pure love, forgiveness, and compassion. The divine presence within emerges, and they perceive reality through the lens of absolute truth and wisdom. As our loved ones review their life on earth through this enlightened perspective, their wounds and imbalances are healed and they attain clarity and understanding into their life lessons and purpose. Reunited with family and friends already in the spirit realm, those on the other side continue to love and support their loved ones who are

1   Daniel Ladinsky, trans., *Love Poems to God* (New York: Penguin, 2002).

• • • • • • • •

still participating in the earth life. They do their best to send signs and let their loved ones who are still in the physical realm know that they are present and guiding and watching over them.

Love is like air in the spirit realm. It nurtures, uplifts, and motivates our loved ones to ascend into the higher vibrations of bliss. One of the ways they experience increasing levels of love and continue to evolve is by watching over and guiding those still on earth. Strengthened with a better understanding of their true self and aware of the importance of the challenges that they underwent while here, they are also better able to assist and guide us in our everyday challenges and experiences.

Your loved ones on the other side are likely doing their best to reach out, support, and guide you in your earthly pursuits. Your openness to receiving their messages and your attempts to connect and communicate with them are seen, felt, and appreciated. Continuing your relationship with a loved one on the other side will empower you to experience the totality of life and tap into the power of your spirit. Physical death does not end your relationship with a loved one; instead, it takes it to a higher dimension where profound healing, love, and forgiveness are possible.

Angels and Archangels

Throughout time and in most spiritual traditions, angels have played an essential and important role in human evolution. Angels embody pure, divine love. They have never been human, although at times angels will inhabit the body of an animal, child, or adult for a specific purpose. Everyone has a guardian angel who has been assigned to them before their birth into the physical world. Angels protect, guide, support, comfort, love, heal, and remind us that we too are love. They inspire and help us to develop compassion and to forgive and express unconditional love to ourselves and others.

Angels transcend the limitations of time and space. Their presence can be felt in the lowest vibration of hatred, war, and suffering and in the highest experiences of love and enlightenment. Wherever you are and whatever you are doing, an angel is present, yet they cannot offer positive energy, guidance, and protection unless you open the door and request their help.

An angel's heart and mind are one with the divine presence. They know who you are in ways that you may not know yourself, and they love all of you. While you perceive the human you— your desires and hopes and flaws and failures—they know you as spirit and love. Their depth of compassion has no limit, as they are never judgmental and they support you in your soul's plan and purpose.

Archangels embody the highest vibration of divine love and power in the angelic realm. While angels watch over individuals, archangels are given the task of reinforcing and upholding higher values and accomplishing specific missions. For example, Archangel Michael is said to purify negative energy and take lost and dark wandering negative spirits into the pure energy of divine love.

Some religious and spiritual texts mention many archangels by name. An archangel's name often provides insightful clues as to their purpose and mission in the world. As an example, Archangel Uriel's name means "God is my light." Uriel dispels confusion and illusion and shines the light on truth and wisdom. Archangel Raphael, whose name means "God heals" or "he who heals," supports and guides us in matters of health and healing.

Archangels guide, support, and infuse humanity with the vital life force rays of love: positive energy, compassion, and wisdom. They reinforce our best and highest qualities of goodness and truth, and although they are tasked with collectively guiding humanity, they can be called upon for personal assistance.

Spirit Guides

Belief in the existence of spirit guides may be more difficult for some to accept and understand. Spiritual traditions all over the world have acknowledged the presence of angels and archangels. The idea that the soul survives death and continues to exist and live in another dimension is as old as time itself, yet the belief that we are being guided, watched over, and taught by spirit guides is not always easy to embrace and trust. Perhaps this is because we feel a familiarity and warmth for our loved ones who are now on the other side. We miss them and not only accept their presence but hope and even yearn to feel their presence close to us. This is also true of angels. Despite our hesitation to completely accept that there are divine and loving angels who attend to us, in times of grief, despair, fear, and loss we often find ourselves asking for their grace. Frequently, it is not until we have a personal encounter with a spirit guide that we trust and further develop this special relationship.

I first became aware of one of my spirit guides when I was young and camping with my family in a mountainous area named after the Native Americans that inhabited it. Because of my youth and naivety in such matters, I welcomed the misty, ghostlike apparition that I spotted near the river one morning. In part, my acceptance of this Native American spirit was due to the feelings of love and peace that I felt in his presence. No words were exchanged that first day I saw him or in the encounters that followed, but there was a tangible sense of knowing and the feeling that he was watching over me, which felt safe and inviting. I now recognize that he is a spirit guide and have felt his guiding presence and support for many years. Along with several other spirit guides, he is who I depend on for guidance in many areas of my life and is part of what I consider my extended family.

· · · · · · ·

Spirit guides have had many earth lives and have evolved beyond the need to return to earth in physical body. However, at times, a highly evolved soul who has served as a spirit guide will choose to return in physical form for a specific purpose.

One of the ways that spirit guides continue to evolve after their earth lives is to help and assist those of us still in the physical realm. Although we do not "know" spirit guides like we would know a family member or friend who is now on the other side, spirit guides are part of our soul group. Our family members, friends, lovers, and even people we meet and interact with for just a brief period are part of the collective group of souls that we incarnate with over and over from life to life. Although the type of relationship that we have with a specific soul changes from life to life, the dynamics and lessons inherent in the relationship tend to be similar.

For instance, imagine that you have had power struggles with your father. Even as you get older, you continue to butt heads over issues, even insignificant ones of little importance. Unbeknownst to either of you, your power struggles with your father are a carryover from a recent past life when he was your husband and exerted control and power over you. Until you both learn and resolve your common lessons, you will continue to incarnate with one another. Similarly, you have had past lives with your spirit guides. However, they were likely a positive influence on you and helped and supported you during crucial times of challenges and growth. They continue to do this once in the spirit realm. At times, a spirit guide is your soul mate who has opted to stay in the spirit realm and send you unconditional love and healing, and guide your efforts in creating a harmonious earthly experience.

Although spirit guides watch over individuals, there are some who have a broader scope and are tasked with larger responsibilities. Like archangels, these spirit guides work for the collective good and further humanity's evolution. Some support and guide us in restoring and caring for the earth and healing disease, while others motivate us to seek peaceful solutions to conflict. In larger issues of global concern, spirit guides work together in unison with angels and loved ones who have passed over to collectively contribute to critical earthly issues. For instance, in my work as a medium, several of my clients' loved ones on the other side have shared how they are assisting humanity in developing new energy technologies and aiding in finding ways to clean the air and seas. Working in groups guided by spirit guides, a few have also related their involvement in helping to defuse large-scale environmental and humanitarian disaster and heal areas of the earth that have sustained toxic trauma. Steadfast and devoted to supporting and positively influencing the collective good here on earth, the spirit realm recognizes its oneness with all of life.

The Benefits of Connecting to the Spirit Realm

Having a relationship with the spirit realm can benefit you in multifold ways. Spirit beings lift your consciousness and your energy vibration, heighten your intuitive senses, and expand your

• • • • • • • •

capacity to experience abundance and joy. The awareness that you are being watched over and guided by benevolent forces decreases anxiety and stress and empowers you to be more present in the moment. Opening your heart and intuitive senses to the expanded awareness of the spirit realm encourages mindful living.

Healing Grief with the Other Side

Those on the other side send us compassion when we are grieving, provide guidance when we are confused, and celebrate our success and happiness. Wherever you are and whatever you are doing, the spirit realm is with you and ready to offer support and guidance.

When a loved one passes over to the other side, we can be left with feelings of loss, emptiness, and overwhelming sadness. Even as your loved one reaches out beyond the limitations of time and space in an attempt to let us know that they are at peace, pain-free, and still alive, we grieve. As you become more comfortable with trusting and sensing the presence of loved ones on the other side, a new realm of relationship possibilities unfolds. A faint touch on your shoulder, the surprising smell of their cologne or perfume, or the flickering of lights near their favorite spot on the couch lets you know that your loved one is close.

This is what happened to Julia. After she lost her mother to cancer, she felt more alone than she had ever felt. When her mother was first diagnosed, Julia became her devoted caretaker. A year and a half after her diagnosis, her mother died at home surrounded by family and friends. Although Julia expected to feel grief, sadness, and loss, she did not expect to still feel the intensity of these emotions more than a year later.

I met Julia when she came in for a session to connect with her mother. During the reading her mother shared comforting memories and offered her opinion on a few of the current issues that Julia was confronting. She also shared with her some of the signs that she was trying to send to Julia in an attempt to let her know that she was near. Julia left the session feeling more light-hearted and closer to her mother than she had felt since her death.

I heard from Julia several months after our session. She told me that the grief and profound sense of loss she felt after her mother's passing continued to lessen and dissipate. She enjoyed looking for the signs that her mother was sending her and began to sense her presence. Julia felt particularly close to her while sitting and meditating in her garden among the flowers and butterflies that her mother had loved so much. It was here that Julia could best feel her mother's touch, laughter, warmth, and love. Although it was a very different kind of communication that they now shared, Julia felt she could now carry her mother's presence wherever she went.

"It is hard to describe," Julia said, "but I feel as if I can talk to her at any time and feel her comfort, encouragement, and laughter when I most need it."

. . . .

Career Direction from a Spirit Guide

Although we are not usually aware of their presence and assistance, spirit guides often work behind the scenes in our day-to-day lives. Expert at influencing situations and conditions and creating synchronicities that get our attention and lead us in the direction of our highest good, they help us to find our way through the maze of everyday life. They alert us to opportunities and guide us to experiences and conditions that feed our soul and reinforce our inner truth.

For instance, Joe, a friend of mine, was struggling to find employment. Being laid off from an unsatisfying job initially seemed like a relief, but a few weeks into unemployment he was still confused as to what kind of work to pursue. When a friend of his from college invited him to go on a weekend backpacking trip with a couple of other guys, he jumped at the opportunity. But, as the weekend of the trip got closer, one by one his friends canceled. Restless and still excited about spending time in nature, he decided to go it alone.

Tired after a long day of hiking, he sat in front of a warm fire the first evening of the trip and fell asleep. Startled awake by a dream, he woke up feeling that he was not alone. For the remainder of the trip, he often sensed a presence close by.

On his way home from the trip, Joe gave me a call to share his experiences with me:

"I had a dream—at least, I think it was a dream. I was standing in front of a garage that was full of cars. There was a man who was waving to me and inviting me into the garage with him. I think this might have been a spirit guide. During the trip I could feel him close by and even caught a glimpse of him once or twice through the corner of my eye. Whenever I did, it felt good, like everything's going to work out. Anyway, I think that there is a message in the dream that I need to figure out. My intuition tells me that the garage is important, but I'm not sure why. The only thing I can relate it to is my love of restored classic cars, but I don't have the money or time for this hobby anymore. Besides," he said, "I was never any good at working on them. My father was the real mechanic. I know everything about these cars—how they were originally made, their popularity, and what they are worth—but I can't fix them worth anything. I would love to work with these cars, but that could never be more than a hobby for me."

I reminded Joe that spirit guides tend to work behind the scenes, influencing events and conditions. "Listen to your heart and your intuition, and follow up on where you feel led," I said. "You never know, there could be a few surprises in store for you."

The trip and the dream seemed to rekindle Joe's passion for restored classic cars. One day while searching the Internet he discovered an upcoming classic car show and made plans to attend. Later that month as he walked up and down the aisles of the show, he heard a familiar voice and spotted an old friend. His friend, now a car dealer, saw him at about the same time and called him over.

"It's great to see you," his friend said. "Are you here selling or buying?"

"Just looking," Joe replied. "I haven't been to a show in years."

"That's surprising! You know more about these cars than anyone I know—except for me, of course," he joked.

"Just never thought that I could make a living at it," Joe replied.

"I've been making a good living restoring and selling these cars for years, and I went into this knowing only half of what you do about them," his friend said. "Have you ever thought of putting that charm and knowledge of yours to work selling cars? I have my own dealership now."

"No, never even considered it," Joe said. Then, with a confidence that surprised him, he continued. "But I sure would like a chance to give it a shot. I have been selling technology for almost fifteen years. I bet I could sell something that I really liked."

I talked to Joe again several weeks after he started working at the car dealership.

"I just never thought I could work a job I liked and make a living. I don't know where that belief came from, but I let it control me for too long. I was miserable," he said. "But I followed my intuition and the positive feelings like you suggested and was led to something so much better than what I thought could happen. Of course, I think I got some unseen help. How do I go about thanking my spirit guide?"

"Don't worry," I said. "He is here, and he feels and hears you loud and clear."

Angelic Healing

True health and well-being spring from the depths of the soul. Angels help us to heal from the inside out. They touch deep into the source of illness and support us as we go through the process of healing mind, body, and spirit.

Tara had always been a bit quiet and shy, yet as a second-grade teacher she was charismatic and enjoyed creating fun and interesting lesson plans. Her students loved her. Healthy and vibrant, it was a surprise to everyone who knew Tara when she was diagnosed with breast cancer. Although it was not an overly aggressive form of cancer, Tara opted to have a mastectomy. A year after the surgery there was more bad news. During a routine screening, cancer was discovered in her other breast. Tara scheduled another surgery but intuitively knew that to fully heal, she had to do more.

Tara had been a sporadic meditator for several years. Now, facing another bout with cancer, she returned to meditation with renewed commitment and devotion. Finding solace and peace from the stress of her illness, within a few sessions she already felt its positive affects. It was while meditating, Tara told me, that she felt led to call me for a medical intuition reading to uncover the core issues and reasons behind her illness.

Immediately after beginning our session, I heard and felt the presence of an angel. When I relayed her messages to Tara, she excitedly told me, "The very first time I closed my eyes to meditate, I felt a warm and loving presence. I think it was an angel, but I am not sure. I feel her

• • • • • • •

close quite often. Do you think that the angel that you are talking to could be the same presence that I feel?"

"Yes, she is with you to support and help you to heal," I said. "Have you had any recent insights or memories surface about your childhood? I am getting the message from your angel that your illness stems from trauma and loss early in life."

She began to cry and told me that she had been having flashbacks of a devastating loss that she experienced as a child. When she was just six years old, her home was burglarized one night. She woke up to the sound of screaming and a gun being fired. Hiding under the covers in her bed, she was alone and shaking with fear when a policeman eventually came and carried her out of the house. Later that evening her mother told her that her father had died and was now with the angels.

Tara went on to tell me that she spent many years in therapy working through the trauma and grief. Now with her struggles with cancer, she realized that this trauma and loss was still affecting her. Since she was clearly struggling with this memory, I asked Tara to do an angelic healing meditation with me. She agreed, and we began. During the meditation I could feel the palpable presence of the angels. I coached Tara to breathe deeply and allow the healing to unfold. I encouraged her to trust what she felt, knew, and sensed, without overthinking it.

After the meditation she slowly told me, "The angels were close. I could feel their love and compassion; it helped me to go deeper into the pain. There was a place in me that I have always been afraid to feel, but in their presence I breathed into it and let myself feel the dark depth of my inner pain. Surprisingly, it seemed to let go and dissipate, then it felt as if peace and love were pouring into me. The cancer stems from the pain that was still locked up inside of me; I know this for certain now."

Tara was silent for a few minutes, then tears welled up in her eyes and she continued, "I even felt the presence of my father. Toward the end of the meditation when you asked me if there was anything else that my angels wanted me to know, I saw my father smiling and I felt his love and warmth. I began to cry, it was so good to feel him close. I know that everything is going to be all right. I didn't want my angels and my father to leave when we ended, but they told me that they are always close and I can feel them in my heart."

How to Know When the Spirit Realm Is Close

Even though you may not be aware of their presence, you have loved ones on the other side and spirit guides and angels that are with you and watch over you. The spirit realm is continually intersecting and interacting with the human realm. At times we sense their presence, but they are often subtle and barely noticeable. With a little intuitive development practice, it is possible to better tune into and understand their messages and guidance. Here are some of the common signs and signals that let you know they are close.

· · · · · · · ·

Your Playful Loved Ones

Your loved ones on the other side often devise creative and playful ways to let you know that they are present.

Pay attention to your dreams; your loved ones may pay you a visit. Many have been able to clearly see and communicate with their loved ones while in the dream state. Others sense their presence or wake in the morning feeling as if they have been in the company of their loved ones.

Loved ones on the other side are able to manipulate and affect electrical and telecommunication airwaves. They may turn the lights in your home or office off and on or make them blink. If an appliance spontaneously turns on or off, or a clock, watch, or phone alarm mysteriously buzzes, or a clock changes time, a loved one might be responsible. They may also drop coins on your path or influence a bird or butterfly to come close or send you feathers.

Trust your intuition when it comes to sensing the presence of a loved one. Have you ever smelled the scent of a loved one's perfume or aftershave lotion? Maybe you have carried on an inner conversation and wondered if you might be receiving real advice from your father or mother on the other side? Have you ever suddenly felt the presence of a loved one comforting you during a difficult time? Maybe you have seen streaks of light or orbs and simultaneously felt a familiar presence close by. These kinds of experiences are often real encounters with a loved one on the other side. If any of these or similar types of phenomena happen to you, breathe, relax, and listen. You may want to close your eyes to further tune into any thoughts, feelings, or sensations that are being sent your way.

Spirit Guides and Their Influence

Spirit guides are aware of our soul plan and purpose. They are adept at influencing conditions and circumstances in order to promote our growth and help us learn important lessons. For instance, have you ever done all that you could do to accomplish a goal and experienced one obstacle after another? No matter how much you try, things do not work out the way you had hoped. Have you ever experienced the opposite? One door after another effortlessly opens, and positive outcomes occur that hardly seem possible. In both of these kinds of scenarios, a spirit guide may be trying to steer you in a specific direction, draw your attention to something, or guide you to important opportunities. They might also guide us to certain books, classes, or information, or influence us to cross paths with those that can help or teach us as well as those we can assist and teach. If you find yourself being at the right place at the right time, you may have a spirit guide to thank.

Spirit guides may also use many of the same signs and phenomena that loved ones on the other side utilize to get our attention. This might include such things as ringing bells, setting off alarms, turning the lights off or on, or sending bird feathers or other animals our way.

• • • • • • • •

The Love of the Angels

The presence of angels can often be detected through feelings of inspiration, love, and joy. They emit positive energy; wherever there is an angel, healing will occur. Have you ever felt your heart spontaneously open while gazing at the sunset or while watching a child play? Have you ever been motivated to give to another in a way that surprised you? Have unexpected feelings of comfort, protection, or serenity ever come over you during times of stress, loss, or fear? Angels glide into our lives on the wavelength of divine love. They help us during times of difficulties and pain, and when we call upon them they can banish our inner darkness and restore our spirit. Angels can protect our heart from the harshness of others and help us to forgive, yet they can only intercede and help us when we ask. They will not intrude in our life lessons or go against our will, even when what we are doing is not in our highest good.

A common angelic sign is the observance of numbers. Do you repeatedly look at the clock either at night or during the day and it is 11:11 or 1:11 or any combination of numbers that include the number one? If so, these numbers are symbolic of the angelic gates opening and welcoming you into a closer and more conscious connection with your angels. Sometimes an angel will show up in your life disguised as an animal, a kind stranger, or as someone or something that provides you with exactly what you most need.

Conscious Communication with the Spirit Realm

Consciously communicating with those in the spirit realm can support and reinforce mindful living by providing you with new insights into your true self and the goodness inherent in all of life. You are not just a planetary citizen but a citizen of the cosmos as well. Those in the spirit realm encourage you to be authentic and love the true you. There is no putting on false masks. You do not have to be perfect and without faults and flaws to communicate and connect with the unseen.

To tune into your loved ones on the other side and your spirit guides and angels, enter the inner stillness, open your heart and mind, and intuitively receive. The following exercises strengthen your ability to better tune into the spirit realm.

EXERCISE: **Spirit Invitation Meditation**

Sit or lie down in a quiet and comfortable place where you will not be disturbed. Close your eyes and begin to breathe deep and relaxing breaths, allowing any thoughts or emotions to surface and releasing them through the exhale.

As you continue to breathe, imagine that you are inhaling cleansing light down through the top of the head and exhaling it through the heart. As you exhale, imagine your heart gently opening and a white light bubble gently emerging and completely surrounding you. Each time you inhale and then exhale, imagine the white light bubble becoming stronger and more vibrant. Imagine that you are safe and protected, and that only what is in your highest good can enter into this bubble.

When you feel ready, send a thought message asking for a loving and light-filled spirit being to enter into this bubble with you. Do not specify who you would like this to be; just allow whoever is in your highest good to enter. Continue to breathe down through the top of the head and exhale through the heart. Relax and come into a receptive state. Continue to send a thought message to a loved one, a spirit guide, or an angel, asking for their presence.

Maintain a receptive state and tune into any physical sensations, feelings, thoughts, or intuitive insights that emerge. It is best not to ask questions at this time or try to figure out what or who might be present; just receive.

Common signs of the presence of a spirit being include feelings of warmth or tingling sensations in your head, up your spine, or on your skin. You may also experience feelings of love and comfort and the emergence of positive memories. You may hear a name, phrases, words, or song lyrics with your inner hearing. Sensations of being touched, sensing someone close to you, smelling a fragrance or flowers, and having spontaneous insights or seeing color (especially purple), streaks of light, or orbs are also common signs of a spirit. You might also see flashes of light or an outline or presence with your inner sight.

When you feel as if you have received all that you can at this time, send warm gratitude to whoever is present and open your eyes. Write down all that you received. More insights, sensations, and intuitive knowing may surface while you write.

EXERCISE: Receiving Guidance Meditation

There will be times when you desire more interaction, guidance, and conscious communication with a loved one, spirit guide, or angel. The following exercise is a good way to receive more information and trust that it is coming to you from a spiritual source.

To begin, write down a concern, question, or situation in your life that you would like to receive guidance about. Keep the question short and simple, and make it one that requires more than a yes-or-no answer. After you have written down the question, think of all the possible answers, solutions, advice, and outcomes that you can imagine, and write them down.

When you are finished, relax in a comfortable position. Begin to breathe deep and relaxing breaths. Allow any thoughts or emotions to surface, and release them

• • • • • • • •

through the exhale. As you continue to breathe, imagine that you are inhaling cleansing light down through the top of the head and exhaling it through the heart. As you exhale, imagine your heart gently opening and a white light bubble gently emerging and completely surrounding you. Each time you inhale and exhale, image the white light bubble becomes stronger and more vibrant, allowing only what is in your highest good to enter.

When you feel ready, send a thought message for a spirit being from the light to come close. Once you feel or sense the presence of a spirit being, send your question to them through a thought message. Repeat the question inwardly a few times, continuing to breathe, relax, and become receptive. Listen and tune into any feelings, sensations, thoughts, or images that emerge.

You may be tempted to start asking questions. You may want to try and figure out what you are receiving, but resist overthinking and getting into your head. Continue to breathe, open your heart, and pay attention to any sensations, thoughts, feelings, or images that emerge.

When you feel as if you have received all that you can at this time, send warm gratitude to whoever is present and open your eyes. Write down all that you received. More insights, sensations, and intuitive knowing may surface while you write.

Interpreting Messages from Spirit

It is not always easy to understand and interpret what you receive. This is normal. Do not rush to an interpretation, and try not to overthink your first impressions. At the same time, allow the guidance to unfold. Quite often, when you least expect it, you will have an aha moment of insight and realize the meaning of a message. Keep in mind that even though you may not cognitively comprehend the communication you have had with the spirit realm, you still benefit. Your heart, mind, and spirit are interacting with positive, benevolent energy. Sometimes the spirit realm will answer your request for their presence or guidance through synchronicity or through what you most need or want coming into your life in an unexpected way.

Every request to the spirit realm will be answered. Let go of your expectations as to what you want to receive and how you will receive it. Be patient and allow your connection with the spirit realm to evolve and strengthen.

The Complete Circle

In the spirit realm the interconnectedness of all living beings with one another includes the physical and nonphysical alike. Life on earth provides us with the illusion of separateness from one another. Because of this, many believe that competition, getting ahead, and denying what others may need in favor of receiving more for ourselves are necessary in order to have enough and be

· · · · · · · ·

happy. This is not so in the spirit realm. From the vantage point of nonphysical reality, there is no separation. We are all one, and our well-being, joy, and happiness can only be fully realized through the collective whole.

Spirit beings are involved in your everyday life. While you may feel alone, isolated, or that your life has little meaning or purpose, the spirit realm does not indulge in these illusionary ego-based fantasies. You are essential; what you do, think, and feel, and your influence on others, are part of a greater plan than human thinking can comprehend. Spirit reaches out to you to uplift, support, guide, and love you. All you need do is answer and allow the benevolence of a higher love and wisdom to become a more integrated part of your life. In doing so, the sacred circle of all of life completes itself. Mind, body, and spirit awareness extend beyond the concept of the individual mind, the individual body, and the individual spirit. They include the divine mind of consciousness, the physical body of humanity, and the eternal spirit. This fuller circle of awareness empowers mindful living.

Sherrie Dillard has been a professional intuitive medium, medical intuitive, and author for more than thirty years. She has given over 50,000 readings worldwide and has been featured on radio and television for her work as an author, psychic detective, medical intuitive, and medium. She is the author of the best-selling *Discover Your Psychic Type*. Visit her online at www.sherriedillard.com.

Abigail Blosser

• • • • • • •

CONCLUSION

Mindfulness applies to many areas of your life and is a lifelong practice. It can be incorporated into any area of your life in whatever way best suits you. This book's team of authors contributed unique voices and perspectives so that you could individualize your mindfulness and meditation practices. Be sure to check out the other offerings from these authors and supplement your practice in harmonious ways.

As this book demonstrates, there are many paths to mindful living, and it is for you—the person seeking greater awareness, health, well-being, and presence—to discern your own best path. The variety of techniques, practices, approaches, and philosophies presented here allow you to review the book in your own way, according to your own interests. Continue to revisit this book when you are ready to deepen your practice or if your inspiration wanes. Even if you have already read the entire thing, the next time you open it will be a new experience: you will have been through more in life, learned things, shifted beliefs, and your practice will have transformed. With these new eyes, it may be like reading the book for the first time!

As time passes and your perspectives and needs evolve, the approaches of this book can evolve with you. Each time you read it you will gain something different because you will be different! Any advanced practitioner—be they an artist, an academic, or an athlete—will tell you that in order to advance, it is key to practice fundamentals. Because of this truth, part one is an invaluable support to your mindfulness habit. Throughout life our health builds and wanes. The second section of this book is a precious resource for maintaining, developing, and restoring health. Similarly, the endeavor to love your body through movement, self-care, and sexuality keeps the third section relevant and a vital tool for your mindful well-being. Most people who prioritize their growth and development feel as though there is more for them to do. The fourth section, on reaching your potential, can offer lifelong inspiration and guidance. As you continue to grow in a meditative lifestyle, you may become more interested in or attuned to the spiritual aspects of life and practice. The final section gives you numerous techniques for connecting to subtle energy and your authentic self. Remember to use this book as your own personal resource, following your needs and interests in order to pick up the reading wherever you see fit. May you remain inspired in practice and in life to get the most out of every moment!

LLEWELLYN'S

COMPLETE BOOK OF

CHAKRAS

Your Definitive Source of Energy Center Knowledge
for Health, Happiness, and Spiritual Evolution

CYNDI DALE

Llewellyn's Complete Book of Chakras
Your Definitive Source of Energy Center Knowledge for
Health, Happiness, and Spiritual Evolution

Cyndi Dale

Cyndi Dale, one of the world's foremost experts on chakras and energy healing, presents the most comprehensive, practical, and readable guide ever written on the topic. Lively and accessible, this definitive encyclopedia explores the science, history, practices, and structures of subtle energy systems, with chakras as the center point, distilling and synthesizing 12,000 years of cross-cultural knowledge. It features a wealth of illustrations and a color insert, plus 114 exercises that you can use to immediately experience chakra healing and clearing.

978-0-7387-3962-5

8 x 10, 1,056 pages

illustrations, exercises, glossary, endnotes, index

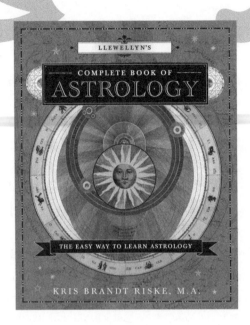

Llewellyn's Complete Book of Astrology
The Easy Way to Learn Astrology

Kris Brandt Riske, MA

The horoscope is filled with insights into personal traits, talents, and life possibilities. With *Llewellyn's Complete Book of Astrology*, you can learn to read and understand this amazing cosmic road map for yourself and others.

Professional astrologer Kris Brandt Riske introduces the many mysterious parts that make up the horoscope, devoting special attention to three popular areas of interest: relationships, career, and money. Friendly and easy to follow, this comprehensive book guides you to explore the zodiac signs, planets, houses, and aspects, and teaches how to synthesize this valuable information. Riske also explores the history of astrology going back to the ancient Babylonians, in addition to the different branches of contemporary astrology.

Once you learn the language of astrology, you'll be able to read birth charts of yourself and others, determine compatibility between two people, track your earning potential, uncover areas of opportunity or challenge, and analyze your career path.

978-0-7387-1071-6

8 x 10, 336 pages

appendices

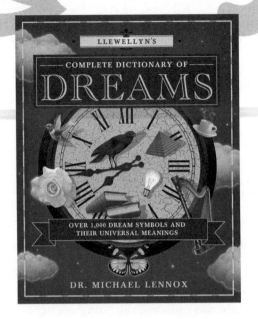

Llewellyn's Complete Dictionary of Dreams
Over 1,000 Dream Symbols and Their Universal Meanings

Dr. Michael Lennox

Dreams have an intelligence and purpose of their own, allowing your soul to reveal itself. By listening to the wisdom of your dreams, you can increase the satisfaction and success you experience in your waking life, make positive changes for a better future, and find a profound connection to your Higher Self.

Llewellyn's Complete Dictionary of Dreams presents more than 1,000 cross-referenced dream symbols and their universal meanings to assist you in analyzing your unconscious mind. Join Dr. Michael Lennox as he explores the basics of interpretation and shows you how to integrate the subtle messages that arise while you sleep. The insights related to the specific symbols in this extensive guide are the keys to creativity, growth, and understanding.

978-0-7387-4146-8

8 x 10, 312 pages

Llewellyn's Complete Book of Names

For Pagans, Witches, Wiccans, Druids, Heathens, Mages, Shamans & Independent Thinkers of All Sorts Who Are Curious About Names from Every Place and Every Time

K. M. Sheard

Parents want the perfect name for their child. Among the baby books available today, none are tailored to the needs of Witches, Pagans, and other seekers like *Llewellyn's Complete Book of Names*.

From Alma and Ash to Zinnia and Zane, this comprehensive and user-friendly name guide offers accurate and extensive information on more than seven thousand names spanning religions, cultures, and centuries. Each impeccably researched entry features factual details on origin, history, and meaning, including magical and mystical associations. Examples of historical figures and characters from mythology, literature, and film are also provided. This essential guide offers everything you need to make this all-important decision, including name selection tips and name lists categorized by theme—the Sun and Moon, the five elements including spirit, the plant world, and more.

978-0-7387-2368-6

8 x 10, 792 pages

appendices, glossary, index, bibliography

To order, call 1-877-NEW-WRLD

Prices subject to change without notice

Order at Llewellyn.com 24 hours a day, 7 days a week!